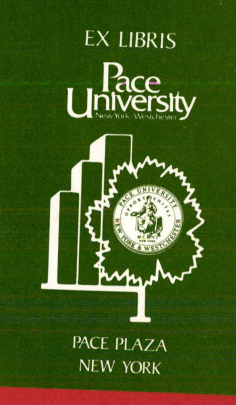

The Pragmatic Imagination

Joseph Wharton. Painting by Julian Story (1906)

The Pragmatic Imagination

A History of the Wharton School 1881–1981

Steven A. Sass

 University of Pennsylvania Press | Philadelphia

Design by Adrianne Onderdonk Dudden

Library of Congress Cataloging in Publication Data

Sass, Steven A. 1949–
    The pragmatic imagination.

    Includes index.
    1. Wharton School — History.   I. Title
HF1134.P46S27   1982   330'.07'1174811   81–51146
ISBN 0-8122-7814-3

Printed in the United States of America

For my parents,
Chaim and Franciska

Contents

List of Illustrations

W. E. B. Du Bois
Leo S. Rowe
James T. Young
Clyde L. King
Roswell Cheney McCrea
Scott Nearing
Arthur H. Quinn
Edgar Fahs Smith
Lightner Witmer
Wharton Barker
William McClellan

following page 162
Charles C. Harrison
Logan Hall
Chalk Board in the Wharton School, College Hall, ca. 1900
Panoramic View of the Campus, ca. 1910
Emory R. Johnson
Emory R. Johnson, *American Railway Transportation,*
    Title Page
Emory R. Johnson, *American Railway Transportation,*
    First Page of Contents
Edward S. Mead
Solomon S. Huebner
John D. Sullivan

following page 200
Emory R. Johnson
Ernest M. Patterson
Raymond T. Bye
Carl Kelsey
James P. Lichtenberger
James H. S. Bossard
Edward P. Moxey, Jr.
George A. MacFarland
Herbert W. Hess
Thomas Conway, Jr.
Grover G. Huebner
G. Lloyd Wilson
Solomon S. Huebner

Gaylord P. Harnwell
Bernard Cataldo
Dorothy S. Thomas
Dan McGill
C. Ray Whittlesey
Irwin Friend
Julius Grodinsky
G. Wright Hoffman
E. Gordon Keith
C. Arthur Kulp
Willis J. Winn
Irving B. Kravis
J. Parker Bursk
Joseph R. Rose
Survey of the Wharton School, Cover
Survey of the Wharton School, First Page of Text

following page 292
Willis J. Winn
Robert Strausz-Hupé
Stephen B. Sweeney
Lester E. Klimm
Michael Dorizas, with Students
E. Digby Baltzell
Marvin Wolfgang
Philip Rieff
Lawrence Klein
Journal of Economic Theory, Volume One,
      Number One, Cover
Journal of Economic Theory, Volume One,
      Number One, Contents
Irving B. Kravis
Arthur Bloomfield
Dorothy Brady
Sidney Weintraub
Richard Easterlin
Oliver E. Williamson
Karl Shell
Edwin Mansfield
Walter Isard

Acknowledgments

This book and I have accumulated a stack of debts that now need to be publicized:

I wish to acknowledge the contribution of my parents, Charles and Franciska, who raised me up.

It has been my excellent fortune to have had Louis Galambos as a teacher. It was he who trained me in the ways of history, and he also read and edited much of this manuscript.

Dean of the Wharton School, Donald C. Carroll, merits special recognition for conceiving the project and lending it his unfailing support. He, his staff, and the members of the Wharton faculty, past and present, have also generously shared their time with me, to discuss the history of the institution. Their remarks, admirable for their candor and insight, were essential to my understanding of the Wharton School.

Archivists, as usual, are the historian's best friend. The archivists at the Friends Library, Swarthmore College, were quite helpful in unlocking the Joseph Wharton Papers. The University of Pennsylvania Archives, directed by James Dallet, provided exceptionally thorough and well-organized support for the entire volume.

The project benefited from the services of several able and energetic assistants: Barbara Copperman, Don and Piyali Ganguly, and Berhanu Abegaz. Three university students, Arthur Charity, Jon Friedman, and David Weinstein, also spent an "independent study" semester with me, studying the history of the school. These associates all contributed to the final product, and did so with their conversation as well as through the execution of their formal assignments and projects.

Several fine editors toughened my arguments and sharpened my prose: the above-mentioned Louis Galambos, Dee Johnson from the Wharton School, my able editor from the University of Pennsylvania Press, Christie Lerch, and my wife, Ellen Golub. Because of the patient and reliable labors of Carole Hawkins and her word processing staff, I was able to fit the criticisms of these and other readers into the manuscript.

To my wife, and newborn Francesca, I owe special thanks for making these past few years a lively adventure.

Foreword

This history of the Wharton School's first hundred years was written to record the events and personalities which helped to shape it into one of the world's leading business schools.

What emerges almost immediately is that the school has never enjoyed the pastoral luxury of standing still; indeed, no academic organization of any stature can afford to rest on past accomplishments. This is immutable.

Thanks to the extraordinary vision of Joseph Wharton, who founded the first business school anywhere, the institution which bears his name was endowed with a spirit and a program still vibrant at our institution. Wharton identified the essential qualifications needed by young businessmen of his day at a time when his contemporaries had little if any formal training. He also saw, with equal prescience, that many senior members of the management were overlooking any thoughtful, disciplined means of bringing their successors along to the point that they, in turn, could perform as effective managers. To redress these defects he established the school. To this day, the Wharton School strives to give its students grounding in the fundamentals, the broad principles of sound management. Intelligently adapted to individual circumstances, they can be of continuing use to young men and women in their developing careers.

This is not only the story of the Wharton School, it is, in some respects, the story of the American business school. Here is how it began, the form and structure it took, the evolutionary stages through which it passed en route to becoming the complex mechanism we behold today.

The Wharton School, having now weathered a hundred years in an arena wracked by cataclysmic events and great change, may safely be said to have stood the test of time. Now for the next century.

DONALD C. CARROLL

A Plausible Introduction

The surname "Wharton" originated in twelfth-century England, with a Hampshire peasant who registered himself as "Quarton" when leasing some acres and a hut from the bishop of Winchester. As indicated by his surname, Quarton made querns, primitive handmills for grinding corn, which he sold to local shepherds and peasants. He now turned much of this income over to the bishop, and he would feed his family with the crops he raised on Winchester's land.

Caught up in the barbarism of the day, in crusading and civil warfare, the bishop of Winchester had neither time nor energy to oversee his sandy Hampshire sheep-walks. Nor had he much use for its products, its wool and mutton, for he needed steel armaments and corn for retainers in Palestine and York. Winchester also hungered after new Asiatic spices, and for textiles far more exquisite than those made by his English serfs. For money, Jews and even stranger businessmen from Flemish and Italian cities would supply Winchester with his needs and his desires. So he divided his pastures into farms and leased them for money.

From the time of the Greeks, who had coined the word, "economics" had meant the art of managing one's household. Economics taught lords the proper manner of treating slaves, planting crops, raising animals, and producing crafts; only secondarily did it consider exchanging goods in markets. From the twelfth century, however, European households, great and small, sought to organize themselves to produce and sell a surplus, and thereby to win purchasing power on markets. No household managed by itself; each came to rely on an expanding business economy to transfer values from querns to rents to textiles to raw produce consumed in cities. Since that time, economics has increasingly become the science of markets.

In areas close to the flow of goods, such as Hampshire, the lords let control of the economy fall out of their immediate grasp. There magnates such as Winchester gave up claims to the labor of peasants such as Quarton; instead they assumed "property" rights over the fertility of land and sovereign claim to a new array of fees and taxes. With one hand this policy promoted peasant initiative, with the other it rented and taxed away its fruit.

Raising money, rather than one's subsistence directly, required new ways of managing affairs. The Italians of the day were then developing the basic mechanisms for handling this economy of trade and credit: double-entry bookkeeping, the bill of exchange, innovative partnership agreements, and commercial law. When Italian businessmen arrived in England at the end of the twelfth century, to collect wool in payment for crusading debts, they paid one of their first visits to the bishop of Winchester. He obliged them with wool, and they in turn helped him systematize his accounts.

To emulate the Italians — to draw commercial contracts, to let property, to keep manorial accounts, and to buy and sell effectively — Winchester was in need of literate and numerate managers. The best were men in the bishop's retinue who had attended the new universities at Paris and Oxford. These schools, which also sprang up in the twelfth century, organized knowledge in a way that had never been done before. Rather than view scholarship as an endless discussion of a unified spiritual tradition, the universities divided knowledge into separable parts. They established "curricula" in the seven liberal arts and in medicine, law, and theology. This program allowed men of the world—men not permanently committed to scholarship — to attend a course of study and then return to their affairs with a systematic understanding of a subject. Universities thus promoted the dissemination of higher learning through society and brought two secular professions, medicine and law, into close contact with scholarship.

Although university education helped the bishop's men grasp the Italians' techniques, it gave them few insights into administrative practice. Aside from the area of law, the new academic world and that of business remained apart. Few university men entered business or political administration and the university did not seriously consider the intellectual issues of economic management. This situation continued for seven hundred years, until Joseph Wharton founded university education for business in the new world of industrial America.[1]

Source Note

1. A Plausible Introduction, factual in its important parts, relies on a letter to Assistant Dean Karen Freedman of the Wharton School from David J. Quarton, 26 Mar. 1979; M. M. Postan, *The Medieval Economy & Society* (London: Weidenfeld and Nicolson, 1972); and Charles Homer Haskins, *The Rise of Universities* (Providence, R.I.: Brown University Press, 1923).

The Pragmatic Imagination

1

Joseph Wharton, Ironmaster

Joseph Wharton's great-great-grandfather, Thomas, followed William Penn from England to his Quaker colony in America in 1685. He prospered as a merchant, died a man of substance, and left a considerable estate. Great-grandfather Joseph also proved to be a "very successful merchant." Grandfather Charles lived for ninety-five years, during which he "was a most successful merchant, and extensively engaged in the importing business of the city." Charles's first cousin, Thomas, Jr., was president of the Executive Council of the Commonwealth of Pennsylvania; his flamboyant half-brother, Robert, was a popular politician and was elected mayor of Philadelphia fifteen times between 1798 and 1824. Other Whartons won distinction as doctors, lawyers, and men of business. For four generations before Joseph, therefore, the family had distinguished itself in Philadelphia society.[1]

Joseph was born in 1826, during the presidency of John Quincy Adams. Missouri had just become a state, the Erie Canal had just reached the Great Lakes, and the old colonial elite, the seaboard merchants such as Wharton's ancestors, and the tidewater planters farther south, were about to lose their control over the nation's government and economy. Joseph's father, William, a respected Philadelphia gentleman, held no position of active authority in business or the professions. He had married Deborah Fisher, a woman whose "equally respectable and successful" Philadelphia ancestry traced back to John Fisher, who had arrived with William Penn on the *Welcome* in 1682. The couple raised a large family which they supported with income from inherited estates, and they spent much of their lives in Hicksite Quaker religious, social, and charitable activities. Deborah devoted herself especially to the cause of the American Indian, a traditional Quaker charity; in this she worked anonymously, also a Quaker tradition. Joseph's parents, and especially his strong-willed mother, passed on to him a deep attachment to his family, to his native city, and to the religion of his ancestors.[2]

William and Deborah provided Joseph with an excellent Hicksite Quaker education. They sent him "to the best private schools of Philadelphia" — Friends' School and Fred A. Eustis's academy. According to Wharton's daughter and biographer, Anna Wharton Lippincott, his parents then expected the sixteen-year-old Joseph to go off to Harvard and prepare for a career in one of the liberal professions. But instead, she continued, he grew ill in his mid-teens, and he stayed in Philadelphia. During winters in the city, Fred Eustis tutored Joseph in French, German, and science. Wharton developed a special fondness for chemistry and through further study in the laboratories of local chemists James Curtis Booth and Martin Hans Boye became quite adept in the subject. Perhaps to regain his health, Joseph spent nine months of the year in nearby Chester County, on the farm of fellow Quaker Joseph Walton. There he developed both a lifelong affection for agriculture and a vigorous physical constitution. Indeed, the regimen succeeded so well that he lived to be eighty-three, old enough to see the election of William Howard Taft as president of the United States.[3]

William Wharton offered his adolescent son Joseph no clear model on how to support himself as a Philadelphia gentleman in the burgeoning nineteenth-century economy. Andrew Jackson and the quick, ambitious men he represented had already wrested control of the nation away from John Quincy Adams and the genteel old families. But William and Deborah still identified with the older ways and decided on a traditional training to fit Joseph to win a livelihood. They chose to apprentice him with the Waln and Leaming counting house, to learn the business of a dry goods merchant. There he was taught the business procedures created by the medieval Italians: book credit and double-entry bookkeeping; the business of insurance, finance, and currency exchange; and the law of contracts.[4]

At the end of one year at Waln and Leaming, the precocious Wharton was head bookkeeper, in charge of eight hundred accounts. Having mastered the "inside part of the business," he looked outside and asked Waln for a chance to go out and sell. The merchant, however, took him aside and assured him that mastering the inside activities — accounting, in particular, but also conveyancing and drawing contracts — would prove more important to his business success. "When you get into business for yourself," he said, "you'll find plenty of men who can do your selling for you, but you'll never succeed unless you can manage your own counting house. That's the place for you to stay." Joseph took the advice and, as it happened, had little reason to regret it. Because most of his businesses were monopolescent or dependent on government contracts, Wharton needed little traditional marketing expertise. His profits relied much more on his ability to control costs, handle high volumes of business paper, and negotiate sound contracts.[5]

Upon leaving Waln and Leaming and for more than fifty years thereafter, Wharton pursued the revolutionary new business opportunities in industrial metallurgy. He combined his business acumen with his earlier training in chemistry to mine, smelt, refine, and sell metals from Philadelphia's great hinterland colony, the Lehigh Valley. Importing foreign technology and using key discoveries of his own, Wharton drew lead, zinc, nickel, iron, and then steel out of the piedmont. He also invested in and served as a director of railroads that operated in the area. In so doing, Wharton kept the family name prominent in Philadelphia. But he also entered a world of business radically different from that of his merchant ancestors, a new industrial world of wage-laborers, corporations, power machinery, and scientific equations.

After a brief venture in white lead manufacturing with his older brother Rodman, Wharton entered the zinc business in 1854. In that year, he and several investors prominent in Philadelphia's growing chemical business (including George T. Lewis and Charles Lennig) bought control of the Pennsylvania and Lehigh Zinc Company, in Bethlehem, Pennsylvania. The assets of the firm were a mine, a plant designed by Samuel Wetherill to extract zinc oxide, and a twelve-year contract with Wetherill whereby he would get ore from the company's mine, operate the works, and sell oxide back to the company. For the past year, the Zinc Company had successfully manufactured zinc oxide under this arrangement and had sold the chemical as a substitute for white lead for making white paint. All members of the Philadelphia group were in the paint business, in a position to gauge the commercial potential for zinc oxide; a member of Lewis's family had even handled the Zinc Company's sales.[6]

The Zinc Company operated much like a traditional commercial partnership. In such a partnership, a small group of merchants would pool their capital to undertake a trading venture too large for any individual. The investors then entrusted entrepreneurial responsibility to two men: a captain, to operate the ship and see that the cargo arrived safely, and a supercargo, to buy and sell goods, to handle the business per se. In the Zinc Company, Wetherill functioned as the captain operating the plant, and Joseph Wharton took the role of supercargo, evaluating the quality of goods received by the company, handling sales, and approving expenditures.[7]

Merchants traditionally saw the supercargo's function as essential and primary. Indeed, such partnerships often confined their activities to assembling and selling cargoes, and hired shipping services from other firms. Merchant investors dominated early industrial enterprises, and they naturally placed the treasurer, who made the financial and commercial decisions, above the operating head of the plant.[8]

Much more than in commercial undertakings, however, industry conflated the business and operating functions of the enterprise. Although Wharton and Wetherill had different interests, they were constantly forced to rely on each other. Wharton complained about the quality of the oxide and objected to Wetherill's policy of making speedy, and therefore costly, repairs. Wetherill wanted to raise output and conduct research on making metallic zinc. Wharton was just as happy to leave the ore in the ground until Wetherill's contract lapsed, and he wanted to slow Wetherill's research until he himself could discover and patent his own process for manufacturing zinc. The solution to the impasse was to eliminate the conflict. Industry had made business dependent upon specialized and ever-changing operating plants. Unless the business firm controlled the productive as well as the commercial and financial processes, it kept within its organization a powerful party with dangerously conflicting interests. So in 1857, the Zinc Company bought out Wetherill's contract.[9]

No sooner had the company resolved its conflict of interest with Wetherill than it ironically established one with Wharton. In 1857 the company faced a severe crisis, as a depression had struck the nation's economy and was pushing the firm toward bankruptcy. Wharton, however, urged new investment to exploit his discovery of an economical process for the manufacture of metallic zinc. The partners hesitated. "Supremely confident of his own business ability," Wharton made a bold proposal. He offered to release the company from its immediate financial burdens by leasing the works for six months. He would pay all expenses and deliver the same eighty thousand tons of oxide a month to the company as had Wetherill. In return Wharton got any surplus production, to be sold only abroad. He later negotiated a contract to build, at a fixed fee, a works for the manufacture of metallic zinc that he would then lease back from the company. Wharton bore all risks of the this venture as well, both in constructing the plant and in producing and marketing the product.[10]

These arrangements allowed Wharton to make a fortune. He expanded zinc oxide output from eighty thousand to two hundred thousand tons a month and successfully sold the difference in Europe. Wharton got his metallic zinc works into production by hiring a Belgian technical consultant, importing skilled Belgian workers, and keeping them sober, disciplined, and on the job. Because of his enterprise, the net value of Wharton's estate grew from three thousand dollars in 1855 to a substantial one hundred twenty-eight thousand dollars in 1862. The company directors, thinking this to be more than sufficient profit, took back operating control of the works and forced an outraged Wharton out of the zinc business. As a man who learned from experience, Wharton noted that "in this country companies often move very slowly and cannot act as resolutely or efficiently as individuals who possess adequate means." Now that he had means, Wharton never again had business superiors or permanent partners.[11]

Even before he wrapped up his affairs with the Zinc Company, Wharton had entered the nickel business. In 1863 he purchased, for his own account, bankrupt remnants of America's early attempt to mine and process nickel. During the 1850s, the Gap Mining Company had opened a mine in nearby Lancaster County and had established a refinery across the river from Philadelphia in Camden. Commercial failure, however, had brought the works to a halt by the end of the decade. But Wharton had confidence in his technical and business abilities and had good reason to believe that a better market now existed for nickel. The business turned out to be more difficult than Wharton expected, but in February 1868 he could finally boast that

the result of the five years of toil . . . and the outlay of a large amount of money (in the aggregate about $300,000), is . . . an establishment of mine, smelting works, and refinery, complete in one ownership, producing the best nickel in the world, and second in magnitude only to one other; that of a wealthy and respectable English firm.[12]

W. Ross Yates, Joseph Wharton's biographer, tells us that when Wharton entered the business he "probably knew as much about the ore deposit there and the metallurgy of nickel as anybody in the United States." He read French and German, in which much of the literature on nickel had been published. He had also become familiar with the metallurgy of nickel firsthand, from various Philadelphia chemists in his acquaintance. Wharton's mentors in chemistry, Martin Hans Boye, James Curtis Booth, and Professor Frederick Augustus Genth, the German-born professor of chemistry at the University of Pennsylvania, had all worked on the mineral and had identified the nickel deposits in the state. Due largely to Booth's discoveries, the United States government began minting small coins from nickel alloys in the 1850s. To help meet the mushrooming demand for small money during the Civil War, the director of the Philadelphia Mint, James Pollock, encouraged Wharton to enter nickel production and assured him the mint's business.[13]

Upon buying the nickel properties, Wharton set out to improve his firm's manufacturing technology. He arranged for the most efficient nickel refiner in the world, the Prussian Dr. Theodore Fleitmann, to reconstruct the Camden refinery according to an advanced design. (He also asked for, and got, Fleitmann's accounting system.) Wharton himself conducted a series of experiments on nickel—exploring the toughness, magnetism, and other qualities of the metal. This work ultimately led Wharton to a new process for producing malleable nickel, an achievement that brought him the gold medal of the Paris Universal Exposition of 1878.[14]

But Wharton had been wrong in his expectation that the United States Mint in Philadelphia offered an assured market for the products of his enterprise. No sooner had director Pollock lured Wharton into the business than he recommended to Washington that the mint abandon nickel coinage for the cheaper bronze. Congress agreed and went even further, authorizing the printing of paper one- and three-cent notes. Wharton struggled along with this unexpectedly reduced demand and fought back with vigor in the political arena. He began lobbying Congress—probably through his friend, Congressman E. J. Morris—for a renewed use of nickel coinage and for a tariff on the metal. He wrote a series of pamphlets praising the virtues of nickel coins to support his case before Congress. Wharton's efforts were in part successful: He won some tariff protection, a new five-cent nickel coin, and moderate profits for his business.[15]

Wharton's big break came in 1871. It was then that Chancellor Otto von Bismarck decided to reform the currency of the newly united Germany and chose to mint small coins with a high nickel content. Wharton and the other four nickel producers in the world allowed Fleitmann to deal with Berlin directly, without their competition. All then sold the metal at the monopoly price that Fleitmann had extracted. In four years of fabulous sales to Germany, 1873 to 1877, the price of nickel doubled and Wharton made $1,239,000. That represented three times his investment in the business as of 1868, and more profit than nickel yielded him in all other years combined. After that, the business turned down. The Germans finished minting their stock of new coins and a Rothschild-backed combine, commonly called "Le Nickel," began supplying the world with cheap metal from its great New Caledonia deposit. Although Wharton continued to fight for his nickel business, his future prosperity was now to come from another metal—steel.[16]

As in the case of nickel, Wharton had entered the iron business while still manufacturing zinc in Bethlehem. In 1857 he had bought stock in the Saucon Iron Company, a local firm soon renamed the Bethlehem Iron Company. By 1863 he had fifteen thousand dollars invested and was named a director of the firm. The company prospered, owing much of its early success to its brilliant engineer, John Fritz, and to a wise decision to buy into the Bessemer patent pool. Because of these advantages the Bethlehem company comfortably survived the depressed decade of the 1870s and reaped a fortune during the huge railroad construction boom of the 1880s.[17]

Until the mid-1880s, conservative local families dominated the company's board of directors. These families perennially rejected John Fritz's ambitious proposals to expand into new products or to buy up the special ores needed by their Bessemer converters. As these ores began disappearing from the market, Wharton and Fritz proposed that the firm enter the arms business. Wharton had been approached by the secretary of the Navy, William C. Whitney, who wanted to establish an American manufacturing capacity for building a new steel navy. Navy Lieutenant William H. Jaques, secretary of the Gun Foundry Board, had secured rights to Sir Joseph Whitworth's forging technology and wanted Fritz to construct and operate the American plant employing that process. Wharton convinced the Bethlehem Company board to go ahead with the project, then traveled to Europe to draw up contracts with Whitworth and the French armor plate manufacturer, Schneider et Cie. Wharton also financed much of the extensive new investment that the Bethlehem Company needed for the venture. He ended up owning one-quarter of the common stock and a majority of the bonds. This investment and his forceful personality made Wharton the dominant force in the prosperous reorganized company.[18]

Wharton's new involvement with arms manufacture raised an apparent conflict with his Quaker beliefs. His black-sheep nephew, Wharton Barker, once approached his uncle after a Friends' meeting at which Wharton most earnestly explained the virtues and necessity of peace. Barker asked his uncle to reconcile these sentiments with his "gun factories on the Schuylkill," to which Wharton reportedly replied, "There are some things that are none of thy damn business." While the story makes good reading, there is no evidence that Wharton ever felt a serious tension between his religion and his business. Indeed, he remained a staunch Quaker until his death. As a later observer reported,

he didn't wear a necktie. He didn't wear collar buttons. He didn't wear studs in his cuffs, you see. No ornaments. A very austere, very superior guy in the sense of doing the thing that he thought was right . . . [H]e was a very sincere man in the sense that he believed in himself and in his cause. And his cause was the steel industry, and making a success of the steel industry.[19]

In his business life itself, however, he was less wedded to tradition. By entering the world of mass raw material extraction and processing, Wharton had left behind much of the business world of his merchant ancestors. Unlike mercantile enterprise, the Bethlehem Company transformed the physical nature of materials, adding tangible economic value to the goods it purchased. For that purpose the company assembled a tremendous fixed plant which represented an unprecedented long-term commitment to products, raw material inputs, and technologies. It employed thousands of workers and put them to work at a tremendous array of specialized tasks. Making a commercial success out of such vast works and labor forces required that businessmen design an efficient organization and maintain continuous high levels of flow through the enterprise. For America's new captains of industry, managing that flow effectively became far more critical than evaluating markets and trading accordingly, the essential tasks of Wharton's mercantile ancestors.

As a captain of industry, Wharton needed a new business persona to replace the now irrelevant "merchant-gentleman." To lay out large amounts of long-term capital, to coordinate vast numbers of men and machines, and to tread the treacherous realms of corporate law and scientific technology, all required forms of business intelligence and authority radically different from those of a trader. In his attempt to nail down what sort of businessman he actually was, Wharton often used the term *ironmaster*. Wharton's relationship to iron stood for all to see, and *ironmaster* was a traditional designation for operators of iron furnaces and plantations. But for a man born in republican America and leading the nation headlong into the modern, highly specialized industrial age, the term had a surprisingly archaic, medieval ring. Indeed Wharton chose the word because he was drawn to the general amalgam of power, craft, and independence wrapped up in the primitive idea of "mastery." He admired Cortez and his conquests and viewed himself as a modern-day "captain" of industrial America. The independence of a "master" appealed to Wharton, a man who forswore partners. He took great pride in his technical accomplishments and identified with a master's craft. Wharton chose to live near Jenkintown, not the most fashionable neighborhood in Philadelphia, but the home of its boldest entrepreneurs— J. B. Lippincott, E. T. Stotesbury, J. B. Stetson, Jay Cooke, John Wanamaker, William Lukens Elkins, P. A. B. Widener, and Cyrus Curtiss.[20]

Like many of his contemporaries, Wharton found the European aristocracy an appealing model of authority. He lived at a time when hundreds of daughters of the American elite were finding aristocratic husbands in Europe; when big country estates and magnificent townhouses (often fitted with reproductions of medieval furnishings) were proliferating; when high Anglican observance satisfied the social and religious sensibilities of the nation's best families. On his frequent European travels, Wharton met and became friendly with aristocrats of several nations. He was especially enamored of the Prussian Junkers, the powerful owners of vast, semifeudal agricultural estates. On an 1873 trip to Europe, Wharton called on Herr Geheimrath Zimmermann, whose estate occupied three thousand acres and included a sugar refinery, oil, flour, and feed mills, and a brick works. Zimmermann employed a thousand peasants full-time, and another thousand at harvest. Wharton wrote home, with obvious approval, of "the people, all orderly and friendly, saluting their chief as he rode about in a sort of semi-military style — it was a sight to remember." The medieval arrangement appealed to the ironmaster. In a rare departure from his typically more prudent business judgment, Wharton later imported an entire village of Prussian peasants to raise sugar beets on his New Jersey land. But to his chagrin, the project failed to thrive on American soil and was soon abandoned.[21]

Wharton's image of mastery caught the crucial transformation in the history of capitalism brought on by the industrial revolution and the subsequent rise of big business. With industrialization, businessman came to organize production directly, controlling the nation's expenditure of labor and the great mass of its immovable productive property. Indeed, the idea of mastery captured the essential similarity between the new bourgeois industrialist and the old landed aristocrat who once had dominated the peasantry and had directed the process of physical production. But mastery only silhouetted Wharton's true business persona. In actual practice he substantially qualified each attribute of mastery that had attracted him.

Wharton's productive powers, which were both real and important, could be identified with a master's craftsmanship only to a limited degree. He made no product with his own hands, as is implied in that notion. Nor could his technical contributions be assigned to his initiation into a craft tradition or mystery. They came, in large part, because of his competence in science, a competence of which he was quite rightly proud. As Wharton appreciated, the productivity of European aristocratic estates in modern times also grew out of a science-based technology. His friend Zimmermann's success depended on applying modern "chemical agriculture" to his traditional estate. Before Wharton called on Zimmermann, he therefore stopped at the nearby University of Halle to discuss scientific sugar beet cultivation with Professor Julius Klein. In all his technical pursuits Wharton was distinctly modern — drawing on the best scientific resources applicable to his undertakings — and not a tradition-bound master of a craft.[22]

Nor could Wharton exercise in his business affairs the power over men implicit in the idea of mastery. Even at the height of his career, Wharton's authority was always constrained. When he controlled the Bethlehem Iron Company, local Bethlehem families that had invested in the company held important management posts; foremen and skilled workmen, and not the company, actually handled the hiring and firing and organized the work process on the plant floor. These men all maintained their areas of prerogative and successfully parried the ironmaster's influence. Wharton yearned for the power of mastery over his subordinates at Bethlehem. But at the end of his career, just as at the beginning when he managed the zinc works, his power often got tangled and muted among the twisting lines of authority in the complex industrial enterprise.

Wharton clearly prized his business independence, but he owed much of his business success to collective actions. He did come to have the dominant voice at Bethlehem, but the firm was a corporation. Other investors put up three-quarters of the risk capital and had much to say about the company's course. Wharton and the Bethlehem Company also cooperated with other firms through the ironmasters' trade association, the American Iron and Steel Association. The AISA lobbied Congress for favors for the industry as a whole and published business and technical information of general value. Wharton also found it profitable to cooperate with his competitors. The Bessemer patent pool, which Bethlehem Iron had joined, kept competition out of the business and divided the market among the eleven participating firms. In the 1870s, Wharton and the other nickel manufacturers allowed Fleitmann to fix the price paid by the Prussian Mint. In the 1890s, Wharton and Andrew Carnegie together set the price they charged the United States government for armor plate.[23]

These compromises of Wharton's independence, and of his authority over men and technology, grew out of the inevitable complications of modern industry. No man, not even one as able and energetic as Joseph Wharton, could fully master the new industrial enterprise. Even though Wharton worked over-full days as compared with the leisurely three hours put in by many colonial merchants, he could not keep up with the demands of his various pursuits. He responded, as best he could, by finding ways to relax the demands on himself in his role as industrial entrepreneur.

Wharton's first strategy was to reduce the pressures of "excess competition." As we have seen, he joined with his fellow industrialists to control markets, prices, and access to technology. Like many nineteenth-century manufacturers threatened by British competition, he also became a protectionist. Wharton suffered from significant foreign competition in both nickel and steel, and self-interest led him to oppose those international channels of trade that had allowed his family to achieve wealth and distinction in the New World.[24]

Wharton's commitment to high tariffs, however, involved more than a businessman's particular claim on the pluralism of America's political economy. Protectionism was Joseph Wharton's great passion, and he vigorously pursued the subject in both the classical and heterodoxical literature of nineteenth-century political economy. On Sunday afternoons he frequented the salon of Philadelphia's mentor in protectionist economics, Henry C. Carey. Carey convinced the ironmaster that protectionism was "no debating club topic," and Wharton became a key leader of the high-tariff forces in this country.[25]

Wharton gave most to the protectionist movement during the years following the Civil War, when his struggling nickel business and iron investments faced stiff foreign competition. A healthy U.S. Treasury — the result of Civil War taxes without Civil War expenditures — made some tax reduction inevitable. As tariff duties thus became a major political issue, Wharton joined with other businessmen relying on protection to form the "Industrial League." He quickly became its "active force," as chairman of its executive committee. Wharton called a representative conference of American manufacturers and presented them with a model tariff bill. The assembly accepted his proposals in the main and sent the draft to the House of Representatives.[26]

Wharton directed the League's political campaign for this and subsequent tariffs. He organized the publication and distribution of a torrent of protectionist literature, including speeches "purchased" from Congressmen and a protectionist textbook that the League placed in all the nation's college libraries. These activities helped direct the inevitable tax reductions away from industrial tariffs and even won higher duties on various manufactures, including nickel and steel.* Many, indeed, considered the 1870 tariff as the foundation of the American steel industry. It fixed the duty on steel rails at twenty-eight dollars per ton just as American Bessemer mills began entering the market, dramatically lowering the cost of steel rail. The result was a sharp increase in

---

*The 1870 tariff replaced *ad valorum* duties with fixed-rate tariffs for many goods. The change offered countercyclic protection to American manufacturers, enhancing the degree of protection during periods of low prices. Fixed-rate tariffs also steadily stiffened duties during the great deflationary era following 1873, a boon to America's industrial sector.

the actual level of protection. Between the Bessemer process and the tariff, the steel industry grew rapidly all through the depressed 1870s and yielded ironmasters an overall return of 10 to 20 percent. With the revival of large-scale railroad construction in 1879, steel manufacturers made enormous profits.[27]

Wharton remained an active leader in the tariff struggle after the great fight in 1870. He continued on the executive committee of the Industrial League and became the vice president of the American Iron and Steel Association in charge of tariff matters. In 1882 he helped institutionalize the entire procedure. Wharton and his allies then won from Congress a bill creating a Tariff Commission that took over the work of the Industrial League: the commission was charged with the responsibility of consulting with the leaders of American industry and then drawing up a tariff bill to be considered by Congress.[28]

Tariffs and other devices that controlled competition raised prices and profits, but the demands on Wharton and other American entrepreneurs remained intense. A more powerful solution to the problem of entrepreneurial overload lay not in reducing the demand for entrepreneurial services but in dividing entrepreneurial labor. At Bethlehem and in his nickel works Wharton delegated his work and his authority to subordinates. In addition to Wharton, the Bethlehem Company had a president, vice presidents, a general manager, a general superintendent, heads of plants, and heads of departments within plants; it had specialists handling the sales, engineering, and legal aspects of the business. Each of these officers, in turn, had assistants of his own. A great many people, organized in a business bureaucracy, now performed as a group the entrepreneurial tasks of planning, coordinating, and controlling the flow of goods through the enterprise. These hierarchies worked more effectively in the smaller nickel works than at Bethlehem, but such a delegation of authority proved necessary at both.

Another mechanism for sharing his responsibilities, and one that Wharton used with great effect, was the rapidly growing market for entrepreneurial services. Tasks and resources that once seemed to be essential attributes of the head of a business were increasingly supplied to the enterprise through markets, by independent firms. Especially valuable in reducing the task of operating a large industrial business were markets in technology, management, investment, and education; Joseph Wharton participated in all four.

An active market in technological processes existed throughout Wharton's business career. He and responsible employees in his firms were more than competent in technical matters and made important contributions of their own. But, as we have seen, Wharton bought the basic technology for each of his major metallurgical enterprises — zinc, nickel, and steel.

Toward the end of his business career Wharton made use of two brand new markets for entrepreneurial services. In 1898 he brought one of the world's first management consultants to the Bethlehem Company, paying him thirty-five dollars a day plus expenses. That consultant was Frederick W. Taylor, an upper-class Philadelphian who had passed up a Harvard education and instead entered industry. By 1898 Taylor was already the most vigorous practitioner of a new economic science that grew out of casting "the engineer as economist." These engineers had developed new techniques of managing the "inside" activities of a manufacturing plant, of handling the planning, coordination, and control of the industrial enterprise. Wharton retained Taylor for three years, to have him install his new system of scientific management at Bethlehem.[29]

When Taylor arrived, he found authority over the flow of materials widely dispersed and inefficiently administered. His basic strategy was "that of taking . . . control . . . out of the hands of the many workmen, and placing it completely in the hands of the management, thus superseding 'rule of thumb' by scientific control." The control that Taylor took from the workmen he placed in a "planning room." There managers laid out and scheduled the flow of materials and tasks and determined the speeds of machines — the rate at which they consumed materials and the volume of each bite. More than at any previous time, the managers in the planning room were also able to develop an accurate accounting of production costs. By centralizing decision making, Taylor achieved greater coordination and had work flowing through the plant at a much faster pace. His methods spread the overhead expenses of the enterprise over more products and dramatically reduced handling costs. In one machine shop alone, Taylor saved the Bethlehem Company a one million dollar investment, and he reduced the firm's corps of yard workers from 400 to 140.[30]

While at Bethlehem, Taylor also developed a novel scheme to divide entrepreneurial labor within the firm. Under the hierarchical chain of delegated authority then in force, each man tended to have one and only one boss. Taylor's "functional foreman" plan, however, called for each worker to fall under the jurisdiction of eight different foremen, each controlling one aspect of the worker's task and no one wielding ultimate authority. He proposed a division of entrepreneurial labor according to functional specialization, with each supervisor becoming an expert in one area and all eight in combination providing improved direction to the worker. Here, as in all his programs, Taylor ostensibly placed his faith in expertise and "science," not strict authority alone. He hoped to solve the general problems of industrial operation through "systematic management, rather than searching for some unusual or extraordinary man."[31]

Taylor's program paralleled, to a degree, the functional specialization of entrepreneurial labor that was then developing at the general corporate level. Industrial firms at the turn of the century were establishing large functional departments such as production, sales, purchasing, law, and accounting. In each unit the company hired men who were expert in the specialized areas. But neither at the corporate level nor on the shop floor did American industrial firms eliminate general executive authority over the various units of the company. In firms such as the Bethlehem Company this power was elusive, shared, divided, and fought over. But it was wielded by men acting as general executives of the enterprise, not specialized professionals. While the Bethlehem Company adopted many of Taylor's improvements, in the end it rejected his functional foremanship idea.

Time, not any functional division of entrepreneurial authority, presented Wharton with the ultimate challenge to his power and the power of his family. When he celebrated his seventy-fifth birthday, in 1901, he knew that no one in his family stood ready to take over his business affairs. He had sired three daughters, none of whom had violated contemporary mores and entered the world of industrial business. Wharton developed close relations with his two sons-in-law, but neither wanted to assume all his business responsibilities. So in 1901 Wharton turned to the greatest market for entrepreneurial services to develop in the nineteenth century, the market for industrial securities that appeared in full blossom after 1896. During the great merger craze at the turn of the century, Wharton sold his power to Big Business. His nickel works became part of the International Nickel Company; the Bethlehem Company was headed for the United States Steel combine before Charles M. Schwab took the company away from the bankers, merged it with other enterprises, but kept the name Bethlehem. Wharton's heirs thus became stock and bond capitalists, not captains of industry.[32]

Twenty years earlier, when he was fifty-five, Wharton had already known that he had no son to keep the family name prominent. In compensation he adopted the sons of his class, America's young men of "inherited wealth and capacity," and assumed responsibility for preparing them to become the nation's next generation of leaders. Wharton's father had not been able to provide young Joseph with a model for how to support oneself as a gentleman and a leader in industrial America. Neverless, Joseph succeeded. "The thing that he was doing and living seemed to him consequential, and he wanted [these] boys . . . to feel that it was consequential" and be prepared to assume his mantle. He knew that the practice of apprenticing young men to established business houses, the system that had trained him in business, no longer functioned. The pace of business had speeded up tremendously in the last forty years, and neither Wharton nor any of his successful peers had time to take on apprentices. If the next generation of business leaders were to receive a proper preparatory education, it would have to be done outside the business firm. For this purpose the ironmaster decided to establish a "Wharton School," to produce a class of "Wharton men." In transferring serious business education to an institution separate from the firm, Joseph Wharton created a new market for an entrepreneurial service—a market for entrepreneurial education.[33]

"Commercial colleges" existed in the 1880s and each year trained approximately fifty thousand of America's youth for business. But Wharton, quite justifiably, complained that these schools trained men to become clerks, not business leaders. Offering a three-month course in business arithmetic, elementary bookkeeping, and penmanship, they altogether failed to give their students an understanding of business life that could compare with that which Wharton had received at Waln and Leaming. Wharton also decided against organizing an independent professional school, analogous to many medical, legal, and theological schools of the country. Instead he turned to the liberal arts college as the place to educate businessmen. Social science was already being taught in liberal arts colleges, and Wharton felt that it provided the best conceptual background for a business career. But most important, Wharton wanted to create a liberally educated class of leaders for American society, and the college was the place to fashion such gentlemen.[34]

Wharton himself was an extremely well-educated man of affairs. Although he had not attended college, Wharton had had a liberal education equal to that of any college-trained gentleman, and he appreciated the value of such training. He made original scientific contributions, spoke several languages, published articles on economics, and wrote verse. Wharton also

knew every in-and-out of technical business. He rarely received a legal paper for execution in which he could not lay his finger on some blemish . . . and he had a vast treasury of knowledge on all the forms for possessing and passing real estate . . . His command of the methods of finance was perfect . . . He knew how to act with deadly swiftness and he knew how to wait—both trading capacities of the highest order.

In contrast to his own accomplishments, Wharton perceived an "intellectual hiatus in the business life of the nation." He expected his Wharton School to address this crisis in the quality of American business leadership and to train young men in his own mold. So in 1881 Wharton offered the trustees of University of Pennsylvania one hundred thousand dollars to organize a "School of Finance and Economy."[35]

Wharton knew that "college life offers great temptations and opportunities for the formation of superficial light-weight characters." He hoped that his school, however, would "instill a sense of the coming strife [of business life]: of the immense swings upward or downward that await the competent or the incompetent soldier in this modern strife." Wharton also knew that colleges harbored free trade economics, a "fungus . . . which healthy political organisms can hardly afford to tolerate," and he dealt firmly with this piece of college foolery. The ironmaster insisted that "no apologetic or merely defensive style of instruction must be tolerated upon this point, but the right and duty of national self-protection must be firmly asserted and demonstrated." Having thus allayed his own hesitations, Wharton brought together business and the university.[36]

The University of Pennsylvania's new provost, William Pepper, announced Wharton's gift at his inaugural, on 22 February 1881. Wharton sent the trustees a formal letter containing his offer on March 1, and, after discussions with a committee of the trustees, he presented them with a "Project," or detailed plan of the new institution. "The main features of the scheme," Wharton wrote,

embodying the fruit of much experience and thought, impressed themselves upon my mind about two years ago, and were then committed to writing; but the many developments and changes of expression which have since occurred to me, have been from time to time carefully incorporated into the paper, so that, as it now stands, it does not lack the *labor limae* which is required by most fabrics of thought and words that are intended to endure.[37]

Wharton declared the "object" of his project:

To provide for young men special means of training and of correct instruction in the knowledge and in the arts of modern Finance and Economy, both public and private, in order that, being well informed and free from delusions upon these important subjects, they may either serve the community skillfully as well as faithfully in offices of trust, or, remaining in private life, may prudently manage their own affairs and aid in maintaining sound financial morality: in short, to establish means for imparting a liberal education in all matters concerning Finance and Economy.[38]

Wharton prefaced his "Project" with a lucid and well-thought-out explanation of his actions. He intended this preamble to become the basic document of the new school, and in this he was not disappointed. Because of its importance the document more than deserves to be reproduced in full:

To the Trustees of the University of Pennsylvania

The general conviction that college education did little toward fitting for the actual duties of life any but those who purposed to become lawyers, doctors, or clergymen, brought about the creation of many excellent technical and scientific schools, whose work is enriching the country with a host of cultivated minds prepared to overcome all sorts of difficulties in the world of matter.

Those schools, while not replacing the outgrown and obsolescent system of apprenticeship, accomplish a work quite beyond anything that system was capable of. Instead of teaching and perpetuating the narrow, various, and empirical routines of certain shops, they base their instruction upon the broad principles deduced from all human knowledge, and ground in science, as well as in art, pupils who are thereby fitted both to practice what they have learned and to become themselves teachers and discoverers.

In the matter of commercial education there was formerly a system of instruction practiced in the counting-houses of the old-time merchants which may fairly be compared to the system of apprenticeship to trades. Comparatively few examples of this sort of instruction remain, nor is their deficiency made good by the so-called Commercial Colleges, for however valuable may be the knowledge which they impart it does not suffice to fit a young man for the struggle of commercial life, for wise management of a private estate, or for efficient public service.

It is obvious that training in a commercial house not of the first rank for magnitude and intelligence must, like trade apprenticeship, probably result in narrowness and empiricism which are not compensated by the hard and practical certainty within limited bounds imparted by the routine of trade or business. Since systematic instruction can not be expected from the over-worked heads of any great establishment, the novice mostly depends on what he can gather from the salaried employes of the house, and, instead of being instructed in the various branches, is probably kept working at some particular function for which he has shown aptitude, or where his service is most needed. Besides, ordinary prudence requires that many things indispensable to mastery of the business should be kept secret from these novices.

There is, furthermore, in this country, an increasing number of young men possessing, by inheritance, wealth, keenness of intellect, and latent power of command or organization, to whom the channels of commercial education, such as it is, are, by the very felicity of their circumstances, partly closed, for when they leave college at the age of 20 to 25 years they are already too old to be desirable beginners in a counting-house, or to descend readily to its drudgery.

No country can afford to have this inherited wealth and capacity wasted for want of that fundamental knowledge which would enable the possessors to employ them with advantage to themselves and to the community, yet how numerous are the instances of speedy ruin to great estates, and indolent waste of great powers for good, simply for want of such knowledge and of the tastes and self-reliance which it brings. Nor can any country long afford to have its laws made and its government administered by men who lack such training as would suffice to rid the minds of fallacies and qualify them for the solution of the social problems incident to our civilization. Evidently a great boon would be bestowed upon the nation if its young men of inherited intellect, means, and refinement could be more generally led so to manage their property as, while husbanding it to benefit the community, or [sic] could be drawn into careers of unselfish legislation and administration.

As the possession of any power is usually accompanied by taste for its exercise, it is reasonable to expect that adequate education in the principles underlying successful business management and civil government would greatly aid in producing a class of men likely to become pillars of the State, whether in private or in public life. An opportunity for good seems here to exist, and fairly comparable with that so largely and profitably availed of by the technical and scientific Schools.

These considerations, joined to the belief that one of the existing great Universities, rather than an institution of lower rank or a new independent establishment, should lead in the attempt to supply this important deficiency in our present system of education, have led to the suggestion of the project herewith submitted for the establishment of a School of Finance and Economy as a Department of the University which you now control, and which seems well suited to undertake a task so accordant with its general aims. In order that the University may not, by undertaking it, assume a pecuniary burden, I hereby propose to endow the school with the securities below named, amounting to $100,000, and yielding more than $6,000 annual interest; these securities not to be converted during my life-time without my assent, and no part of the endowment to be at any time invested in any obligation of the University, viz:

Five hundred shares in the Delaware and Bound Brook Railroad Company. $50,000 second mortgage bonds of the Schuylkill Navigation Company.

I am prepared to convey these securities at the opening of the first term of the School, or at any earlier time when the University shall satisfy me that the School will surely be opened at the beginning of the next term, interest being adjusted to such opening.

The only conditions which I impose are that the University shall establish and maintain the School according to the tenor of the "Project" hereto appended, and that when the University shall by its own desire, or by default established in a suitable Court of Equity, cease so to maintain the School, the endowment shall revert to me or to my heirs, I reserving the right during my life to amend in any way, with the assent of the then trustees of the University, the terms of the said "Project."

To commemorate a family name which has been honorably borne in this community since the foundation of the city, I desire that the School shall be called "The Wharton School of Finance and Economy."[39]

Source Notes

1. Anne H. Wharton, "The Wharton Family," *Pennsylvania Magazine of History and Biography* 1 (1877):325, 459, 324 – 29, 455 – 59, 2 (1878):50 – 57, 211 – 18; Joanna W. Lippincott, *Biographical Memoranda Concerning Joseph Wharton, 1826 – 1909* (Philadelphia: J. B. Lippincott, 1909), 9 – 11.

2. Lippincott, *Wharton*, 13–17; Anne H. Wharton, "The Wharton Family," 213–14.

3. Lippincott, *Wharton*, 21, 21–25; W. Ross Yates to author, 24 Aug. 1980.

4. Lippincott, *Wharton*, 25.

5. B. S. Stephenson, "Eminent Men of Iron World: 2. Jos. Wharton," *Iron Trade Review* (1907):547.

6. W. Ross Yates, "Samuel Wetherill, Joseph Wharton and the Founding of the American Zinc Industry," *Pennsylvania Magazine of History and Biography* 48 (1974):484–88.

7. Ibid.; Frances W. Gregory, "The Office of President in the American Textile Industry," *Bulletin of the Business History Society* 26 (1952):129.

8. Gregory, "President."

9. Yates, "Zinc," 488–92.

10. Ibid., 492–506.

11. Ibid., 496, 505, 512–14.

12. Joseph Wharton, "Suggestions Concerning the Small Money of the United States," quoted in W. Ross Yates, "Joseph Wharton's Nickel Business," *Pennsylvania Magazine of History and Biography* 51 (1977):300–301; Yates, "Nickel," 292.

13. Ibid., 294, 294–95.

14. Ibid., 299–300, 311–13.

15. Ibid., 296–98.

16. Ibid., 308–11.

17. *Dictionary of American Biography* (hereafter *DAB*), s.v. "Joseph Wharton"; John Fritz, *Autobiography of John Fritz* (New York: John Wiley & Sons, 1912); Yates, "Zinc," 514; Peter Temin, *Iron and Steel in the Nineteenth Century* (Cambridge: M.I.T. Press, 1964), 173, 174–75, 208; Stephenson, "Wharton," 548–49; Lippincott, *Wharton*, 58–59.

18. Stephenson, "Wharton," 548–49; Fritz, *Fritz*, 182ff.; Frank B. Copley, *Frederick W. Taylor: Father of Scientific Management* (New York: Harper & Brothers, 1923), 2:7–8; Lippincott, *Wharton*, 58, 136–39; Robert Hessen, *Steel Titan: The Life of Charles M. Schwab* (New York: Oxford University Press, 1975), 164, also see 42–44.

19. Scott Nearing, *The Making of a Radical: A Political Autobiography* (New York: Harper & Row, 1972), 52–53; interview with Scott Nearing, by Barbara Copperman, 24 Dec. 1979.

20. Joseph Wharton, "The American Ironmaster," read at Pittsburgh, 6 May 1879, Joseph Wharton Papers, Friends' Library, Swarthmore College; Emory R. Johnson, *Life of a University Professor: An Autobiography* (Philadelphia: Ruttle, Shaw & Wetherill, 1943), 23; E. Digby Baltzell, *Philadelphia Gentleman* (Glencoe, Ill.: Free Press, 1958; Quadrangle Paperbacks ed., 1971), 210–14; Harrison S. Morris, "Joseph Wharton, Sc.D. LL.D.", *Proceedings of the American Philosophical Society* 48 (1909); lxxv.

21. Lippincott, *Wharton*, 70, 64–72; Baltzell, *Gentlemen*, 232; Francis W. Gregory and Irene D. Neu, "The American Industrial Elite in the 1870s: Their Social Origins," in *Men in Business*, ed. William Miller (Cambridge, Mass.: Harvard University Press, 1952; Harper Torchbook ed., 1962), 200; Edward C. Kirkland, *Dream and Thought in the Business Community, 1860–1900* (Ithaca, N.Y.: Cornell University Press, 1956; Quadrangle Paperback ed., 1964), 29–50. Joseph Wharton, *International Industrial Competition*, (Philadelphia: Henry Carey Baird, 1872), 7.

22. Lippincott, *Wharton*, 64–65.

23. Hessen, *Steel Titan*, 91–97, esp. 94; Temin, *Iron and Steel*, 175.

24. Lippincott, *Wharton*, 41–46.

25. Joseph Wharton, "National Self-Protection," reprinted from the *Atlantic Monthly*, Sept. 1875 (Philadelphia: American Iron & Steel Association, 1875), 35; A. D. H. Kaplan, *Henry Charles Carey* (Baltimore: Johns Hopkins University Press, 1931), 74–75.

26. James M. Swank, "Joseph Wharton," *Bulletin of the American Iron and Steel Association* 43 (1909), Joseph Wharton Papers; "Men and Things," *Philadelphia Evening Bulletin*, 13 Jan. 1909, Joseph Wharton Papers.

27. Frank Taussig, *Tariff History of the United States*, 6th ed. (New York: G. P. Putnam & Sons, 1914), 222 – 24, 227; "Joseph Wharton's Great Work in Aiding to Firmly Establish Protection as Country's Policy," *Philadelphia Press*, 24 Oct. 1904, and obituaries of Joseph Wharton, *Philadelphia North American*, 13 Jan. 1909, *Philadelphia Public Ledger*, 13 Jan. 1909, "Joseph Wharton File," Archives of the University of Pennsylvania (hereafter Archives); Temin, *Iron and Steel*, 113, 171, 213.

28. Joseph Wharton, "Shall the Tariff Be Revised by a Convention?", address before the New York Tariff Convention, 30 Oct. 1881, and Joseph Wharton, "Brief Statement of the Action in Behalf of the Eaton Bill for a Tariff Commission and Measures for Renewing the Movement," June 1881, Joseph Wharton Papers; Joseph Wharton, *International Competition*, 26 – 31; Taussig, *Tariff History*, 231 – 32.

29. Henry R. Towne, "The Engineer as Economist," *Transactions of the American Society of Mechanical Engineers* (1886):428 – 32; Copley, *Taylor*, 2:1 ff.; Daniel A. Wren, *The Evolution of Management Thought* (New York: Ronald Press, 1972), 111 – 46, esp. p. 127.

30. Frederick W. Taylor, "On the Art of Cutting Metals," quoted in Copley, *Taylor*, 2:120; Copley, *Taylor*, 2:1 – 164.

31. Frederick W. Taylor, *Principles*, quoted in Wren, *Management Thought*, 141; Daniel Nelson, "Taylorism and the Workers at Bethlehem Steel, 1898–1901," *Business History Review* 51 (1977):487 – 505.

32. Hessen, *Steel Titan*, 147 – 50; Yates, "Nickel," 319 – 20.

33. Joseph Wharton to the trustees of the University of Pennsylvania, Minutes of the University Trustees, 24 Mar. 1881.

34. *Report of the U. S. Commissioner of Education (1886 – 87)*, cited in Michael W. Sedlak, "The Emergence and Development of Collegiate Business Education in the United States, 1881 – 1974; Northwestern University as a Case Study" (Ph.D. diss., Northwestern University, 1977), 16.

35. Morris, "Wharton," lxxii, lxxv.

36. Joseph Wharton, "Is College Education Advantageous to a Business Man?", address before the Wharton School Association, 20 Feb. 1890 (Philadelphia: Wharton School, 1890), 15; Joseph Wharton, "National Self-Protection," 8; Wharton to the trustees, Minutes of the University Trustees, 1 Mar. 1881.

37. Wharton to the trustees, Minutes of the University Trustees, 24 Mar. 1881.

38. Ibid.

39. Ibid.

Joseph Wharton as a young man

Joseph Wharton, ironmaster

Joanna W. Lippincott, *Biographical Memoranda Concerning Joseph Wharton, 1826–1909*

Ontalauna, winter home of Joseph Wharton

Marabella, summer home of Joseph Wharton

Joseph Wharton, his wife, Anna, their daughters,
and nephew, William R. Wharton, in the early 1880s

Joseph and Anna Wharton, with their children and
grandchildren, at their golden wedding anniversary, 15 June 1904

INTERNATIONAL

INDUSTRIAL COMPETITION:

A PAPER READ BEFORE THE

AMERICAN SOCIAL SCIENCE ASSOCIATION.

AT THEIR

GENERAL MEETING IN PHILADELPHIA, OCTOBER 27, 1870

BY

JOSEPH WHARTON.

PHILADELPHIA:
HENRY CAREY BAIRD,
INDUSTRIAL PUBLISHER,
406 WALNUT STREET,
1872.

INTERNATIONAL INDUSTRIAL COMPETITION.

Man hat Gewalt, so hat man Recht,
Man fragt um's Was? und nicht um's Wie?
Ich müsste keine Schifffahrt kennen:
Krieg, Handel, und Piraterie,
Dreieinig sind sie, nicht zu trennen.—*Faust, Part 2, Act 5.*

Having the power, you have the right.
One asks but what you've got, not how?
Talk not to me of navigation:
For war, and trade, and piracy,
These are a trinity inseparable.

I CHOOSE as a motto these words, put by Goethe into the mouth of Mephistopheles, because they express what I think has been too much overlooked by many writers upon the subject of International Commerce, *i. e.*, the essentially antagonistic nature of trade. It has of late years been rather the fashion to omit from consideration those aspects of the case which become apparent when the several nations are regarded as competing organisms, each of which struggles to better its condition both absolutely and relatively to the others, just as each individual of a community strives to rise in the social scale.

Much is said, upon the one hand, of the higher wages which the protective system affords to the producer; and, upon the other hand, much concerning the cheaper goods offered to the consumer by unshackled commerce; but if either the free-trader or the protectionist could prove to demonstration that his policy insured to either class a larger allotment of personal comforts during the current year, with a larger surplus at its end, than under the opposite policy it could enjoy, the question as to which course is most expedient for the State would still not be exhausted. The statesmen must look beyond individuals or classes, and beyond the immediate present; not content with noticing that certain parts of the body politic are properly nourished, he must see that the body as a whole possesses vigor and symmetry; that development and robustness attend upon nutrition; that the whole organism enjoys fair play and good guidance in its strife with similar artificial bodies, and above all, that its present course is leading on to future health and power.

The advocates of unrestricted commerce in particular seem to

3

Joseph Wharton, *International Industrial Competition*,
title page and first page of text

Works of the Bethlehem Iron Company, ca. 1890

Frederick W. Taylor

Joseph Wharton at the end of his life

2

The Philadelphia School of Finance and Economy

When Joseph Wharton approached the University of Pennsylvania with his project, control of its liberal arts college lay in the hands of the Board of Trustees.* Luckily for Wharton, the trustees were men of his own class. They came from prominent Philadelphia families and traveled in the leading political, social, and religious circles of the city; and like the ironmaster, the trustees spent their days in active pursuit of business success. Philadelphia was always the most heavily industrialized of the old colonial port cities, and never would such activities play so prominent a role in the city's business life as they did in the 1880s. Industrialists, as a result, then dominated the university's Board of Trustees more than at any other time in its history. Like Wharton, most were engaged in building large-scale manufacturing, mining, and railroad enterprises; the rest were the lawyers and bankers who served these industrialists. Joseph Wharton had developed personal relationships with many trustees, including William Sellers, the prominent Philadelphia machine-tool maker; Frederick Fraley, lawyer and one of the most successful Philadelphia busi-

---

*Traditional European universities knew nothing of boards of trustees — such bodies were an American innovation in university control. Unlike the University of Pennsylvania's schools of medicine and law, which were controlled by their faculties, in the college of liberal arts the trustees could pass judgment on matters as fine as individual student discipline when they chose to do so.

27

nessmen of the nineteenth century; publisher J. B. Lippincott; and the railroad magnate John Welsh. Sellers and Fraley had also helped Wharton organize the Industrial League, with Sellers serving on its executive committee. Like Wharton, these manufacturer-trustees believed that their careers were "consequential," and they quickly approved the ironmaster's plan to train their sons to take charge of the society they were in the process of creating.[1]*

For several years before the founding of Wharton's school, many of the trustees had been working on developing new systems of leadership suitable for managing the industrial business economy. Most promising were the organizations that they had established in cooperation with the nation's university-educated professionals. During the Civil War, for instance, trustees Frederick Fraley and Stephen Colwell, along with Charles J. Stillé, university provost between 1868 and 1880, had served with university-trained physicians and scientists on "the largest, most powerful, and most highly organized philanthropic activity that had ever been seen in America," the United States Sanitary Commission. The commissioners and their staffs had had to operate a large and complex organization whose mission was to care for the sick, wounded, and lonely soldiers of the Union armies. When faced with this vast managerial task, the commissioners, like Joseph Wharton at his business, responded to primitive urgings for control and mastery and insisted upon rigid administrative structures and total obedience to their directives. Stillé, a friend of Wharton's who made a wide reputation for himself as the commission's historian and propagandist, wrote that the commission "subordinated all its plans, even for the relief of suffering, to the maintenance of that discipline in its strictest form." Due to their

---

*The university also needed Wharton's money. Penn had far fewer resources than other major universities, and the trustees were no doubt also drawn to Wharton's project by its one hundred thousand dollar endowment. Indeed, in the 1882-83 academic year, income from the school's endowment covered fifty-five hundred dollars in salaries that the university would normally have had to pay on its own. So interested were the trustees in adding to the assets of the institution that in 1883 they accepted a sixty thousand dollar endowment for a chair in philosophy from Henry Seybert, on condition that the incumbent investigate the claims of spiritualism upheld by Mr. Seybert. (After four years of thorough investigation the university, very quietly, issued a report skeptical of these spiritualist beliefs.)

contact with professionals, the commissioners also made a cult out of "science," the source of authority of professional men. They tried to apply "scientific" rationality to charity management as well as to their medical chores, and they organized a rather hard-hearted board of experts to allocate the nation's philanthropy "scientifically."[2]

After the conclusion of the Civil War the American Social Science Association (ASSA), founded in 1865, broke new ground in the relationship between professionals and businessmen. Wharton and various university trustees soon took part in its activities. Whereas the Sanitary Commission had been an operating organization, the ASSA brought the genteel community of business and professional men together for "scientific" discussions of social problems and to formulate programs of reform. Businessmen made up half of the association's membership, and their views were actively solicited and respected. But the ASSA was essentially a professional institution, and it organized committees on social problems according to the old professional division of labor. Physicians took care of public health; lawyers formed a committee on jurisprudence; and college teachers assumed responsibility for education. Businessmen were crowded into the association's Social Economy division along with the clergymen and a few random academics and public officials. There they hoped to devise model policies for handling the economic and financial problems—broadly conceived—faced by the state.* Wharton himself delivered a paper on "International Industrial Competition" before the ASSA in 1870. The society's Philadelphia branch, the Philadelphia Social Science Association (PSSA), was led by his good friends chemical manufacturer Joseph Rosengarten and University of Pennsylvania historian Henry C. Lea.[3]

For most members of the association, the central political goal of the social science movement was to establish a sound civil service in government. The nation's genteel elites recognized both the expanding administrative responsibilities of the modern state and the dismal performance of American government, then controlled by cantankerous and corrupt political machines. In con-

---

*The Social Economy division dealt with public finance, banks and currency, tariffs and taxation, labor issues, poverty, museums and libraries, and the morality and administration of charity.

trast to this spoiled state of democratic government, they pictured the civil servant as the ideal amalgam of the professional and the businessman — an educated, disinterested man of affairs whom the nation could trust with public power. This new official would stand aloof from political squabbles, "scientifically" examine issues and formulate policy, and then execute his authority with skill and discipline.[4]

The Philadelphia group shared this clean-government ideal, but at a somewhat lower pitch of enthusiasm than elsewhere in the nation. In Philadelphia, "social science" did not primarily refer to civil service reform, but to the "Philadelphia School" of political economy and its principal program—protectionism. The city's guru of high tariffs, Henry C. Carey, had set out the fullest justification of protection ever produced in the city in his three-volume magnum opus, the *Principles of Social Science*. Almost every self-respecting Philadelphia gentleman lived and breathed this gospel. Carey championed Philadelphia's favorite cause at the second meeting of the ASSA, held in predominantly free trade Boston, and proved to be the "star attraction" of the program. When the Philadelphia branch of the Social Science Association was organized in 1868, the city's protectionist crowd swelled its meetings and made it the largest and most independent local chapter in the nation.[5]

While the University of Pennsylvania's trustees and provost took an active interest in local political and economic affairs, the university itself did not then play an important part in the leadership of the city. In the years immediately following the Civil War, the university's professional schools trained lawyers and physicians, but not business or political leaders per se. It is best to think of the university's college of liberal arts at this time as resembling a modern-day, small-town high school. Only 150 students attended, with many entering at the tender age of fourteen and graduating at eighteen. These students followed a completely spelled-out curriculum that differed suprisingly little from the course of study taught in the Middle Ages at Oxford or Paris. Comprised of classics, mathematics, philosophy, and some science, it represented the established core of Western culture. The college saw as its primary function the teaching of these liberal arts and graduating broadly cultured young gentlemen without any particular practical competence.[6]

When the study of society and questions of leadership did appear in the old college curriculum, they did so primarily as part of the course on "moral philosophy." Most colleges taught this course to seniors, as a capstone of their education and as a bridge to positions of social leadership as college-educated gentlemen. Penn's antebellum professor of moral and intellectual philosophy and sometime provost, Henry Vethake, had taught a traditional course in moral philosophy. He had called on his students to look within themselves, to discover the salient attributes of human nature, and then to construct a model of the well-ordered moral society. Vethake's introspection had emphasized the social significance of "character," that elusive substance that lay at the heart of nineteenth-century moralizing. Like most American moral philosophers, he had also used the introspective technique to teach two fundamental principles of political economy. First, Penn's professor had demonstrated the existence of a natural harmony of interests in free market economies, whereby the pursuit of private gain would produce the greatest good for all. The second great principle that Vethake had taught his students was the direct connection between the righteousness of a nation and its material prosperity. The moral character of a people, Vethake had argued, determined the quality of justice, the degree of frugality, and the respect for property; these, in turn, determined the wealth of the nation.[7]

Despite the overriding concern for righteousness, economic theory had developed suprisingly far under the auspices of moral philosophy, and Vethake had given his students a fair grounding in what we today call "classical economics." Here he had followed Adam Smith, the greatest of all moral philosophers, and Smith's disciple, J. R. McCulloch. Following Smith and McCulloch, Vethake had translated two basic aspects of human nature, desire and rationality, into an analysis of free markets and into arguments for laissez-faire as the policy of peace and prosperity. Vethake had also taught the economics of David Ricardo, presenting Ricardo's arguments for free international trade to the sons of protectionist Philadelphia. By explicitly confounding the theories of Henry C. Carey, he had deprived the "Philadelphia School of Economics" of a home at the University of Pennsylvania.[8]

Aside from the economics taught in the moral philosophy course, and the prestige and general intellectual facility offered by an education in the traditional curriculum, the college did little to prepare its students for business and political leadership. Nor was the free trade political economy of Henry Vethake considered of much value by the local establishment. After the Civil War, however, the larger movement to reorganize Philadelphia's leadership took hold of the university and made it more responsive to the practical needs of the city. Pushed along by Provost Stillé and several of the trustees, especially Fraley and Welsh, the university cut its moorings to the traditional curriculum and slipped into the fast-flowing academic streams of the nineteenth century. The major reform came with the adoption of the elective system in the winter of 1866-67. That change allowed students to reduce the time that they devoted to the classical curriculum and gave them the opportunity to pursue more vocational or more present-minded studies. The old professors of Latin and Greek quite naturally objected to this rude and radical departure from the ancient unities of Western culture. But they lost the battle everywhere, not only at Penn. And whereas before the elective system a college education had meant one thing, after the reform it could mean many things.[9]

With the adoption of the elective system at the university, all students took the same subjects during their first two years and then specialized as juniors and seniors. They chose among ancient or modern languages, the scientific course, or one in history and English. With the establishment of the Towne School in 1872, the scientific offerings of the university were revitalized and organized into a three-year course of study that prepared students in chemistry and engineering. When Wharton designed his school, a decade later, he conceived of business education as a three-year elective. And in his formal communications with the trustees, he explicitly used the Towne program as his model.[10]

In line with this general changeover to a more practical-minded university, the trustees also set out to improve, to their way of thinking, the quality of instruction in economics. In 1860-61 the college began teaching the mild protectionist arguments of Francis Bowen, and four years later, in 1864-65, students studied the theories of Henry C. Carey in their new "political economy" classes. In the first year of Stillé's administration as provost, 1868-69, Careyite "social science" was made a required senior-year course in the new "English" elective curriculum. The provost quickly hired a fiery and energetic young instructor, Robert Ellis Thompson, to teach this "social science."[11]

Born an Ulsterman in 1844, Thompson had immigrated to Philadelphia with his parents as a child, soon after the potato famine of 1845. His parents had arrived with some money and were able to send young Robert to Philadelphia's leading educational institutions: Central High School, Faires' Classical Institute, and the University of Pennsylvania. He had graduated first in his class at Penn in 1865, completed his master's degree there in 1868, and the university then appointed him to the faculty as an instructor of Latin and mathematics. While in high school and at the university, Thompson had also studied theology in Presbyterian schools, and he had entered the clergy as an ordained minister in 1874. But suprisingly, neither his education at Penn nor his theological training drew him into the American moral philosophy tradition of political economy, a tradition that owed much to Scotch-Irish Presbyterianism. Thompson instead found his "social science" in Philadelphia, in the protectionist theories of Henry C. Carey. In fact, he soon became one of the most vigorous apostles of the Philadelphia School of economics. This, of course, made him eminently acceptable to the university trustees.[12]

Although Thompson at first taught Latin and mathematics, as well as "social science," he soon abandoned the two traditional liberal arts to specialize in the new branch of academic knowledge. So new, in fact, was Thompson's course in social science that no other American college of the day offered any instruction by that name. In 1871, trustee Stephen Colwell, iron manufacturer, Careyite economic writer, and friend of Joseph Wharton, died and left his famous library of six thousand works on political economy to the university on condition that it further expand its program in social science and set up a chair in the subject. Colwell's chair never materialized,* but in 1874 the trustees did make Thompson a professor of social science, the first in the nation. Moral philosophy continued to be taught at Penn, but Thompson's appointment and his rapid promotion finally gave Philadelphia's own school of political economy a proper home at the city's leading university.[13]

Unlike Penn's classical moral philosopher, Henry Vethake, Thompson became a key figure in the local "social science" movement. Even as a very young man he had regularly attended Carey's Sunday afternoon salons, where Philadelphia's leading reformers and manufacturers came to know and appreciate his ideas. With Carey's help, Thompson organized a new instrument for publicizing the views of the Philadelphia School, the *Penn Monthly Magazine*, and for two years, 1870 to 1871, he edited the journal and wrote much of its extensive copy. The magazine kept local genteel opinion informed on a wide array of subjects, offering lively, opinionated, and protectionist views of history, society, and politics. Thompson also used the *Penn Monthly* to support the work of the Philadelphia Social Science Association, announcing association activities and publishing papers read at its meetings, including Wharton's "International Industrial Competition." Thompson would later edit various other journals of opinion, and in each he vigorously presented the views of the Philadelphia School.[14]

It is not clear where or when Joseph Wharton and the young professor of social science first struck up an acquaintance. Perhaps it was at Carey's salon, perhaps at a meeting of the Philadelphia Social Science Association or through the *Penn Monthly*. In any case, the two met in the early 1870s and found each other useful. At the time, Wharton was chairman of the Industrial League's Executive Committee and in desperate search of a protectionist college textbook. He felt a pressing need to present the

---

*The university got Colwell's library, even though it did not establish his chair in social science. Together with the collections that Henry C. Carey and a Mr. McCalmont of London gave to Penn, the Colwell bequest would form the heart of the Wharton School's library. Wharton's early announcements always emphasized these holdings and boasted that they comprised "the largest and most complete library of works on economic science that is to be found in any educational institution in the world." To remind all users of the library's "Philadelphia" roots, portraits of Colwell and Carey were hung on its walls.

case for high tariffs before the nation's genteel youth, to counteract the free trade theories of American moral philosophers. He therefore encouraged Thompson to write out the lectures of his course in social science for publication as a text. Thompson took this advice and authored *Social Science and National Economy*, which appeared in its first edition in 1875. Wharton eagerly read the manuscript and made numerous prepublication suggestions; his Industrial League then sponsored the production of the book and sent copies to the nation's colleges and libraries. As Thompson wrote in his preface, the work was primarily designed "for those teachers — in colleges and elsewhere — who approve of our national [that is, protectionist] policy as in the main the right one, and who wish to teach the principles on which it rests and the facts by which it is justified." When Wharton established his business school in 1881, he could thus rely on Thompson and his course in social science as the mainstay of the program.[15]

Wharton began his serious work of designing a business school in 1879, and he labored on its structure for two years before formally approaching the trustees. During that period he studied the history of higher education, especially its recent development, and acquired a radical enthusiasm for the vocationally oriented university. The elective system and courses such as Thompson's in social science inspired Wharton to envision a new relationship between business and higher education and the creation of a new class of university-educated businessmen. These men would be an amalgam of the professional and the man of affairs, similar to the civil service ideal that captivated so many of Wharton's contemporaries. In fact, as he had said in describing his "Project," Wharton had designed his new school to "fit a young man . . . for efficient public service" as well as for "the struggle of commercial life." Wharton's college-educated businessman and the new civil servant would hold critical positions of power in society and could rely on the liberal arts education that they would receive at Penn as a source of prestige, perspective, and personal character. Both would also use the "social science" and vocational training offered in the new Wharton course to manage practical problems. Likening the managerial preparation offered at his school to the lowly fruit of the earth, Wharton would "let students have . . .

what they will of fine college fare, but let them also have potatoes."[16]

Wharton spelled out the program of his new school in great
detail, and as the trustees oversaw the college, so did the ironmaster intend to supervise his latest venture. The carefully outlined "Project," included in his contract with the university,
specified a faculty of seven, including a dean, and described the
three-year curriculum and the moral tone to be maintained at the
institution. In the event that the university failed to establish and
operate the school as outlined, Wharton reserved the right to sue
Penn to recover his money. To maintain this control and to prevent
the university from supporting another branch of learning with
his endowment, Wharton required that the new school's "funds
. . . be kept absolutely separately invested by the Trustees of the
University in the name of this School; to be applied only to its
own uses."[17]

As outlined in his "Project," Wharton's new school of business was to serve two kinds of potatoes in addition to the "fine
college fare" offered in the first two years of the Pennsylvania
program. As a first course, the "Project" specified instruction in
accounting and mercantile law. These comprised the basic skills
of business practice that Wharton had learned during his apprenticeship with Waln and Leaming. The Italians had first developed
these tools in their modern form in order to control operations
and to facilitate business partnership, investment, and exchange.
Thirty generations of businessmen and their lawyers had further
refined the rules, reasons, and procedures of law and accounting,
and together they comprised the cultural heritage of business.
Wharton "laid special stress" on instruction in accounting and
called for training in "the simplest and most practical forms of
book-keeping" for a wide array of uses — for individuals, commercial houses, banks, industrial firms, trustees, and for various
government officials. He himself had a thorough grasp of the law
and made constant use of it; even his communications with the
university were clear, proper, and legally enforceable documents.
To give students at his school such facility, Wharton prescribed
the study of the state and federal constitutions and the "principal
features" of the law of industry, commerce, navigation, and real

estate; of partnership and corporations; and of insurance and inheritance.[18]

The science of economics comprised the second pot of potatoes that Wharton thought necessary in the business student's diet. The ironmaster conceived of economics as a policy tool, not as abstract speculation for its own sake. But despite its practical uses, economics was an entirely different kettle of spuds from training in law and accounting. Unlike the latter subjects, the economy was not a mental product; it was not an outgrowth of human reasoning alone. Growing out of human needs and interactions and the physical characteristics of the environment, the economy behaved in ways no one fully understood. A professor of law or accounting could hope to hold the fundamental framework of his subject in his mind, and to transmit a goodly portion of that knowledge to his students. A professor of the economy, however, found his discipline more elusive, requiring the discovery and explanation of often surprising forms of behavior. Students of the economy did not unfold a chain of rules and reasons as did accountants and lawyers; they had to use the apparatus of scientific investigation: induction and deduction — the interpretation of evidence and logical reasoning.

Wharton identified three different areas of economics that he wanted taught in his new school: taxation, money, and "industry, commerce, and transportation." In each subject he wanted instruction on the history of the field and on how present practices could be improved. In addition, Wharton directed his instructor in "money" and "currency" to teach "the necessity of permanent uniformity or integrity of the coin unit . . . how an essential attribute of money is that it should be hard to get"; this professor would also explain the causes of panics and business cycles and the modern uses of credit and securities. The "industry, commerce, and transportation" professor had perhaps the most extensive task of all. He had to present the Philadelphia School's theories of how industries and nations increase in wealth, as well as

the nature and origin of money wages; the necessity, for modern industry, of organizing under single leaders or employers great masses of laborers, and of maintaining discipline among them; the proper division of the fruits of organized labor between the capitalist, leader, and workman; the nature and prevention of "strikes."[19]

Finally, Wharton spelled out a series of measures to insure that graduates of his school would have a vigorous and conservative business character. "Lazy or incompetent students," he wrote, "must be dismissed." "Elocution should be taught. The *general tendency of instruction*," Wharton wrote, "should be such as to inculcate and impress upon the students . . . the immorality and practical inexpediency of seeking to acquire wealth by winning it from another rather than by earning it through some sort of service to one's fellow-men." Wharton also wanted the students to feel the necessity for "system and accuracy in accounts, a thoroughness in whatever is undertaken, and of strict fidelity in trusts." He would make the students cautious about debt and prompt in repayment. They should understand "the necessity of punishing by legal penalties and by social exclusion those persons who commit frauds, betray trusts, or steal public funds." He also expected loyalty to the Union and, of course, contempt for "the sentimental notion . . . that international trade between competing nations is or may be carried on upon the principles of universal brotherhood." To round off the student's education, Wharton specified that all seniors had to write an original, "lucid, terse, and sincere" thesis. For the best thesis and for the best all-around academic performance Wharton wanted the school to give "annually a gold medal weighing about one ounce, to be called respectively 'Founder's Thesis Medal,' and 'Founder's Proficiency Medal.'"[20]

After some preliminary discussions, the trustees accepted Wharton's project on 24 March 1881, and then asked the faculty to work out the details. The professors organized a committee* that met several times with the trustees' committee, and once with Wharton himself. The college faculty as a whole had no great enthusiasm for the business program, and committee members no doubt expressed their concerns at these meetings. At the end of the discussions, Wharton agreed to a "brief experimental period" — which turned out to be two years — before proceeding with his full program. During that time the Wharton course consisted of

---

*The faculty committee was chaired by Charles P. Knauth (vice provost and professor of moral and intellectual philosophy) and included Thompson and Professors E. Otis Kendall (professor of mathematics) and Francis A. Jackson (professor of Latin).

the old social science college curriculum, with only two classes added in "Elementary, Mercantile and International Law" and "Mercantile Practice." Law, of course, was a university subject of long standing, and its appearance presumably posed few problems to the faculty. Wharton's "Project" had made no mention of "mercantile practice," and it was here that the faculty piled all of the controversial new "instruction in business procedure, in management of trusts, and in the routine of banking."[21]

In addition to cutting down the number of offerings, the experimental design also narrowed the span of Wharton's school of finance and economy as outlined in the "Project." Course titles in both law and practice emphasized the "mercantile" aspect of business, thus focusing attention on traditional trading functions and minimizing the newer industrial and managerial activities of business. Joseph Wharton had not expected the school to begin full operation in September 1881, but he had certainly expected a grander approximation to his proposed three-year course.

Before returning to their former routines, the faculty quite reasonably elected Professor Thompson dean of the newborn "school." During the "experimental" first two years, Thompson's instruction in social science constituted nearly the entire course of potatoes on the Wharton menu. He taught "subjuniors" basic social science, using his own text. Juniors took four semester-long courses with Thompson, courses that delved more deeply into the areas of economics specified in Wharton's "Project": the "Wage Question"; "History and Functions of Money"; "Municipal, State, and National Taxation"; and "Industry, Commerce, and Transportation." Thompson then lectured seniors on "Living Issues" (from money and tariffs to communism and education), taught them a course on Elisha Mulford's *Nation*, and directed their original research on economic questions, as called for in Wharton's "Project."[22]

As Wharton wanted, Thompson went over the history and principles of taxation, banking, and monetary instruments. But he did not teach "hard money" (as Wharton directed). Instead, Thompson followed Carey's lead and instructed his students that credit was an essential stimulus to cooperation and output. Where there was "more money," he reported, there was "more production."[23]

On the relationship between entrepreneurs and laborers, Thompson taught, as Wharton desired, that "the capitalist is the captain of industry, who takes the unorganized mob of men, drills it into a disciplined army, supplies them with weapons, ammunition and a commissariat, and leads them to industrial conquests." But Thompson also taught that "grave injuries have been inflicted on the laboring classes by the conflict between labor and capital." As a mechanism to restore the "essential harmony of interests," he thought that workers ought to share in the profits of the enterprise. Thompson, however, rejected schemes for industrial "cooperatives" because he believed that they could not develop the "singleness of purpose, the clearness of outlook, and the energy that large industrial operations demand . . . [and that] it has been found difficult to secure the right sort of men to take the place at the head of cooperative establishments."[24]

The essence of Thompson's instruction, of course, was the economic theories of Henry C. Carey and his followers in the Philadelphia School of political economy. Like much serious economic theorizing of that day, the work of the Philadelphia School had developed in opposition to the Ricardian classical orthodoxy of the first half of the nineteenth century. David Ricardo had been a practical businessman, a London stock-jobber, whose analysis of the dynamics of capitalist economies had captivated nineteenth-century economic thought. He had presented his readers with a simple abstract schematic of the current economic system, a set of unrealistic assumptions about the interactions among its parts, and tortuous numerical manipulations — and had then shown them their economic future. So potent was Ricardo's "comparative static" method of analysis that it (although not his specific theories) survives to this day as the fundamental mode of academic economic reasoning.[25]

Ricardo's vision began with the Malthusian spectre: that a growing population pressing against limited natural resources yielded ever-diminishing returns to man's economic activity. The manner in which the market economy distributed income, Ricardo continued, made matters worse: Competition for the increasingly scarce fertility of the earth would shift all nonsubsistence income to the rentier owners of those resources. The share going to the productive capitalist classes would shrivel up, halting all further development of the economy. This gloomy stagnation could be postponed, the Englishman had reasoned, by an occasional technological innovation or by opening up a new channel of trade. His theory of comparative advantage claimed to show that the expansion of international trade benefited both parties of the exchange, even if one nation was economically much less developed than the other. But inevitably, Ricardo assured his nineteenth-century audience, population growth would halt economic progress.[26]

The earliest classes of the Wharton School were filled with Thompson's tirades against Ricardo's system and demonstrations of the superiority of the Philadelphia brand of economics. Thompson, Carey, and the entire Philadelphia School took their initial premise from Adam Smith, the fountainhead of modern economics. Smith's basic axiom was that the division of labor lay at the root of the wealth of nations. As Thompson explained, "a *division of labor* separates the functions of the human members of society, and each species of work is done more effectively and productively for employing the whole time and attention of the men employed in it." As population grows, Thompson argued, so does the division of labor and thus the productivity of the economy. Growing numbers thrust "men into closer and more helpful association, and [force] them to adopt wiser and better methods." More people also meant a larger market for novel goods and services. As Adam Smith pointed out, it then became worthwhile for men to invest in capital and skills to fill these demands in a more specialized and therefore more efficient manner. Of the two results of a growing population, this increased productivity and Ricardo's rising scarcity of fertile land, Thompson felt sure that the first overpowered the second. Increasing returns, not decreasing returns, was the Philadelphia School's great principle of economic history.[27]

To support his theories, Thompson turned to the evidence of the past. He claimed that "at every step in . . . man's industrial development, the growth of numbers and of wealth has gone on with equal strides." He produced a great deal of evidence from the long history of European agriculture that showed productivity increasing with the growth of population. More people meant more specialization, and therefore more blacksmiths, shepherds, millers, and other skilled workers in the economy. "Till the grist mill is erected the labor of a thousand arms is expended in grinding grain; the work then becomes the business of a few persons, the rest have the more time for better work than turning hand-mills or pounding wheat in *querns*." Equipped with the resources of a diversified and a more productive economy, farmers armed with iron plows could then come down off the sandy hilltops and exploit the more fertile but less tractable soils of the valleys. The Philadelphia economists were convinced that richer natural resources lay ever ready to be unlocked, awaiting only the growth of society's productive power. Certainly the experience of the nineteenth century did not teach otherwise.[28]

The Philadelphia School began by extolling the virtues of the division of labor. But at the conclusion of its theorizing, as we all know, it opposed the extensive division of international labor as advocated by the English classical school. What made national boundaries such critical economic phenomena? How could they negate the advantages of the division of labor in which Thompson himself had put so much faith? Thompson gave his students at the Wharton School two different explanations for this apparent inconsistency.

Thompson began by challenging the moral philosophy of the classical English school. As an ordained Presbyterian minister, he took such things seriously. Thompson told his students that Adam Smith and his followers had reasoned from a world composed of independent actors, of men existing without significant social relationships. Smith then derived the intricate web of divided labor from man's natural "propensity to truck, barter, and exchange one thing for another." According to Thompson, it was only the pernicious influence of Enlightenment atheism that led Smith to ignore an essential characteristic of human nature: a tendency to associate and to live in society. In Careyite economics, the division of labor derived from this power of association. It was association that created organizations and markets, institutions that allowed individuals to specialize in their own areas of competence and to rely on others for the rest of their needs. For Adam Smith, the division of labor was limited by the extent of the market. But for Thompson and the Philadelphia School, specialization was essentially limited by the degree to which society allowed the power of association to operate. A righteous nation—one that maintained peace and justice, protected the weak, and promoted health and education—instilled trust among its people and thereby fostered the mutually advantageous association of one person with another. Like many of his fellow American academic moralists, Reverend Thompson cited the Old Testament history of the Hebrew people as the foremost example of such righteousness. Thompson thus concluded that nations, as the dominant social units of the day and the frameworks for modern association, were justified in protecting themselves from unwanted external disruptions.[29]

In his second line of attack on free international trade, Thompson sounded much like a modern "third-world" critic of the market economy. He argued that such commerce generated an ugly tributary system rather than an ongoing exchange among equals. According to his reading of economic history, trade accelerated the division of the world into what we today call "core" and "periphery" areas, with all the wealth, power, and skilled industry, all the extensive division of labor, concentrated in the core. Thompson outlined to his students the reduction of India, Portugal, Turkey, and other once-flourishing nations that saw their industry, trade, and prosperity decimated by British competition in a free international market. These shattered nations of the periphery, Thompson concluded, could now obtain industrial products only from the core, in exchange for huge amounts of toil and raw materials.

The rich nation becomes, for a time at least, richer by the exchange; the poor nation permanently poorer. The former, through its command of cheap capital, and, by consequence, its greater division and efficiency of labor, can continually undersell the latter in whatever it chooses to export to it. . . . The process of accumulating capital in the poorer country is decisively checked; its people are reduced from what variety of industry and mutual exchange of services they had possessed, to a uniformity of employment in which no man needs or helps his neighbor. Their power of association is destroyed; money, the instrument of association, is drained out of the country. Nothing is left them but production of such raw materials as the richer nation chooses to buy.

In the end, Thompson concluded, the question of free trade versus protection was really the question of whether the United States would be a developed nation with diversified industry or an agriculture country monotonously producing raw staples for the international market.[30]*

Thompson offered Wharton's first students a good helping of social science, but business courses formed only a small part of their collegiate education. Resistance among the faculty to appointing nonacademics to their ranks and the short span of time between the adoption of the initial program in May and the opening of the school in September 1881 contributed to this result. In addition to Thompson's economics, Wharton offered only a single, one-semester commercial course when it opened its doors and inaugurated university instruction in business. William D. Marks, a promising but underemployed professor of "dynamic engineering" from the Towne School, greeted the school's first students in their class in mercantile practice. According to the *Catalog*, he gave "oral instruction in business procedure, in the management of trusts, and in the routine of banking." Marks himself would enter business life in 1884 with the Philadelphia Electric Light Company, and would become the firm's president eight years later. But as an instructor of business at Wharton he performed rather dismally, and managed to teach the subject only until the first semester of the school's second year.[31]

Joseph Wharton, who was keeping a close eye on the school, soon found fault with such progress. Problems in the business course and the lack of improvement no doubt troubled the founder. Furthermore, a proposed university reorganization threatened to eliminate his school's autonomy (and Thompson's deanship), placing the program under the control of the college. An irate Joseph Wharton warned the board that

I have no objection to urge against the judgment of the Trustees . . . so long as the School is conducted substantially as laid down in the "project" which forms part of the contract between the University and myself.

---

*Thompson also justified protection by arguing that a healthy economy consisted of a balance among commerce, industry, and agriculture. To separate these sectors with international trade, Thompson told his students, would foul the natural functioning of an economy. Here he cited one of Carey's favorite examples: Separating agriculture from industry clogged the cities with garbage while depriving farms of the "return" of municipal refuse to fertilize their fields. In a balanced system, the stuff of the economy would flow in a regular and productive circuit.

You will readily perceive that it would be imprudent to endanger the foundation by any such lapse.

The assimilation of the Wharton School into the college went ahead, and Thompson lost his title as dean. But two days after Wharton's letter was sent, on 26 January 1883, the trustees strengthened the school's offerings in business by appointing the sedate and conservative Albert S. Bolles as the world's first true professor of such subjects. They named him professor of mercantile law and practice, in charge of all work in the field, and even gave him a salary greater than Thompson's.[32]

Before this appointment Bolles had never served on a college faculty, but he came to his new post as a mature and experienced man of affairs with an impressive set of credentials. He had begun his career as a lawyer in Connecticut, and four years after his admission to the bar, at the age of twenty-four, he had become judge of the Court of Probate for the district of Norwich. He had sat on the bench for six years before resigning in 1875 to edit the local daily newspaper, the *Norwich Bulletin*. Upon becoming a journalist he had begun writing on economic issues, a subject that had interested him his entire life. In 1880, after five years at the paper, Bolles had resigned and became editor of *Bankers Magazine*, a journal that had already published many of his articles.[33]

In the context of the 1880s, the editor of a major trade magazine was the closest approximation to a modern professor of business. Such journals first appeared in the nineteenth century and grew up rapidly in the major branches of business activity; their editors emerged with them as the nation's major purveyors of business rationality. These men served as information brokers, statistics collectors, history writers, guardians of morality, and general spokesmen to the outside public. They had a bird's-eye view of their industry, saw its common problems and the various attempts at solving them, and informed businessmen of what should be done. Henry Varnum Poor, editor of the *American Railroad Journal*, became perhaps the best known of these business journalists through his history of American railroads, his statistical and analytical *Manual*, and his campaigns to reform railroad management and information reporting. While he edited the *Bankers Magazine*, Bolles wrote a three-volume *Financial*

History of the United States and led a campaign advocating greater public disclosure of bank statistics. Men in the field wrote to him asking for information on a variety of matters, including training in banking practice. When Harvard chose its first professor of economics, it not surprisingly chose the well-known editor of the *Boston Advertiser*, Charles F. Dunbar. Wharton's selection of Bolles made equal sense.[34]

At Wharton, Bolles taught business law and practice, but not accounting. As it was taught at the time, the latter subject did not demand his talents, and in the 1883-84 academic year it was farmed out to Chester N. Farr, Wharton's first instructor of accounting. Farr stood before his class of juniors at the school, dictating lengthy examples of normal accounting practice and then drilling his students on this material. If we can believe the *Catalog*, he gave instruction not only in traditional mercantile accounting, but also in that for "Factories, Banks, and other Corporations, and in Municipalities." Joseph Wharton had specified such a broad exposure to accounting problems, many of which were new to the nineteenth century. This course, however, was not a success. In 1885 Bolles even decided that the manner in which it was taught caused "grave injury to the School," and he recommended that "in view of the ill odor surrounding bookkeeping at present in the University," the subject be dropped for a year "until the students had somewhat forgotten how it had been mistaught." The authorities at the university followed Bolles's recommendation and offered 1885-86 as a respite from course work in accounting.[35]

As a former judge of probate, Bolles was admirably prepared to teach his students business law. But he faced a basic problem in that hitherto academic education in business law had been designed for students intending to become lawyers. As a result texts in business law were organized around legal principles and, because they could assume some knowledge of the law from their readers, were filled with unexplained legal terms. They were carefully documented with citations to cases, a help for lawyers who had to make arguments before a court. Most businessmen, of course, had not been initiated into the linguistic world of the law and had no use for extensive case citations. When they sought to understand their legal environment, they relied on rather simple treatises that explained the "dos and don'ts" of common business practices. When Bolles first taught his course in mercantile law, he used both a book designed for businessmen, *Commercial Law* by George Sharswood, and one for lawyers, *Elements of Mercantile Law* by Theophilus Parsons, a well-known lawyer and legal writer. Luckily both authors agreed that "business law is really the law of merchants" and that "all mercantile business begins with or terminates in contracts of some kind." Using these books Bolles thus gave his students both a practical and technical review of contracts for sales, debt, partnership, insurance, shipping, and real estate — all matters very familiar to medieval Italian merchants.[36]

In Bolles's second year of teaching business law he adopted Parson's new *Law of Business*, a book written for businessmen and admirably suited for Wharton students. This book avoided technical terms, assumed no legal background, and provided Bolles's students with a large number of sample legal forms covering common business procedures. As Parsons explained, he found it relatively easy to write for his new audience because "the laws of business are generally free from mere technicality and obscurity; and the reason is, that they are for the most part and substantially, nothing more than the actual practice of the business community, expressed in rules and maxims, and invested with the authority of law." As such, nearly all of this law was part of the common law tradition, the law that emerged from the actual usages of businessmen and lawyers, with only minor statutory refinements added by various legislatures.[37]

In addition to law, Bolles taught that amorphous catch-all subject, mercantile practice. He introduced his students to many of the various business "practices," including banking, merchandising, and transportation. But as the editor of *Banker's Magazine*, Bolles had particular knowledge and interest in finance, and it was that subject that he emphasized in his classes. In the 1883-84 academic year he even offered special instruction in finance, using as textbooks elementary introductions to money and credit by two of the leading economists of the day, William Stanley Jevons and Henry Fawcett. No simple guide to the actual business of operating a bank remained in print, so after he arrived at Wharton Bolles wrote *Practical Banking* for use in his courses.[38]

Bolles's instruction in finance drew heavily on his background as editor and judge. As a journalist of many years' experience, he presented the material in his books and lectures in a clear and lively style. Using colorful anecdotes from history and the current scene, Bolles gave his students fine descriptions of the complicated credit and monetary exchange systems; his *Practical Banking* laid out the organization of contemporary banks, simply but precisely detailing the various divisions of authority in such nineteenth-century enterprises. Bolles's work in finance also paid special attention to the law. His *Financial History of the United States* thoroughly explained the legal rights and procedures surrounding banking and their development through time. He followed monetary and banking legislation through Congress, quoting in profuse detail the opinions of leading bankers and politicians on contested points of law. When advising an aspiring banker, he naturally thought it essential for him to acquire "a sufficient legal knowledge to make him aware of defects in proffered securities," and to make him conscious of his legal powers and obligations.[39]

The strength of Bolles's instruction in finance lay in its solid, conservative grounding. He knew and gave thorough instruction in the traditional aspects of this business practice — the law governing finance and the systems and procedures of commercial banking. Clearly, what Bolles taught remained essential to commercial success in the nineteenth century. But of the new developments in the field, Bolles taught less. He gave his students no serious theory of money, prices, interest, or output. He used no mathematics. (Even the section on accounting in his *Practical Banking* was written by someone else.) The revolutionary new field of investment banking, then in the 1880s enjoying the beginning of its greatest period of prestige, received scant attention. Finally, Bolles focused entirely on the domestic financial system. He paid little attention to the banking in Europe and other parts of the world with which American businessmen were increasingly involved.

Like Wharton, Bolles emphasized the virtue of conservative business attitudes and through all his teachings on finance he projected a sober tone. A "hard-money man," Bolles used history to expose inflationist Congressmen as self-interested debtors; he pictured the "gold-bugs" in Congress and the Treasury as harried defenders of the public credit, the guardians of the economic republic. Although a reformer, Bolles advocated only the most conservative changes: a uniform national banking law and the publication of banking statistics to protect the business community from deception and speculation by unscrupulous bank officers. He told his students that prudent caution will, more than any other characteristic constitute the criterion of their merit as a banker. His *Practical Banking* declared the youth, who

in childhood, stole slyly to the closet for his mother's sweetmeats, who was never content at the table with the share of niceties allotted to him, who shirked his known tasks, and imposed their performance upon a younger and more dutiful brother, and who, as years wore on, evinced a disposition to rely upon others, and to earn nothing for himself, but yet who showed a determined purpose to feed on the best, and to dress in the finest — such a youth, though as quick at figures as Colburn himself, should never be placed in a bank.[40]

Bolles thus fulfilled Joseph Wharton's pedagogic expectations and, along with the Reverend Thompson, got the new school off to a respectable start by the spring of 1883. This faculty of two, one trained in academe, the other in affairs, naturally brought quite different perspectives to the new institution. Nowhere was this better illustrated than in their uses of the past. Thompson used history to demonstrate the truth of his economic theories and to inspire a return to justice and community. Bolles had neither subtle economic theories nor ministerial obligations in mind; a true lawyerlike, nineteenth-century business conservatism motivated his interest in history. At back of his three-volume *Financial History* lay an impulse to find precedents and analogies to current problems and to explain the spirit and intentions of past legislators and bankers. To Bolles, the collective past represented the full-blown account of business culture and practice and should, he thought, guide the decisions of the current generation. This distinction between the search for justice and theoretical truth and that for tradition and procedure defined the two foundations of the Wharton School. The genius of the institution, and of the larger movement begun in 1881, was that it brought these two traditions together in a productive fashion.

During the "experimental period," however, the Wharton School educated only a small portion of the nation's young businessmen. In its first year of operation, 1881-82, the school drew thirteen students. By 1883-84, the enrollment reached only twenty-one, and it was decided to scale the Wharton program down from three to two years. At the end of that academic year, in June 1884, Wharton awarded its first five graduates Bachelor of Finance degrees. They were Robert Adams, Jr., Edward Potts Cheyney, Shiro Shiba, Charles Winrod Finck, and William Redwood Wharton (a nephew of the founder). Adams became ambassador to Brazil; Cheyney went on to become a distinguished historian at the university; and Shiba, a native of Japan, returned to his country, became a member of the Diet (the Japanese parliament) and then assistant to the minister of agriculture. Only William Wharton made a mark in business — as a manufacturer of railroad supplies.[41]

Most of Wharton's enrollment at this time, however, consisted of "specials"—part-time or nonmatriculating students who primarily sat in on the business or social science courses. Many of these "specials" would become prominent, especially in business, but during their college days a rather large proportion found themselves caught up in undisciplined adolescent hijinks. In a college that was none too strict in the first place, Wharton students established a reputation as a bunch of misfits and failures. Penn undergraduates came to call the Wharton School "Botany Bay" — the refuge "down under" for their less serious-minded colleagues. No doubt the slurs contained some measure of youthful hyperbole. They also reflected the deep and somewhat justified suspicions of traditional liberal scholars about Penn's new program in pragmatics. Wharton thus began life at the nether end of the university's status scale.[42]

Despite its initially poor reputation, the Wharton experiment had important support at the university. Not only did the trustees maintain their interest in business education, but the Wharton School had the backing of the new strong man on campus, Provost William Pepper. Pepper, a physician, naturally had great respect for professional education in the abstract. It is unclear whether in 1883 he had much attachment to the idea of collegiate education for businessmen or whether he simply wanted to hold on to the

Wharton School's endowment. In any case, the provost backed the program and served as an important counterforce to faculty opposition to the new school.

Pepper had become provost in 1881, the same year in which the Wharton School was established, and with his appointment the office had become powerful at the university. The longtime provost who had preceded him, Charles J. Stillé, was a proud and bellicose Philadelphia patrician who had resented his lack of authority in relation to the trustees. Just as Joseph Wharton had complained that "companies often move very slowly and cannot act as resolutely or efficiently as individuals," Stillé had told the trustees that their collective management of the university was impeding its growth. He had insisted that the university needed one professional "head . . . one organizing brain . . . as an organizer, a leader whom we shall trust because we know he has been specially trained, and that he will give all his energy and capacity to the work in which he is engaged." Such special training, according to Stillé, involved "familiarity with the work of all the Faculties" and with "all that is going on in the world of education . . . As well might you look for advice worth taking on matters of Banking and Insurance from our Professors," he had continued, "as to suppose that the members of the Board could manage intelligently the details of our University."[43]

In a showdown with the trustees, Stillé had demanded that he be declared the single "head" of the university. He lost, and subsequently resigned. The faculty, however, had unanimously supported his position. They had pointed to strong university presidents, such as Daniel Coit Gilman at Johns Hopkins and Charles William Eliot at Harvard, who were then leading their schools to new positions of greatness in American culture and society. Acceding, somewhat, to the logic of the faculty and to the current trends in higher education, the trustees decided to surrender some of their power. They made Pepper, the new provost, the "chief executive officer of the University" and gave him a seat on their board and broad discretionary powers over university life. The year 1881 thus paradoxically marked both the entree of business into the university curriculum and the beginning of a recession in the influence of businessmen at the University of Pennsylvania; it saw the introduction of collegiate management education and the origins of modern management at the university.[44]

At once heartened by the promise of business education and concerned about Joseph Wharton's threats and the school's reputation, Pepper decided that the university's business program had to move beyond its "experimental period." He instructed Bolles to recruit more faculty for the school, and at this Bolles succeeded magnificently. His efforts, in fact, soon changed the Wharton School's character from that of a struggling provincial experiment to a school of national importance and international reputation.[45]

Source Notes

1. This chapter and the following two chapters owe much to an extended conversation with Thomas M. Jacklin; *Dictionary of American Biography*, s.v. "William Sellers," "Frederick Fraley," "J. B. Lippincott," and "John Welsh"; Edward P. Cheyney, *History of the University of Pennsylvania* (Philadelphia: University of Pennsylvania Press, 1940), 280 – 81, 319; Industrial League, "Industrial League" Tariff Tract no. 1, 1885, 1 – 2, and Sellers to Wharton, 7 Feb. 1881, Joseph Wharton Papers; Bruce Laurie and Mark Schmitz, draft of "Manufacture and Productivity," in *Toward an Interdisciplinary History of the City*, ed. Theodore Hershberg (New York: Oxford University Press, 1981); Minutes of the University Trustees, 5 June 1883.

2. Charles J. Stillé, *History of the United States Sanitary Commission* (New York, 1868), quoted in George Fredrickson, *The Inner Civil War* (New York: Harper & Row, 1965), 98; Fredrickson, *Civil War*, 105, 98, 101 – 2, 111 – 12; *DAB*, s.v. "Charles J. Stillé," "Frederick Fraley" and "Stephen Colwell"; Joseph Wharton, *International Industrial Competition* (Philadelphia: Henry Carey Baird, 1872), 31; Thomas L. Haskell, *The Emergence of Professional Social Science* (Urbana: University of Illinois Press, 1977), 93.

3. Haskell, *Social Science*, 100 – 18; Edward C. Kirkland, *Dream and Thought in the Business Community, 1860 – 1900* (Ithaca, N.Y.: Cornell University Press, 1956), 15 – 16; also see Joseph G. Rosengarten, "Work of the Philadelphia Social Science Association," *Annals of The American Academy of Political and Social Science 1* (1890-91):708-19.

4. Haskell, *Social Sciences*, 91, 115 – 17, 119 – 21.

5. Haskell, *Social Science*, 118; E. Digby Baltzell, *Puritan Boston and Quaker Philadelphia* (New York: Free Press, 1979), 372 – 83; Henry C. Carey, *Principles of Social Science* (Philadelphia: J. B. Lippincott, 1858 – 59).

6. Cheyney, *History of the University*, 249, 259.

7. Donald H. Meyer, *The Instructed Conscience* (Philadelphia: University of Pennsylvania Press, 1972), 99 – 105; Gladys Bryson, "The Emergence of Social Science from Moral Philosophy," *International Journal of Ethics* 42 (1932):514 – 18.

8. Carl W. Kaiser, Jr., *History of the Academic Protection – Free Trade Controversy in America Before 1860* (Philadelphia: University of Pennsylvania, 1934), 90 – 97; A. D. H. Kaplan, *Henry Charles Carey* (Baltimore: Johns Hopkins University Press, 1931); Anna Haddow, *Political Science in American*

Colleges and Universities, 1636–1900 (New York: D. Appleton-Century, 1939), 125–26; James McLachlan, "American Colleges and the Transmission of Culture: The Case of the Mugwumps," in *The Hofstadter Aegis: A Memorial*, ed. Stanley Elkins and Eric McKitrick (New York: Alfred A. Knopf, 1974), 184–206.

9. Francis N. Thorpe, *William Pepper, M.D., L.L.D. (1843–98)* (Philadelphia: J. B. Lippincott, 1904), 160–61; Cheyney, *History of the University*, 276–77.

10. Cheyney, *History of the University*, 276–77; Joseph Wharton, "Project," in Wharton to the trustees, Minutes of the University Trustees, 24 Mar. 1881; Thorpe, *Pepper*, 183.

11. Haddow, *Political Science*, 126, 185; Charles J. Stillé, *Reminiscences of a Provost, 1866–80* (Philadelphia: privately printed, 1880).

12. Richard Montgomery, "Robert Ellis Thompson: A Memoir," *Barnwell Bulletin [of Central High School of Philadelphia]* 12 (Oct. 1934):15–28.

13. James H. S. Bossard, "Robert Ellis Thompson — Pioneer Professor in Social Science," *American Journal of Sociology* 35 (1929):239–42; *DAB*, s.v. "Stephen Colwell"; *Catalog of the University of Pennsylvania (1881-82)*, 39; *The Pennsylvanian*, 25 Jan. 1887, 254.

14. Montgomery, "Thompson," 29; Joseph Wharton, "International Industrial Competition," *Penn Monthly Magazine* 1(1870):476–93.

15. Robert E. Thompson, *Social Science and National Economy* (Philadelphia: Porter & Coates, 1875), iii; "Joseph Wharton's Great Work in Aiding to Firmly Establish Protection as Country's Policy," *Philadelphia Press*, 24 Oct. 1904, Joseph Wharton Papers, Friends' Library, Swarthmore College.

16. Wharton, "Project"; Joseph Wharton, "Is a College Education Advantageous to a Business Man?" (Philadelphia: Wharton School Association, 1890), 19.

17. Wharton, "Project."

18. Albert S. Bolles to Wharton Barker, 25 Apr. 1885, "Wharton School File," Archives; Wharton, "Project."

19. Wharton, "Project."

20. Ibid.

21. Minutes of the University Trustees, 24 Mar. 1881, 3 May 1881; Wharton to the trustees, 23 Jan. 1883, Minutes of the University Trustees, 24 Jan. 1881; Wharton, "Project"; *Catalog (1881–82)*, 39–40; *(1882–83)*, 43–44; Minutes of the University Trustees, 3 May 1881.

22. "Announcement" of the Wharton School, Minutes of the University Trustees, 3 May 1881; Elisha Mulford, *Nation; the Foundation of Civil Order and Political Life in the United States* (New York: Hurd, 1870).

23. Thompson, *Social Science*, 163, 157–205.

24. Ibid., 149, 146, 151.

25. Marc Blaug, *Economic Theory in Retrospect*, 3rd ed. (Cambridge, England: Cambridge University Press, 1978), 140–42. David Ricardo, *Principles of Political Economy and Taxation* (London: Murray, 1819).

26. Ricardo, *Principles.*

27. Thompson, *Social Science*, 50.

28. Thompson, *Social Science*, 50, 69, 70–129; Kaplan, *Henry C. Carey*, 49–50.

29. Adam Smith, *The Wealth of Nations* (New York: Modern Library, 1937), 13, 16; Thompson, *Social Science*, 12, 13, 19, 32ff., 232, 400–403; see Kaplan, *Henry C. Carey*, 61.

30. Thompson, *Social Science*, 234–35, 249, 40, 46–48.

31. *Catalog (1881–82)*, 37, 39; *(1882–83)*, 43; Bolles to Barker, 25 Apr. 1885; Joshua L. Chamberlain, ed., *The University of Pennsylvania, Its History, Influence, Equipment and Characteristics with Biographical Sketches and Por-*

traits of Founders, Benefactors, Officers, and Alumni (Boston: R. Herndon, 1901), 1:376.

32. Wharton to the trustees, 23 Jan. 1883; Minutes of the University Trustees, 24 Jan. 1883, 26 Jan. 1883, 5 June 1883; E. Otis Kendall [Dean of the College Faculty], *First Annual Report of the Wharton School of Finance and Economy*, 1 May 1884, "Wharton School File," Archives, 2–3.

33. "Albert S. Bolles," in Chamberlain, ed., *University of Pennsylvania*, 1:386–87.

34. See Alfred D. Chandler, *Henry Varnum Poor: Business Editor, Analyst and Reformer* (Cambridge, Mass.: Harvard University Press, 1956); Frank W. Taussig, "Introduction" to Charles F. Dunbar, *Economic Essays*, ed. by O. M. W. Sprague (New York: Macmillan, 1904), vii; Arthur H. Cole, "A Conspectus to the History of Business and Economic Literature," *Journal of Economic History* 17 (1957):333 – 88; Albert S. Bolles, *Practical Banking* (New York: Homans, 1884); Albert S. Bolles, *Financial History of the United States*, 3 vols. (New York: Appleton, 1879–86).

35. *Catalog (1883 – 84)*, 31; *(1885 – 86)*, 55 – 56; Bolles to Barker, 25 Apr. 1885; Wharton, "Project."

36. Theophilus Parsons, *Elements of Mercantile Law* (Boston: Little, Brown, 1862), x; George Sharswood, *Commercial Law* (Philadelphia: Hayes & Zell, 1856); Theophilus Parsons, *Law of Business* (Hartford: S. S. Scranton, 1881), 28.

37. Parsons, *Law of Business*, 25.

38. Kendall, *First Annual Report*, 3, 4; Bolles, *Practical Banking*, v.

39. Lorenzo Sabine, "Suggestions to Young Cashiers on the Duties of Their Profession," reprinted in Bolles, *Practical Banking*, 302; see Bolles, *Financial History*.

40. Sabine, "Suggestions," reprinted in Bolles, *Practical Banking*, 309.

41. Minutes of the University Trustees, 13 June 1884; biographical files of "Shiro Shiba," "Robert Adams, Jr.," "William Redwood Wharton," and "Edward Potts Cheyney," Archives.

42. Eric Goldman, *John Bach McMaster, American Historian* (Philadelphia: University of Pennsylvania Press, 1943), 51; *Catalog (1881–82)*, 41; *(1882–83)*, 44.

43. Stillé to Frederick Fraley, 30 Jan. 1880, Minutes of the University Trustees, 3 Feb. 1880. 4

44. Ibid.; "Report of Committee," Minutes of the University Trustees, 12 Jan. 1881.

45. Goldman, *McMaster*, 50; Richard A. Swanson, "Edmund J. James, 1855–1925: A 'Conservative Progressive' in American Higher Education" (Ph.D. diss., University of Illinois, 1966), 76–77.

Henry C. Carey

Frederick Fraley

J. B. Lippincott

Stephen Colwell

John Welsh

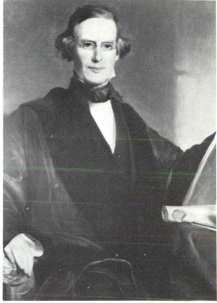

Charles J. Stillé

Henry Vethake

Henry C. Lea

William D. Marks

College Hall

University of Pennsylvania Chapel, Room 200, College Hall, ca. 1885

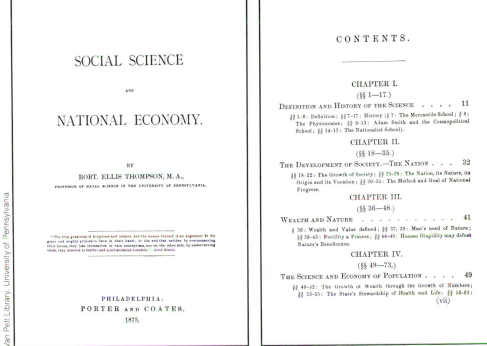

SOCIAL SCIENCE

AND

NATIONAL ECONOMY.

BY

ROBT. ELLIS THOMPSON, M. A.,

PROFESSOR OF SOCIAL SCIENCE IN THE UNIVERSITY OF PENNSYLVANIA.

"The true greatness of kingdoms and estates, and the means thereof, is an argument fit for great and mighty princes to have in their hand; to the end that neither by overmeasuring their forces, they lose themselves in vain enterprise, nor on the other side, by undervaluing them, they descend to fearful and pusillanimous counsels."—*Lord Bacon.*

PHILADELPHIA:
PORTER AND COATES.
1875.

CONTENTS.

Robert Ellis Thompson, *Social Science and National Economy,*
title page and first page of contents

Robert Ellis Thompson

Albert S. Bolles

William R. Wharton   Edward P. Cheney

Robert Adams, Jr.   Shiro Shiba

3

The School of Practical Affairs: The College of Political and Social Science

When Albert Bolles set out to recruit faculty for the Wharton School in 1883, he found a tremendous revolution under way in the nation's academic institutions, with a new vision of the future possessing the ambitious leaders of American higher education. Inspiring this excitement was the image of the great German universities, at the time enjoying a tremendous reputation for practicality, erudition, and discovery. American reformers held up Germany's dedicated and proficient university-trained civil service as a model for their own government administration. The levels of scholarship in German schools established an entirely new standard of achievement. But most impressive, to laymen and to scholars alike, was the flood of new contributions to scientific and cultural studies that flowed from these universities. At the root of this success lay two powerful engines of intellectual advance that German academics had developed in the nineteenth century: the research laboratory and the research seminar. Following the opening in 1876 of the Johns Hopkins University, a school that from the beginning modeled itself on the German research design, a craze to domesticate the German achievement took hold of the nation's campuses. By the early 1880s, American "captains of erudition" were busily establishing new institutional structures, new standards of scholarship, and a new leadership role in society. Professor Bolles and Provost Pepper realized that the future success of the Wharton School required that it find some way to join with this dynamic new university system. Among the professors to be brought to Philadelphia, Bolles hoped to find a leader to take Wharton out of the traditional era of the college and into the burgeoning world of the university.[1]

Bolles first tried to recruit Herbert Baxter Adams, professor of history at Johns Hopkins. Under the direction of Baxter Adams, the Johns Hopkins historical seminar had already established itself as America's most prominent academic school of social interpretation. Building on German historical research, Adams's group had traced the genius of political democracy in the United States back to tribal Teutonic institutions of local government. Like Bolles, in his *Financial History of the United States*, Adams sought to recapture the past human purposes that lay behind contemporary institutions. Like Robert Ellis Thompson, he hoped that historical study would inspire a revival of civic virtue. But more than a particular type of interpretation, and more than an approach to cultural commitment, Adams's discipline of history was the leading method of inquiry of the German school of social research. This "historical method" brought original documents and carefully gathered statistical series before a critical seminar, where they served as empirical evidence for or against conjectures on the development of social institutions. The historical method explicitly challenged the methodological foundations of the moral philosophers and classical economists — psychological introspection and reasoned deduction. By abandoning the "self" as the ground of inquiry, the German strategy avoided the individualist-laissez-faire bias in traditional Anglo-American social thought. It thus opened the way for more "organic" and statist ideologies.[2]

As the preeminent academic historian in America, Herbert Baxter Adams was the big academic prize of the day. Recruiting him would have brought the university tremendous prestige. But when Bolles approached Adams with his offer, the historian was already at the head of a thriving operation. He had just begun editing the influential *Johns Hopkins University Studies in Historical and Political Science*, and his seminar was sending into the world a stream of thoroughly trained young professional scholars. With such success in Baltimore, Adams declined Bolles's invitation to come to Philadelphia.[3]

Although Bolles was anxious to hire Adams, the historian's work actually had little to do with the immediate training of business and political leaders or the formulation of policy. German scholars had great faith in the value of historical research for leadership training and to assist policymaking. But Adams's program was entirely academic, concerned mainly with the pre-revolutionary beginnings of American political history and far removed from the practical concerns of the Wharton School. Bolles was clearly carried away with the new rage for scholarship when he made this offer. Giving Adams a prominent place in the Wharton School, in fact, would have invited a conflict with the founder over the direction of the school. Much more suitable, however, were the two young academics that Bolles did recruit. In John Bach McMaster he found a professor of history more interested in the economic and social development of nineteenth-century America than any other leading historian. In Edmund Janes James, who became Wharton's new professor of public administration and finance, he located a scholar with not only a German Ph.D. (and a German wife), but also with a commitment to reproduce in the United States the vaunted German system of generating civil servants and public policies.[4]

John Bach McMaster had come to history in a roundabout manner. The son of a New York business family more cosmopolitan than prosperous, he went through that city's public schools and graduated from the New York Free Academy in 1872.* Five years later, after working at various odd jobs and earning a degree in engineering, he accepted a position teaching that subject at Princeton. With leisure time and a secure income, McMaster was now able to redeem his patrician ancestry and take up the genteel vocation of historian; he embarked right away on his life's work, a multivolume narrative *History of the American People*. Unlike other American historians, who wrote only of politics, McMaster wanted to capture the social and economic life of the nation as well. As he declared at the beginning of his study, "the history of the people shall be the chief theme" and he would "describe the

*This academy later became the City College of New York.

dress, the occupations, the amusements, the literary canons of the times." When his first volume appeared in 1883, it won an immediate and enthusiastic reception, and McMaster soon had offers to teach history from three good universities. He chose the University of Pennsylvania and the Wharton School.[5]

At Wharton, McMaster taught his students American economic and social history and had them write historical essays using original source materials. But despite McMaster's pioneering interests and sources, his teaching and his writing never broke free of traditional historiography. Although he discussed the history of finance, transportation, and manufactures, of education and social habits, he found his central theme in the nation's political history — in the development of individual freedom and national unity and power. In courses on the Constitution of the United States and on the political development of the nation, McMaster taught the standard interpretation of the nation's political history of the 1880s: that prosperity, moral sensibility, and freedom in the United States had grown in tandem with the strength of the Union; that the Constitution and centralized government had been the great bulwarks of American liberty and civilization, and the essential framework for opportunity. McMaster introduced his students to the thinking of the founding fathers; he explained how the institutions that they had fashioned defended achievement and property against irresponsible democrats who would fill government office with spoilsmen and undermine the monetary standard with inflated currency. Finally, McMaster presented the Civil War as the great test of constitutional government in the United States, as the triumphal vindication of the Revolution.[6]

The addition of McMaster's pedagogy and thought, those of an accomplished and thorough scholar, gave the Wharton program much-needed weight. Under his direction historical studies grew steadily through the 1880s and two junior historians, his students Edward Potts Cheyney and Francis N. Thorpe, had to join McMaster on the faculty to satisfy the expanding demand for the subject. Bolles and Thompson also taught historical courses, so that in 1887, instruction in history made up half of the Wharton curriculum.[7]

Despite McMaster's erudition and the obvious demand for history, McMaster never became a forceful presence at the school. Cheyney, the finest historian to win a Wharton degree in the 1880s, reported that McMaster was more successful in print than in the classroom; Cheyney's own "master" instructor in history had been Thompson, not McMaster. Neither McMaster, nor for that matter Thompson, succeeded in weaving historical work at Wharton into the emerging academic system. Neither attempted to establish history as the basic method of inquiry in the social sciences as it was in Germany, nor did they establish a strong research seminar. McMaster, modeling himself not on Germany's great academic scholars but on England's great amateur social historians Thomas Babington Macaulay and Henry Thomas Buckle, wrote his history as a self-contained narrative intended for popular audiences. He did not see himself in the German academic tradition, writing "contributions" to a scholarly "literature" read primarily by fellow professionals. So when Herbert Baxter Adams organized these professionals into the American Historical Association in 1885, McMaster did not participate. In any case, McMaster and his courses passed out of the Wharton School in 1891, establishing themselves first as the Institute of American History and Institutions and then joining the Department of History in the college. There McMaster stayed until his retirement in 1918, finishing his *History of the American People.*[8]

Bolles's recruitment of Edmund J. James proved far more important to the history of the Wharton School. At the time of his appointment in 1883, James was a promising twenty-eight-year-old social scientist with good German credentials, zeal for his profession, and a winning manner. He arrived with a firm vision of how to organize a professional school of affairs, one combining scholarship and pragmatics. Furthermore, James had the ability to realize ambitions. Vigorous, charming, and obviously intelligent, he easily attracted students to his classrooms, faculty to his programs, and business and civic leaders to his causes.

Born in 1855, James was the son of a circuit-riding Methodist preacher from Illinois. Apart from religion itself, the great interests of his father, the Reverend Colin Dew James, were education and the preservation of the Union. He was a devout Republican and through the dark days of the Civil War impressed upon his son the historical significance of the American republic. The elder James believed in education as a great moral and civilizing process and served as a trustee of three Illinois colleges; indeed, he moved his family to Bloomington so that his children could attend the excellent practice school operated there by Illinois Normal School. There young Edmund enrolled in the classical program, but already exhibited a particular interest in economic policy. It is said that in preparation for a debate, he once devoured all books in the school's library on the subject of the tariff. Upon graduation he went on to study for a year at Northwestern University and then for another year at Harvard. But the educational frontier lay still further eastward. In 1875, at the age of twenty, James set out for Germany and the University of Halle to study economics.[9]

Before James left for Europe, his mother advised him to attach himself to a great teacher and to absorb his genius. He obeyed, and chose as his mentor Johannes Conrad, a vigorous young professor of economics at the University of Halle, who was then at the beginning of a long and distinguished career. Conrad had first made his reputation in 1864, when he had published a careful statistical refutation of Ricardo's pessimistic prospect for agricultural production. His documentation of the growth of agricultural productivity paralleled the work of Carey's Philadelphia School. But in explaining the expansion of per capita output, Conrad stressed the development of applied agricultural knowledge — chemical discoveries, crop diversification, and farmer education. He made no use of Adam Smith's principle of the division of labor and even thought that birth control was an economic boon. Conrad also felt no need to use such deductive "principles" of human behavior as Smith's little theorems. To discover new economic knowledge, he relied on methods of empirical investigation that he had learned from Germany's great historical scholars — Leopold von Ranke and Gustav Schmoller. Conrad, however, concentrated less than his mentors on documentary criticism and more on statistical analysis.[10]

Most of the students taught by Conrad and his fellow "historical economists" were intent on careers in the civil service, not in scholarship or the old liberal professions. This German school of economics thus began with the premise that the state had a positive role to play in economic and social affairs. While British political economists puzzled over the proper economic sphere of government, the German school taught students how to formulate and administer policy, how to maintain and improve the applied intelligence of the state. This German program made a powerful impression on James because it combined the two critical values that he took from his midwestern Republican upbringing — passions for education and for the unity and power of the federal government.[11]

The tradition of preparing government officials in German universities can be traced back to the eighteenth-century "cameralists," who taught public finance and administration and served as advisors to the state. Conrad still taught public finance and administration and maintained the cameralistic tradition of consulting on policy matters. To advise the nineteenth-century state more effectively, Conrad and his fellow historical economists founded the *Verein für Sozialpolitik*. This organization, like the American Social Science Association, brought professionals and men of affairs together to investigate social issues and to agitate for reform. Unlike the ASSA, however, it was controlled by the esteemed German professoriate, not by men of affairs and the traditional professional groups. With scholars in control, the *Verein* sponsored a series of admirable research projects on the controversial issues of the day. Its work especially influenced government policy toward problems created by the new urban-industrial economy, on matters such as housing, labor conditions, and social insurance.[12]

In Conrad's classroom James learned the cameralistic disciplines of public finance and administration. In Conrad's seminar James practiced the new methods of inquiry — evaluating historical documents and gathering and examining social statistics — and then wrote his Ph.D. dissertation on the American tariff system. Conrad also introduced his student to the activities of the *Verein* and encouraged him to organize a similar association in the United States. Although James's German education lasted only two years, the experience had such vibrancy as to shape his entire subsequent career.[13]

James returned to the United States in 1877 with his Ph.D., but could find no job at an American university. Instead he found employment in his native Illinois as a high school principal, first in Evanston and then at the Illinois Normal School's new Model High School in Bloomington. High school education was a fairly prestigious field at the time and not very different from American collegiate instruction. But fresh from the world of German universities and fired by greater academic ambitions, James began publishing articles in order to widen his reputation. He and a friend even bought a pedagogical journal in which to print their essays. At the same time James wrote a series of long articles in the *Cyclopedia of Political and Social Science and of the Political History of the United States*, edited by Chicago newpaperman John J. Lalor. Among his contributions were surveys of the "history of political economy," "labor," "insurance," the "science of finance," and "factory laws." Written in vigorous prose, these articles were among America's first and finest expositions of German economic thinking. They attracted Bolles's attention and led to the realization of James's aspirations: his appointment as Professor of Public Finance and Administration at the Wharton School.[14]

As soon as James arrived in Philadelphia he established himself in the image of a German professor. On Sunday afternoons he and his wife maintained a European-style "open house" for students and fellow faculty. In class James used the German professorial lecture rather than the contemporary collegiate routine of rote, recitations, and drills. In September of 1885 he introduced the first research seminar at the University of Pennsylvania, the "Seminary for Political and Economic Science," thus bringing to Philadelphia the new German institution for evaluating and creating social knowledge. The young professor also played a central role in organizing a German-style, research oriented graduate school at the university. Like Conrad, James also put his erudition, his energy, and his new academic eminence at the head of local reform activities, becoming an active member of the Philadelphia Social Science Association. More than Thompson and Bolles, with their outside journalistic interests, or McMaster, who never fully engaged his students, James thus made the Wharton School and professional social science the center of his life.[15]

The instruction that James himself offered at Wharton covered the traditional cameralistic areas of study — public finance and administration. Having written his dissertation on the tariff, the chief source of federal revenue at the time, James was well prepared to teach public finance. Through the 1880s James taught seniors a one-year course on the subject, using Bolles's *Financial History* for the first semester and lecturing in the second. There he reviewed in great detail the structure and administration of federal, state, and local revenue systems. He also presented his students with the taxation and expenditure theories of the German authorities and of the leading British economists — Smith, Ricardo, McCulloch, and John Stuart Mill. Through James, Wharton's graduates thus acquired a background in cameralistic economics, an education akin to that of German aspirants to civil service positions, not the classical, moral-philosophical learning absorbed by their fellow American bachelor degree-holders.[16]

James's true love, and the major part of his work at Wharton, dealt not with public finance but with general problems of policy: the theory of the state, constitutional structure, and public administration. Indeed, James stopped offering his course in public finance in June 1892 and thereafter concentrated on issues of general politics. In September 1889, he organized the major portion of his instruction into a two-year course, covering political constitutions in the junior year and public administration in the senior. Whereas McMaster went over much of the same material in historical perspective, James did so with a German variant of the "historical method" — the "comparative method." He presented the American material in the first semester and then offered European examples of constitutions and administrations in the second. His comparisons both highlighted general characteristics of all such political systems and the peculiarities of the American situation.[17]

The essential conclusion to be drawn from such an extended examination of nineteenth-century politics, James impressed upon his classes, was that there was a new necessity for positive state administration. Joseph Wharton, Henry C. Carey, and Robert Ellis Thompson, of course, had offered long arguments for state promotion of economic development in the form of tariff legislation. McMaster and voices in the American past, such as Alexander

Hamilton and Henry Clay, had also justified government promotion of roads, canals, and banks. But James went further. He taught his students that the proper sphere of government continually expanded, paralleling the growth of social complexity, economic interdependence, and collective enterprise. In modern industrial society, he argued, justice, equity, and the long-run vitality of the community had become much more problematic than in the past. Only the state, as the expression of popular consciousness and will, and not some moral crusade by itself, could protect these national interests. The American people, he reasoned, now had to rely on government to bring them fully out of barbarism and into civilization.[18]

James explained that the major opponents of his position, Adam Smith and his nineteenth-century liberal followers, held an "untenable theory of the state and its functions." Like Thompson, James criticized this school for picturing extensive social cooperation as growing "naturally"—as a manifestation of some natural law governing "economic men"—and in no fundamental respect dependent upon good political administration. James faulted Smith for ignoring

> that deeper conception of the higher spiritual essence of the state and national life; for nations are to him [Smith] nothing but aggregates of individuals controlled by merely material and economic motives, and not communities of souls who have and pursue moral, political and spiritual ends and aims. . . . Out of this view rose a political theory which leads to fatalism, in which the ethical power and freedom of the human will are utterly powerless in the grasp of natural law.[19]

James had important tasks for "the ethical power and freedom of the human will," and liberalism's practical effect of inducing "fatalism" bothered the minister's son even more than did the purely academic nature of the dispute. "Human progress depends," he wrote, not on any automatic market mechanism but "largely on conscious human effort, put forth in accordance with a conscious purpose." James saw his social science as part of a larger revival of American civic righteousness and as providing the nation with a "conscious purpose." The blind and dissolute politics in contemporary America, where "the lowest form of institution known to civilized society — the corner saloon, controls the government of a great people," horrified James. He staunchly believed in popular government, but the populus had to be educated in social science and power entrusted to the best people of the land. With such government, the republic could proceed to the tasks of ordering its industrial affairs: The state could regulate the economy so as to prevent corporate directors from defrauding stockholders, railroads and other monopolists from gouging consumers, employers from overtaxing their workers, and loggers from despoiling the nation's forests; such government could operate the public utilities, protect labor unions, and generally care for the weak and dependent.[20]

Reflecting the influence of his Midwestern Republican origins and his German experience, James placed the need for better education and research above all other issues. His most important schemes for reform were efforts at improving the quality of intelligence that was applied to social, political, and economic problems. In 1885, two years after his arrival in Philadelphia, the thirty-year-old professor advanced two programs to that end: plans for an association of professional economists and a new design to make the Wharton School a "School of Political and Social Science." Neither proposal met with success at the time. But because of James's persistence and his entrepreneurial skills, both projects came to have a significant impact on the Wharton School.

In 1885 James and two former classmates from Halle, Simon N. Patten and Richard T. Ely, decided to establish a national association for academic economists like themselves. With Ely handling the organizational chores, James and Patten wrote a constitution for a "Society for the Study of National Economy." Their proposed organization would encourage and publish research and "combat the widespread view that our economic problems will solve themselves and that our laws and institutions, which at present favor individual instead of collective action, can promote a better utilization of our material resources." James and Patten concluded their constitution with a list of governmental activities that the new society ought to endorse. These included aiding education, regulating transportation, "lumbering", and working conditions, promoting agricultural and industrial research, and insuring "the symmetrical development" of the nation's resources (i.e., high tariffs).[21]

James's and Patten's proposals for the Society for the Study of National Economy never materialized. Ely drew up an alternative and somewhat less statist plan and saw to it that it became the basis for the American Economic Association. At its first meeting, held in conjunction with the American Social Science Association and the fledgling American Historical Association, only ten economists attended.* Young economists soon arrived in larger numbers. But only after eliminating all of those ideological and direct research-sponsoring functions that James and Patten had outlined did the nation's economists join en masse and make the AEA their central professional association.[22]

At the same time that James was working to establish the American Economic Association, he presented, in an address to the Philadelphia Social Science Association (PSSA), his plan to redesign Wharton into a "School of Political and Social Science." Typically combining his experiences in Germany with the values that he had learned from his father, James envisioned a much closer interaction between the school and the work of the world. He emphasized the value of Teutonic research and specialization for in-depth understanding of practical problems. In addition, James's plan obeyed his father's injunction to establish learning throughout the land. His proposed Wharton School would elevate a whole new class of human activities into university-based professions. By organizing the intellectual components of particular occupations into a curriculum and setting up a research program to develop this "knowledge," he hoped to bring the enlightenment and dynamism of the university to all practical affairs. Such was the promise, according to James, of Germany's academic innovations and their diffusion into society.[23]

In his paper, James made a series of specific proposals. First he would have Wharton become a "center" for the "most detailed and patient investigation of facts and principles" underlying the pressing social and economic issues faced by the government. He listed as urgent areas of research the problems of railroad regulation, the growth of industrial monopoly, and relations between labor and capital. James then turned to the undergraduate pro-

---

*Albert Bolles appeared on the first published list of members, but he did not attend this meeting.

gram. In addition to the general training that every businessman required—the accounting, law, and general business practice that Wharton then offered — James also wanted to start educational programs in various particular industries. He specifically mentioned "the great departments of business, such as banking, railroading, merchandising, manufacturing and other similar branches." James's Wharton School would also offer courses of study in pedagogy and journalism, as well as in business and politics. In a popular democracy, he reasoned, those who instructed and informed the people needed special academic preparation equal to that of the men who handled affairs.[24]

James thus proposed to push the newly established elective principle further than anyone had ever intended. Academe had just given up the grand unity of its curriculum to provide a place for schools such as Wharton. Now James advocated a truly infinite number of collegiate programs. In a passage strikingly reminiscent of Conrad's and Carey's history of agriculture, James wrote that

opening new lines of study which reach down into the mass of the people is like sinking new shafts in a mining district. It opens up entirely new veins of unsuspected wealth, which might have remained concealed forever if this particular shaft had not been sunk. There is an infinite variety of tastes and types of mind, and an infinite variety of science. The infinitude of the one corresponds to the infinitude of the other, and we shall achieve the highest results in utilizing all the variety of talent, only when we have placed within its reach all the variety of Art and Science.

James even went so far as to credit the recent diversification of education as the major cause of modern economic progress, claiming

that the explanation of the wonderful material progress of modern free communities lies, to a large extent, in the simple fact that we have begun at last, for the first time in the history of the world, to utilize a small part of the infinite intellectual power of the race.[25]

James thought that his specialized, professional program would draw into the university young men aspiring to business careers. It thus addressed "one of the great problems of higher education[:] to secure its diffusion among the business men of a community." The well-educated and diversely trained business and political class produced by such a school, James predicted, would then invigorate American society. Management of the nation's affairs could be taken out of the dull hands of uneducated "routinists" and placed into those of alert "professional students," men who constantly searched for new opportunities and recognized them when they appeared. He expected that his School of Political and Social Science would soon achieve a status akin to schools of medicine and law, "except that it should insist on a higher grade of acquirement for admission." James ended his address to the PSSA with a plea for support. "Philadelphia needs such a school . . . . The State, nay the Nation, needs such an institution." When added to Wharton's endowment and tuition income from students, James thought that a mere twenty-five thousand dollars would be needed to open its doors.[26]

In one respect, James spoke for the whole Wharton faculty: The professors were unanimous in their support for a journalism program. Earlier in the year, in fact, they had petitioned the trustees to hire another faculty member in order to develop a course of study in the field. Thompson and Bolles remained practicing journalists throughout their careers at Wharton; James regularly wrote essays for the popular press, and McMaster relied on newspapers as a source of truth about the past. All knew of the journalist's critical responsibilities in handling ideas in the world of affairs. But the trustees, who were concerned about a shortage of students and funds, took no action.[27]

Despite faculty support on this one issue, James's performance at the Philadelphia Social Science Association was quite brash. At the time, James was a thirty-year-old academic who had been in the city for just two years. Not a powerful research scholar of the German or Johns Hopkins type, he gave little indication that he could manage the proposed "centers" of research. His work was abundant, thorough, well-written, and accurate, but it was not original; aside from his dissertation, itself an essay of less than 100 pages, James would never contribute a book-length monograph to the scholarly literature. Meanwhile, the exotic undergraduate panorama that he proposed involved a further expansion of both Wharton and the elective principle, each a new and controversial innovation.[28]

Joseph Wharton looked with cold jealousy on James's effort to redesign his newborn school. He thought the proposed School of Political and Social Science "unlikely to be established, and if established, liable to disappoint its founders." The project, he sneered, simply required too much money and too much management. Wharton also saw in James's scheme a purpose for the school different from his own. "My object," he pointed out, was simply "to provide if possible a way for young men to fit themselves for the management of affairs — to acquire sound knowledge of the principles of what is called 'business.'" The founder saw no reason to attach other forms of instruction. The science of pedagogy aroused his skepticism and

as to journalism, why set out to train boys for that any more than for grocery: if the boy is trained to quick apprehension of statements or occurrences, to rapid and easy connections of arrangement and expression, he may become a journalist or succeed in another career.

Wharton clung to his original program, to educate a class of responsible leaders. He objected to any effort to proceed with James's plans unless, of course, the faculty could find a separate endowment for the purpose. It could not.[29]

With James's proposals thus tabled, the school's expansion came to an end, remaining comfortably within the lines laid down by the founder. Although instruction in history marked a departure from Joseph Wharton's "Project," the addition of James fleshed out his program by providing the designated "Professor or Instructor upon Taxation." As Joseph Wharton had envisioned, the school also attracted students from families that had long been prominent in Philadelphia business and society, young men with names such as Jayne, Woodruff, McGeorge, Brooke, Griscom, Busch, Houston, Welsh, Milne, and Jones. When not embarked on furniture-busting adolescent rampages, these young gentlemen "of inherited intellect, means, and refinement" received instruction in social science, business law and practice, history, and cameralistics. Perhaps as many as one-half of the school's graduates in the 1880s joined their fathers' firms and quickly rose to positions of executive authority. The same proportion, although not the identical graduates, went on to become "prominent" in Philadelphia business, politics, and learning.[30]

James had no argument with Joseph Wharton's ambitions for the school. He sincerely agreed that providing a professional collegiate education for society's business and political elite was a valuable and legitimate task. But James never abandoned his ambition to make the Wharton School itself a dynamic, leading force in society. While Joseph Wharton attended to the affairs of the Bethlehem Company and its venture in arms manufacture, James worked steadily to establish his own program. The Philadelphia ironmaster could never take direct charge of the school that he had founded, but, as at Bethlehem Steel, was forced to rely on others. As a result, his design for the Wharton School soon lost its grip on the institution, while that of Edmund James grew increasingly influential.

James found important support for his program among Wharton's upper-crust student body. A vigorous, lucid, and inspiring teacher, he naturally attracted a following among students with a serious turn of mind. Walter Weyl, who later became a founding editor of the *New Republic*, was one such student. He later wrote to James:

It may be out of place to express at this time my deep sense of personal obligation to you but I have wanted to thank you so often for the very great impetus you have been to me. . . . I am only one of many men who have gone through the Wharton School and are trying more or less successfully to be what you have told them to be.

James won the lasting loyalty of a great many of his students, including those who entered business after college. But the greatest testament to his teaching success is that during the 1880s four out of ten Wharton graduates actually followed James's message of enlightenment and righteousness into careers as academics and reformers. Well-connected and well-to-do young men, such as Weyl, Ellis P. Oberholtzer, and Clinton R. Woodruff, could afford careers in journalism, letters, and reform. Those with fewer resources, such as Roland P. Faulkner, Leo S. Rowe, and Samuel M. Lindsay, turned to scholarship. Over 10 percent of Wharton's early graduates became college professors and approximately half of these young men followed their mentor's path to Germany for graduate training. James guided the best of them to Halle and Conrad.[31]

Such success among students must have encouraged James, but to establish his program for the Wharton School required more basic changes. James's influence over events improved dramatically at the end of the 1886-87 academic year, when Bolles resigned his position to become Pennsylvania state statistician. Provost Pepper then officially placed the school in James's hands, naming him chairman of the Economics Department of the college. Bolles had been a conscientious scholar, a man of broad experience, and an important member of the faculty. As his successor James chose a former student, Roland P. Faulkner, a young man with no exposure to the world of affairs, but one trained in the methods of the new academic system. Like James, Faulkner was the son of a minister and had graduated from a public high school — Philadelphia's Central High. He had continued on to Penn and, while studying at Wharton during James's first two years on the faculty, had decided on an academic career. No doubt directed by James, he had gone off to Halle to study economics and statistics with Johannes Conrad. In 1888, at the tender age of twenty-two, he won his Ph.D. Faulkner then returned to Philadelphia, to teach at the Wharton School.[32]

Although Faulkner took over all the business subject areas — accounting as well as business practice and law — his primary expertise, and the chief reason for his appointment at Wharton, was his thorough training in statistics. Quantitative reckoning had already assumed major importance in the world of political and industrial affairs and Conrad in Germany had shown James this power of statistical analysis. In 1885-86 someone at Wharton, perhaps Bolles, had offered a ten-lecture course in statistics. No doubt Faulkner, still an undergraduate, attended the series. But at Halle, Conrad led Faulkner much further into the growing literature of statistics. He showed him in detail how the new quantitative tools and information could help businessmen and public officials measure their environment. Duly impressed, Faulkner made the subject his own and, when he returned to Philadelphia, made it a regular part of the Wharton curriculum.[33]

At that time statistics was barely taught in American colleges and universities. Faulkner, in fact, was one of the first two American professors whose title included the word *statistics*. There being no suitable introductory textbook to the subject, Faulkner provided one of his own, a translation of August Meitzen's *History, Theory and Techniques of Statistics*. It was quickly apparent that the Wharton School had broken ground in an important area of research and instruction, and Faulkner soon found his skills in great demand in the world of affairs. During the 1891-92 academic year he was called away from the classroom to serve as statistician of the U.S. Senate Finance Committee. There he oversaw "the most exhaustive investigation of prices and wages in the United States to that time," a pioneering seven-volume study known as the "Aldrich Reports." The next academic year, 1892-93, also found Faulkner on leave, this time to serve as secretary of the American delegation to the International Monetary Conference. With his statistical skills afforded such a dramatic reception in the world of affairs, Faulkner dropped his other teaching responsibilities upon his return to Wharton and became the nation's first full-time professor to specialize in the subject. He then offered graduate as well as undergraduate instruction on gathering and using economic and social statistics.[34]

James's second change in Wharton's faculty proved to be even more important than the addition of Faulkner. It did not, however, come so easily. In November 1887, the students complained that they were not getting the kind of instruction they would like in political economy. Robert Ellis Thompson was perhaps appearing a bit too romantic or old-fashioned. In the meantime, the Central Committee of the alumni of the university had proposed that a lecturer favoring free trade be invited to the campus. The Philadelphia School of political economy was clearly in trouble. So too was Joseph Wharton's endowment, since the controversy challenged instruction in protectionism at the school. In the fall of 1887, Provost Pepper held a series of "anxious deliberations" and then decided to ease certain prominent professors, including Thompson, out of their critical positions on the faculty. With the trustees' approval, the chair in political economy was declared vacant on 6 December 1887 and Thompson was asked to devote most of his time to literature and history, not economics. Trustee Henry H. Houston donated six hundred dollars for a series of lectures on political economy (conducted under the auspices of the undergraduate Philomathean Society!) until the university found a permanent professor.[35]

The man brought in to teach economics, beginning in September 1888, was James's good friend, Simon Patten. The two had gone through Conrad's seminars at Halle and had worked together on the organization of the American Economics Association. James used his considerable influence at Wharton to bring Patten to Philadelphia, even going so far as to fudge his curriculum vitae to have him appear more active in recent years. James's confidence in his friend proved worthwhile. Although Patten had not previously held a university post, he had published his protean *Premises of Political Economy* in 1885. His appointment brought to the faculty one of the most imaginative economic minds in the history of the discipline, and he soon became a fixture of the Wharton curriculum. Patten taught his students the economic principles of Smith, Ricardo, and Mill with a masterful touch and conducted a graduate seminar in economics which quickly won fame for its brilliance and novel thinking.[36]

As James went about his business of recruiting a Halle-trained faculty, he was also at work making his talents useful to the local elite. Bolles and Thompson had lived in the larger society as journalists, and journalism was perhaps the most common way for men of ideas to take part in the handling of affairs in nineteenth-century America. But James was true to the *Verein* idea and hoped to influence events as an academic, through research and command of the scholarly literature. He found the old Philadelphia Social Science Association the most hospitable arena for these ambitions.

James became noticeably active in the Social Science Association in 1885. In that year he presented the Philadelphia group his plan for establishing university-level "Instruction in Political and Social Science."' He also became the secretary of the national organization's Department of Social Economy, a position he kept until 1890. But James's great success came in 1886, when he read to the Philadelphia society a long and detailed analysis of *The Relation of the Modern Municipality to the Gas Supply, with Special Reference to the Gas Question in Philadelphia*.[37]

James's paper addressed the problem of administering utilities, a question which had long perplexed government administrators. Throughout history certain economic functions, such as maintaining transportation systems and administering justice, were naturally controlled by a central authority. The nineteenth century saw the rise of new municipal "utilities"—water and sewer, gas, electricity, and mass transit systems. The economic vitality of the city economy came to be critically dependent upon the cheap and efficient provision of these services. But each new utility had its own esoteric, patentable, and enormously expensive technology. Each impinged on the rights and powers of the state in a myriad of different ways. In 1886 the question facing the citizens of Philadelphia was how they ought to control their gas system: Should the municipality own and operate, lease, regulate, or merely license the works?

Late nineteenth-century Philadelphia government had lost whatever administrative grasp it had once had on the efficient delivery of urban services. The city-owned gas works had been leased to a venal group of politically well-connected "managers," known as "the Gas Ring," and had become just another source of enrichment in the wide-open "Great Barbeque" of America's gilded age. The "Gas Ring" had operated the enterprise as a fiefdom, employing thousands of political hangers-on and passing the cost of this payroll on to the utility's customers. The lease on the gas works had just terminated, and the future of the utility was now a public question. The situation was fluid, and all possibilities, including continued control by the powerful Gas Ring, remained open.[38]

Philadelphia's band of genteel reformers, led by Joseph Wharton's good friend and University of Pennsylvania historian Henry C. Lea, had for years agitated for the return of the works to municipal hands. Now, in 1886, James contributed his seventy-six-page academic essay to this party of good government. James's "Gas Supply" laid out, in lucid detail, the city's various options; it reviewed the experience of several leading cities, and concluded that Philadelphia would indeed do better to manage its own property. Leasing the works, James argued, would double the price of gas, strengthen monopoly power in the city, eliminate the incentives for innovation at the utility, and generally reduce Philadelphia's ability to compete with more efficiently run cities. He met the inevitable objection, the city government's corruption and inefficiency, with a favorite argument: Adding administrative functions to the government would induce the citizenry and their civic leaders to pay closer attention to City Hall. They would then insist that public business be in the hands of responsible officials, civil servants of the type that the Wharton School stood ready to supply.[39]

"Gas Supply" won James a solid reputation among Philadelphia's civic-minded gentlemen and received wide notice both locally and nationally. After James read the piece at the Philadelphia Social Science Association, it was published by the American Economics Association. "Gas Supply" unquestionably helped Lea's crusade succeed. And for years afterward, civic-minded Philadelphians commonly cited the Wharton professor as their champion who had kept the utility in municipal hands.[40]

Despite James's success with the Philadelphia Social Science Association and his work at the national organization, the American Social Science Association (ASSA) failed to attract the same sort of participation from other new professional economists. Instead, these men invested their energy in the American Economic Association and steadily pushed that society away from reform activities and contact with nonacademics. As a result, the ASSA lost stature and effectiveness, and the wedding of scholars and civic leaders seemed an increasingly unlikely union. But James persisted in his commitment to policy-oriented research and research-based reform. Rather than join his colleagues in their chosen isolation or continue with the foundering ASSA, he established a new organization, the "American Academy of Political and Social Science," in December 1889.[41]

James, by this time, had assembled a strong constituency in Philadelphia. The large group of Wharton faculty, students, and alumni that had gathered around him formed the core of his new academy and dominated its proceedings. They unanimously elected James as president of the organization, while its council included Simon N. Patten, Clinton R. Woodruff, Roland P. Faulkner, Edward P. Cheyney, and Samuel M. Lindsay.* Of Wharton's "prominent" graduates, an impressive 40 percent joined the academy. The Philadelphia Social Science Association, acknowledging James's new leadership in the city, immediately dissolved itself into the academy. A large portion of its prosperous membership joined the new association. That, and perhaps a subsidy from the university, made James's academy an instant financial success.[42]

---

*The last four were alumni, and the last three also became members of the full-time faculty.

The American Academy declared in its handbook that

membership is open to those who by reason of their interest and position in the community are desirous of aiding in the right solution of social, political, and economic questions. The membership is at present composed of business and professional men and government officials.

Despite the similarity of aims and constituency between the new Academy of Political and Social Science and the American Social Science Association, James actually intended to significantly reorganize the way in which professionals and businessmen studied public issues and campaigned for reform. James naturally chose Conrad's *Verein* as his model, and he made the academy the nearest American replica of that German institution. Because of the central role that James and the Germans gave to formal research, both the academy and the *Verein* placed professional academics at the head of their organizations. Implicit in this design was the notion that academics, those who produced and handled policy research, ought to direct society's organized intelligence on issues of reform. This was in contrast to the primacy of the practicing professionals—doctors, lawyers, clergymen, and teachers—in the ASSA.[43]

The new academy also scrapped the ASSA division of labor, which had organized its work around the different practicing professions. But the shift to academic social science, in 1889, entailed no other division of labor. In pedagogy the apostle of specialization, James wanted the new organization to survey the various issues facing the nation and deal with them all as problems in political administration. Any major development in social science would be brought before the academy's monthly forum of businessmen and professionals and publicized through its journal, the *Annals of the American Academy of Political and Social Science*. In this James acted no differently from other American social scientists. Aside from the historians, all professional students of society were then organized into only one professional association, the American Economic Association, and no other societies were formed until the twentieth century. James, however, would also bring into the discussion the nation's powerful men of affairs.[44]

The meetings of the academy and its journal, the *Annals*, provided important vehicles for academic research on contemporary economic and social issues. Wharton faculty and alumni were frequent contributors to the *Annals*, but the list of authors also included prominent social scientists from around the world, scholars such as J. B. Clark, John Hobson, Leon Walras, Georg Simmel, and Gustav Schmoller. Articles ranged from Edward P. Cheyney's historical study of "The Medieval Manor," to Emory R. Johnson's immediately relevant analysis of "River and Harbor Bills," to general essays such as Patten's on "The Decay of Local Government," to self-conscious studies of academic work such as "The Study of Political Science at Oxford" by D. G. Ritchie. The *Annals* also included reports on important academic and reform meetings, biographical notes, book reviews, and lengthy monographs issued as supplements. The exceptionally high quality of the academy's activities and its solid financial foundation insured a healthy beginning for James's new organization. Indeed, the academy exists to this day and is the only remnant of the old Social Science Association still functioning.[45]

In the latter part of 1891, James, his academy, and the Wharton School group played a key role in establishing the Municipal League of Philadelphia, a mini-*Verein* focusing on issues of city government. The league was committed to the traditional recipe for good clean government — establishing a thoroughly professional civil service that would "conduct the city's affairs by enlightened business principles." But more than just a seat of genteel political agitation, the league also promoted scholarly investigations into Philadelphia's problems. Clinton Rogers Woodruff, Wharton School alumnus and an original counselor of the American Academy, became secretary and de facto leader of this new society. As Woodruff, James, and their friends were organizing the Philadelphia League, the academy spent an entire meeting discussing "How to Improve City Government." The *Annals* then published two papers presented at this session, together with the League's bylaws and declaration of principles; later issues carried more articles on urban problems and notes on league activities. James first made his mark in Philadelphia with his analysis of the gas supply — a municipal concern; it was in the same arena that his program of applied social science would have its greatest practical impact.[46]

In December 1893, Woodruff and the Philadelphia group assembled the nation's leading civic associations to organize the National Municipal League. Many of America's most prominent scholars and reformers came to Philadelphia to join the NML, but the Wharton faction stood out.* Woodruff became the secretary of the League, serving for more than twenty-five years as "its organizing genius, its motivating force, its guiding spirit." James and a young new professor at the Wharton School, Leo S. Rowe, became fixtures of the new organization, delivering papers and serving on committees to design model charters and accounting systems for the nation's cities. The *Annals*, furthermore, published regular accounts of league activities.[47]

This work outside the classroom came to have an important effect inside the Wharton School as well, as James brought his concern for municipal reform into the curriculum. He taught courses on municipal government, and while he himself worked on a model city charter for the National Municipal League, his class made a comparative study of existing charters. In 1893, the members of the senior class researched Philadelphia's municipal departments as their graduation theses. Published under the title of *The City Government of Philadelphia*, their essays won well-deserved praise for their thorough descriptions of the workings of the city administration. All students also participated in mock legislatures — one year the United States Congress, the alternate year the Philadelphia City Council. Although this program seems never to have been fully successful, with comic relief too often overwhelming the political melodrama, the exercise did familiarize students with problems involved in handling the public's business. Throughout their extensive education in politics, Wharton's students learned of the new and pervasive responsibilities of government in the modern urban and industrial economy. Many of the school's more sober-minded young gentlemen formed "a vigorous and permanent interest and pride in the purity and efficiency of . . . city administration." Because James brought his outside activities into the classroom, Wharton students not only

---

*Among those who lent their support to the National Municipal League were Theodore Roosevelt, Herbert B. Adams, Charles Elliot Norton, Washington Gladden, Richard T. Ely, Daniel C. Gilman, Frances A. Walker, and Edwin L. Godkin.

witnessed but were invited to participate in the rise of America's administrative state, one of the great transformations in the history of capitalist civilization.[48]

While James was establishing a German-style Wharton School, complete with a Halle-trained faculty at work on the major issues of reform, he was also active in spreading this new academic learning across the nation. With Provost William Pepper in the lead, James worked hard to organize the Philadelphia (later American) Society for the Extension of University Teaching, an organization that arranged for professors from all faculties of the university to offer short, off-campus courses of approximately six lectures each. In 1891, after James replaced Pepper as president of this society, university extension became an especially important part of his life. The program grew to tremendous size under his administration, and between 1890 and 1898 it sponsored 1,714 short courses at 343 different locations. Robert Ellis Thompson's discourses on history, literature, and the tariff were extremely popular. The society also brought speakers from as far away as England to instruct the community on such "Wharton School topics" as "Sociology" and "Geography in Relation to Commerce." Hoping to influence the curricula of local colleges and bring them into Wharton's expanding orbit, James sent them the syllabi from these courses.[49]

In 1889, William H. Rhawn, a local banker and member of the executive council of the American Bankers' Association, presented James with a great opportunity to further influence the educational system of the nation. Much impressed with both James and the Wharton School, Rhawn got the ABA to set up a committee, with himself as its chairman, to investigate "the establishment of schools . . . of general scope and character like that of 'The Wharton School of Finance and Economy.'" Rhawn's committee, in turn, appointed James to carry out the actual study. At the ABA convention of 3 September 1890, James presented a vigorous argument in favor of collegiate education for business. Businessmen were taking over the dominant positions in American society, and for the nation to flourish, he argued, they had to be properly educated.

The higher aspects of human society—the liberal support of science and art, the intelligent direction of charity and benevolence is to be expected chiefly from an educated class, and just in proportion as our ruling sets became educated may we expect to see these finer things increase and multiply.

James disputed the common opinion that college was just "a fine dessert . . . a pure article of luxury," and he dismissed Andrew Carnegie's well-known observation that he had never met a successful businessman who had gone to college. James presented the Wharton School curriculum to the convention and argued that its training in history, politics, economics, and business skills would be useful to young bankers and other businessmen. He then outlined plans for improvement, reviving his proposals of 1885. Putting words into the mouth of his audience, James said,

It will doubtless have occurred to you that more instruction in the practical details of the banking business would be desirable in the curriculum. In this the Faculty would doubtless fully concur. We need very much a lecturer on banking. . . .

The ideal of the Faculty, it may be said, is a great institution, comprising many different courses, one looking to business, another to journalism, still another to politics, another to the university—all composed alike of two elements: a common one . . . and a professional one. . . . The [professional] business course itself should be subdivided according to the intention of the student, and should comprise not merely the fundamental branches we now have, but many others, such as railroading, commerce, insurance, etc.[50]

The bankers loved it. They unanimously adopted Rhawn's resolution that

the American Bankers' Association most earnestly commends not only to bankers but to all intelligent and progressive citizens throughout our country the founding of schools of finance and economy for the business training of our children, to be established in connection with the universities and colleges of the land, upon a like general plan as that of the Wharton School . . . [Such schools] would give us the best system of training for business, journalism, — in a word for citizenship, which the world has yet seen.

At the request of the ABA, James prepared even more studies of the subject, reporting on business education in Europe and in American high schools. (The ABA, of course, paid all expenses for his trip to Europe.)[51]

At the university, as well as on the stump, James kept pushing his 1885 plans for a School of Political and Social Science. In 1892 he again petitioned the provost to proceed with his design, but now James embellished his original proposal with a call to extend the Wharton program over all four college years. The school had abandoned its three-year course in 1883-84 and now occupied only the last two years of a normal four-year college course. But James thought that more time, and access to all four years, was needed to give adequate coverage to the "core" social science disciplines, to the general business courses, and to final training in the proposed areas of practical specialization. To teach these new, specialized courses, James also asked permission to hire associate professors in banking, transportation, insurance, merchandising, business law, business practice, commerce, accounting, and journalism. The canny James was quick to predict financial, as well as academic, success for his plans. Through discussions with local high school principals, he came to believe that if the new program were enacted, many of the high school graduates who then went straight into business would enter the Wharton School instead. The lure of practical education in the freshman year, he reasoned, would induce a whole new group of students to come to the university, and once there, many would stay on through the completion of a professional training course. He assured the provost that tuitions from this new clientele alone would pay the cost of the new program.[52]

By the early 1890s the energetic James had gathered enough influence to do more than just air his pedagogical ideas, as he had done in 1885. Service to the university and to the "gospel of extension" had made James "one of the most trusted advisors" of the provost. The student body of the Wharton School had grown from 21 in 1884 to 59 in 1892, and was generally receptive to his dynamic leadership; they had even petitioned the trustees for James's pet cause, a course of study in journalism. By then James had also assembled a faculty with his own training and persuasions. His outside activities, which brought prestige and important research opportunities to the school, also brought Wharton independent sources of money for hiring new faculty. James could support young professors with jobs at the American Academy and with funds from the pockets of wealthy friends who had come to take the cause of the Wharton School as their own. The academy afforded salaries to sociologist Franklin H. Giddings, "social economist" Edward T. Devine, and historian James Harvey Robinson. Benefactors of the school gave James money to hire William Draper Lewis to teach legal institutions and Emory R. Johnson to give instruction in geography and transportation. In 1893 James found a place on the faculty for Joseph French Johnson, a good friend and fellow student from Halle who, upon his return to the United States, had been a superintendent of schools and then a newspaper editor. At Wharton, Joseph Johnson took over many of the business courses, freeing Faulkner to specialize in statistics, and organized the long-sought program in journalism. Although the separate, specialized course of study won final approval from the Academic Council of the university only in 1895, Johnson was teaching everything from correcting proof to newspaper law as soon as he arrived. Such was James's new power at the Wharton School.[53]

Only two obstacles stood between James and the full realization of his program—Robert Ellis Thompson and Joseph Wharton. Thompson, especially, opposed James's ideas about education. Although clearly outside the mainstream of the new Wharton School, Thompson was "easily the best-known and most admired teacher in Philadelphia" and had a strong following among students, alumni, and in the community at large. And the formidable Wharton still had to be won over. As James fully understood, the authorities at the university thought that they "ought not to extend the scope of the Wharton School unless Mr. Wharton will advance funds for the purpose."[54]

Thompson had long objected to James's ambition to make the Wharton School over along the lines of the German universities. He thought that the American college was of a lower educational level and that its students needed basic, general education. Thompson considered it premature and a fraud to give them a specialized program. James's curriculum, he once said, would make it Wharton's business merely "to furnish high-class servants for rich men and corporations."[55]

But Thompson's continued tenure at Wharton soon came into question. In 1892, at the behest of Pepper, James presented a long report on Thompson and his place at the Wharton School. Asserting his "highest possible respect for Professor Thompson's abilities," he reported that the faculty all thought that the school's first "dean" had no place in the current institution. Thompson ignored Wharton's research, its seminars, and the new organizations that were growing up around it. He "uniformly refused to co-ordinate his work with that of his colleagues"; his lectures "wandered, in the most indiscriminate though usually most brilliant way, over the whole field of instruction . . . thus making it impossible to plan or carry out a systematic course of work." Attempting to grasp the bigger picture, Thompson tended to "overlook" detail; James's Germanic approach, on the other hand, sought truth in the careful examination of details. This new academic brand of social studies had no appeal for Thompson, who totally ignored the activities of the American Economic and Historical Associations. Because of his other outside activities, largely journalism and religion, Thompson gave no time to his students, his colleagues, or his scholarship, aside from the time he spent in the classroom. What the Wharton School needed, according to James, was a professor "imbued with the feeling that developing a great department in a great university is a career worthy of the best that a man has to give." As to the fear that, if Thompson should resign, the doctrine of protection would be in danger, James reassured Pepper that "Dr. Patten . . . can be trusted to look after that. He is regarded by nearly all economists . . . as the leading scientific representative of this policy."[56]

Using James's report, Pepper forced Thompson's resignation. Instantly students, alumni, and other Thompson admirers raised a huge protest before the Board of Trustees. The board, however, felt compelled to support their provost. Thompson then appealed to Joseph Wharton, claiming that his forced resignation was actually the eviction of the Philadelphia school of economics from its rightful home. Joseph Wharton had his longtime business associate, Cyrus Elder, investigate Thompon's charges. Unfortunately for Thompson, James completely won Elder over. His report, which was full of praise for James and Patten, found the school "animated by a common spirit[,] . . . a fresh and progressive spirit." "There is no question," he insisted, "of the value of its degrees." He went on to highlight the American Bankers' Association endorsement and the interest in the Wharton School idea recently expressed by the Universities of Wisconsin, Chicago, and California. As to protectionism, Elder described Patten as "a distinguished representative of the younger scientists who have been influential in giving the science of Political Economy its new character of nationalism," and asserted that his students "can show that the [ultimate] mission of protection is not free trade" but, as claimed by the Philadelphia School of "high" protectionism, to put "all our land and labor . . . to their most productive uses.'" He concluded by endorsing James's plan to add "additional practical courses" as the "natural order of development."[57]

Joseph Wharton by no means shared Thompson's hostility to practical and Teutonic education. He was himself a cultured Germanophile who had long considered professional training in German universities as a proper model for America. Moreover, James's program of specialization, as well as the quality of his leadership, had by this time won Wharton over. In 1890 Wharton had literally rhapsodized over the new possibility that "to be a doctor, a *doctus*, or learned man, is thus no longer to be a recluse separated from his fellow-men," and that soon there could be such a "doctus" of "some service in trade, or finance or legislation, some organization of industry, some problem in social life." After Elder reassured him as to Patten's soundness and the stature that James had brought to the school, Wharton decided to do nothing to help Thompson.[58]

As a further indication of his support for James, Wharton gave the school an additional endowment of seventy-five thousand dollars in November 1893. This gift and the sanction of the founder induced the trustees to approve James's four-year curriculum four months later, on 6 March 1894. The success that James had prophesied for his plan materialized immediately. In the academic year 1894-95 the student body (now including freshmen and sophomores) expanded overnight from 71 to 113. Courses in accounting, geography, history, and current issues in economics, society, and politics were now scheduled in Wharton's new freshman and sophomore years. To handle this expanded program the school hired new faculty: Leo S. Rowe in municipal government, Samuel M. Lindsay in sociology, and Henry R. Seager in economics. The larger staff allowed the older professors to specialize more completely.[59]

But before James had time to work out the implications of the four-year course, a new provost had come into office and disrupted his progress. Charles H. Harrison, Pepper's replacement, was a very wealthy man who, as a member of the Board of Trustees, had nearly single-handedly kept the university solvent. He would now endow the institution, and especially its graduate school, with truly huge amounts of money. But over the years Harrison had acquired a strong distaste for Professor James; he resented the independent authority and the huge salary of six thousand dollars a year that James had extracted from Pepper — a salary higher than that of any other faculty member. Harrison's vice provost, George F. Fullerton, was a Thompson loyalist and for a long time had been suspicious of James's influence. Both, moreover, looked down on the Wharton School and its practical work.[60]

On New Year's Day 1895, Harrison's first day as provost, he called James into the privacy of his office and demanded his resignation. He accused James of neglecting his work and producing nothing of scholarly value. Regardless of the truth of these charges (and they did have some justice), James had no recourse. It was now Harrison's university, and James had to resign. Unlike Thompson, he left discreetly, without any public notice. Thompson, a creature of Philadelphia, had remained in the city to become the principal of Central High School; James, however, was a creature of the new academic profession, and he promptly moved on to a post at the University of Chicago. There he helped organize the nation's second collegiate school of business in 1898. Later he went on to serve for many years as the president of the University of Illinois. But when he left Philadelphia at the age of forty, he had largely completed his self-appointed task. He had decisively taken Joseph Wharton's school out of the ranks of the American college and had redesigned it along modern university lines. In so doing he had given the institution a position of leadership in American higher education and in the administration of public affairs. Long after James had gone, his vision of the practical university would remain the foundation of the Wharton School program.[61]

Source Notes

1. Richard A. Swanson, "Edmund J. James, 1855 – 1925: A 'Conservative Progressive' in American Higher Education" (Ph.D. diss., University of Illinois, 1966), 77 – 78; see Donald Fleming, *William H. Welch and the Rise of Modern Medicine* (Boston: Little, Brown, 1954), 32; Frederick Rudolph, *The American College and University* (New York: Alfred A. Knopf, 1962), 264–86, 329–54.

2. Eric Goldman, *John Bach McMaster, American Historian* (Philadelphia: University of Pennsylvania Press, 1943), 51; Albert Somit and Joseph Tanenhaus, *The Development of Political Science: From Burgess to Behavioralism* (Boston: Allyn & Bacon, 1967), 25ff.

3. Somit and Tanenhaus, *Political Science*, 25ff.

4. See William Roscher, "Roscher's Programme of 1843," translated by William J. Ashley, in William J. Ashley, *Surveys Historic and Economic* (London: Longmans, Green, 1900), 33–34. Roscher was the founder of the German historical school of economics.

5. John B. McMaster, *A History of the People of the United States from the Revolution to the Civil War*, 8 vols. (New York: Appleton, 1883–1913), 1:1; Richard Hofstadter, *The Progressive Historians: Turner, Beard, and Parrington* (New York: Knopf, 1968; Vintage Books ed., 1970), 25; John Higham et al., *History: The Development of Historical Studies in the United States* (Englewood Cliffs, N.J.: Prentice Hall, 1965), 150–51; Thomas J. Pressley, *Americans Interpret Their Civil War*, 2nd ed. (New York: Free Press, 1962), 217–18. Goldman, *McMaster*, 51 and passim; Ellis P. Oberholtzer, "John Bach McMaster," reprinted from *Pennsylvania Magazine of History and Biography* 57 (1933):1–12.

6. Hofstadter, *Historians*, 26–29, 193; Higham et al., *History*, 151ff.; Goldman, *McMaster*, 39 – 40; Pressley, *Civil War*, 217 – 26; E. Otis Kendall, *First Annual Report of the Wharton School of Finance and Economy*, 1 May 1884, 1; Edmund J. James, *The Education of Business Men* (New York: American Bankers Association, 1891), 15 – 17; *Catalog of the University of Pennsylvania (1883 – 84)*, 31; (1884 – 85) 35 – 36; (1887 – 88), 61 – 62.

7. *Catalog (1887 – 88)*, 61 – 62.

8. Hofstadter, *Historians*, 41; Higham et al., *History*, 157; Goldman, *McMaster*; Edward P. Cheyney, *History of the University of Pennsylvania*, (Philadelphia: University of Pennsylvania Press, 1940), 290; Minutes of the University Trustees, 7 Apr. 1891.

9. Swanson, "James," 5 – 21.

10. Swanson, "James," 22 – 25; Daniel M. Fox, *The Discovery of Abundance: Simon N. Patten and the Transformation of Social Theory* (Ithaca, N.Y.: Cornell University Press, 1967), 21 – 23.

11. Swanson, "James," 25; Fox, *Patten*, 23 – 25; Edmund J. James, "Political Economy in German Universities," *Nation* 35 (1882):261 – 62.

12. Brian Chapman, *The Profession of Government* (London: George Allen & Unwin, 1959), 23 – 24, 100; Fox, *Patten*, 23 – 24; Swanson, "James," 25.

13. Swanson, "James," 25, 27, 94.

14. Swanson, "James," 27 – 37, 41, 59, 70 – 71, 77; Bolles also contributed to Lalor's *Cyclopedia*. See his article on "Finance, History of," 2:196.

15. Cheyney, *History of the University*, 297, 290, 298; Swanson, "James," 86 – 89.

16. *Catalog (1883 – 84)*, 31; (1887 – 88), 62; Kendall, *First Annual Report*, 2; Edmund J. James, "The Science of Finance," *Cyclopedia of Political and Social Science*, 2:196 – 206.

17. *Catalog* (1889 – 90), 76 – 77; (1893 – 94), 108 – 11; Anna Haddow, *Political Science in American Colleges and Universities* (New York: D. Appleton – Century, 1939), 187.

18. Swanson, "James," 42–45; see Thomas L. Haskell, *The Emergence of Professional Social Science* (Urbana: University of Illinois Press, 1977), 24–47, 234–56.

19. James, "Factory Laws," quoted in Swanson, "James," 41; James, "History of Political Economy," quoted in Swanson, "James," 39–40.

20. James, "The Relationship of the Modern Municipality to the Gas Supply," *Publications of the American Economic Association* 1 (1886):61; James, "State Interference," quoted in Swanson, "James," 47; Swanson, "James," 43, 57ff.

21. Edmund J. James and Simon N. Patten, "Society for the Study of National Economy," reprinted in Richard T. Ely, *Ground under Our Feet* (New York: Macmillan, 1938), 297. Fox, *Patten*, 37 – 39; Swanson, "James," 95 – 97.

22. Fox, *Patten*, 37–41, 39 n. 14; Swanson, "James," 97–99; Mary Furner, *Advocacy and Objectivity* (Lexington: University Press of Kentucky, 1975).

23. Edmund J. James, *Instruction in Political and Social Science* (Philadelphia: Philadelphia Social Science Association, n. d. [1885?]).

24. Ibid., 6, 14.

25. Ibid., 10, 10 – 11.

26. Ibid., 14, 20, 23.

27. Albert S. Bolles to Wharton Barker, 25 Apr. 1885, "Wharton School File," Archives.

28. Swanson, "James," p. 35.

29. Wharton to Martin Barker, 15 Apr. 1885, "Wharton School File," Archives.

30. "Wharton," Project, in Wharton to the trustees, Minutes of the University Trustees, 24 Mar. 1881; Minutes of the Wharton Faculty, Dec. 1888; Emory R. Johnson, "The Wharton School," Minutes of the Wharton Faculty, 5 June 1939, p. 3; Jonathan Pollard, "The Wharton School — Its Early Graduates," term paper, Connecticut Wesleyan University (1980); "Information File: Wharton School," Archives. The figure for alumni entering family enterprises is Pollard's. He extrapolated from Bossard and Dewhurst's findings for later classes back to the 1880s. I have followed a similar procedure, albeit admittedly arbitrary, to arrive at the number in positions of executive authority. James H. S. Bossard and Frederick Dewhurst, *University Education for Business* (Philadelphia: University of Pennsylvania Press, 1931), 200 – 201. The calculation of "prominent" graduates relies on Pollard's research and his classification as "prominent" of those alumni listed in either *Who's Who in Philadelphia*, *Who's Who in Pennsylvania*, or Joshua L. Chamberlain, ed., *The University of Pennsylvania: Its History, Influence, Equipment and Characteristics* (Boston: R. Herndon, 1901). This calculation eliminates from consideration alumni who died before 1900 and those who left the Philadelphia area. It includes among the "not prominent" those for whom Pollard could find no information, less the proportion of "prominent" alumni that died before 1900 or moved away from the city. (The assumption used is that the same proportion of "prominent" and "not prominent" graduates died or left Philadelphia.)

31. Weyl to James, 4 Oct. 1912, quoted in Swanson, "James," 90; Pollard, "Wharton School," 6 – 10.

32. Minutes of the University Trustees, 7 June 1887; Paul J. FitzPatrick, "Leading American Statisticians of the Nineteenth Century, 2" *Journal of the American Statistical Association* 53 (1957):698.

33. *Catalog* (1885 – 86), 56; (1888 – 89), 60.

34. FitzPatrick, "Statisticians," 697 – 99; "Dr. R. P. Faulkner, Economist, Dies," *New York Times*, 29 Nov. 1940; Faulkner's translation of Meitzen's book,

History, Theory and Techniques of Statistics, first appeared as two supplements to the *Annals of the American Academy of Political and Social Science* 2(1891). The translation became widely used in other schools as they added instruction in statistics.

35. Minutes of the Wharton Faculty, 12 Nov. 1887, 19 Nov. 1887; Minutes of the University Trustees, 5 Jan. 1886, 2 Feb. 1886, 6 Dec. 1887, 7 Feb. 1888.

36. Minutes of the University Trustees, 29 May 1888; Fox, *Patten*, 25–26, 36; Simon N. Patten, *The Premises of Political Economy* (Philadelphia: J. B. Lippincott, 1885).

37. Philadelphia: Philadelphia Social Science Association, n. d.(1886?); Haskell, *Social Science*, 182, 188 n. 49, 196; Swanson, "James," 105.

38. Philip S. Benjamin, "Gentleman Reformers in the Quaker City," *Political Science Quarterly* 85 (1970):65–67; Frank M. Stewart, *A Half Century of Municipal Reform: The History of the National Municipal League* (Berkeley: University of California Press, 1950), 9; Swanson, "James," 105.

39. Benjamin, "Reformers," 65–67; Swanson, "James," 105.

40. James, "Gas Supply"; Swanson, "James," 105.

41. Swanson, "James," 102–4.

42. Ibid.; Haskell, *Social Science*, 215–16, 216–18; J. R. Rosengarten, "Work of the Philadelphia Social Science Association," *Annals* 1 (1890):719; Pollard, "Wharton School."

43. *Handbook of the American Academy of Political and Social Science* (Philadelphia, 1891), printed as a supplement to, and bound with, *Annals* 1 (1891):20.

44. Haskell, *Social Science*, 215.

45. *Annals* 4 (1893–94):275–92; 2 (1891–92):782–813 and 85–102; 1 (1890–91):26–43; Haskell, *Social Science*, 232–33.

46. Clinton R. Woodruff, "The Municipal League of Philadelphia," *American Journal of Sociology*, 10 (1905):337; Arthur B. Woodford, "The Municipal League of Philadelphia," *Social Economist* 2 (1891–92):21–22; Clinton R. Woodruff, "The Philadelphia Municipal League," *American Journal of Politics* 5 (1894):287–94; William D. Lewis, "The Political Organization of a Modern Municipality," *Annals* 2 (1891–92):458–87; Frank P. Prichard, "The Study of the Science of Municipal Government," *Annals* 2 (1891–92):450–57; "By-laws of the Municipal League of Philadelphia," *Annals* 2 (1891–92): 573–76.

47. Woodruff, "League of Philadelphia," 356; Stewart, *National Municipal League*; "The National Conference for Good City Government," *Annals* 4 (1893–94):850ff., esp. 852; also see *Annals* 5 (1894–95):636–39; 8 (1896): 188–90; 13 (1899):267–69; James H. Potts, "The Evolution of Municipal Accounting in the United States," *Business History Review* 52 (1978):518–23.

48. Edmund J. James, "Introduction to Members of the Senior Class of the Wharton School of Finance and Economy," *The City Government of Philadelphia* (Philadelphia: Wharton School of Finance and Economy, 1893), 16; Swanson, "James," 106; *Catalog (1892–93)*, 155–156; *Catalog (1893–94)*, 111; "The City Government of Philadelphia. A Study in Municipal Administration," *New York Independent*, 1 Feb. 1894, "Wharton School File," Archives; "Wharton School Senate," *Pennsylvanian*, 13 Dec. 1892; "Mock Congress," *Pennsylvanian*, 11 Dec. 1894.

49. Francis N. Thorpe, *William Pepper, M.D., LL.D. (1843–1898)* (Philadelphia: J. B. Lippincott, 1904), 117–20; James to Pepper, 3 Feb. 1893, "Wharton School File," Archives; Richard Montgomery, "Robert Ellis Thompson: A Memoir," *Barnwell Bulletin [of Central High School of Philadelphia]* 12 (Oct. 1934): 15–28.

50. "Introducing Plan of the Wharton School of Finance and Economy," in James, *Education of Business Men*, 27; ibid., 14, 10, 20 – 21, 9 – 19.

51. "Proceedings of the American Bankers' Association Relative to Address of Professor James, and upon the Founding of Schools of Finance and Economy," in James, *Education of Business Men*, 37; James, *Education of Business Men*, 4: *Education of Business Men in Europe* (New York: American Bankers' Association, 1893).

52. James to the provost and trustees, 29 Nov. 1892, "Wharton School File," Archives; also see James to Pepper, 3 Feb. 1893, and James to the provost and trustees, 14 Jan. 1894, "Wharton School File," Archives.

53. Thorpe, *Pepper*, 385; Minutes of the University Trustees, 28 May 1889; Swanson, "James," 81, 82, 84, 103 – 4. Chamberlain, ed., *University of Pennsylvania*, 388 – 90; Minutes of the Wharton Faculty, 20 May 1895, 17 Oct. 1895; "Student's Practice Paper," *Philadelphia Record*, 11 Jan. 1894; "Wharton School File," Archives; "Professor Elected to Fill a Wharton Chair," *Pennsylvanian*, 9 (10 Mar. 1893); *Catalog (18 – 94)*, 111; *(1894 – 95)*, 67; Haskell, *Social Science*, 215.

54. Montgomery, "Thompson," 36; James to Pepper, 3 Feb. 1893.

55. Montgomery, "Thompson," 37.

56. Swanson, "James," 90 – 92; James to Pepper, undated, "Robert Ellis Thompson File," Archives; Edward Shils, "The Order of Learning in the United States from 1865 to 1920: The Ascendancy of the Universities," *Minerva* 16 (1978):186 – 87.

57. Swanson, "James," 90 – 94; Montgomery, "Thompson," 36; Thompson to Wharton, 16 Apr. 1892, "Robert Ellis Thompson File," Archives. Elder to Wharton, 23 May 1892, "Wharton School File," Archives.

58. Wharton, "Is a College Education Advantageous to a Businessman?" (Philadelphia: Wharton School Association, 1890), 9; Swanson, "James," 93.

59. Swanson, "James," 84, 84 n. 22; *Catalog (1894 – 95)*, 65 – 69; *(1895 – 96)*, 75 – 79.

60. Swanson, "James," 120 – 22, 122 n. 104.

61. Swanson, "James," 121 – 23; Montgomery, "Thompson", 38ff; Bossard and Dewhurst, *Education for Business*, 252.

Edmund Janes James

William Pepper

Campus of the University, ca. 1890

John Bach McMaster

Simon Nelson Patten

Joseph French Johnson

ANNALS

OF THE

AMERICAN ACADEMY

OF

POLITICAL AND SOCIAL SCIENCE.

ISSUED QUARTERLY,
WITH SUPPLEMENTS.

VOL. I.

JULY, 1890—JUNE, 1891.

Editor:
EDMUND J. JAMES.

Associate Editors:
FRANKLIN H. GIDDINGS,   ROLAND P. FALKNER.

PHILADELPHIA:
AMERICAN ACADEMY OF POLITICAL AND SOCIAL SCIENCE.
1890.

CONTENTS.

Title page and first page of contents, *The Annals of the American Academy of Political and Social Science*, volume 1, number 1

Roland P. Faulkner, Samuel L. Lindsay, Simon N. Patten, and Leo S. Rowe

4

On the Firing Line
of Civilization

I

With James gone, the "chairmanship" of the economics department and leadership of the Wharton School fell to Simon N.
Patten, perhaps the greatest mind in the history of the institution.
James and Patten had been close friends and collaborators since
their school days at Halle, where they shared Midwestern Republican upbringings and a commitment to the new academic life.
Despite this bond, however, there were important differences between Patten and James. James possessed far more social effectiveness and organizational skill, and his great contributions to
the Wharton School — redesigning the program, setting up aux-
iliary organizations, and winning support from the Philadelphia
leadership — depended upon these abilities. Such accomplishments were beyond the reach of Simon Patten, who cultivated a
sheepish, ploughboy demeanor. But what Patten lacked in political sophistication, he made up in intellect. His imagination, orig-
inality, and brilliant analytical vision into economic affairs stood
in stark contrast to the well-wrought but completely derivative
writings of Edmund James. Patten relentlessly pushed outward,
always incorporating new insights into his schema. After thirty
years at the Wharton School, he had wedded economics, history,
sociology, psychology, religion, and philosophy into a grand vision of human development and a manifesto for his times. So
powerful were his ideas that they led the Wharton School itself

directly into that great American watershed at the turn of the century known as *Progressivism.*Understanding the school during Patten's twenty years of leadership, 1895-1917, thus requires a rather careful examination of his ideas and purposes.[1]

Simon Patten was born in 1852 and grew up in Sandwich, Illinois, a far more provincial setting than James's hometown of Bloomington, Illinois. Patten's mother died when he was four years old, but his father, William, remarried and provided him with a stable and strict Presbyterian upbringing on the prairie. William was a leader of the Sandwich community: He farmed his land with the most progressive techniques in use in De Kalb County, served as an elder in the local Presbyterian church, and represented his district in the state legislature. Like the Reverend Colin Dew James, William Patten believed that education, religion, and the Republican Party were the essential forces making for progress in American society. But Patten had come to his Republicanism from a different background than did the Reverend Mr. James. Sandwich farmers had always been Democrats, believing that the party of Andrew Jackson best represented the nation's enterprising farmers and small businessmen. They abandoned this affiliation only a few years before the Civil War, when they decided that Southern slave owners had taken control of their party. This "Slave Power," they feared, was preventing God's children from exercising their given rights to settle the free soil of Kansas and other parts of the great continental heartland. With Abraham Lincoln as the new champion of American opportunity, William Patten led the farmers of Sandwich into the Republican crusade.[2]

While serving in the state legislature, William Patten had been embarrassed at his own lack of formal schooling. He became an ardent believer in education, and he made sure that his son received the training that he lacked. Simon went to the Jennings Seminary and then to Northwestern University, with his father expecting him to take up law. While working his way through the classical curriculum at Jennings, however, Simon developed a close relationship with a fellow student, Joseph French Johnson. Young Patten admired this dashing blade who had all the social grace that he himself lacked; Johnson, on the other hand, was the only one at Jennings who appreciated Simon's intellectual creativity. While Patten continued his education at Northwestern, his friend went off to Halle and Johannes Conrad's seminar. From there he wrote letters describing marvelous things in Germany, and convinced Simon to cross the ocean. Although William Patten was probably not enthusiastic, in 1875 he agreed to pay his son's way to Halle for two years' study.[3]

Patten never entered the social whirl of German student life, where his staunch Presbyterian refusal to smoke or drink dampened his access to *Gemutlichkeit*. Instead Patten devoured economic theory. On the basis of intellectual rapport he revived his ties with Johnson and befriended Johnson's new comrade, Edmund James and their common mentor, Johannes Conrad. (Conrad, in fact, later said that he had learned more from Patten than he had from any other student.) Despite his limited social experience, Patten found his sojourn intellectually exhilarating, and he set his rising ambitions on an academic career. He also developed a lifelong attachment to German efficiency, which he someday hoped to be able to combine with Anglo-Saxon liberty and democracy. After writing a slim doctoral dissertation explaining the virtues of the property tax as the fiscal base of American local government, Patten sailed home to America in 1878.[4]

Awaiting him in America were academic unemployment and a father intent on seeing him a lawyer. After Simon had spent a year mucking about on the family farm, William sent his reluctant son to law school in Chicago. But he had been there for only six weeks when his eyesight mysteriously failed, and he returned home to Sandwich in darkness. There he remained for three years, alone and unable to read, to work, or to satisfy either his or his father's ambitions. Only the ministrations of a Philadelphia oculist, whom he saw while on a visit to James, were finally able to clear up the problem. He then went to work: teaching school in Illinois, designing the new American Economic Association, and writing a treatise on economics, the *Premises of Political Economy*. When Patten sent his manuscript to Johnson in Chicago, his friend was appalled. Johnson found the draft completely bereft of punctuation and its first sentence spread across fifteen pages. Johnson hammered the text into a semireadable state and passed it on to James, who convinced the Lippincott company to publish it. On the basis of this book and several articles, James got Patten his place at the Wharton School in 1887. He was then thirty-five years of age and had been home in America for eight years.[5]

The economic analysis that Patten taught at the Wharton School was rooted in the now well-established anti-Ricardian tradition. Like Thompson, Carey, and Conrad, Patten challenged the classical "law" of decreasing returns with a "law" of increasing productivity. As the sources of expanded per capita output in industrial nations, he listed the growing division of labor and diversification of industry, ongoing adaptation to the environment, new technological combinations, and larger, more powerful organizations. He cited the now familiar course of agricultural history to illustrate the power of the forces of progress. To these traditional considerations Patten added a thoroughly original and extended analysis of consumption,*introducing a law of increasing returns exactly analogous to the anti-Ricardian law of increasing returns in production. Like the earlier German and Philadelphia economists, Patten argued that in a progressive society the power of variety and new combinations overcame any tendency toward stagnation. In dynamic economies, he reasoned, the variety of new delights grew far faster than the ability of the citizenry to consume and thus tire of their goods. Progressive societies, he continued, were constantly devising ingenious recipes that combined existing products into savory new objects of consumption. As an example, he pointed out that eating beef with salt yielded much more pleasure than munching up either staple by itself. When Patten combined these tendencies toward steadily increasing pleasures from consumption with the traditional anti-Ricardian belief in steadily increasing output, he uncovered a tremendously optimistic picture of economic history. Armed with this joyous vision, he thereafter worked to protect the dynamism

---

*The issue of consumption was then in the forefront of economic speculation: Ernst Engel, the head of the Prussian Royal Statistical Bureau, had recently begun an important series of empirical studies to chart out this previously murky field. William Stanley Jevons and Karl Menger were in the process of reconstructing classical economic analysis on the basis of subjective "utility" theory, which made consumers the ultimate arbiters of economic values. Jevons and Menger preserved Ricardo's essential assumption of decreasing returns to economic activity: Ricardo's decreasing returns in agricultural production became their decreasing utility in consumption: these "neoclassical" economists assumed that people relished their second helpings less than their first.

of the American economy and to understand the implications of its burgeoning abundance.[6]

Patten's mastery of current economic analysis and his original contributions made him one of the most distinguished economists of his day. But what made him especially valuable to the Wharton School was the fact that he was the only leading academic economist to defend the doctrine of protection. In 1890 he published *The Economic Basis of Protection*, which gave the policy perhaps its most sophisticated and interesting theoretical defense to that time. The book won wide popular and scholarly notice and immediately established Patten as the nation's leading academic champion of the tariff.[7]

At the center of Patten's argument for protection lay his vision of a dynamic, ever-expanding economy. He argued that such economies had special properties and needs which negated the fundamental defense of free trade, Ricardo's law of comparative advantage. According to Ricardo, differences among nations in overall productive power had no impact at all on the desirability of trade; the only thing that mattered were the *relative* prices among goods in one country as compared with another. Patten argued that Ricardo's theorem applied only to technologically stagnant economies. A dynamic economy, he pointed out, would constantly improve its productive processes, and this progress would always occur in different industries at different times: Thus the steel industry could experience a burst of productivity in one decade and then see sluggish advance in the next. In agriculture, the timing could be reversed. If free trade developed between this dynamic economy and a static one in the first decade, the progressive nation, according to the law of comparative advantage, would specialize in producing steel. It would import agricultural goods and reduce or even dismantle its agricultural industry. That society, and perhaps the world as well, could then miss out on an agricultural revolution. Patten concluded that technical dynamism was the fruit of a developed society and not tied in any way to particular industries. "Civilization causes intelligence," he claimed, "and intelligence gives productive power." According to Patten's tough reasoning, to place any industry in static, "distant lands," would blunt the impact of new scientific methods and reduce the long-run success of the economy. And thus a new rationale for high tariffs.[8]*

Patten's defense of the tariff gratified the school's founder. When Joseph Wharton sent Cyrus Elder to the campus in 1892 as his "observer," Elder found students reading Patten's work, hearing him lecture, and all enthusiastically upholding protectionist doctrine. What Elder did not observe, however, was that Patten was not a doctrinaire instructor after the fashion of Thompson and Carey. Protectionism occupied only a secondary position in his thought, and he gave Wharton students a broad familiarity with the various schools of economic theory and policy. Patten had great regard for the classical economists and believed that the school "cannot too much emphasize Ricardian clearness." He likewise relished the work of his neoclassical contemporaries, who were brilliantly extending Ricardo's vision of decreasing returns and his "marginal" analysis of rent determination to all parts of economics. Wharton students read these mainstream analysts and also studied economic history and the history of economic theory. In all cases Patten used these authors and subjects as points of departure for class discussion and prized imagination and independent thinking above any orthodoxy.[9]†

*Patten ironically constructed his most elegant defense of the high American tariff by combining Ricardo's two classic theories of rent and comparative advantage. The United States had a great abundance of land relative to Europe, and free trade with the Old World would result in greater demands being placed on those plentiful natural resources. Ricardo's theory of rent predicted that this demand would then substantially raise the proportion of national income going to landlords. Patten and Ricardo both viewed landlords as a parasitical and unenterprising lot, the great antagonists of enterprise and labor; in Patten's mind they were akin to the evil antebellum Southern plantation owners, and he continually chastised rentiers as "the owners of natural monopolies" and the "classes in society exempt from competition." Following Ricardo, Patten argued that to increase the landlord's share of national income would dampen the dynamism of the economy. Increased productivity, he continued, reduced man's dependence on natural resources and lowered rents; thus dynamic nations would have low rents and stagnant nations exorbitant rents. Wharton's economist concluded, and even Ricardo may have concurred, that with free international trade, rents paid by developed nations would rise: "This is the real burden of free commerce. The more progressive nations must continually pay to the owners of natural monopolies a sum equal to the full value of their natural resources to the less progressive nations."

†Already in the early years of the 1890s, the school had escaped the paternal "protection" of its powerful sire. The founder could only command a general deference toward the tariff, and by the first decade of the twentieth century even this taboo had vanished.

Patten's educational program was the pedagogic equivalent of his theory of economic dynamism. Simply because he himself had fashioned a good theory provided no reason to limit the development of other lines of analysis: diversity and novel interconnection remained Patten's prescription for vitality. Here he, like his friend James, clashed with traditional collegiate pedagogy, the program that hoped to discipline the various mental faculties through drills and recitations on the established core of Western culture. Patten carefully outlined his position in an article published in 1890, the same year that he issued *The Economic Basis of Protection*. There he claimed that "educational value" — the ability to excite students' interests and to develop their powers of reasoning for everyday life—ought to replace "disciplinary value" as the criterion of pedagogic success. In a vigorous attack against the Wharton School's enemies on the Pennsylvania college faculty, Patten claimed that neither humanistic nor scientific study yielded sufficient educational value. The former lacked the rigorous deductive reasoning that Patten thought essential to any well-developed mind; the college sciences, while of undoubted precision and utility, were largely finished and deductive and therefore offered little opportunity for developing creative imaginations. Patten argued that political economy, then in the process of transition from an inductive to a deductive science, stimulated curiosity and trained the student in "reasoning similar to that which he has to do in every-day life." He pointed out that economic theory "is of great value in giving to the pupil a confidence in reasoning"; the factual premises of theories and their relation to particular economic problems, however, were all open for discussion; statistical investigations gave "the student a love for fact" and posed stiff challenges to his imaginative and reasoning abilities; and the study of economic history and the history of economic thought gave insight into the policies of other people and nations and developed "a catholic feeling which . . . is not possible to obtain in any other way." A Wharton School education, he concluded, thus provided the greatest educational value at the university and best prepared students for a rich and creative life.[10]*

*In order to maximize the educational value of political economy and to prevent common errors, Patten explicitly warned of several potential dangers in handling economic science. In the process he revealed a sophisticated understanding of the subject, one that he no doubt passed on to his best students. Patten was quite protective of the theoretical achievements of his science. When predictions

Patten inspired a generation of Wharton undergraduates, but over time he gave up these chores to specialize in graduate instruction. It was here, as a graduate professor surrounded with advanced students, that Patten found his true home and his imaginative intelligence had its opportunity to soar. As early as 1894-95, when Patten and James were still sending Ph.D. students to Halle, they each devoted over half their classroom hours to graduate instruction.* When James left, the economist became the dominant factor in Wharton's graduate effort. Beginning in the late 1890s, he began turning out Ph.D.'s on a regular basis and building an academic reputation for the school sufficient to establish a truly significant program. Many aspiring academics came from middle-class families, not so different from Patten's and James's, and were able to attend Wharton's graduate seminars only as the school found funds to support them. When Provost Harrison endowed the university with a host of fellowships for graduate students, some of the nation's most promising doctoral candidates were drawn to Patten's tutelage. An enlarged Wharton student body, growing

---

failed to materialize, he would often uphold the validity of analysis, claiming that because of the complexity of economic events "direct verification of certain theories is impossible." He would abandon a theory only when its assumptions were shown to have no foundation in fact. On the other hand, Patten cautioned against "teaching political economy as a compact whole, like mathematics." Treating the science in that fashion, he charged, encouraged the student to "overlook all economic phenomena which do not fit nicely into the economic scheme which he has formed." He insisted that such instruction induced a false belief that theory defined all possibilities, a dangerous assumption that allowed one to "prove" a thesis by disproving all other options defined by a theory. But his essential objection to this mode of thought was educational, that "it cramps the mental development of the student, instead of aiding in his progress."

Patten gave Wharton's students a broad and diverse sampler of economic science. He began juniors with Adam Smith's *Wealth of Nations*, Francis A. Walker's *Political Economy*, and his own work on *Protection* or *Dynamic Economics*. Seniors studied John Stuart Mill (and later, Alfred Marshall) and the history of the science using Ingram's *History of Political Economy* (later Gide and Rist). When Wharton went to the four-year program in 1894-95, the school added a freshman course in "practical economic problems" to ease the student's way into the dismal science. These classes covered many of the issues named in Wharton's "Project" and formerly taught by Robert Ellis Thompson at the culmination of the Wharton course: the tariff, wages and labor controversies, currency questions, and problems of transportation. During the first decade of the twentieth century the school set up a sophomore theory course, using Frank Taussig's standard textbook, and required most of its students to take it.

*Officially the Wharton School had no Ph.D. program and all such courses in the university were organized into a separate graduate school. But Wharton professors ran their own programs and awarded Ph.D.'s (in economics) in Wharton subjects. Intellectually, if not administratively, Wharton had a graduate school.

from 150 in 1901 to 625 in 1912, created another source of support for graduate students: They served as discussion section "quiz-masters" and assumed some of the teaching burden. Instead of sending its best students to Halle, Wharton now kept them at Penn and drew others to the new program. In short order, a vigorous and independent academic enterprise grew up around the school's economist.[11]

What the American Academy of Political and Social Science was to James, the graduate program was to Patten. The close intellectual contact with graduate students, in seminars and small classes or over breakfast at the University Club, became the natural environment for this otherwise shy, socially inept man. In such company the gangling, ill-dressed Patten, whom most freshman at first took to be the janitor, became a brilliant conversationalist and one of the greatest of teachers. Patten inspired his graduate students not only to organize for reform but to think, at least for a while, as intellectuals. In his graduate seminars Patten found an arena where he could squeeze all the "educational value" out of economic science, where he could

treat the relation of doctrines to one another and of the whole as a unit. The student has now acquired the culture and mental power needed for such work, and can pursue it without that detriment which he would have received had he followed some rigid system from the start.[12]

Patten's seminars emerged at a critical time in the history of Western social science. The neoclassical school of economics was then closing in on the central riddle of the discipline: the analysis of market price. This achievement, however, came at the cost of narrowly concentrating attention on short-run economic problems, for only there could economists assume that human responses and productive relationships conformed to some simple, stable pattern. Moral philosophers such as Adam Smith and economists such as John Stuart Mill had been vitally interested in long-term issues of economic progress and had given extended consideration to religious, moral, social, and psychological issues. Patten and other analytically talented economists of his day resented the fact that theoretical work in their field had come to mean an ever more exclusive diet of symbols and attention to marginal phenomena. Some, such as Alfred Marshall, nevertheless went ahead with the analytical work at hand and hurried the neoclassical revolution on to its deductive conclusions. Others, including Patten, Max Weber, Vilfredo Pareto, and Joseph Schumpeter, kept their gaze fixed on the historical horizon. Patten claimed that there could be "no full discussion of economic problems without bringing political and moral principles into relation with the economic." In fact he defined the "laws" of economics not as explanations of any purely economic behavior but as an enumeration of "what qualities must be impressed upon men in the struggle for that higher civilization which the conditions of life permit." In order to provide his students with a "full discussion" of economic problems — with all its educational value — and to participate in the formulation of such economic laws, Patten kept his focus on the traditional issues of the profession.[13]

Patten held a pragmatic philosophy of knowledge that gave him a special impetus to take the broad view. Thought, to the economist, was the basic means of human adjustment to a changing environment; it grew out of the combination of particular experiences and basic human needs, not out of some vision of universal truth. When the socioeconomic environment shifted dramatically, Patten expected the basic categories of social philosophy to come unglued and lose their contemporary relevance. Narrow-focusing specialists would scurry about their tasks of reconstruction, only to be checked by obsolete ideas that they had borrowed from other areas of thought. From the vantage point of his analysis of economic history, Patten had detected an epoch-making event: the arrival of a new era of abundance. Current social philosophy and "economic law," however, were still based on what Patten viewed as the obsolete axiom of scarcity. So, in the mid-1890s, he and his graduate students embarked on an extended study of psychology, sociology, and history, to find "what qualities must be impressed upon men" in the current age of abundance. Within a decade, Patten's effort in this area would usher in a radical transformation of the Wharton School — in its intellectual life, its professional purposes, and its relationship to society and to the Philadelphia elite.[14]

Patten's epic work in his search for the new economic law, *The Development of English Thought*, appeared in 1899. The volume opened with a simple psychological typology based on the dichotomy of will and rationality, or he put it, "motor intelligence" and "sensory intelligence." Patten divided mankind into four psychological groups: *clingers* — the timid and unthinking folk who would willingly trade all for survival; *sensualists* — a vigorous, powerful group, but one whose ability for calm, clear thinking was crippled by insatiable "strong appetites" for crude gratifications; *mugwumps* — an intelligent, analytical class, but without much will to act; and *stalwarts* — who both cultivated rational approaches to problems and had the drive to actualize their programs.[15]*

These types, and the material conditions of life, constituted the foundation of Patten's vision of history. Beginning with the great stretch of time when economic scarcity dominated human existence, Patten saw the struggle for survival as intense and localized. He argued that calm and generalizing stalwarts and mugwumps could find no niche and that society was peopled only by feeble clingers and a dominating class of sensualist lords and priests. But with the appearance of a larger economic surplus in fifteenth-century Europe, Patten saw a sudden proliferation of rational types. As they grew more numerous, they soon challenged the sensualist lords for European leadership.[16]

Patten identified his religious ancestors, the Calvinist Protestants, as the principal agents of the new rationality, the "first modern stalwart[s]." Essential to the psychology of these Puritans, Patten explained to his students, was their well-developed sensory intelligence: their capacity to form and handle symbolic concepts which they then placed "above custom and tradition." This capacity for abstraction, he continued, led the Puritans to develop democratic ethical standards and to create the modern moral community of equals:

Democracy could not have its present force if the common qualities of men had not been idealized. Only when the differences and defects of men are overlooked can the concept of free citizens, born with certain natural rights, become vivid enough to control society. The citizen is taught to pride himself on these common qualities. . . . It is upon these

*Patten's contemporary economist-cum-sociologists, Weber, Pareto, and Schumpeter, also employed a psychological typology based on the dichotomy of will and reason. Each writer, however, had a different ideological point of view and colored his portraits quite differently.

instincts that modern societies are built; without them no co-operation would be possible.

According to Patten and the entire anti-Ricardian tradition, such cooperation was the great source of increased abundance in the modern age. In Patten's history, the Puritans and their stalwart culture thus presented the sensualists with a powerful rival for authority in society.[17]*

Patten's hope for mankind lay with the triumph of these active, rational stalwarts. But before the stalwarts could succeed, Patten believed they had to develop a new form of consumption, the "weak appetite." Scarcity had encouraged the "strong appetites" of the sensualists and clingers, who stuffed their mouths full of any food readily available. But now, in the age of surplus, men would find greater fulfillment with weak appetites: They could rationally avoid excess, patiently search for a variety of pleasures, and fashion new delights. In these modern times, Patten thought that the infinite variety of intellectual and spiritual pleasures offered especially appealing alternatives to more meat and potatoes.[18]

Despite progress, Patten believed that the outcome of the struggle between the stalwarts and sensualists still lay in doubt. Weak appetites and democratic beliefs were far from universal, and sensualists and clingers still abounded. A spectre of a new industrial slavery, in fact, haunted Patten's mind. He feared that buccaneering, sensualist capitalists, exploiting a mass of unskilled and uneducated clingers, could defeat the stalwarts in the marketplace. In the production of staples these brutish entrepreneurs and their proletariat, with their single-minded energy, could outproduce those with weak appetites. Since such staples best satisfied the simple tastes of strong appetites, the competitive success of sensualists and clingers would stimulate demand for the very products that they themselves most effectively produced. Con-

---

*Both the lords and the Puritans, according to Patten, failed to negotiate the new economy of abundance. The sensualist lords could neither constitute a modern cooperative, productive nation nor handle its pleasures, falling prey to gluttony, war, and the plague. The Calvinist conception of a wrathful God and their belief in predestination, he thought, induced passive mugwumpery and ultimately rendered the Puritans historically irrevelant. He also claimed that Calvinism vainly restricted appreciation of the newly abundant pleasures and had ultimately "died of consumption."

versely, the economist reasoned, those with weak appetites also sought out the same type of products that they created. They were the skilled artisans and professionals, the producers of esoteric goods. Patten thus portrayed his contemporary American society as balanced precariously between the forces of good and those of perdition. The new economic abundance could usher in an age of abundant and varied consumption, or the surplus could be wasted in competitive struggles among a new set of industrial lords. The conflict had all the trappings of the spiritual civil war that America had fought in Patten's childhood.[19]

Patten defined the essential task of contemporary economics as leading the nation's stalwarts "in the struggle for that higher civilization which the conditions of life permit." Accordingly, Wharton's economist made it his first order of business to bring his vision of events to the attention of the public and see that it became the basis of action. He did use the institutions that James had established for influencing opinion — the American Academy and the National Municipal League. But by the early 1900s the social elite that James had gathered into these organizations had lost much of its enthusiasm for reform; these "best people," commonly known as mugwumps, had been nearly as ineffective in politics as the mugwumps of Patten's typology. In any event, Patten had neither the talent nor the inclination to cultivate established elites. He wanted to go directly to the people, to address and to energize middle-class, democratic opinion.[20]

Contemporary psychologists had convinced Patten (if he really needed any convincing) that esoteric academic arguments mattered little in the history of humanity. In keeping with this observation, his presidential address before the American Economic Association in 1908 thundered that the place for economists was "on the firing line of civilization," that they were "by education and tradition revolutionists," and that their "vehicle should be the newspaper and magazine, not the scientific journal." Patten had taken this course himself, and had written sharp, vivid articles that boldly raised issues of national survival. He published in the *Independent, Charities and Commons* (later renamed *Survey*), the *New Republic,* and *Science.* In 1907 he issued a popular version of his theories, *The New Basis of Civilization,* that went through eight editions in sixteen years. These writings all laid before the public his vision of an age of surplus, an obsolete culture based on scarcity, and the necessity of immediate social adjustment.[21]

Patten saw the nation suffering from "cultural lag," and he busily set out to fashion new beliefs appropriate to the times. First he called for recognition of the moral community of equals as the foundation of modern society and of the cooperation so vital to economic growth. But he went on to insist that free competition, which grew out of this belief system, often sacrificed the "lower classes" in the competitive struggle among the "equals." The democratic community, as a result, needed protection. Patten wanted society to "recognize the existence of a dependent class who lacked inherited qualities needed to enable them to enter into a state of free competition." He called for the general maintenance of wage levels and working conditions against ruthless and powerful "sensualist" employers who could grind the nation's populace — men, women, and children — into a shapeless mass of proletarian "clingers." Although lauding large-scale industry for producing a vast cornucopia of goods, he would sanction big business only if the government regulated monopolies to protect the dependent consumer.[22]*

Patten's pursuit of social reform ultimately took him into the realm of religion. Having been raised in a strict Presbyterian household, and now an active member in his local Baptist church, Patten took his religion seriously. But his economic interpretation of history made ideas, even religious ideas, dependent on environmental conditions; only the basic religious desire for meaningful relationships persisted through time. From his economic perspective, Patten saw social cooperation replacing individual struggle as the source of economic production, and the human community replacing harsh nature as the true economic environment of man. This perception justified his belief in social solidarity and human brotherhood as viable articles of contemporary faith. But more radically, Patten declared that the new plentitude

---

*Observing that modern industry outproduced women at home in their traditional tasks, such as making clothes and preparing foods, Patten urged women to get jobs, buy these goods, and thereby adjust to the new prosperity. He became a leading champion of both the place of women in the larger economy and the need for special protection of their working conditions.

now allowed society to adopt the religious message that he took from Jesus Christ; it could embark on a sweeping "social regeneration" that would reintegrate all outcasts back into society. To achieve the redemption at hand, Patten urged Christians to emulate Jesus. As Jesus had descended to earth in order to raise mankind, Patten would have modern believers journey into the lower classes to help and to educate those who had been ground down. All progress, he claimed, involved just such descent. The dawning age of abundance created the potential for raising all the downtrodden, and Patten called social regeneration "the religious need of the day." It would replace that Old Testament righteousness that had dominated nineteenth-century American Protestantism and that Robert Ellis Thompson had preached in the early years of the Wharton School.[23]*

During the period of his leadership, from 1895 to 1917, Patten's ideas had a profound influence over the development of the social sciences at Wharton. Economics texts written by his students — Henry R. Seager, Edward T. Devine, and Scott Nearing — all highlighted issues of consumption with exceptional thoroughness. Patten's sociological, ethical, and religious views exerted an even greater impact than his economic theories. After a vicious economic depression struck the nation in 1893, causing intense and widespread suffering among the poor, the country awoke to the fact of mass industrial poverty. Patten and his new seminar in "Problems of Sociology" examined existing remedies to this modern misery, a condition that challenged the nation's conscience and its basic democratic ideology, and found them all inadequate. But Patten's analysis of social development and his vision of social regeneration brought on by Christlike agents gave hope to his students. In their seminar they developed an alternative program of "social work," and their enthusiasm sparked a rapid growth of sociology and social work education at Wharton.[24]†

---

*As Patten had become an active journalist to promote his economic views, he became an "active myth-maker" for his religious ideals. Toward the end of his life he wrote a redemptive novel, *Mud Hollow*, and a large number of hymns for the new religion of joy and solidarity. All, unfortunately, were as uninspired as they were well-intentioned.

†In the 1880s Patten and James had been most impressed with the work of the English Christian Socialists in dealing with the problem of poverty. They

According to some, Patten actually coined the term *social work*. But even if he did not, he insisted upon its use, played a central role in fashioning its ideological justification, and assured it a place in the language, thought, and politics of the nation. Before social work, support for the poor had been in the hands of "charity workers," usually "middle-aged women desirous of doing good in the world," who dispensed alms and "neighborly" advice. But Patten wanted to equip a new army of "Christlike" social workers with state money and then send them down into the masses of the poor. Their mission, quite simply, would be to free the nation from the unnecessary horrors of scarcity and to bring the urban masses into the "stalwart" community of equals. He saw three good meals a day and the acquisition of the weak appetite — not charity or kindly advice — as the remedy for pauperism and for strong-appetite maladies such as alcoholism and crime. Instead of aiding just those who had already slipped off the edge of subsistence and civility, Patten wanted to prevent any collapse into misery. He would insure every citizen an adequate diet, an education in proper consumption, and decent working and living conditions. As members of society, Patten argued, the impoverished had a right to share in the socially produced surplus.[25]

As the Wharton School program expanded to a four-year course, Patten was able to hire his former student Samuel McClune Lindsay as the school's first full-time professor of sociology. Lindsay, a "practical economics" major, had graduated from Wharton in 1889, continued his education at Halle, and had taken his degree there in "social economics." (Lindsay later recalled that from Patten and Thompson's "practical economics it was not a very long jump to Social Economics.") Upon his return as a committed young Ph.D., Lindsay immediately began teaching "Descriptive Sociology," "Sociological Theory," "Practical Problems,"

were especially taken with English educational extension and social settlement house programs. These efforts gave the humble the cultural tools and the community support thought necessary for adjustment to industrial civilization. Indeed, in the realm of extension education, James could be counted as one of the most fervent followers of English practice in the United States. In 1891, he and Patten brought Englishman Frederick W. Moore to Wharton for a year, to teach the school's first course in "sociology." Patten took up the subject after Moore left, conducting his graduate seminars in "Problems of Sociology."

and "Field Work."* The purpose of his instruction was to "stir up interest in the questions of practical philanthropy" — issues such as crime, alcoholism, and pauperized immigrants and minorities. Through friends in social welfare agencies, and especially in the New York City Charity Organization Society, Lindsay and Patten placed students in summer jobs where they could get real-world exposure to social work practice. In 1899 the Wharton School announced a "two-year course in 'Social Work,'" in all probability the first formal university program in the United States.† It was designed for "those who cannot pursue the full four-year college course, but who desire a technical training in sociology, economics, history and allied branches of liberal culture"; the school expected to educate clergymen interested in reform, as well as "superintendents, secretaries and responsible officers" of "educational and philanthropic societies." Through the commitments of Lindsay, Patten, and Provost Harrison (whose father had been president of the State Board of Charities), Wharton entered a brand new academic territory—the professional realm of "practical philanthropy" and the work of social regeneration.[26]

Lindsay soon left Wharton — at first teaching only on a part-time basis and then resigning in 1907. His successors, however, continued along the same path. Carl Kelsey, a professional social worker who took his Ph.D. under Patten and Lindsay, joined the

---

*Lindsay worked on the staff of the American Academy, becoming its president and editor of the *Annals* between 1900 and 1902. He also helped found and direct the Philadelphia Toynbee Society, a group named after a prominent English Christian Socialist and dedicated to improving the lot of working people through conciliation, arbitration, and the creation of a favorable public opinion toward labor organizations. In addition to Lindsay, Patten inspired many others of his best students to enter social work. These included Edward T. Devine, prominent leader of the New York Charity Organization Society and editor of *Survey* magazine, and Frances Perkins, Secretary of Labor under Franklin Delano Roosevelt and the first woman member of an American presidential cabinet.

†Toward the end of the 1890s, leaders in the field of social welfare felt the need for such formal training programs. The predominant opinion seemed to favor the establishment of schools independent of universities. One such leader feared that in universities "the immediate needs of charity might not be so much considered as the traditions of the institution"; another thought that universities would raise difficulties for such a program, especially on the matter of awarding degrees. Led by Wharton graduate Edward T. Devine, the New York Charity Organization Society began the first formal social work training program in the summer of 1898, a year before Wharton announced its two-year course. The organization soon expanded this course into the New York School of Philanthropy. Devine, Patten, and Lindsay all lectured at the new school, and Wharton graduate Roswell McCrea also served on its faculty.

faculty in 1903 and assumed responsibility for the school's course in "Social and Civic Work."* Six years later the school added James P. Lichtenberger, who was also influenced by "a philosophic approach and not a little also by the religio-philanthropic bent." Wharton's two new sociologists thus felt comfortable with the school's practical reform-oriented curriculum: sociological theory; social economy (using Patten's *Development of English Thought*); classes on a host of social problems; social and vital statistics; and sociological field work. This last course, the capstone of the program, was described as "a study of actual social conditions and of methods employed in the care of dependent and delinquent classes."[27]

The major emphases of Wharton's sociology program were practical and action-oriented; research was not a principal activity. Indeed, the one significant sociological research project conducted at the Wharton School before 1920 was not the result of the faculty program. It originated with Susan P. Wharton, a relative of Joseph, who had become interested in the work of the English Christian Socialists. In 1896 she approached Provost Harrison with money to finance an English-style survey of the black population in the environs of her social settlement house in North Philadelphia. Harrison went to Lindsay, who then offered the job to W. E. B. Du Bois, a brilliant twenty-eight-year-old black sociologist who had just completed his Ph.D. at Harvard. Du Bois quickly accepted the offer, for he was eager to "study the facts, any and all facts concerning the American Negro and his plight and by measurement and comparison and research, work up to any valid generalizatons which I could."[28]

During his fifteen months in the city, Du Bois produced his classic study, *The Philadelphia Negro*. Du Bois made a careful collection of community data in the best traditions of English social survey work. But more important, he issued the first public statement of his views on racial politics, ideas that stood in sharp contrast to those then circulating at Wharton. To achieve racial equality in the United States, Du Bois argued, the black commu-

---

*The Wharton School dropped instruction in social work with the organization of an independent Pennsylvania School of Social and Health Work. Kelsey, however, maintained "an active connection" with the new institution. In 1935 the Pennsylvania School again became a part of the University of Pennsylvania, but with no formal ties to the Wharton School.

nity would have to develop an open, talented, and responsible elite that could help the race overcome its difficulties and win the respect of the dominant whites. The young sociologist claimed that his research showed such an elite to exist in embryo in Philadelphia, but that it had developed neither the responsibility nor the recognition needed to begin the long struggle for equality. Du Bois thus provided a different prescription for reform from that proposed by Patten. For Du Bois, dedicated social workers were no substitute for strong and responsible "native" elites in ethnic communities. Du Bois portrayed contemporary society as essentially stratified into classes and divided into racial groups; he rejected Patten's stalwart community of equals as a fanciful utopia. But since Du Bois soon left Philadelphia to teach and to set up a research program at black Atlanta University, his revolutionary ideas had no further impact at Wharton. The school thus continued with Patten's program for the nation.[29]*

II

Just as Du Bois traveled south, to train the "talented tenth" of his race for leadership, relations between the Wharton School and the Philadelphia Establishment began to come apart. Patten, the bookish, rustic reformer and proper Philadelphia had never really been comfortable in each other's presence. Nor did the economist's program include the local elite among the forces of reform. The young political scientists who had assumed James's teaching and administrative responsibilities, Leo S. Rowe and James T. Young, also failed to maintain the close relationships that James had developed with the city's Establishment. Graduates of Wharton and Halle, both young men were well prepared

---

*Although named assistant instructor, Du Bois never had any real standing at the school. He had almost no contact with students, little with the faculty, and neither an office nor an official listing in the catalog. On his slim salary of eight hundred dollars he lived in a slum where "murder sat on our doorstep, police were our government, and philanthropy dropped in with periodic advice." Du Bois naturally resented the thoughtlessness of his employers and suspected their motives for hiring him. In his analysis of the situation,

> Philadelphia was having one of its periodic spasms of reform . . . The underlying cause [of the political malaise] was evident to most white Philadelphians: the corrupt semi-criminal vote of the Negro seventh ward. Everyone agreed that here lay the cancer; but would it not be well to elucidate the known causes by a scientific investigation, with the imprimatur of the University? It certainly would, answered Samuel McClune Lindsay.

for active academic careers: Rowe, the nation's first professor of municipal government, worked closely with the National Municipal League and served as president of the American Academy from 1902 to 1930. Young took over James's courses in administration and became "administrative director" of the school in 1904. But Rowe and Young were inexperienced. Despite their positions of authority and the pertinence of their subject matter to the interests of the leaders of society, they could not replace James as a bridge between Wharton and genteel Philadelphia.[30]

Once James was gone, the reform organizations that he had established quickly lost their function as a meeting grounds for academics and the elite. The American Academy and the Municipal League continued to explore the leading political issues of the day, but after James left their programs became so technical and specialized that they lost their appeal among genteel audiences. After 1898 the academy devoted its entire annual meeting to a single topic, and the *Annals*, after 1901, focused each issue on an in-depth analysis of one problem. The Municipal League became even more esoteric. Beginning with its first model "municipal program" in 1897, it chased the intricacies of municipal charters, accounting systems, utility management and taxation with devotion that drove off all but the most dedicated academic specialists and city officials. Both in content and constituency the league came to resemble a professional association of city administrators. Increasingly, the league provided academicians with a bridge not to the social elite but to municipal officials and to academically trained professionals working in new bureaus of municipal research. (The New York Bureau of Municipal Research, headed by a Wharton Ph.D., William Allen, served as the model institution of this type.) Aside from advocating honesty, efficiency, and strong administration, there was little left for the genteel amateur to do.[31]

Elites in the city and in the nation, however, did not sit idly by while Wharton's academics were off pursuing technical detail and "social regeneration." With a tremendous display of energy and purpose, the upper classes themselves went out between 1896 and 1905 and reorganized American society, making it much more to their liking. In 1896 they led the movement to stop William Jennings Bryan's campaign for the presidency and placed conservative William McKinley in the White House; Provost Harrison served as treasurer of McKinley's Pennsylvania organization. With a sympathetic president, the return of prosperity, and the retirement of many of the great nineteenth-century entrepreneurs, America's leading investment bankers then began consolidating the nation's industrial companies at a frantic pace. By 1903 they had gathered nearly half of all corporate assets into one hundred giant firms and thereby properly ushered in the age of modern corporate capitalism. To maintain their wealth, power, and culture, the nation's patricians quickly came to rely on corporate monopolies, oligopolies, and, where necessary, government regulatory commissions. As these new institutions stabilized the industrial economy, gentility found it expedient to ignore or to buy out the nation's corrupt and localistic urban political machines. Occupied in their larger tasks, the elite had little energy left for an untrustworthy and rather stale movement for political reform.[32]

Nothing revealed the aggressive new strategy of Philadelphia's upper class as much as the controversy over the city gas works in the late 1890s. In 1885 James had been among the leaders of patrician Philadelphia in its fight to place the utility under municipal management. After twelve years of city operation, however, the price and quality of gas service still left much to be desired. Attempting to fill James's role, Professor Rowe conducted an admirable study of the situation. By comparing the accounts of the municipal authority with those of other gas utilities, he showed that progress had been made and that the major source of continuing inefficiency lay outside the management of the works. For reasons of personal gain and political influence, Rowe claimed, members of the City Council had raised wages and raw material costs, lowered prices for by-products, and ignored needs for prudent investment and maintenance expenditures. He concluded that the traditional program of reform still applied: Remove administration from the corrupt influence of the legislature, install a professional civil service, and performance would greatly improve.[33]

Philadelphia's Establishment, however, had lost patience with reform. A private corporation, the United Gas Improvement Company, promised to lower prices, deliver better gas, and pay solid dividends to investors. All it needed was a lease on the utility. Backed by the city's business interests and using less than honorable means, UGI neatly rushed a lucrative thirty-year lease through City Council. As stock in UGI quickly found its way into most proper Philadelphia fortunes, the genteel elements in the city lost "interest" in the schemes of Wharton professors.[34]

Rowe correctly perceived that abandonment of municipal management reflected a decline of "civic ideals" in the city. He argued that in addition to giving up a source of great potential income at a bargain price, the community had lost an important instrument for progress. He pointed out that enlightened municipal utilities in England underwrote the spread of gas to the poor, to the ultimate benefit of society as a whole. Using the logic of Simon Patten, he reasoned that

the wastefulness of the coal stove and the comparatively high cost of its maintenance . . . had given to uncooked foods an important place in the standard of life of these classes, a fact that seriously affected their industrial efficiency and physical vigor. The widespread use of alcoholic liquors was largely to be explained by the crude diet of the poorer classes.

Raising the general standard of living and civilization did not, however, concern UGI, and Rowe concluded that such "private corporations performing quasi-public functions constitutes the greatest danger to American local institutions."[35]

The faculty thus awoke to find their old ally in uplift now arrayed among the opposition. Feeling betrayed, Rowe complained that

in those very classes that should furnish leaders in our civic life, we find waging the conflict between private interests and public welfare which usually results in the triumph of the former. Attachment to the city is not sufficiently strong in American communities to withstand the temptation of private gain.[36]

Challenged by the new political situation, the faculty expressed renewed enthusiasm for their educational work. In an article representative of the general opinion at Wharton, Rowe claimed that the school's program cultivated the civic spirit that the times so desperately needed. He thought that a traditional collegiate education, in contrast, developed those critical and analytical "faculties" that hampered the ability of a student "to cooperate with his fellow citizens in the struggle for civic improvement." Wharton's program of instruction in practical issues and student investigations into the workings of society, Rowe claimed, expanded the "constructive powers" of mind and contributed "toward the development of civic instincts" and "the strengthening of civic effort"; it equipped students with a knowledge of public affairs, a sense of social reponsibility, and the personal confidence essential for them to become progressive young stalwarts. Especially effective, he thought, was the school's emphasis on original student reports. "The zeal, ingenuity, persistence and attention to detail with which the college students will take up a work of special inquiry is one of the most inspiring as well as the most hopeful indications of the civic effects of these special investigations."[37]*

In 1905 Rowe's vision seemed to be confirmed, for when the gas issue reemerged the students at Penn did rally around the banner of civic righteousness. The UGI and its political allies in City Council then attempted to grab still more privileges from the municipality, and much of the local Establishment either supported the company's claims or quietly looked the other way. But Mayor Weaver and the progressive newspapers of the city raised a huge fuss and successfully stopped the deal. A political bloodbath ensued. When elections were next held, the Republican machine, with the city police in their corner, threatened to turn Weaver out. The Penn student body, many of whose parents supported UGI and the Republicans, valiantly rushed to the aid of the mayor. Students manned offices, canvased neighborhoods, and on election day formed mobile squads with flags and cameras to guard the polling places. With beefy Penn wrestlers and football players prominently displayed, these squads faced down the city police, who were intent on coercing the voters to back the machine.[38]

---

*Rowe proposed that all courses in municipal government in the United States adopt this format, and he developed a program through the National Municipal League whereby all university students in the nation conducting such investigations would explore the same topic. "A spirit of mutual helpfulness will thus be aroused which will add considerably to the educational value of these courses."

Patten practiced the same "investigation method" pedagogy at the graduate level as Rowe did among his undergraduates. The implications, however, were different. With undergraduates, the program challenged the older patterns of American collegiate instruction; at the Ph.D. level it was the conservative technique that resisted a growing emphasis on fundamental research and complete reviews of the scholarly literature. In the 1870s and 1880s a brief essay of thirty or forty pages had been sufficient to win a German doctorate. By the 1900s, however, careful and exhaustive three-hundred-page dissertations had become common American practice. Patten abhorred such esoteric exercises and wrote that a "three hundred page thesis not only does not fit a man to be an economist: it really incapacitates him for work." He thought the graduate school an inappropriate setting for extended research, preferring instead large independent institutions such as the New York Bureau of Municipal Research or agencies of the federal government. With their large staffs of trained economists, Patten thought that these specialized agencies were much more capable of gathering reliable data and of wringing out sound interpretations than universities. He wanted his own graduate students to address the issues of the day and to write for popular audiences. They had to know that "there can be no economic literature apart from general literature" and that while in the past the "college has stood for culture and science[, i]t must now stand for efficiency." Patten thus remained within the engaged, pragmatic pedagogy championed by Edmund James. But now with James gone, and with huge corporations transforming the nature of power in America, Patten led Wharton's graduate program into the rising "Progressive" movement of the times. His graduate students

left his classroom to investigate the doings of the United Gas Improvement Company, the Philadelphia Electric Company, the Hard Coal Combine, and the other aggregations of capital that held the city and the state in the hollow of their hands. One standard was set up in these classes— the public welfare, and it was in light of these class discussions that Patten's men attacked the problems that lay around them.[39]

In their dissertations and in their later interests, "Patten's men" each developed expertise on a separate social problem; in dividing their investigative labor they thereby magnified their impact on society. Scott Nearing, the school's long-time instructor of freshman economics and "probably the favorite faculty member of much of the class," concentrated on the child labor issue. To Patten and his students, child labor was an especially vicious aspect of contemporary American life, one that resembled antebellum slavery in its systematic denial of education and opportunity to a whole class of Americans. The state of Pennsylvania at the time was the nation's leading employer of children, with the practice especially prevalent in its coal fields and textile mills. In addition to authoring studies of the situation, Nearing also served for a while as director of the state Child Labor Committee. Thomas Conway, young professor of finance, investigated street railway operations and found a pattern of mismanagement and excessive charges in the Philadelphia transit system. An instructor in business law, W. Ward Pierson, scrutinized the Pennsylvania Railroad; Professor of Geography J. Russell Smith championed the cause of conservation; political scientist Clyde King took on the Philadelphia Electric Company and the local food distribution system. All of these young members of the Wharton faculty resolved "to learn the truth, to teach the truth, and to build the truth into the life of the community."[40]

As in the 1905 "Gas War," Wharton's activists found their most effective allies among government administrators and sympathetic molders of public opinion — the press, church groups, and popular reform organizations. The most effective years for reform came during the administration of independent mayor Rudolph Blankenburg, from 1912 to 1916. Blankenburg himself had no direct associations with Wharton, but several of his deputies, especially Director of Public Works Morris L. Cooke, developed close ties with the school. Cooke, a protege of Frederick W. Taylor, resolved to bring "efficiency" to Philadelphia. He had "no hesitation in saying that many accomplishments of our department would have been impossible had it not been for the help I received from the experts on the faculty of the Wharton School of the University of Pennsylvania."[41]*

---

*Clyde King investigated the local food distribution system at Cooke's request and found inefficient middlemen raising prices to consumers and lowering returns to farmers. His report recommended a city-operated system of public markets and a trolley system of freight transportation to bring farmers and con-

The campaign for efficiency heated up in 1914, after Cooke became convinced that the Philadelphia Electric Company (PECO) had systematically "mulcted and fleeced" its consumers. He went to City Council for funds to sue PECO to lower its rates. But the council denied Cooke's request, instead cutting his administrative budget. Cooke then surprised everyone and took on the utility as a private citizen. Among his most faithful allies were Clyde King and Ernest M. Patterson of the Wharton economics department. William Draper Lewis, a Wharton Ph.D. who taught business law at the school before becoming dean of the university law school in 1896, argued the case before the Pennsylvania Public Service Commission. Cooke's suit succeeded, and PECO lowered its rates by over one million dollars annually.[42]

While professors campaigned for progressive causes, Scott Nearing's course in economics, required of all Wharton freshmen, introduced the student body to the swift currents of reform at the school and in the world. Patten took special interest in Nearing's work, encouraging him to teach a course with critical punch and to write a new textbook to match. Nearing willingly complied. His new text on *Economics* and his introductory survey covered the standard topics in such courses; additionally, he devoted a great deal of time to monopolies and utilities, to programs of reform, and to Patten's central theoretical interest—consumption. Nearing also distributed a list of the leading progressive books of

sumers closer together. The Republican organization politicians in City Council, however, denounced the plan as "municipal socialism" and killed it. W. Ward Pierson worked to establish a city Department of Wharves, Docks and Ferries and then investigated price fixing in the shipping industry. Pierson also studied the cost of transporting coal to Philadelphia utilities, a cost that was passed directly on to the consumer. He found tremendous gouging and served as attorney in a suit before the Pennsylvania Public Service Commission to lower these charges.

During these years of high reform, Cooke often addressed Wharton classes and arranged field trips to various city offices so that students could get a practical, close-up view of municipal government. He also hired King and others at Wharton on a part-time basis for municipal research projects. Highly enthusiastic about the results, Cooke declared in his book on the civic awakening:

> It would be a good thing if we could have in this field some part-time teachers and professors — men who would serve the city, say six months in the year and teach the rest of the time. We tried this experiment and it proved a wonderful success. For instance, Dr. Clyde King of the Wharton School, University of Pennsylvania, was several different times entrusted with important city work and each time he rendered an exceedingly valuable service. His experience as a city employee inevitably broadened his usefulness as a teacher.

the day,* requiring each student to read and write reviews of three books on the list; "quizmasters" assigned the freshmen additional readings "in popular magazines of an ultra-radical character." This economics survey course thus served as the school's primary introduction to Patten's program of engaged social science.[43]

Discussions in Nearing's class and in the sections conducted by his quizmasters were always lively. Especially spirited "quarrels" sprang up when students considered the current distribution of income in the United States and the "adequacy" of the standard of living of the poorer classes. Nearing used this topic as an occasion for vigorous assaults on "natural monopolies under private control" and to expatiate on how "private enterprise capitalism had created a distribution system that was unethical and anti-social." His stirring portrayals of poverty at the hands of cruel monopoly had a great effect on the freshmen passing through the course. His arguments stimulated students' sympathies for the oppressed, engaging their sense of justice and their resentment of privilege. But the great strength of the lectures came from Nearing's mastery of fact and the intensity with which he argued his positions. He filled the lecture room with detailed exposés of corruption and painted each piece of dirty business in stark moral terms: good in this corner, bad in the other. Simon Patten, who feared that American collegiate education dangerously overemphasized passive "sensory" as opposed to active "motor" intelligence, could take heart in the work of his young instructor.[44]

Wharton's aggressive program of reform was intellectually exciting but politically dangerous, exposing the school to the rapidly shifting tides of power in "progressive" America. The campaign for social regeneration isolated the school from its traditional supporters and alienated it from rising interests. The faculty found itself increasingly vulnerable to external pressures, forces which eventually shattered the traditions that had been built up at the school since the 1880s.

A scandal attending the death of Joseph Wharton, in 1909, served as an ironic portent of the final collapse. The old ironmaster had kept a close eye on the school, especially in its early days;

---

*Nearing's list included works by Lincoln Stephens, Gustavus Myers, Jane Addams, Thorstein Veblen, John Dewey, Charles Beard, and Herbert Croly.

he spoke at functions, reviewed plans, and sent inspectors through its halls. During his lifetime Wharton had raised his endowment from the initial one hundred thousand dollars to five hundred thousand dollars and now, upon his death, the faculty expected a further portion of his estate. The eagerly anticipated reading of the will revealed that the founder had indeed originally included another five hundred thousand dollars for the school. But for some unknown reason he had removed this provision in a 1906 codicil. Rumor mills offered several explanations, including a few that accused the Wharton School of excess radicalism or some peccadillo in etiquette. Wharton would no doubt have difficulty accepting all that now went on at the school. But the majority of observers laid the blame elsewhere; they pointed to a tiff between the Wharton family and the Philadelphia Establishment that controlled the university. Proper Philadelphia, with Provost Charles C. Harrison in the lead, had denied Wharton's son-in-law, Harrison S. Morris, a seat on the board of the Pennsylvania Academy of Fine Arts. Angered at this snub and apparently to spite them, and not his school, Wharton rescinded his bequest to the university. The school's leaders were caught unawares, because no one in recent years had developed a close relationship with the founder. To allow the ironmaster so callously to dismiss the interests of the Wharton School was an oversight of shocking financial proportions. If the story were true, then Joseph Wharton had come to identify the school that he had founded with the established Philadelphia elite — with the provost who had banished James and with the trustees whose interests the faculty were busily assaulting.[45]

After Provost Harrison stepped down in 1911, the school's situation did not improve; indeed, at that point the position of Patten's program at Penn began to deteriorate quite rapidly. Harrison had financed the university during his tenure in office, and now that he was gone new sources of funds, bringing with them new influences, had to be found. In pursuit of new benefactions, the university added as trustees men whose affairs lay in the direct line of fire of Wharton's progressive reformers — businessmen with lucrative interests in utility companies and upstate coal fields and Republican politicians with access to the state treasury. Harrison's successor as provost, Edgar Fahs Smith, was an intimate of the city's notorious Republican machine, which he often defended in public. Through his connections, the university began receiving large state appropriations in 1911, funds that remain a major source of its support to this day. Members of the Wharton faculty, however, saw in Provost Smith a "reactionary of the most mulish sort." Smith favored the classical curriculum of Greek, Latin, mathematics, and philosophy, with a dash of modern languages and science to finish off a college education. As for politics, he was said to have asked three Wharton teachers:

Gentlemen, what business have academic people to be meddling in political questions? Suppose, for illustration, that I, as a chemist, should discover that some big slaughtering company was putting formalin in its sausage; now surely that would be none of my business.

Thus when Wharton's reformers began their most effective period of activity — with the Blankenburg administration — they found themselves faced with a radically hostile administration in the university.[46]

From the first, the new men in power at the university attacked the activities at Wharton. They denied promotions to Nearing, Pierson, and Conway, despite their obvious accomplishments and enthusiastic recommendations for advancement from the Academic Council of the university. To pressure the faculty to tone down its progressivism, the trustees held up funds for the Wharton School in general and for its Political Science Department in particular; Nearing, in response, did stop his child labor agitation for a while. When the trustees reorganized the university in 1912 and made the Wharton School independent of the college, they seriously considered naming a conservative professor of *English*, Arthur Hobson Quinn, as the school's first dean since Robert Ellis Thompson. Quinn, however, took on the more prestigious and powerful post of dean of the college. But the progressive forces were not without their victories. During the 1912 university reorganization they finally succeeded in abolishing the Greek requirement in the college. More important to Wharton, Roswell Cheney McCrea, a Patten student and professor of economics at the university since only 1911, was named dean of the school. McCrea held impeccable progressive credentials; he had been associate director of the New York School of Philanthropy between 1907 and 1911, and he believed that "as capitalism increases, misery and unemployment and low wages increase unless there is some sort of social action." The conflict, however, had not been resolved with the selection of McCrea as dean.[47]

Tensions between the camps reached a climax in the 1914-15 academic year, both at the university and in the city. The war in Europe, ending the 100 years' peace in Western civilization, unnerved the entire nation, while in Philadelphia Patten's pacifism and sympathy for German efficiency enraged the city's thoroughly Anglo-Saxon Establishment. The suit against the electric company, then reaching a decision, further exacerbated local frictions between the propertied and the progressives. In apparent reaction to these anxieties, one hundred thousand militant white Protestant Philadelphians marched under the banner of the paramilitary "Stone Men's League," an organization hostile to immigrants, Jews, Catholics, and racial minorities. Blankenburg's director of public safety, George D. Porter, actually endorsed the league's activities and reviewed its mass parade. Meanwhile a broad array of sponsors, with members of the city's genteel elite at the forefront, brought the reactionary revivalist Billy Sunday to Philadelphia for a triumphal four-week crusade. For an entire month, the evangelist used Jesus to praise patriotism, civil obedience, and an overriding concern for one's own salvation. When the Reverend Mr. Sunday came to the University of Pennsylvania and addressed the entire student body in a special assembly, he received a very gracious welcome from Provost Smith and Trustee George Wharton Pepper, a prominent high-Anglican layman. Smith and Pepper believed the revival of religion on American campuses to be the most important university event in recent years and hoped that Sunday would turn student attention to personal redemption and away from the muck of the city. It was perhaps no accident that the revivalist's visit coincided exactly with the final victory of Cooke and the party of social regeneration over the electric company. Progressive papers in the city carried the utility rate case on their front pages while across town the conservative press headlined Sunday's activities.[48]

During this same academic year, 1914-15, Scott Nearing emerged as the most vocal champion of the progressive cause at

Wharton. He renewed his efforts to abolish child labor and wrote a sharp public letter to Billy Sunday. Nearing told the revivalist,

the chief priests, scribes and Pharisees of Philadelphia will never crucify you while you deal in theological pleasantries. Has it occurred to you that their kindness is a return for your services in helping them to divert attention from real, pressing worldly injustice to heavenly bliss? Turn your oratorical brilliancy for a moment against low wages, overwork, unemployment, monopoly and special privilege.

In class, Nearing achieved more notoriety with an especially stinging sermon of his own against "real" injustice and privilege. He posted on a bulletin board a long newspaper article describing a lavish dinner at the mansion of Edward Townsend Stotesbury, J. P. Morgan's Philadelphia partner. With telling effect on his students, Nearing contrasted the splendid affair with the diet, dress, and housing of the city's unemployed. He went on to describe the child labor, utility corruptions, monopolies, and financial frauds that Stotesbury and his guests had employed to raise themselves up into the lap of luxury. The issue was no longer introductory economics, but sin and social salvation. And at the end of his sermon, the freshmen gave Nearing a rousing ovation.[49]

Among the students in Nearing's class was the son of Mrs. Stotesbury, J. H. R. Cromwell. Lately young Cromwell had been having a rough time at Wharton defending himself and his family. Everyone listening to Nearing's lesson was quite aware of Cromwell's presence, and Nearing's direct accusations and the subsequent student response left young Cromwell even more embarrassed and isolated. But inasmuch as his stepfather, Edward Stotesbury, sat on the Board of Trustees of the university and was clearly the most prominent businessman in the city, Nearing's performance proved to be highly impolitic; yea, academically suicidal.[50]

On 15 June 1915, without formal charges or a proper hearing, in violation of normal university practice and ignoring the recommendations of the faculty, the trustees fired Scott Nearing, effective immediately.

The trustees never officially explained their reasons for dispatching Nearing, and their motives can only be surmised. The immediate instigators of Nearing's dismissal may actually have been those employers in the state who were clearly upset over his criticism of child labor. When Nearing was fired, Joseph Grundy, the powerful representative of upstate coal interests in Harrisburg, seems to have been holding up the university's state appropriation in order to force the professor out. These threats may have been the proximate cause of Nearing's departure. But the trustees and their close business and social associates, the alumni organized as the "General Alumni Society," had reasons of their own. One trustee, ex-Attorney General of Pennsylvania John C. Bell, resented a slurring reference that Nearing had cast on the Episcopal Academy, a local elite private school. Referring to such incidents as the humiliation of young Cromwell, other trustees objected to Nearing's stridency and intolerance. They criticized him for failing to appreciate

the extent of his responsibilities to young students, and . . . the importance given to his words by the mere fact that the University has commissioned and trusted him to teach, and has conferred upon him the right to use her name in addressing either students or the public.

They claimed that his "methods, language and temperament provoke continued and widespread criticism alike from parents of students and from the general public" and that he had not been "tolerant of the opinions of other students of life as it exists." Where Nearing saw intolerable sin, the trustees found a legitimate matter for personal judgment.[51]

In the end, it was the trustees who were themselves intolerant. Trustee Joseph G. Rosengarten, who had known the late Joseph Wharton well and had once served as his "observer" of the Wharton School, thought it an outrage that

men holding teaching positions in the Wharton School introduce there doctrines wholly at variance with those of its founder and go before the public as members of the Wharton School faculty and representatives of the University, to talk wildly and in a manner entirely inconsistent with Mr. Wharton's well-known views and in defiance of the conservative opinions of men of affairs.

Leader of the Alumni Committee of the Wharton School and prominent Philadelphia banker, Thomas S. Gates, informed the public that his group was squarely opposed to the use of the fair name of the University as a point of vantage for utterances foreign to the scheme of its teaching and ideals in education, and recommends that where such members of the teaching staff are not willing to subscribe to its policies their services should be dispensed with.[52]

The trustees' firing of Nearing prompted a huge and instant protest. Using his experience at political organizing, Nearing immediately sent out a mimeographed fact sheet to fifteen hundred newspapers, influential organizations, and individuals throughout the nation. Meanwhile, two trustees who had opposed Nearing's dismissal publicly attacked the board; ironically, they were Joseph Wharton's nephew, Wharton Barker, and the founder's aggrieved son-in-law, Harrison S. Morris. Unlike the upper-class General Alumni Society, other Penn alumni groups joined the chorus of protest, as did much of the local press and the Philadelphia Central Labor Union. The newly formed American Association of University Professors, organized in response to similar incidents at many other major American universities, set up a committee to investigate the affair. Lightner Witmer, Wharton alumnus and conservative professor of psychology at the university, declared, "I don't give a damn for Nearing. He and I disagree on almost everything, but this is my fight. If they can do that to him they can do it to any of us. It is time to act." And Witmer spent the entire summer producing a book that bitterly criticized the trustees and their presumption upon academic matters.[53]

The Wharton faculty had left campus for the summer before the trustees fired Nearing. But immediately upon hearing of the dismissal, Dean McCrea demanded from the trustees "a frank statement of the grounds of their action" and went on to point out that "the present apprehension and public expressions of indignation are jeopardizing not only the interests of the Wharton School but of the University at large." When the Wharton faculty reassembled, it unanimously resolved

to protest against the manner of and the assigned reasons for the removal of Assistant Professor Nearing . . . the failure of the Board of Trustees to reappoint an instructor or an assistant professor, when recommended by the faculty of which he is a member, without a hearing, without specific charges and without due notice . . . [,and] the policy formulated by the Board of Trustees relating to utterances of members of the faculty[.]

The Wharton professors took up a collection that gave Nearing an income for the rest of the year. The students, for their part, covered the campus with placards from fall through spring to protest the dismissal.[54]

But the trustees remained adamant and uncompromising. Simon Patten had prepared the faculty for this showdown, and urged "no resignations. If they come after us let them drag us out one at a time with hooks." Despite their mentor's call to battle, key men nevertheless left the university. Dean McCrea, Professor of Geography and Industry J. Russell Smith, and others on the faculty accepted appointments at Columbia. Professor Leo S. Rowe resigned after the trustees angrily refused to extend his leave of absence while he was working for the federal government. Clearly, the school was losing some of its best minds.[55]

To replace the stalwart McCrea, the trustees named William C. McClellan dean of the school in 1916. A prominent Penn engineering graduate, McClellan had made a successful career for himself in the very municipal utility companies that Wharton's progressives had so successfully assaulted. His major qualification for the deanship was his presidency of the Associated Pennsylvania [Alumni] Clubs, a conservative group that had pressured the trustees to change the political profile of the school. Neither an academic nor learned in the social sciences, McClellan was the trustees' man. He tried to enforce their claim of a right to veto extracurricular faculty activities, infuriating the professoriate by asking them to report all such engagements.[56]

The faculty, however, refused to do business with the new dean. Among themselves they called McClellan the "gorilla" and plotted against him.

They did not intend to be worsted again and they devoted themselves singlemindedly to the enemy until he withdrew . . . [The faculty] led him into every embarrassing ambuscade possible and then enfiladed his forces with an absolutely demoralizing fire of publicity. He never had a chance. And they had more fun than they had ever had in their lives.[57]

Faced with such skilled resistance, McClellan and the trustees finally relented. The dean rescinded his memorandum, and the trustees gave up their claim to control extracurricular activities. Much more important, the faculty at Wharton and throughout the university won the right to determine the tenure of their staff without interference from the trustees. McClellan himself stayed on through the war years, dividing his time between the Wharton School and his business interests in Washington, D.C. But continued faculty hostility and threats by Wharton Barker and Harrison Morris to begin a formal investigation of the school finally forced McClellan out in 1919.[58]

Before McClellan left, the trustees delivered a culminating blow to progressivism at Wharton. In 1917 Simon Patten reached the age of retirement — sixty-five. The trustees customarily extended the tenure of distinguished faculty, and in that very year they did so for John Bach McMaster, Patten's old colleague from the early days of the school. But the board saw Patten as the source of Wharton's mischief and was anxious to see him go; it refused to continue his contract and terminated his connection with the university. The faculty, of course, protested. They called Patten an economist of "national and international reputation" whose work "shed lustre on the University." But unfortunately they voiced their objections on the same day that America entered World War I, and their protest was lost amid the resulting din of militant nationalism.[59]

For Patten it must have been the final scene of a great tragedy. His Wharton School lay crushed by what he saw as the evil "sensualist" forces of history. They were the exploiters of child labor and the masters of monopoly; they had corrupted the democratic processes of the republic and had employed obscurantist priests to confuse the legitimate religious aspirations of the people. No longer would eager young scholars at Wharton create and publicize practical programs of reform for the "stalwart" community. The great task that Patten had assigned for contemporary American civilization — to integrate the German principle of organization with the Anglo-Saxon tradition of democracy — lay defeated not only at Penn but in the great slaughterhouse of World War I. Patten left his professorship "a lonely and isolated man," spending "the last five years of his life . . . in a cluttered apartment in Philadelphia, in a one-room cabin in East Alstead, New Hampshire, or at a hotel in Browns Mills, New Jersey."[60]

In the aftermath of the Nearing affair and the disgrace of Patten, a stench lay over the university. The scandal prevented the Wharton School from attracting any first-rate, critical mind to replace Patten and it raised serious questions about the future of the institution. In 1917 the school lost its intellectual, a man who lived for ideas. Thereafter it had to make do with professionals, men who lived off ideas.[61]

Source Notes

1. Daniel M. Fox, *The Discovery of Abundance: Simon N. Patten and the Transformation of Social Theory* (Ithaca, N.Y.: Cornell University Press, 1967), 19; John R. Everett, *Religion in Economics* (New York: King's Crown Press of Columbia University Press, 1946), 99–134; Rexford G. Tugwell, "Notes on the Life of Simon Nelson Patten," *Journal of Political Economy* 31 (1923):170.

2. Fox, *Patten*, 13–18; Everett, *Religion in Economics*, 99–102; Tugwell, "Patten," 158–65.

3. Fox, *Patten*, 18–20; Everett, *Religion in Economics*, 102–4.

4. Fox, *Patten*, 20–24; Everett, *Religion in Economics*, 103–5.

5. Simon N. Patten, *The Premises of Political Economy* (Philadelphia: J. B. Lippincott, 1885); Fox, *Patten*, 24–31; Everett, *Religion in Economics*, 105–7.

6. E. K. Hunt, "Simon Patten's Contributions to Economics," *Journal of Economic Issues* 4 (1970):40–48; James Boswell, *The Economics of Simon Nelson Patten* (Philadelphia: University of Pennsylvania Press, 1934), 46–101; Fox, *Patten*, 44ff.

7. Simon N. Patten, *The Economic Basis of Protection* (Philadelphia: J. B. Lippincott, 1890).

8. Ibid., 127, 20, 66, 53, 7–13, 37–38, 51–53, 90–91, 123–33, 162–69.

9. Scott Nearing, *Educational Frontiers: A Book about Simon Nelson Patten and Other Teachers* (New York: Thomas Seltzer, 1925), passim, esp. (ix–19, 45; Tugwell, "Patten," 193–94; see Edward T. Devine, *Economics* (New York: MacMillan, 1898), Henry R. Seager, *Introduction to Economics* (New York: Henry Holt, 1904), and Scott Nearing and Frank D. Watson, *Economics* (New York: MacMillan, 1908).

10. Simon N. Patten, "The Educational Value of Political Economy," *Publications of the American Economic Association* 5 (1890):473, 477, 494, 484; 491, 486, 487, 495; *Catalog of the University of Pennsylvania (1892–93)*, 154–6; *(1893–94)*, 109–11; *(1894–95)*, 66–69; Rexford G. Tugwell, "To the Lesser Heights of Morningside," MS memoir, 144, 144n.

11. Minutes of the Wharton Faculty, 9 Oct. 1895; Roswell C. McCrea, "The Wharton School," *Alumni Register* 17 (1915):294–95, 298; Emory R. Johnson, *The Wharton School: Its First Fifty Years, 1881–1931* (Philadelphia: Wharton School, 1931), 20; Edward P. Cheyney, *History of the University of Pennsylvania* (University of Pennsylvania Press, 1940) 299, 337–39.

12. Patten, "Educational Value," 487; Nearing, *Educational Frontiers*, 7–11, 17–19; Fox, *Patten*, 2.

13. Simon N. Patten, "The Formulation of Normal Laws," *Annals* 7 (1896): 426–34; Patten, "Educational Value," 481, 496–97; Simon N. Patten, *The Development of English Thought: A Study in the Economic Interpretation of History* (New York: MacMillan, 1899), 406; see Talcott Parsons, *The Structure of Social Action* (New York: McGraw-Hill, 1937) and Joseph Schumpeter, *The Theory of Economic Development* (Cambridge, Mass.: Harvard University Press, 1934 [1911]).

14. Patten, "Normal Laws," 434–49.

15. Patten, *English Thought*, 1–31; Fox, *Patten*, 71–72.

16. Patten, *English Thought*, 57–88.

17. Ibid., 122, 118, 123, 124, 123, 140, 134–42; Patten, "Normal Laws," 435.

18. Ibid., 142–363; Boswell, *Patten*, 46–48; Everett, *Religion in Economics*, 111–12.

19. Boswell, *Patten*, 125–27.

20. Fox, *Patten*, 83–85, 94, 103.

21. Simon N. Patten, "The Making of Economic Literature," in *Essays in Economic Theory by Simon Nelson Patten*, ed. Rexford G. Tugwell (New York: Alfred A. Knopf, 1924 [1909]), 244, 247, 244; Everett, *Religion in Economics*, 108–9; Fox, *Patten*, 51, 63–65, 71–72, 83–85.

22. Patten, "Normal Laws," 442; Fox, *Patten*, 48.

23. Simon N. Patten, *The Social Basis of Religion* (New York: MacMillan, 1911), 210; Everett, *Religion in Economics*, 117–28; Fox, *Patten*, 108; Simon N. Patten, *Mud Hollow: From Dust to Soul* (Philadelphia: Dorrance, 1922); Fox, *Patten*, 112, 112 n.39; Tugwell, "Morningside Heights," 156–57, 157n.

24. Devine, *Economics*; Seager, *Introduction to Economics*; Nearing and Watson, *Economics*; Fox, *Patten*, 95; Tugwell, "Morningside Heights," 72; James H. S. Bossard, "A History of Sociology at the University of Pennsylvania," *General Magazine and Historical Chronicle* 33 (1930–31):411–16.

25. Mary E. Richmond, "Training of Philanthropic Workers," address before annual meeting of American Academy of Political and Social Sciences, Apr. 1898, quoted in Samuel M. Lindsay, "The Study and Teaching of Sociology," *Annals* 12 (1898):19, 20; Nearing, *Educational Frontiers*, 32; Fox, *Patten*, 89, 95–105, 112–13.

26. Samuel M. Lindsay to James H. S. Bossard, quoted in Bossard, "History of Sociology," 512; Lindsay, "Sociology," 24; "Circular of Information, M," University of Pennsylvania publications, May 1899, quoted in Bossard, "History of Sociology," 417; "Course in Social Work," attached to Minutes of the Wharton Faculty, Dec. 1900; Richmond, "Training of Philanthropic Workers," 21; Bossard, "History of Sociology," 416–18, 512–14; Samuel M. Lindsay, "Social Work at the Krupp Factories," *Annals* 3 (1892):330–62; Fox, *Patten*, 69, 97–98, 196 n. 10, 204 n. 1; *Catalog (1894–95)*, 66–69; "Sociological Notes," conducted by Samuel M. Lindsay, *Annals* 6 (1895):187–88; editorial, *Annals* 19 (1902):256–57; Lindsay, "Sociology," 18–28. Patten's *New Basis of Civilization* (New York: MacMillan, 1906) grew out of a series of lectures that he delivered to the New York School of Philanthropy.

27. Lichtenberger to Bossard, quoted in Bossard, "History of Sociology," 514; *University Bulletin, The University of Pennsylvania, The College: Wharton School of Finance and Commerce, (1909–10)*, 19, 8, 19–20; Bossard, "History of Sociology," 416–17, 512–13; Cheyney, *History of the University*, 428.

28. W. E. B. Du Bois, *Dusk of Dawn*, 51, quoted in E. Digby Baltzell, introduction to the 1967 edition of Du Bois's *The Philadelphia Negro* (New York: Schocken, 1967 [1899]), xviii.

29. W. E. B. Du Bois, "My Evolving Program for Negro Freedom" in *What the Negro Wants*, ed. Rayford Logan, 44, quoted in Baltzell, Introduction, xix; Baltzell, Introduction, xvi–xxix; Du Bois, *Philadelphia Negro*, 316–19; 385–93; *Dictionary of American Biography*, s.v., "W. E. B. Du Bois."

30. "James T. Young File" and "Leo S. Rowe File," Archives.

31. Lindsay, "Sociology," 1; Frank M. Stewart, *A Half Century of Municipal Reform: The History of the National Municipal League* (Berkeley: Uni-

versity of California Press, 1950), 28ff.; Emory R. Johnson, *The Life of a University Professor* (Philadelphia: privately printed, 1943), 67–68.

32. For an earlier instance of private corporations taking over from government, see Louis Hartz, *Economic Policy and Democratic Thought: Pennsylvania, 1776 – 1860* (Cambridge, Mass.: Harvard University Press, 1948); Professor Louis Galambos first brought to my attention the idea that the new power of oligopolistic corporate business at the turn of the century made the resort to government intervention less necessary to American elites.

33. Leo S. Rowe, "The Municipality and the Gas Supply: As Illustrated by the Experience of Philadelphia," *Annals* 11 (1898):301 – 23; Clinton R. Woodruff, "The Philadelphia Gas Works: A Modern Instance," *American Journal of Sociology* 3 (1898):601 – 13.

34. Woodruff, "Gas Works," 601 – 13; Rowe, "Gas Supply," 30 – 33, 313 – 14, 322 – 23; E. Digby Baltzell, *Philadelphia Gentleman* (Glencoe, Ill.: Free Press, 1958).

35. Rowe, "Gas Supply," 320, 322.

36. Ibid., 322.

37. Leo S. Rowe, "University and Collegiate Research in Municipal Government," *Proceedings of the Chicago Conference for Good City Government* (Philadelphia: National Municipal League, 1904), 242–43, 247.

38. Edwin O. Lewis, "College Men in Philadelphia Politics, from a City Party Point of View," *Red and Blue* 19 (January, 1907):2 – 7; Lloyd M. Abernathy, "The Insurgency in Philadelphia, 1905," *Pennsylvania Magazine of History and Biography* 87 (1963):3 – 20.

39. Patten, "Economic Literature," 245; Simon N. Patten, "University Training for Business Men," *Educational Review* 29 (1905):232; Patten, "Economic Literature," 244; Nearing, *Educational Frontiers*, 16 – 17. Patten also mentioned the Russell Sage Foundation and government agencies as large institutions capable of useful empirical work.

40. Nearing, *Educational Frontiers*, 16 – 17; taped statement by George Friedlander, 15 Feb. 1980; Nearing, *Educational Frontiers*, 33; Nearing, *The Making of a Radical* (New York: Harper & Row, 1972), 56–58; Lightner Witmer, *The Nearing Case* (New York: B. W. Huebsch, 1915), 113 – 17.

41. Morris L. Cooke, *Our Cities Awake* (New York: Doubleday, Page, 1919), 153 – 54, 150 – 51; 150 – 57, 174; Tugwell, "Morningside Heights," 67 – 68. King verified Cooke's claim as to the beneficial effects of his government service in his "Public Service of the College and University Expert," *Annals* 67 (1916):291 – 96; Witmer, *Nearing Case*, 115; Clyde King, "Municipal Markets," *Annals* 50 (1913): 102–17; Donald W. Disbrow, "Reform in Philadelphia under Mayor Blankenburg," *Pennsylvania History* 27 (1960):386; Jeffrey S. Feld, "The Whartonians: An Examination of the Relationship between Philadelphia Municipal Reform and Professors of the Wharton School, 1906–1916," table 5 – 2, (senior thesis, Department of History, University of Pennsylvania, 1980), 87–88.

42. Kenneth E. Trombley, *The Life and Times of a Happy Liberal* (New York: Harper, 1954), 44, 36 ff.; Cooke, *Our Cities Awake*, 260; "William Draper Lewis File," Archives.

43. Minutes of the Wharton Faculty, 1 June 1910; Nearing, *Making of a Radical*, 53; Nearing and Watson, *Economics*; Tugwell, "Morningside Heights," 37 and addendum I.

44. Tugwell, "Morningside Heights,"61; Nearing, *Making of a Radical*, 56; Nearing, *Educational Frontiers*, 31.

45. *Philadelphia Inquirer*, 14 Jan. 1904, 17 Jan. 1909, 20 Jan. 1909, and *Philadelphia Bulletin*, 16 Jan. 1909, "Joseph Wharton File," Archives.

46. Tugwell, "Morningside Heights," 80; Smith to Wharton professors, quoted by Upton Sinclair, *Goosestep* (Pasadena, Calif.: published by the author,

1923), 98, 97 – 101; Witmer, *Nearing Case*, 63, 103 – 6; Nearing, *Educational Frontiers*, 48, 78 – 79; Cheyney, *History of the University*, 371 ff.

47. Witmer, *Nearing Case*, 113ff.; *Philadelphia Public Ledger*, 14 Aug. 1912, and *New York Herald*, 10 Sept. 1912, "McCrea File," Archives.

48. Fox, *Patten*, 117 – 22, 126; Trombley, *Happy Liberal*, 44 – 45; Witmer, *Nearing Case*, 52 – 59; Disbrow, "Reform in Philadelphia," 392 – 93, 395; Simon Patten, no doubt out of his great respect for the religious sensibility, sat on the platform as one of Billy Sunday's sponsors when the revivalist came to the university. Fox, *Patten*, 125.

49. Nearing to Sunday, *Philadelphia North American*, 2 Feb. 1915, quoted in Witmer, *Nearing Case*, 54 – 55; Nearing, *Educational Frontiers*, 45.

50. Nearing, *Educational Frontiers*, 45: Tugwell, "Morningside Heights," 131.

51. Resolutions of the University of Pennsylvania Board of Trustees, 14 Oct. 1915, in Edward Robins (secretary of the university) to Roswell McCrea, 12 Oct. 1915, Minutes of the Wharton Faculty, 22 Oct. 1915; Witmer, *Nearing Case*, 3, 31.

52. Witmer, *Nearing Case*, 84, 75.

53. Nearing, *Making of a Radical*, 87, 83 ff.; Witmer, *Nearing Case*, 1 – 14, 32 – 36.

54. McCrea to Provost Edgar Fahs Smith, 22 June 1916, in Minutes of the Wharton Faculty, 22 Oct. 1915; interviews with Joseph Willits and William Hockenberry; Disbrow, "Reform in Philadelphia," 391.

55. Nearing, *Educational Frontiers*, 13; "J. Russell Smith File" and "Roswell C. McCrea File, " Archives; Sinclair, *Goosestep*, 96.

56. Feld, "Whartonians," 96; interview with Willits; Tugwell, "Morningside Heights," 243; McClellan to members of the instructional staff, 2 Nov. 1916, Minutes of the Wharton Faculty, 11 Nov. 1916.

57. Interview with Willits; Tugwell, "Morningside Heights," 243.

58. "Lawsuit Avoided When Dean Quits," newspaper clipping dated 28 Apr. 1919, "William McClellan File," Archives; Cheyney, *History of the University*, 371; Minutes of the Wharton Faculty, 12 Jan. 1916.

59. Fox, *Patten*, 126.

60. Ibid., 142.

61. Tugwell, "Morningside Heights," 134; Richard Hofstadter, *Anti-Intellectualism in American Life* (New York: Alfred A. Knopf, Vintage Books, 1962), 26 – 27.

Simon Nelson Patten

Simon N. Patten, *The Development of English Thought*,
title page and first page of contents

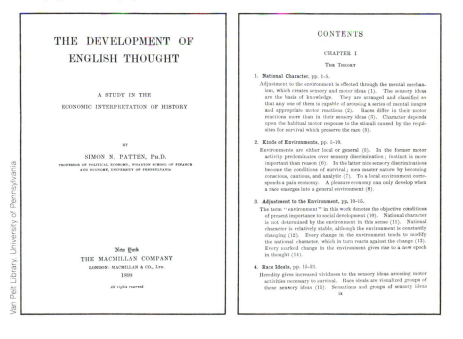

THE DEVELOPMENT OF
ENGLISH THOUGHT

A STUDY IN THE
ECONOMIC INTERPRETATION OF HISTORY

BY

SIMON N. PATTEN, Ph.D.
PROFESSOR OF POLITICAL ECONOMY, WHARTON SCHOOL OF FINANCE
AND ECONOMY, UNIVERSITY OF PENNSYLVANIA

New York
THE MACMILLAN COMPANY
LONDON: MACMILLAN & CO., Ltd.
1899

All rights reserved

CONTENTS

CHAPTER I

The Theory

ix

Samuel M. Lindsay

W. E. B. Du Bois

Leo S. Rowe

James T. Young

Clyde L. King

Roswell Cheney McCrea

Scott Nearing

Arthur H. Quinn

Edgar Fahs Smith

Lightner Witmer

Wharton Barker

William McClellan

5

Getting Down to Business

During the very years of Simon Patten's leadership at Wharton, while he and his band of progressive social scientists were battling poverty, inefficiency, and privilege, the school also took up in earnest the mission assigned by the founder: to educate business-men. Between 1895 and 1915, Wharton established an extensive business curriculum according to the pedagogic program laid down by Edmund James: The school developed specialized courses of study in finance, transportation, economic geography, account-ing, insurance, marketing, business law, and industrial manage-ment. Young faculty, fresh out of Wharton's new Ph.D. program, began to specialize in these areas, soon became expert, and helped build up a new set of academic disciplines. As could be expected, these young instructors received more support from the university trustees, from the Philadelphia business community, and from ambitious students than did Wharton's contentious social scien-tists. They rose quickly through the academic ranks, and in the outside world of entrepreneurial affairs found rich extracurricular opportunities for themselves and employment for their students. Each year Wharton's business section grew larger and more di-verse. Well before the time when Scott Nearing was fired, in 1915, these practical programs had overwhelmed the social science por-tion of the school. Their success insured that even after the defeat of Wharton's progressives at the hands of the university trustees, the institution would survive as a first-class school of business.[1]

The Wharton School, of course, had taught technical business subjects from its beginnings. Joseph Wharton had stipulated in his "Project" that the school teach finance, accounting, and business law. But such courses had been few, and as late as the early 1890s students took only a year's course in business law, another in accounting, and a semester of banking and commercial "mercantile practice." Occasionally the school had found outside instructors who gave short courses of up to ten lectures on business subjects (such as railroading and taxation in the state of Pennsylvania), but this had resulted in no permanent additions to the faculty or curriculum. James had also induced local businessmen to lecture to Wharton classes, appearances which both flattered prominent Philadelphians and stimulated their interest in James's other activities. These presentations, however, had been "recognized as inadequate for purposes of discipline and instruction and no substitute for a well-planned course of study."[2]

The approval of James's program for the school and the adoption of the four-year course in 1894 opened the way for the expansion of Wharton's business curriculum, at least on paper. The faculty moved preliminary material, such as elementary economics, business law, accounting, and a new class on commerce and geography, into the first two years of college and allowed students to pursue more sophisticated matters as juniors and seniors. The faculty then devoted a substantial amount of time and effort to working out the implications of the four-year course and charting the future of professional education at Wharton. In 1896, they finally adopted a new curriculum that provided for three "parallel courses," or majors, in business. Students electing these practical programs took an additional year of accounting and business law in their sophomore year and then four or five special classes under the direction of one professor. The plan assigned Joseph F. Johnson the banking course, newcomer Emory R. Johnson commerce and transportation, and Roland P. Faulkner insurance.[3]*

---

*Students in banking were to take two years of banking and one in "corporation finance"; the insurance curriculum called for one year of insurance theory, practice, and law, followed by classes in vital statistics and corporate finance. The course in commerce and transportation required two years' work in the subject, in addition to the survey required of all students in the school. The 1896 plan also included a prelaw "parallel course" that emphasized the old Wharton menu of history and political science.

Various factors, however, slowed the development of this program. Enrollments at the school between 1894 and 1899 failed to rise, and classes in the projected programs were not filled. More importantly, Faulkner and J. F. Johnson never got their courses up and running. Faulkner was then spending most of his time on statistics, his primary interest, and probably resisted conscription as the new guru of insurance. He never did teach the subject at Wharton. J. F. Johnson seemed more interested in finance, and offered classes in banking. But he was also in charge of the four-year journalism course and the school's senior research program, and had no time to develop a new curriculum. In any case, both men left the university at the turn of the century. And with them went Wharton's programs in statistics, journalism, and senior research, as well as these early programs in finance and insurance.[4]*

Only Emory Johnson truly relished the opportunity offered by his "parallel" business course. After winning his Ph.D. at Wharton, Johnson had joined the faculty in 1893, to teach geography, commerce, and transportation.† Patten had thought that training in economic geography provided the best foundation for a business education and wanted to introduce such courses at the school. If one considers economic geography a commercial subject, as did Patten, then Emory Johnson was the only regular faculty member in the early 1890s to teach business subjects alone. Moreover, Johnson had ambitions to develop the purely practical fields of commerce and transportation as areas of study distinct from the more general field of economic geography. He took great pride in the fact that his courses in commerce and transportation

---

*J. F. Johnson moved on to the new school of commerce at New York University and in 1903 became its dean. Faulkner joined the U.S. census.

†Emory Johnson had first come to James and Patten's attention as a graduate student in economics working with Richard T. Ely at Johns Hopkins. He had written a fine paper on the development of the Great Lakes transportation system and had published the piece in the *Annals*. (This paper, Johnson's dissertation, and indeed his life's work, all stemmed from an undergraduate senior honors thesis that he wrote for historian Frederick Jackson Turner at the University of Wisconsin.) James then had given Johnson introductions at Halle and had hinted at employment at Wharton should he study in Germany and return for his Ph.D. at Penn. Johnson took the offer. The university trustees, however, at first refused to fund the young man's salary. But James found money from "friends" of the Wharton School, some part-time work at Haverford College, and after one year was able to employ Johnson full-time at Wharton.

were the first of their kind in the nation. But like Faulkner and J. F. Johnson, Emory Johnson left Wharton before his parallel course had much of a chance to develop. In 1899, even before the commerce and transportation curriculum had been sanctioned by the proper university authorities, Johnson accepted an offer to join the U.S. Isthmian Canal Commission. For two years he stayed away from Philadelphia, investigating the possibilities of building an interocean waterway across Central America.* He then returned to Penn with valuable experience and important connections, but the sojourn postponed his development of the commerce and transportation specialty.[5]

Observing the difficulty in staffing these commercial programs and noting the mood of reform at the school, one might well imagine that Wharton's progressive social scientists had drawn some taboo around business studies. Such was not the case. The two groups — the progressives and the business professors — suffered together from the sneers and suspicions of the older Arts and Sciences faculty and fought side by side for status and resources in the still hostile academic world. The social scientists also had a substantive appreciation for the new disciplines. Patten's curiosity about all things socioeconomic and his attraction to efficient "motor" activity drew him to the problems and procedures used in practical affairs. He thought it useful for reformers to have mastered business skills,† and confided to his students

---

*Like Wharton professors Rowe and Lindsay, who left the school to work for the federal government in Puerto Rico, Johnson joined the employ of the state as it attempted to sort out the aftermath of the Spanish-American War. All three apparently owed these opportunities to the patronage of Provost Harrison, whose efforts on behalf of William McKinley during the 1896 presidential election had earned him important considerations in Washington.

†Political scientist Leo S. Rowe best exhibited this transfer of business skills to public uses. Like many reformers, Rowe came to see the problems of city administration as "essentially and primarily a business matter, to be managed in the same way as large corporate enterprises." Unfortunately, he thought that the "directors of a business corporation would not for a moment tolerate" the operating procedure of major American cities. Working as part of a National Municipal League program in 1897, Rowe therefore pioneered in adapting "the methods of accounting to the increasing complexity of city administration and the widening sphere of city functions." He set up an orderly scheme of categorizing receipts and expenditures, of entering interest and amortization, and of distinguishing extraordinary expenditures from the ordinary. As he demonstrated in his 1898 investigation of the Philadelphia gas works, such business techniques enabled reformers to draw "fruitful comparisons of the finances of different cities" and to identify inefficiencies and corruption. Leadership in municipal accounting soon shifted from Wharton to the New York Bureau of Municipal Research, where

that Wharton ought to train more experts in business practice than the corporate interests could employ, so that a few would be available for public service.[6]

In addition to such political uses of managerial techniques, Patten championed university training for business because he believed in the beneficent power of higher education. He shared James's faith that education "uplifts" practice from the level of a "devitalizing routine," creating "progressive" businessmen who "break through restraint." Such dynamism was needed now more than ever, Patten feared, because of the growth of the large corporation. He believed that these giant organizations tended

to put each man into a fixed group defined by its unvarying duties; his associations are more and more with his fellow members; he is horizoned by the same street, the same club, and the same restraints of rank. The deeds of other men at other tasks go on beyond his view, and the educative experiences of democracy, as it was expressed in business two generations ago, are withdrawn from him. . . .

It is the school, and only the school, that can restore the individuality, personal integrity, and democratic equality so often stifled by the growth of large-scale production.[7]

Despite such encouragement to business education, Patten and the other prominent Wharton professors focused their efforts elsewhere. They had little to do with the immediate development of business studies. Much more important were the students, administrators, and younger professors. They, in turn, were themselves responding to a rapidly changing environment — to the tremendous growth of national income, big business hierarchies, and the American educational system.

The growth of corporate enterprise and urban affluence during the lush years of prosperity between 1896 and 1914 provided an essential stimulus to the development of academic business training. As large bureaucracies took over firms formerly controlled by individual proprietors, they divided the entrepreneurial labor into a new array of esoteric specialties. Legions of newly propertied Americans, with funds to invest and dependents to protect, also provided a healthy demand for a variety of business

Wharton Ph.D.s William H. Allen and Frederick Cleveland developed the more sophisticated system of revenue and expense accrual accounts to replace Rowe's cash receipt/expenditure system.

services. Suddenly, the functional activities of accounting, finance, marketing, factory management, and insurance became much more sophisticated subjects, and new opportunities opened up overnight for "professionals," specialists with a command of advanced business techniques and usages. Even businessmen with general executive responsibilities, in small firms as well as large, needed greater understanding of these new areas of knowledge. For such intricate training, classroom education became a much more efficient teacher than practical experience. Employers now encouraged their precocious workers to return to school, and parents advised their children to get a business education at college. Entrepreneurial university administrators and professors, at Wharton and elsewhere, stood ready to provide the necessary courses. Between 1897 and 1917 the nation's population of business schools went from one — the Wharton School — to thirty, helping the new mass of college students accept the opportunities offered by twentieth-century capitalism.[8]

No one at the University of Pennsylvania better understood the implications of the triumph of corporate enterprise than Provost Charles H. Harrison. When Joseph Wharton had first gone to the university with his proposal, in 1881, Harrison had just been appointed to the Board of Trustees. Like many of his colleagues, he had been an active industrialist in charge of a substantial private company, the largest sugar refinery in the city. But in 1892, after many years of guiding the firm through prosperity and "ruinous competition," he and his family sold out to the American Sugar Refinery Company trust; they exchanged their property and their business for ten million dollars in negotiable securities. Harrison thus converted his "real-world" power and authority into paper claims and, in 1895, retired into provostship. Thereafter he and his family maintained their fortune through corporate industrial enterprises, stock and bond markets, banks, and insurance companies. Unlike his sugar refinery, each of these businesses employed large numbers of skilled white-collar workers and specialized "business professionals." Harrison therefore knew of the opportunities that such companies offered to college graduates. During his tenure in office, 1895-1911, he, more than any other university official, promoted the development of practical business education at the Wharton School.[9]

While the American world of affairs became concentrated and bureaucratic, the nation's educational system expanded and grew more democratic. Between 1896 and 1915, the annual number of American high school graduates increased from seventy-five thousand to two hundred and forty thousand, and many now presented themselves at the nation's universities for vocational training. The older professions chose not to accommodate such a crush of new labor, and leaders in medicine, law, and other established professions responded by raising entry and training requirements to unheard-of levels. They improved standards of competence in their fields, made professional status more sought after, and, in the process, turned this vast new supply of would-be competitors to other occupations. Many students thus excluded now turned to business as a source of livelihood.[10]

Undergraduate enrollments at Wharton expanded from 150 in 1901 to 916 in 1914, and this increasingly worldly, not especially high-minded student body sent up a clear call for more business material in the curriculum. The Wharton course remained the easiest at Penn, and many of these new undergraduates found themselves in the school not because of its reputation, but as water finds the sea. Those with ambition, moreover, usually chose arenas more lucrative than academe or reform. Between 1894 and 1914, 60 percent of Wharton's graduates went immediately into business; another 30 percent went to law school and then entered the world of affairs. Of those going straight into business, half joined family firms, many starting out as proprietors or corporate officers. These well-connected students from business families had been passing through Wharton since its beginnings and by and large had been satisfied with the old historical and social science curriculum. But students who had to make their own way in the business world, without the aid of family connections, represented a relatively new and rapidly expanding group. To become successful, these young men had to equip themselves at Wharton with expertise in some functional area. Indeed, most of Wharton's student body in the years immediately before the First World War came with the intention of staying only one or two years, enough time for them to get a rudimentary training for business. Fully two-thirds failed to complete the full four-year course, and most of these, one can imagine, were not so well connected. Wharton's new evening school, organized in 1904, added to this demand for practical business instruction. Night students were interested in vocational education alone, and with 450 enrolled in 1907 and 700 by 1914, they further stimulated the development of the functional curriculum. As the business world became more sophisticated and as Wharton's program added advanced courses in business practice, even students from leading families sought out a more thorough commercial education. If they joined family firms, they would bring important new resources, and if they chose careers with large public corporations, they could qualify for advanced positions.[11]

Meanwhile, the influence of Wharton's social science professors over their charges steadily declined. The school's controversial and stimulating faculty stuffed their undergraduates with shocking information, had them read progressive literature, and assigned investigations of issues currently before the public. Wharton students did cheer Scott Nearing, stood up for civic virtue in the 1905 "Gas War," and impressed visitors as an especially curious and questioning group. But the days of Edmund James, with its close contact between students and faculty and shared ambitions, no longer existed. Ever-increasing numbers of new undergraduates, the resulting large lecture classes, and a growing commitment to the Ph.D. program constantly expanded the distance between the school's major professors and its students.[12]

As the Wharton faculty lost much of its old influence, a powerful undergraduate subculture developed in its place. During Provost Harrison's regime the university put up acres of new buildings that gave students an impressive new stage on which to play out their dramas. Penn erected a huge athletic stadium, its first dormitories, and the first student center in the nation — Houston Hall. The Wharton School, in sharp contrast, became increasingly cramped in its original quarters in College Hall. In 1904 Wharton moved "temporarily" into Logan Hall, the refurbished former home of the medical school. While the school patiently waited for a new building, students jammed the corridors and four to seven professors shared each office. Neither Joseph Wharton's purse nor the univerity's own brick and mortar came to the rescue, and as enrollments grew, students fled from the crush of Logan Hall to the new and more hospitable campus outside.[13]

In the fresh extracurricular air of West Philadelphia, Wharton students found an undergraduate life that was often quite unruly. Mobs of students periodically joined in

the official feuds of the classes, the bowl and poster fights in which students are stripped naked or sent to the hospital, and the Sophomore raid on the Freshman banquet in which hundreds of dollars worth of furniture and pictures are destroyed, and other rough and vulgar displays of animal spirits.

Sparked by midnight cries of, "Rowbottom!!! Rowbottom!!!" commemorating a legendary ne'er-do-well of that name who specialized in nocturnal mischief — gangs of undergraduates periodically spilled from the dormitories in aimless riot. The students delighted in setting off false fire alarms and then, from behind the protective gates of the university, taunting the police and firemen who arrived.[14]

Students also found themselves swept up in the craze for football, fraternities, and the other provincial enthusiasms that then excited all American college campuses. The tone of student life at the university was set clearly by its twenty-six fraternities, one for each two hundred undergraduates. The frats at Penn, as elsewhere, established a status system that glorified athletic success and included "some snobbishness, family or financial, [a]ntisemitism, . . . prejudice against women as students, . . . some aversion to foreigners and considerable antipathy to negroes." Penn was nevertheless more cosmopolitan than most major campuses, with more foreign students and more commuters, and such student pretensions never quite overruled a general mood of "informality and congeniality."[15]

This convivial student culture prepared Wharton undergraduates for business careers perhaps better than the old curriculum of the Wharton School itself. Campus life provided a young man with those essentials of success, training in how to "be a gentleman with ready powers of conversation and . . . a host of friends among the men of his class." Such social arts and assets were precisely what much of the school's social science faculty lacked. And what most Wharton students expected from their formal schooling was not uplift or intellectual excitement, but a useful business training.[16]

The Wharton School found its instructors in business not at Halle, but at home, among its own doctoral students. At the turn of the century Wharton had begun turning out a steady stream of Ph.D.'s (such as sociologist Carl Kelsey and economist Scott Nearing), and among this group were several ambitious young men who wrapped their passions and professional identities around business studies. As Wharton's student population began to grow, the school could support even more such graduate students as "quizmasters" and could bring onto the faculty even greater numbers of its own Ph.D.'s. In this manner Wharton produced its business professoriate. These new doctors of practical affairs quickly developed each of the three "parallel courses" outlined in 1896, as well as several others devised in the new century. By 1910 Wharton Ph.D.'s directed eager undergraduates through courses of study in finance, commerce and transportation, geography, insurance, factory management, marketing, business law, and accounting.

This explosive growth of the business subjects resembled the "saltation," or "quantum speciation" process found in biological evolutions: The sudden opening up of a new mode of survival spawned a broad array of new species of study, not the simple expansion of the older forms. Wharton's original business subjects —law, accounting and business practice—lost their former status as the essence of the professional curriculum; studies such as insurance, finance, and marketing became the basic units of instruction. Like journalism, Wharton's first separate professional course, these new specialized business programs included work in the law, accounting, and practice specific to their particular areas of concern. A new organizing principle now controlled the structure of Wharton's disciplinary array. The founder's original scheme had called for a single business program, composed of courses teaching the skills needed by all businessmen. Now the school mirrored the emerging divisions of entrepreneurial labor in the nation's economy, as both students and faculty sought niches in the new lines of commercial specialization then opening up.

The school had the habit of placing one professor "in charge" of a subject, making the size of each discipline depend primarily on the ability of one man to control its material. As business enrollments mushroomed after 1900, and as business itself grew increasingly esoteric, the amount of professional material offered at Wharton expanded apace. Professors found themselves with too much work on their hands, and they then turned whole fields in their responsibility over to ambitious and able Ph.D.'s coming out of Wharton's doctoral program. The first decade of the new century thus offered entrepreneurial business scholars the unique opportunity to take over a new academic specialty at its beginnings. For these young professors, as for their social science colleagues, the "progressive" era was indeed a heady time.

The men who seized the challenge to organize a new field of study had to assemble a curriculum from scratch. For lecture materials they went out and collected testimony from men of affairs and reports from the business press. Since no textbooks then existed, they wrote the pioneering surveys in their fields. As they proceeded in this activity, they took over from nineteenth-century business journalists much of the responsibility for handling ideas in their respective areas of study. The move into academe clearly enhanced the execution of such intellectual tasks. Business professors explained the "best practice," but in textbooks rather than magazine articles; they served as experts in public discussions, but often with long leaves of absence and time off from their other chores. By the coming of the First World War, Wharton's business professors had had a decade or more in which to establish themselves in their respective fields. Although still young men in their twenties and thirties, they could already challenge—and in some cases had actually replaced—traditional business journalists as the leading voices in their specialties.

In the fall of 1900 the school's full-time business faculty included the two Johnsons—one absent on leave to Panama and the other soon to depart from the university — and two new Wharton Ph.D.'s, Frederick A. Cleveland and Edward S. Mead.* Cleveland immediately took over the special banking course, giv-

---

*Early in his life Mead spelled his name with a final e. For consistency, I have used the spelling that he later and more commonly chose.

ing all of the instruction in this field; J. F. Johnson now offered only the finance course in the general curriculum. Mead substituted for E. R. Johnson in commerce and geography but was interested in all business skills and taught accounting, industrial management, economics, and finance. The last, however, was his true interest, and when Cleveland left Wharton in 1903, Mead took over as head of instruction in finance. As the school grew, E. R. Johnson and Edward Mead became the fountainheads of the new business specialties. When more Wharton Ph.D.'s joined the faculty, Johnson and Mead gladly parcelled off whole pieces of their official teaching loads in order to concentrate on their primary interests. They also found new sources of support to sustain their junior colleagues and fledgling specialties. Using his connections outside the university, Emory Johnson won research grants, jobs on government investigations, and book contracts for graduate students and young professors. By founding and directing Wharton's Evening School, one of the first collegiate evening schools of business in the nation, Mead provided the expanding commercial faculty with work.[17]

Mead's Evening School of Accounts and Finance, established in 1904, proved to be especially important to the growth of business studies at Wharton. Catering primarily to clerks without the time or resources to attend college during the day, it opened up an entirely new market for the school's young professors. In 1913 the Evening School added an Extension School, which took Wharton's business faculty by train to Harrisburg, Wilkes-Barre, Scranton, and Reading. Under Mead's direction, the Evening School offered courses at night that equalled, and in some cases even surpassed, the quality achieved in the traditional program. Its graduates won premium jobs, and employers encouraged their office workers to take its classes. Enrollments grew rapidly, and as they did, so did the health of the business program and the degree of specialization at Wharton.[18]*

---

*Mead and Cleveland had discussed the Evening School idea together, but before the project had advanced very far, Cleveland left the university. Mead nevertheless took the proposal to Provost Harrison, who liked it and gave his authorizaton to begin. Originally the Evening School was organized as a separate unit of the university, administratively independent of the Wharton School. In 1913, however, Wharton took jurisdiction over the night program.

Emory Johnson had been Wharton's original full-time business specialist (Albert Bolles being Wharton's first full-time generalist), and he thrived in the school's new environment. Johnson had never been interested in geography nor especially fond of commerce. He had taught these subjects because he had to, and used them as springboards for discussing his true passion: the structural patterns and practical techniques of the transportation business. As the school expanded and Johnson's Ph.D. students took over responsibility for teaching all of geography and much of commerce, he seized the opportunity to specialize further. He began by teaching a course on railroads and another on waterways; he then added advanced, graduate-level classes on each topic. Beginning with the publication of his *American Railway Transportation* in 1903, Johnson issued a steady stream of texts for use in his own courses and others like them in the nation's new business schools. These books, published in the Appleton Company's pioneering series of business texts, were the first such volumes in the field and offered general descriptions of existing transportation systems, common business practices, and regulation by government. Books such as *Railroad Traffic and Rates*, an outgrowth of Johnson's advanced course, were addressed to college students and railroad men alike and provided "information as reliable as possible and as complete as practicable, regarding the intricate and detailed work of those who have to do with railroad traffic and with rate making." By concentrating so intently on transportation issues, Johnson soon made himself master of the details of the business.[19]

Johnson's personal dignity and his command of the intricacies of transportation gave him the stature of a disinterested professional, a man who spoke with the authority of unbiased knowledge. He quickly became one of the nation's leading experts in the field, with his services in constant demand. In 1911 he returned to Central America to set the tolls on the Panama Canal, then under construction. Soon after his return to Philadelphia in 1913, the governor of Pennsylvania appointed him to the new Public Service Commission, the state regulator of railroads.*

*Johnson thought that the author of the PSC legislation, university trustee and state attorney general John C. Bell, had recommended him for the post. (Bell was, incidentally, the trustee who was outraged by Scott Nearing's favorable

Johnson's career as a transportation expert culminated in 1918-19, with his work on the Executive Committee of the Chamber of Commerce's National Transportation Conference.* Under Johnson's leadership, the shippers on the nation's railroads hammered out a common program which, after some changes, was enacted into law as the landmark Transportation Act of 1920.[20]

While Johnson became prominent as a specialist on transportation, his students took over the other parts of his original set of responsibilities. The more ambitious among them imitated Johnson and his management of his career. They likewise specialized as much as possible, mastering one subject area in great detail. While none had public careers as illustrious as Johnson's, several became prolific writers of college texts and established themselves as highly visible experts at the head of their chosen fields.

Geography was the first nontransportation area that Johnson was able to shed. In 1901 J. Paul Goode, a Johnson Ph.D. who

comparison of an education in hell to one offered by Philadelphia's Episcopal Academy.) The PSC assigned Johnson the job of organizing its Bureau of [Railroad] Rates and Tariffs, and he appointed George P. Wilson, a longtime official at the Pennsylvania Railroad, as director of the new bureau. Despite the potential for a conflict of interests, Johnson viewed Wilson's office as a neutral, professional post and he found the man's work to be "successful and efficient." During World War I Johnson himself did the same kind of professional work for the U.S. Shipping Board, investigating costs in order to control transportation charges during the conflict and to prepare for the process of regulation after the war.

*During the First World War, the federal government had taken over direction of the nation's railroads, and the problem of how to dispose of these properties in the postwar period raised some of the most fundamental issues in American economic life. Labor unions called for government ownership, while business groups wanted a return to private control and government regulation. These business interests, however, differed among themselves. The railroad companies argued for greater power to pool traffic, to cut expensive services, and in general to operate more efficiently and profitably. The shippers, however, demanded better service and lower rates. During the war, the powerful and rather arbitrary government board controlling the industry had been quite responsive to the cost-cutting suggestions of railroad executives. The operators hoped for a similarly powerful, sympathetic, and cost-conscious administrator in the future. The shippers, represented by the Chamber of Commerce, had not thrashed out a common position. Most, however, wanted power returned to the Interstate Commerce Commission, which had respected their needs for sometimes expensive services. The Chamber of Commerce had convened its conference to harmonize the position of the shippers so as to present a united petition to Congress—just as Joseph Wharton had done much earlier with the tariff lobby. Like Wharton, Johnson prepared much of the agenda and wrote many of the final recommendations. The conference called for a return of the rails to private hands; the organization of larger, stronger systems; traffic pooling supervised by the government; strengthened ICC regulation; and a guaranteed 6 percent rate of return to the operators.

specialized in geography, took over the chores of teaching the subject. Goode left in 1903 but was immediately replaced by another Wharton Ph.D., J. Russell Smith.* In his first year on the faculty Smith taught two courses in economic geography and one on "The Organization of Ocean Commerce," the subject of his dissertation. He soon dropped his class in commerce, concentrated on geography, and by 1909 offered separate classes on nine different geographical areas. With this level of specialization, Smith was able to produce work that had an important impact on the development of his discipline while making the subject more useful to both businessmen and government officials. Most previous work in geography had focused on the physical characteristics of the earth's surface or on political boundaries and descriptions. But coming to the subject from the perspective of the Wharton School, Smith emphasized the role of material interests in creating the characteristics of the landscape. His lively and readable texts, especially his *Industrial and Commercial Geography*, were pioneering works in the fields of economic and human geography. In class, Smith provided Wharton undergraduates with a valuable and broad-ranging perspective on the play of economic and business forces within the physical context of Planet Earth.[21]

Immediately after Smith entered the graduate program, in 1903-4, the lure of the Harrison Fellowship brought Solomon Huebner to the university. The son of a prosperous, progressive, and evangelical Wisconsin farmer, Huebner had gone off to the state university, where he studied under Richard T. Ely and Frederick Jackson Turner. He then came to Wharton, where he took graduate courses in economics, political science, sociology, history, accounting, and transportation; of all his professors, he was most comfortable with Emory Johnson. Both men were from Wisconsin, were alumni of its great university, and had studied under

*Smith had been an outstanding undergraduate at Wharton in the 1890s and had continued into the master's program to study under Johnson. When his appointment to the Isthmian Canal Commission in 1899 allowed him to hire an assistant, Johnson chose Smith. The two worked together for the full two years of the project, and then Smith went off to Germany for graduate study in geography. Dissatisfied with his experience abroad, Smith accepted a fellowship to the Wharton School for the academic year 1902-3. He resumed his studies with Johnson, finished his degree within the year, and was hired as an instructor in geography.

Ely and Turner. Both were interested, above all, in the field of transportation, and Huebner chose Johnson to direct his dissertation. After finishing his Ph.D. in 1904, Huebner hoped to remain at Penn to continue working with his mentor, and he induced his younger brother, Grover, to follow him to Philadelphia and study with Johnson.[22]*

Like Solomon, G. G. Huebner became a close friend and associate of Emory Johnson's. But from the beginning the two brothers pursued radically different career strategies. Solomon was "a wheel-horse kind of a guy" who relished challenge and new responsibilities. With Johnson's encouragement, he soon lit out on his own and took charge of one of Wharton's new areas of instruction, insurance. To Solomon's perpetual amazement and annoyance his brother Grover, who had a retiring personality, exhibited no such ambition to lead a new academic enterprise. G. G. instead remained in commerce and transportation studies, becoming his mentor's right-hand man. He helped Johnson periodically revise his original texts, and together they wrote the more advanced handbooks on transportation; when Johnson was

---

*Solomon Huebner had stayed on at Wisconsin after graduation to win a master's degree, working with the noted transportation authority Balthasar Meyer. His thesis on "The Distribution of Stock Holdings in American Railroads" had found its way to Wharton, perhaps as part of his Harrison Fellowship application, and it so impressed the faculty that they published it in the *Annals*. (They also awarded Huebner the fellowship.) Huebner had heard of his successful application only in the fall of 1903, while he was in Europe preparing to enroll in the University of Berlin. But because of the Harrison money and the opportunity to work at Wharton, he immediately sailed for America and Penn. Upon completing his degree, Huebner had hoped to be the first Ph.D. in Johnson's new Department of Transportation, with a degree "in economics in transportation." A technicality, however, frustrated this wish, and the university declared him a doctor "in economics in economics."

In 1904 Johnson could find only one course for Solomon to teach in transportation, hardly enough work or income for an ambitious young academic. But just then Johnson fortunately accepted an offer from the Carnegie Institution that allowed him to augment Huebner's salary and to support even more graduate students in commerce and transportation. In 1904 Carrol D. Wright, a friend of Johnson's and member of the Executive Committee of the Carnegie Institution Board of Trustees, was parcelling out funds and research responsibilities for a large-scale collective project on the economic history of the United States. He got scholars such as John R. Commons to write the history of American labor and Victor S. Clark to describe the development of American manufacturing. Emory Johnson took responsibility for preparing a history of the nation's domestic and foreign commerce. Johnson did little of the writing himself, and divided the job among seven young scholars, including Solomon Huebner. Four of Johnson's remaining six collaborators, including Huebner's brother Grover, were also his students in transportation and commerce.

asked to set the tolls on the Panama Canal, he naturally took G. G. Huebner with him. Wharton students, hyperbolizing this fraternal difference, referred to the two Huebner brothers as "Sunny Sol" and "Gloomy Gus."[23]*

While Grover Huebner toiled in the fields of his mentor, his brother, "Sunny Sol," developed his portion into one of the leading branches of the Wharton School. He brought great powers of showmanship to his work, combining vigorous energy, years of training in public speaking, and moralizing zeal. (Both in appearance and in his forceful manner of address, the elder Huebner reminded many who met him of President Teddy Roosevelt.) Firmly convinced of the beneficence of his subject, Huebner soon had his students worked up into a positive frenzy for insurance. He purposely deemphasized the abstruse, actuarial mathematics of the subject, concentrating attention on its practical value. He explained many little-understood business uses of life insurance: how it helped make men's financial promises credible, how it could render corporate success less dependent on the life of a key executive. He taught his students that insurance represented the only secure discharge of a family man's financial responsibilities, was "a bulwark of the home," and was "in compliance with

---

*As Solomon recollected in later years, he came upon the idea of teaching insurance quite suddenly one night while perusing the *New York Journal of Commerce*. Huebner was struck by the attention that the *Journal* gave to the business of insurance and by the absence of instruction in the subject at Wharton. He then supposedly went to Johnson, the two talked to Patten, and then the three to Harrison. Johnson, Patten, and Harrison all supposedly listened to the plans of the eager twenty-three-year-old, confessed that his courses seemed appropriate for the Wharton program, and regretted that they themselves had not thought of it earlier. They asked him to proceed with his course on insurance, with another on organized security and produce exchange markets, and annointed him "assistant in commerce" at an annual salary of five hundred dollars.

Huebner's narrative, however, requires some qualification. Johnson and Patten, if not Harrison, had clearly known about the 1896 plan for a course in insurance with Roland P. Faulkner as instructor. Huebner had also written his dissertation on marine insurance, and that certainly offered a more reasonable entree into the new field than any nocturnal inspiration from the pages of the *New York Journal of Commerce*. Johnson may very well have decided on that dissertation specifically to prepare Huebner to take over the stillborn 1896 course. With the provost having sat on the board of the Insurance Company of North America for ten years and often thinking of what he could do to help Philadelphia's young men get ahead in business, the chances were quite good that the university would allow Huebner to take up the field. In any event, when Huebner began teaching in 1904, he offered the world's first university-level instruction in both the business of insurance and that of organized securities and exchange markets.

Christian duty." Each year "a fair percentage of the boys induce their fathers to take out insurance on their lives, and some take it themselves for protection of a parent." Huebner explained how students could secure their personal note with a life insurance policy, thereby helping finance their education, and each year "a number in the class" followed this course of action. After experiencing Huebner's lectures, Wharton's students literally burst out of his classroom inspired to sell insurance to their families, to their friends, and, indeed, to the entire world.[24]

Unlike the efforts of the great "progressive" moralizers then on the Wharton faculty, Solomon Huebner's crusade for insurance stood the business in good stead. And this was quite useful to the industry. Although growing enormously, quadrupling between 1890 and 1905, the reputation of the insurance trade had then reached its historical nadir. It was in 1905 that the New York State Armstrong investigation exposed a pattern of questionable practices in the industry, including excessive sales commissions, subordination to those investment bankers who sold securities to insurance companies, and agents pandering to the gambling impulses of the populace.* While agreeing that there had been serious abuses, Solomon Huebner stood foursquare in defense of the sobriety and righteousness of insurance contracts. He claimed, in fact, that insurance "is the antithesis of gambling" and the foundation of family thrift and financial independence. He belittled many other investments, especially common stocks, and each time that he sent a premium check to one of his insurance companies (he had several), he would announce to his class, "There goes x dollars removed from my own incompetence!" Conjuring the spirit of the founder to justify his enterprise, Huebner had printed, framed, and hung in his office Joseph Wharton's injunc-

---

*Certain religious people, including Huebner's own parents, shunned life insurance because they viewed it as a wager against the Providence of God. In the broader society, the insurance industry had become notorious for its widespread promotion of "tontine" policies. Under the terms of the tontine agreement, failure to keep up with one's premium payments resulted in forfeiture of all claims against the company. The resulting funds were then placed in a jackpot and distributed by the insurer in claims paid out to its remaining clients. These tontines were obviously a risky form of insurance, an ironic gamble on one's future financial responsibility. Huebner, like most sober Americans, frowned on tontines and never viewed insurance as a wager. That was fortunate, because between inflation and his own longevity, the value of Huebner's premium payments far exceeded that of his insurance estate.

tion that the school give its students an appreciation of "the deep comfort and healthfulness of pecuniary independence whether the scale of affairs be small or great."[25]*

In addition to teaching, Solomon Huebner followed his mentor into service with the government. Apparently on Johnson's recommendation, the House Merchant Marine and Fisheries Committee appointed Huebner to investigate competitive conditions in the steamship business. He found serious monopolistic practices that probably violated the nation's antitrust laws. Rather than suggest legal action to restore competition, he recommended government regulation of agreements among steamship and railroad companies, and the United States Shipping Act of 1916 enacted many of his proposals. The next time the government called on Huebner, in 1918, it requested his services as an expert on insurance, not transportation and commerce. The war had put unbearable pressure on the nation's marine insurance industry, and during the emergency the government itself had gone into this business. After the war, the government wanted to return the industry to the private sector, but unfortunately only English, not American, companies stood ready to underwrite most risks. Congress hired Huebner to put the trade in American hands. After five years of work he produced a well-regarded text on *Marine Insurance* (published in the Appleton series), a model marine insurance law, and a plan which Congress adopted, that a syndicate of American companies take over the business and operate without regard to the nation's antitrust laws. Like Wharton with the tariff and Johnson with the Interstate Commerce Commission, Huebner recognized that a free, competitive market was not always in the best interest of business.[26]

While Johnson and his students developed the disciplines of geography, transportation, commerce, and insurance, Edward Mead served as the fountainhead for instruction in finance, accounting,

---

*Student scuttlebutt explained Huebner's taste in personal finance with tales of huge gains, but ultimately huge losses, in the stock market. The story, however, may have only been a bit of fancy. Huebner's biographer reported no such speculations, and the boys typically liked to associate their instructors with the grand gyrations of high finance. They told another tale about a brother of Simon Patten who had cornered the wheat market. But in actual fact it was not Patten's brother, but his cousin James Patten, who had gleaned substantial sums from grain corners in 1908 and 1909.

and industrial management. He and his colleague Frederick Cleveland had gone through the Wharton Ph.D. program at the turn of the century, Cleveland getting his degree in 1900 and Mead his one year earlier. Although studying social science and banking with Patten, Seager, Rowe, and J. F. Johnson, both men were primarily interested in the rapidly growing field of corporate finance. And insofar as they became expert in their chosen field of study, they did so largely by themselves.[27]

Cleveland and Mead's subject, the funding of corporations through securities markets, was essentially a nineteenth-century addition to the business world. Only since the 1850s had specialized American "investment" bankers dealt in private stock and bond financing, primarily for railroad companies. This business differed significantly from traditional commercial banking, the funding business that had been a central part of the capitalist system since the Middle Ages. The new investment bankers accepted no deposits and extended loans only as an ancillary part of their business; they dealt in equity shares and long-term debt, not traditional short-term paper; they held securities only as inventory, to be sold to clients. Investment banking had not been taught in the early years of the Wharton School. Although courses in "finance" were taught since the early 1880s, the term "finance" then referred primarily to government operations — taxes, tariffs, public expenditures, and the like. Courses in private funding covered only the traditional business of commercial banking. James, who had written an article on "The Science of Finance" and had taught finance at Wharton, discussed only the affairs of the state. Bolles had lectured on commercial banking in his "Mercantile Practice" class and covered both banking and government funding in his financial history course. Only with the development of the "parallel course" in banking and the more extended treatment of finance that it allowed did the Wharton curriculum call for work in corporation finance. But between 1896 and the turn of the century the subject took on an entirely new importance in the business world. The great wave of industrial mergers in those years rendered "banking" a totally anachronistic title for any parallel course in the private funding business. Wharton students demanded far more training for this dramatic new occupational niche in the world of affairs, and Cleveland and Mead prepared themselves to supply it.[28]

Cleveland and Mead collected lecture materials from cooperative investment bankers* and from the financial press. They then compiled this information into pioneering textbooks—*Trust Finance, Funds and Their Uses,* and *Corporate Finance*—all published in the Appleton series. Their books and lectures offered careful descriptions of the laws, accounts, and procedures involved "in the promotion, capitalization, financial management, consolidation, and reorganization of business corporations." Cleveland's *Funds and Their Uses,* the more elementary text, included over a hundred illustrations of monies, securities, and financial instruments. In all of their work, Wharton's pioneer professors of corporate finance focused primarily on the man-made, procedural aspects of the business, not on explaining the impersonal forces that moved financial markets. Neither man

attempted to deduce from facts of Corporation Finance any new laws or principles. All that [they] have tried to do is to describe in as much detail as the subject permits, the methods employed in Corporation Finance, to indicate the working rules of procedure and management which govern those methods, and to show some of the dangers which lie in ignorant and careless financial management.[29]†

Although Mead had graduated before Cleveland and the two had worked together on the new program in corporation finance, Cleveland taught all of the early courses: He was much older and more experienced than his colleague, having graduated from college in 1890 and worked as a lawyer before coming to Wharton

---

*This brought them into contact with local financiers, including the son of Provost Harrison, officers of the Brown Brothers investment banking house, and the Fidelity Mutual Life Insurance Company.

†Mead did, however, make claims about the efficiency of big business, an issue that took him outside the procedural mainstream of his course. Although suspicious, like Solomon Huebner, of common stock investments, Mead thought that the rise of large corporations advanced business efficiency. Their ability to integrate the production process and thereby to control the flow of resources, he reasoned, resulted in a reduction of costs; their size, he argued, offered great advantages in serving foreign markets and in developing new products. He also applauded the ability of public utility corporations, such as the Philadelphia Street Car Company, to distribute their stock throughout the community and thus ally "public opinion" to their interests. Like Emory Johnson, Solomon Huebner, Simon Patten, and Joseph Wharton, Mead thus presented his own arguments for limiting the competitive forces of the market economy.

for his Ph.D. In 1903, after Cleveland left the university, Mead took on his responsibilities. Until his retirement in 1944, Mead remained the major figure at Wharton in the field of finance.

While Cleveland taught corporation finance at Wharton — between 1900 and 1903 — Mead gave instruction in accounting and industrial management. Although he was teaching accounting because others qualified to teach it had left the university, he had been drawn to both of these subjects by his primary interest in corporation finance. Financial accounts reported essential information about a corporate enterprise, and any student of the subject had to be able to interpret these statements. The success of large-scale industrial corporations, the stuff for which investors searched, depended critically on managerial ability. At the time, when much of America's manufacturing capacity was being merged into huge combinations, the question of whether these industrial behemoths enhanced or diminished productive efficiency concerned all observers of the business scene.[30]

Mead's instruction in management marked the beginning of such courses at the school, and as such it represented a most impressive achievement. In 1901-2 Mead offered his first class in "Industrial Management," vaguely described in the *Catalog* as discussing the "organization and management of industry and trade." While no other documentation on the course remains, we do know some of the managerial issues that passed through Mead's mind at the time. He was then in charge of a new section in the *Annals*, "Notes on Industry and Commerce," where he discussed various aspects of industrial management; no doubt, he brought much of this material before his students. In these "Notes," Mead reported on topics such as the findings of the United States Industrial Commission, an important investigation of large-scale manufacturing enterprises; labor-management relations from the management point of view; the work of trade associations; and the internal accounting system of a large department store and how it facilitated control and communication in the organization. Students taking his course therefore must have had an impressive review of managerial problems and the sources of industrial efficiency in large organizations.[31]

In the next academic year, 1902-3, Mead added courses entitled "American Industries," later known as "Manufacturing Industries of the United States," and "Field Work in Industry." The first course surveyed the important technologies and power sources used in American manufacturing operations and became a basic course in the school's curriculum. Mead's other addition, "Field Work in Industry," served as the culmination of his three-course program in industrial management, helping students bridge the gap between academe and business life. Mead and his successors took students on inspection trips through industrial plants in the city, showing them actual manufacturing conditions and some of the innovative work in factory management. Philadelphia then claimed to be the "Workshop of the World," and the city offered Wharton's students exposure to a tremendous variety of industrial processes and problems. By 1916 the class was visiting firms such as Curtis Publishing, Atlantic Refining, Campbell Soup, Baldwin Locomotive, Midvale Steel, J. B. Stetson, Remington Arms, Scott Paper, and various smaller companies. They also toured plants that had installed various forms of "scientific management," including the Tabor Manufacturing and the Link Belt companies. To sharpen their experience and to develop analytical and perceptual skills, the students wrote a report on each plant visited. This course became one of the most important and memorable at Wharton. It was a clinic that gave the school's students a chance to think like managers and to build up confidence in their own abilities.[32]

While not so dramatic an innovation as his courses in management, Mead's contribution to the development of the accounting curriculum was also quite significant. Here he emphasized instruction in preparing and evaluating *corporate* financial statements; all other material, including mercantile, banking, and manufacturing accounting, he concentrated in the first-year course which he renamed "Bookkeeping and Office Methods." With these issues out of the way, Mead was able to devote the entire second year to a course on "Corporation Accounting." In this class he discussed problems in accounting for corporate mergers and dissolutions, issuing securities and depreciation.[33]

Mead stopped teaching management and accounting when he took up Cleveland's duties in 1903, and his former courses were assigned to eager young graduate students. Edward P. Moxey, Jr., was soon placed in charge of Wharton's accounting program.

Mead, however, remained close to the subject and had an important impact on its development at Wharton. When accounting
and finance left the jurisdiction of the Economics Department in
1912, they were grouped together in one department, with Mead
as chairman. Even more important to the growth of accounting
education at Wharton was Mead's work as founder and director
of the Evening School of Accounts and Finance. As indicated by
its name, Mead's specialties of finance and accounting were the
main potatoes served up by the new institution. But in accounting, the evening school offered a far more advanced menu than
the regular Wharton day program. Mead brought into the night
school a pre-existing course (established a few years earlier by
Philadelphia's leading accounting firms) to train young men to
become "certified public accountants." Wharton's day program
had never attempted to educate professional accountants, but only
to provide the basic skills needed by any businessman. As Patten
and others in the city immediately recognized, the "Night School
of Accounting had solidified and energized the group of men
interested in business accounts" and made the Wharton School a
focus of professional activity in Philadelphia.[34]*

*The rapid rise of corporations had created a great demand for financial
information and interpretation supplied by professional accountants. This demand, however, had encouraged large numbers of quacks and poorly trained men
to sell their services to an ignorant public. To maintain the reputation of their
profession and to suppress this nuisance competition, Pennsylvania's leading
accountants had convinced the state to set up licensing examinations and to allow
only "certified public accountants" to prepare the more sophisticated financial
statements. A large part of the business then flowed quite naturally to the established firms, and they suddenly faced a great shortage of qualified employees. To
meet this demand they set up the course which soon became part of the Evening
School of Finance and Accounts.

More remarkable, although not more important in accounting education,
was young Thomas W. Mitchell's introduction of a course in "cost accounting" in
1904. Costs were not a major concern of the profession, which at the time was
fully occupied with measuring the assets and incomes of business corporations.
In fact, cost accounting was not developed by professional accountants at all, but
by engineers working inside industrial plants. These engineers, the early leaders
of the "scientific management" movement, had developed methods of measuring
costs, including ways to assign overhead charges to the various products manufactured in the plant. Their accounting systems not only measured the use of labor,
tools, and inventories, but also became the basic means of managerial control and
communication on the factory floor. Mead had discussed such methods in his
course in industrial management, but Mitchell's class probably represented the
first time that these issues were presented as part of a collegiate curriculum in
accounting. That they were taught there at all probably owed something to Mead's
continuing influence over the accounting program. But as Mead's attention drifted

While Wharton's program in corporate accounting blossomed magnificently, the curriculum that Mead had begun in industrial management fell into stagnation. The young graduate student who took over Mead's courses in 1903* did not work out, and geographer J. Russell Smith took over as a last-minute replacement. Smith, of course, was not trained in industrial management nor was he especially interested in the subject. His management courses took on a decidedly "geographic" flavor, emphasizing questions such as where to locate an industrial plant. Smith also saw fit to drop "Field Work in Industry," the culminating course in Mead's old design. That class made its way back into the curriculum in 1907 — but only after Mead recommended its revival.[35]

Smith's chance assignment, however, hardened into institutional fact. Protected by Patten's belief that geography was the best introduction to a management education, Smith retained jurisdiction over the field and became chairman of the independent "Geography and Industry" department. Although Smith taught management until he left Wharton in 1919, he always devoted most of his energies to the study of geography. His 1915 textbook on *The Elements of Industrial Management* emphasized the significance of the landscape (and Smith's belief that kindness spurred worker productivity). As late as the academic year 1916-17 the geography and industry curriculum required only the same three courses that Mead had introduced by 1902. It listed, however, nine geography classes as early as 1909-10 and its curriculum for a major in "manufactures" then included three geography courses as well as the three in management.[36]

That management education should receive such neglect cries out for explanation. Training for industrial leadership had been

away from managerial issues and settled on problems of corporate finance, and as the Certified Public Accountant program came to dominate the accounting curriculum, the cost accounting course became an isolated appendage. By the time that Mitchell left the school, in 1909, the course had disappeared from the Wharton curriculum.

*Mead's replacement, Walter E. Kreusi, seemed to have a background suitable for developing a program in industrial management. In addition to a classical education, Kreusi was trained as a machinist, an electrician, and an iron molder; his father was a long-time associate of Thomas A. Edison, a great entrepreneur as well as a great inventor. For two years Kreusi taught Mead's courses and also had the distinction of introducing marketing to the Wharton curriculum, with a 1904 class on "Marketing Products." But Kreusi left the school in 1905, without completing his degree.

Joseph Wharton's primary purpose in founding the school, and he himself had employed the father of the scientific management movement, Frederick Taylor, only a few years earlier. Taylor and several of his followers resided in Philadelphia and could have been employed as lecturers at the Wharton School. A lack of expert faculty, however, cannot bear the entire responsibility for the failure of Wharton's management curriculum. Although J. Russell Smith specialized in geography, in time he induced several fine students to enter academic careers in the field of management. They were on the staff and offering effective instruction before the outbreak of the First World War.[37]

More light can be shed on our anomaly by contrasting the striking success of the accounting program with the dismal performance of management. More than any other curriculum at Wharton, accounting led to a well-defined vocational competence and professional career, and students took these courses because of their clear value in providing a livelihood. To a lesser extent, an education in finance, insurance, or transportation likewise led to job opportunities. Had law not been taught in separate schools at the time, it too would have been a logical candidate for rapid development at Wharton.[38]*

Marketing and management were different, however. In marketing, a stable occupational structure had not crystalized, and courses appeared in Wharton's *Catalog* sporadically and late.†

---

*From 1899 to 1905, Wharton's courses in business law were taught on a part-time basis by the distinguished Philadelphia lawyer Thomas Raeburn White, who wrote a widely used textbook on *Business Law*. The law curriculum began to grow rapidly when John J. Sullivan joined the full-time faculty in 1905. Sullivan and W. Ward Pierson, who came in 1907, were extremely popular teachers and soon taught three year-long courses that covered traditional issues such as commercial contracts, corporate law, estates, and litigation procedures. Students got from these classes a fine sense of Anglo-Saxon traditions as well as a survey of the legal structure of the marketplace. But the law program remained what it had been in the past: a part of the general business background necessary to all men of affairs. Preempted by existing law schools, Wharton never even considered offering a professional course in the subject. The school's professors likewise stayed close to the traditional curriculum of commercial law. They left the recent additions to the law of business arising from the new industrial economy — antitrust law, labor law, and the rulings of regulatory commissions — to their colleagues in Wharton's Political Science Department.

†Kreusi offered a lone course on "Marketing Products" in 1904, but the field began its continuous development at Wharton only in 1909, with the addition of Herbert Hess and his courses on advertising and salesmanship. Two earlier pioneers in marketing education, Paul T. Cherington, later of Harvard, and James E.

Management, as well, was only beginning to be seen as a distinct professional category. Most contemporaries viewed management as essentially tied to a specific industry or function; they saw railroad or bank management, sales or production management, but not management as an independent activity by itself. Most managers owed their positions to family control of the enterprise or long service with the company, not some professional skill. Few therefore saw any value in academic training or mastery of general managerial principles. Frederick Taylor's great manifesto, which announced his claims of discovering *The Principles of Scientific Management*, appeared only in 1911 and even then restricted its focus to the factory floor. Taylor, moreover, considered his professional enterprise as a part of engineering, not business. He and his colleagues published most of their articles in the *Transactions of the American Society of Mechanical Engineers*, and Taylor's most prominent appearance at the University of Pennsylvania was a speech that he made at the dedication of the new engineering building in 1906.[39]

Only one business school in the period developed a successful management program, the Harvard Graduate School of Business, founded in 1908. Set up from the beginning as a graduate school and headed by historian Edwin F. Gay, Harvard took an entirely different tack to the problem of business education. Rather than hoping to develop management as a technology, as a procedural science, or to promote the various functional areas as independent specialties, Harvard wanted to cultivate skills of integrated executive judgment, decision, and leadership. To develop these traits of personality, Harvard adopted its famous case method of instruction, modeled after Dean Gay's "historical method" of inductive reasoning and the instructional technique made famous in the Harvard Law School. Equipped with good family connections, an undergraduate liberal arts education, and a "Masters of Business Administration" degree, many of Harvard's graduates became "gentlemen" leaders of America's established corporations and financial institutions.[40]

Hagerty, later of Ohio State, had both won Wharton Ph.D.'s and had written theses on the institutional structure of the marketing process. After graduation, both had worked for a time at the Philadelphia Commercial Museum, only two blocks away from the Wharton campus. But probably because of low student interest in their rather academic, nonprocedural work, neither was added to the faculty.

In the new universe of American business schools, Harvard won preeminence in the field of general management and Wharton established itself as the leading exponent of specialized business studies. By the outbreak of the First World War, the nation's first business school was offering the most diverse array of business courses and professional training programs anywhere. Rather than cultivate overall executive ability, Wharton offered training in the various divisions of entrepreneurial responsibility. Specialization was its response to the fact that the sum of business knowledge and skill had far outgrown individual capacity. Wharton's professors pushed aside problems of ultimate economic coordination and busily organized books and courses on the law, accounts, and practices of the various divisions of business. With this great assembly of expertise, Wharton emerged as the best place in the nation to explore the practical intricacies of business activity. Prepared by their education at Wharton, thousands of young men soon joined the business world as professionals, relying on ideas and expertise, rather than corporate office or the ownership of property, as a basis of income and economic authority.[41]

Source Notes

1. Rexford G. Tugwell, "To the Lesser Heights of Morningside," MS memoir, 3; Scott Nearing, *Educational Frontiers* (New York: Thomas Seltzer, 1925), 74–75.

2. Roswell C. McCrea, "The Wharton School," *Alumni Register* 17 (1915):292; Joseph Wharton, "Project," Minutes of the University Trustees, 24 Mar. 1881; *Catalog of the University of Pennsylvania (1892 – 93)*, 153 – 56; (1884 – 85), 36–37; (1887 – 88), 63.

3. Minutes of the Wharton Faculty, 13 Nov. 1896, 27 Nov. 1896.

4. Edwin E. Slosson, "Great American Universities, 11: University of Pennsylvania," *Independent* (1 Jan. 1908):1013; Emory R. Johnson, *Life of a University Professor* (Philadelphia: privately printed, 1943), 25, 161; Minutes of the Wharton Faculty, 26 Sept. 1901.

5. Johnson, *University Professor*, 17 – 27, 33ff.; Simon N. Patten, "University Training for Business Men," *Educational Review* 29 (1905):229; Richard A. Swanson, "Edmund J. James, 1855 – 1925: A 'Conservative Progressive' in American Higher Education," (Ph.D. diss., University of Illinois, 1966), 184 n. 22; *Catalog* (1893 – 94), 109, iii.

6. Leo S. Rowe, *The Problems of City Government* (New York: Appleton, 1915), 182; "Notes on Municipal Government," conducted by Leo S. Rowe,

Annals 12 (1898):43, 436, 437; James H. Potts, "The Evolution of Municipal Accounting," *Business History Review* 52 (1978):522–28; Leo S. Rowe, "The Municipality and the Gas Supply," *Annals* 11 (1898):301–28; Nearing, *Educational Frontiers*, 13, 20, 33; see George Burnham, Jr., "Philadelphia Bureau of Municipal Research," *National Municipal Review* (1917):467.

7. Patten, "Training for Business," 220, 221.

8. Ibid.; Willis J. Winn, *Business Education in the United States: A Historical Perspective* (New York: Newcomen Society in North America, 1964), 7–9.

9. Alfred S. Eichner, *The Emergence of Oligopoly* (Baltimore: Johns Hopkins University Press, 1969), 73, 80, 163, 169–87.

10. Slosson, "University of Pennsylvania," 1013, 1015, 1016; McCrea, "Wharton School," 294–95, 298; Tugwell, "Morningside Heights," 60; James H. S. Bossard and J. Frederick Dewhurst, *University Education for Business* (Philadelphia: University of Pennsylvania Press, 1931), 164, 187, 198–201; Patten, "Training for Business," 218; U.S. Bureau of the Census, *Historical Statistics of the United States* (Washington, D.C.: 1957), 207.

11. Bossard and Dewhurst, *Education for Business*, 198–201.

12. Slosson, "University of Pennsylvania," 1014–15.

13. Ibid., 1008–10, 1016; n.t., *Philadelphia Evening Bulletin*, 12 Aug. 1904, 16 Jan. 1909, and *Philadelphia Inquirer*, 14 Jan. 1904, 17 Jan. 1909, 20 Jan. 1909, "Joseph Wharton File," Archives; Nearing, *Educational Frontiers*, 20; McCrea, "Wharton School,"299.

14. Slosson, "University of Pennsylvania," 1021; Tugwell, "Morningside Heights," 46, 50–51.

15. Slosson, "University of Pennsylvania," 1020, 1019, 1022; Tugwell, "Morningside Heights," 39–40.

16. Patten, "Training for Business," 223.

17. *Catalog (1900–1)*, 146, 150–51; *(1901–2)*, 150, 152–54.

18. Murdoch K. Goodwin, "[Edward S. Mead?]," clipping from *Red and Blue*, March 1928, "Edward S. Mead File," Archives, 12–13; Slosson, "University of Pennsylvania," 1015, 1016.

19. Johnson, *University Professor*, 271, 25–27, 66–75; Emory R. Johnson, *American Railway Transportation*, 2 vols. (New York: Appleton, 1903); Emory R. Johnson and Grover G. Huebner, *Railroad Traffic and Rates* (New York: Appleton, 1911).

20. Johnson, *University Professor*, 103, 47–65, 76–130; K. Austin Kerr, *American Railroad Politics* (Pittsburgh: University of Pittsburgh Press, 1968), 194–95.

21. Virginia M. Rowley, *J. Russell Smith* (Philadelphia: University of Pennsylvania Press, 1964), 17–25, 45–60, 72–73; J. Russell Smith, *Industrial and Commercial Geography* (New York: Henry Holland, 1913).

22. Mildred F. Stone, *The Teacher Who Changed An Industry* (Homewood, Ill.: Richard D. Irwin, 1960), 11–54; Solomon S. Huebner, "The Distribution of Stock Holdings in American Railways," *Annals* 22 (1903):63–78; Johnson, *University Professor*, 71–74; Emory R. Johnson, Thurman W. Van Metre, Grover G. Huebner, and David S. Hanchett, *History of Foreign and Domestic Commerce of the United States* (Washington, D.C.: Carnegie Institution of Washington, 1915).

23. Interview with Scott Nearing by Barbara Copperman, 24 Dec. 1979; Johnson, *University Professor*, 66–75, 89–100, 228; Stone, *Teacher*, 54–56, 95–96; Marquis James, *Biography of a Business: 1792–1942; Insurance Company of North America* (Indianapolis: Bobbs–Merrill, 1942), 381; Charles C.

Harrison, "Autobiography of Charles Custis Harrison, 1844–1929," typescript, Archives.

24. Solomon S. Huebner, "Life Insurance Education," *Proceedings of the National Association of Life Underwriters' Annual Convention* 25 (1915), quoted in Stone, *Teacher*, 127; Solomon S. Huebner, "Human Life Value in Business Compared with the Property Value," *Proceedings of the National Association of Life Underwriters' Annual Convention* 35 (1924), quoted in Stone, *Teacher*, 130.

25. Huebner, "Life Insurance Education," quoted in Stone, *Teacher*, 127; taped statement by George Friedlander, 15 Feb. 1980; Stone, *Teacher*, 48–49, 92–103; Douglass North, "Capital Accumulation in Life Insurance between the Civil War and the Investigation of 1905," *Men in Business*, ed. William Miller (Cambridge, Mass.: Harvard University Press, 1952), 238–52; "James A. Patten," *Webster's Dictionary of Biography* (Springfield, Mass.: Merriam, 1948), 1153.

26. Stone, *Teacher*, 104–23.

27. "Edward S. Mead File" and "Frederick A. Cleveland File," Archives.

28. Minutes of the Wharton Faculty, 9 Feb. 1901.

29. Edward S. Mead, *Corporation Finance*, 5th ed. (New York: Appleton, 1923 [1910]), ix–x; Frederick A. Cleveland, *Funds and Their Uses*, rev. ed. (New York: Appleton, 1905), vii; Edward S. Mead, *Trust Finance* (New York: Appleton, 1901); Edward S. Mead, "The Trust Danger Exaggerated," clipping from *Collier's Weekly*, 23 July 1904, "Edward S. Mead File," Archives.

30. *Catalog (1900–1)*, 146, 150; *(1901–2)* 150, 152; *(1902–3)* 134, 135, 138, 139.

31. *Catalog (1901–2)*, 152; Edward S. Mead, "Notes on Industry and Commerce," *Annals* 18 (1901):88–91, 574–78; 19 (1902):317–26.

32. *Catalog (1902–3)*, 134, 135, 138, 139; taped statement, including list of plants visited in "Field Work in Industry Course," by George Friedlander, 15 Feb. 1980; Frank B. Copley, *Frederick W. Taylor*, 2 vols. (New York: Harper & Brothers, 1923), 2:175–85.

33. *Catalog (1900–1)*, 150; *(1901–2)*,152; as a text, Mead used D. A. Kiester, *Corporation Accounting and Auditing*, 7th ed. (Cleveland: Burrows Brothers, 1899).

34. Simon Patten, "University Training," 221; Slosson, "University of Pennsylvania," 1016; Goodwin, "[Mead?]"; [Oscar S. Nelson?], "History of the Accounting Department of the Wharton School of Finance and Commerce," mimeographed, files of the Accounting Department, Wharton School, 4–6; *Catalog (1904–5)*, 214; "University Bulletin: Wharton School of Finance and Commerce, 1909–1910," 19–21.

35. "Walter Edison Kreusi File," Archives; Rowley, *Smith*, 80–81, *Catalog (1904–5)*, 213; Minutes of the Wharton Faculty, 14 Mar. 1907.

36. Rowley, *Smith*, 74, 80–84; J. Russell Smith, *The Elements of Industrial Management* (Philadelphia: J. B. Lippincott, 1915); *Catalog (1916–17)*, 117; "University Bulletin: Wharton School, 1909–10," 3, 12–13, 19–20.

37. Rowley, *Smith*, 76, 80, 85–90; Tugwell, "Morningside Heights," 85.

38. *Catalog (1899–1900)*, 240, 246; Emory R. Johnson, "History of the Wharton School," mimeographed, 1939; Minutes of the Wharton Faculty, 5 June 1939, 5; Frederick C. Kempin, "A History of the American Business Law Association" (St. Paul, Minn.: West, 1974), 5–6; Thomas R. White, *Business Law*, with a foreword by Roland P. Faulkner (New York: Silver, Burdett, 1900); Tugwell, "Morningside Heights," 83; "University Bulletin: The Wharton School, 1909–10," pp. 20, 24, 26.

39. *Catalog (1904–5)*, 213; *(1909–10)*, 268, 281; H. H. Maynard, "Marketing Courses Prior to 1910," *Journal of Marketing* 5 (1941):382–84; James E.

Hagerty, "Experiences of an Early Marketing Teacher," *Journal of Marketing* 1 (1936): 21 – 23; Thomas C. Cochran, *200 Years of American Business* (New York: Basic Books, 1977), 125; Frederick W. Taylor, *Principles of Scientific Management* (New York: Harper & Row, 1911); Copley, *Taylor*, 2: 260 – 65.

40. Morris T. Copeland, "The Genesis of the Case Method in Business Instruction" in *The Case Method at the Harvard Business School*, ed. Malcom P. McNair (New York: McGraw-Hill, 1954), 25 – 27.

41. McCrea, "Wharton School," 292.

Charles C. Harrison

Logan Hall

Panoramic view of the campus, ca. 1910

Chalkboard in the Wharton School, College Hall, ca. 1900

Emory R. Johnson

AMERICAN RAILWAY TRANSPORTATION

BY

EMORY R. JOHNSON, Ph. D.

PROFESSOR OF TRANSPORTATION AND COMMERCE
IN THE UNIVERSITY OF PENNSYLVANIA
MEMBER OF THE ISTHMIAN CANAL COMMISSION 1899 TO 1904
AUTHOR OF "OCEAN AND INLAND WATER TRANSPORTATION"

SECOND REVISED EDITION

NEW YORK AND LONDON
D. APPLETON AND COMPANY
1915

CONTENTS

vii

Emory R. Johnson, American Railway Transportation, title page and first page of contents

Edward S. Mead

Solomon S. Huebner

John D. Sullivan

6

Cranking Up the Professional Machine

I

Following the end of World War I, the Wharton School accompanied the rest of the nation in its pursuit of "normalcy," and a new flood of practical-minded students surged through Logan Hall in search of business training. With Simon Patten retired and young firebrands like Scott Nearing gone from the faculty, little stood in the way of the triumph of such a utilitarian use of the university, and the school soon accommodated these student ambitions with an expanded variety of commercial courses and professional programs. Between 1917 and 1928, the detailed study of specialized business subjects flowered luxuriantly, and the number of course topics increased one-third, from 87 to 118. But as these courses on specific aspects of business practice came to dominate the curriculum, a portion of the faculty became uneasy. Their Wharton School had shaken off the moral burdens of Patten's nineteenth-century ideology and the somewhat unprofitable rigors of his economic theory. But Patten's theoretical vision, his passion for investigation, and commitment to efficient technique had given the school its character. Now that his combination of theory, research, and practice had fallen apart, "normalcy" became more a desire than a description of conditions at the school.[1]

In 1919 Dean William McClellan resigned, and his departure brought to an end the bitter struggle between the progressive reformers on the Wharton faculty and the university trustees. But much of the prewar social science faculty had also resigned, and morale at the school lay at a low pitch. Wanting to restore the confidence of the faculty and to make a new beginning for the school, the trustees chose Emory R. Johnson as Wharton's new dean. The senior professor at the school and the mentor of many other instructors on the staff, Johnson had a warm personality, a dignified presence, and a true concern for the welfare of his colleagues. While not a powerful thinker, he had nevertheless won a national reputation as a transportation expert and thereby gathered important contacts in Wharton's two major constituencies, government and business. Over the course of his fourteen years as dean, Johnson would vindicate the trustees' judgment, proving to be a popular leader and preparing the school to meet its responsibilities to a new wave of students.[2]

World War I had marked a watershed in the size and character of the school's student population. During the war, Wharton's enrollments had actually fallen, and to keep classes full the faculty had resolved to admit women and younger students and to launch an advertising campaign. Wartime jobs with the government and the quick return of peace and prosperity, however, had saved the professoriate from such drastic remedies. The twenties, however, brought the greatest movement of labor into business employment in the eighty years between 1870 and 1950; the number of workers in banking, finance, and insurance alone grew more than 80 percent between 1920 and 1930. The nation's business schools, which helped build this huge increase in the stock of businessmen, saw their enrollments explode sixfold between 1915 and 1926 and include a far more democratic slice of the American population than ever before. Such trends, which had begun at Wharton as early as 1900, accelerated at this time and succeeded in giving the school an entirely new face.[3]

A sea of ambitious young men now swept through Wharton, looking for their entree into the expanding world of finance and commerce. Already granting more undergraduate degrees than any school at the University of Pennsylvania in 1915, by 1924 the Wharton School saw its graduating class grow by a factor of 4, from 147 to 570. The evening school likewise expanded, as the number of degrees jumped from 62 in 1916 to 152 by 1924. These young men who flocked to Wharton in the 1920s were, moreover, far less privileged and came from a much broader range of society than their counterparts before 1914. The school drew relatively fewer of those students of inherited position and ability whom Joseph Wharton had hoped to educate; many of their places were now taken by sons of South European and East European Catholic and Jewish immigrants who came looking for means of survival and advancement. Fewer Wharton graduates of the 1920s were headed for traditional professional careers, for positions in family businesses, or for first jobs as corporate officials or proprietors of their own businesses. Barely 1 out of 4 eventually joined family firms, compared with a third of the old student body. The numbers who were to start their business careers as corporate officers or proprietors fell even more, from 13 percent of the graduates to a mere 5 percent. The new students shunned the social sciences, and a greater proportion chose their fields of business specialization on the basis of available economic opportunity. More worked their way through college, and at jobs carrying less prestige and responsibility than those held by prewar students: they were salesmen, laborers, and waiters, rather than camp counselors, teachers, and journalists. Clearly, the school was now a predominately middle-class, rather than elite, institution.[4]

Graduates from former years observed this change, both at Wharton and at the university in general, and resisted it. Conservative alumni leaders, who seemed most upset by progressive reform before the Great War, now mounted a determined campaign against what they called "mass education." They protested the sheer size of the new student body, its composition, and its blatant ambition. Wharton's evening and extension schools drew their concentrated fire, including calls for eliminating these, the school's most practical of programs. The alumni hoped, above all, to maintain their alma mater as a small, upper-crust liberal arts college with a good football team. They rallied around the slogan "education for leadership," by which they meant an education that would fashion their children into a clubby American gentry. Like Joseph Wharton, they wanted the university to cater to those with "a superior inheritance or promise, either of money, of vigor, of health, of mental equipment, or of family, social or political influence [who would be] more apt to be given or to secure positions of executive responsibility in later life than those without these advantages." Of Penn's most prominent alumni, many backed up their complaints with action. Rather than threaten their children's chances for success, they increasingly sent them to Harvard, Princeton, and Yale — not the University of Pennsylvania. The founder's grandson, Joseph Wharton Lippincott, had graduated from the Wharton School in 1908, but in 1918 his younger brother Bertram took his college degree at Princeton.[5]

Dean Johnson shared many of the concerns of the alumni. In his distinguished career as a transportation expert, Johnson had met and established friendships with many prominent politicians, businessmen, and military officers. Without any great effort, he became an initiate in the culture of the elite. He adopted much of their social vision, even abandoning the evangelical Baptist faith of his parents for the Episcopalian ritual of the Eastern Establishment. For several years Johnson served as president of the National Institute of the Social Sciences, which he himself described as

on the whole, a conservative organization. It was felt by the officers that there was no need for a radical society that would break new paths in social theory, but that there was a real necessity for an organization whose publications should be essentially candid and sane . . . Its management had been careful not to give public expression to new ideas until they have been carefully weighed, and until a reasoned opinion can be obtained upon public questions of vital moment.

Oddly enough, Johnson's organization grew out of the remains of the old American Social Science Association; his institute, and Edmund James's American Academy of Political and Social Science, were in fact the only direct twentieth-century continuations of the nineteenth-century ASSA. But unlike the academy, which remained a vehicle for academic leadership on social issues, Johnson's institute had no organic relationship with the university. It served primarily as an instrument to dispense status to useful citizens and to give them an entree into high society. During Johnson's regime as president, meetings became primarily an occasion for bestowing gold medals and eating at the tables of leading New York City bankers, and he induced Mrs. Henry P. Davison, Mrs. William Salomon, Mr. and Mrs. Otto Kahn, Mrs. Andrew

Carnegie, and Mrs. Ripley Hitchcock to host the annual meetings of the institute in their homes.[6]*

As the new dean of the Wharton School, Johnson moved quickly to improve the "tone" of the program and to respond to alumni critics who wished to preserve the social prestige of the institution. At the request of the university, he limited the school's enrollment, beginning in 1926. Rather than accepting all who qualified for admission, the school now prescribed the number of students that it wished to admit and took only so many. Johnson and his colleagues also promised to give these students "character training" and "individualized instruction," not "mass education." For the alumni he organized various conferences, where faculty and prominent businessmen lectured returning graduates on current topics. This allowed Wharton alumni to keep up with new developments in business while renewing old ties and repairing their faltering confidence in the school.[7]

Despite Johnson's general sympathy with the American upper classes, he did not heed all of the alumni's complaints. Under his regime Wharton's student population did not return to prewar levels, but stabilized at about 2,200. The evening and extension schools also remained intact. In addition to providing an important educational service to the city and state, these programs were the financial pillars of the school, and their elimination was unthinkable. More important, Johnson ignored alumni suggestions to reverse the process of professional specialization and to move the university back toward a general liberal arts curriculum. On the contrary, he encouraged the proliferation of practical programs. Johnson's own success had come through specialization, by concentrating his attention on his primary area of interest and shucking off other areas of responsibility to his students. Thus in 1916 he told the Wharton faculty that the purpose of the sopho-

---

*Johnson made special note of the award granted in 1924 to Mrs. G. Lorrilard Spencer:

> She was then dividing her time between New York, Newport, Rhode Island, and the Island of Jolo, in the southern part of the Philippine Islands where Bishop Charles Henry Brent had established the school which she, with other Americans, has continued to support and which for more than twenty-five years has carried on its work of converting a hostile and lawless people into a friendly one with higher standards as to what is right and wrong.

more year ought to be "to get men into specialized courses." Under his leadership as dean,

greater emphasis was placed upon the departmental organization of the faculty. The number of departments, or subject groups, was increased, and the chairmen of the several departments were given added responsibility for the educational development and the personnel of their respective departments.

Johnson believed in authority, but saw professional specialization, not general leadership skill, as the surest path to excellence.[8]

Johnson proposed accounting, with its rigorous discipline, practical value, and professional certification, as his model for the various specializations at the Wharton School. Businessmen accorded the Certified Public Accountant (CPA) certificate great respect, and Johnson would have each discipline develop a similar program of in-depth training and licensed expertise. Upon becoming dean in 1919, he gave accounting a department of its own and appointed the suave Edward P. Moxey, Jr., its chairman. No longer a graduate student, but an elegant gentleman with a finely waxed mustache, Moxey was a business professional of the first rank. He had taken over his father's prestigious accounting firm, E. P. Moxey & Co., and managed a thriving professional practice in addition to his classroom duties at Wharton. As a leader in the area of cost accounting (a field largely controlled by "scientific managers" before the war), he had established a national reputation as well. Moxey and his instructional staff, several of whom were employed in his accounting firm, combined intellectual subtlety with a wealth of up-to-date experience to provide an excellent training for business. Accounting soon became the school's most popular major and attracted many of Wharton's finest students. Scores of these young men did take the state CPA examination and then established useful professional practices. Others found that their training in accounts opened still further opportunities in business. Not a few continued on to the university's law school, combining thorough training in the two fields of business study that Joseph Wharton had thought most essential, and from there embarked on spectacularly successful careers. The CPA, Dean Johnson's telos, was not the goal of most majors in accounting. Nevertheless, the intellectual rigor of the CPA program and the social stature that came as an accoutrement of professionalization clearly established accounting and the CPA as a legitimate model for business education in general.[9]*

Insurance was by far Wharton's most vigorous business specialty in the 1920s and other than accounting, was the one that advanced the farthest on the road to professionalization. Led by Solomon Huebner, Johnson's former student and fellow member of his National Institute of Social Science, the department had a distinguished faculty of fourteen by 1932, and its courses were among the most widely elected at the school. By then the Wharton department had become the dominant center of insurance education in the world and the major force in the professionalization of the trade. Huebner concentrated his attention on the major analog to the public accountant in the industry — the insurance agent — and during the 1920s he led a remarkably successful movement to raise the business of life insurance sales to the level of a profession. He used education to "uplift" this segment of the industry, and thereby helped bring relatively sophisticated insurance services to much of the nation's population. For such outstanding contributions, Dean Johnson proudly singled out Huebner for a special Doctor of Science award at Wharton's fiftieth anniversary celebration in 1931.[10]

Huebner's remarkable career in the insurance industry had begun before the war, when he forged close ties with the National Association of Life Underwriters (NALU). In 1914 a student introduced Huebner to his uncle, Ernest J. Clark, Baltimore general agent for the John Hancock Mutual Life Insurance Company and the president of the NALU. The professor and the underwriter quickly established a warm friendship, which soon developed into the most powerful alliance between business and the university ever achieved at the Wharton School. Clark engineered numerous speaking engagements for Huebner before the NALU, where

---

*Accounting, not suprisingly, had a reputation for difficulty, and, aside from those majoring in the subject, most undergraduates avoided it after finishing their required freshman survey. But all students had a taste of this, the "syntax" of business, and they did so at the hands of one of the great teachers in the history of the Wharton School, George MacFarland. In later years nearly all alumni considered this training in accounting among the most valuable courses in their Wharton education.

he gave insurance men a fresh perspective on their work and championed the cause of education. Clark also persuaded the association to publish Huebner's 1915 text on life insurance, a pioneering volume. But most important, the two set their sights on designing a program of education and professional certification in life insurance similar to the CPA in accounting. The underwriter was thrilled that Huebner, speaking with the authority of the university, had set out to raise the standards and reputation of the industry; the professor seized on the opportunity now open to have his ideas influence business practice.[11]

In 1924 Huebner delivered the virtuoso performance of his career, his keynote address to the NALU convention in Los Angeles. His speech, "Human Value in Business Compared to Property Value," "became as familiar to life underwriters in the 1920s as Lincoln's Gettysburg Address." With ingenuity and linguistic flair, an impassioned Huebner outlined the core idea of his entire approach to life insurance, the protection of the "human life value." Anticipating by decades the "human capital" notion in theoretical economics, Huebner contended that the productive power of individual human beings represented a tremendous asset, "six to eight times the aggregate of the nation's material wealth." Large professional income streams, he pointed out, were altogether dependent on the life of the practitioner, and "where business property values exist, life values are inseparably interwoven with them." But the professor charged that this, the greatest store of wealth of the nation, was the country's least recognized and most poorly managed resource. Huebner claimed that the time had come to handle "life values" with skill and intelligence, and that insurance was the key instrument for performing such a task. He told the assembled underwriters,

the time is not far distant when, in wholesale fashion, we shall apply to the economic organization, management, and conservation of life values the same scientific treatment that we now use in connection with property. We shall do so to the extent of capitalizing them with bonds to give them perpetuity as a working force and fluidity as a source of credit, of subjecting them to the principles of depreciation, and of using the sinking-fund method to assure realization of the contemplated object wherever man has a future business or family obligation to fulfill that involves the hazard of uncertainty of the duration of working life. I also believe that Life Insurance alone affords the medium through which such scientific treatment can be applied, and that it has no competitor.[12]

This 1924 address clearly established Huebner as a leader of the insurance industry and allowed him to proceed with his ambitious plan of professionalization. With the active encouragement of Dean Johnson, Huebner and Clark designed an educational program to train and certify "Chartered Life Underwriters," the professionals who would handle the "economic organization, management, and conservation of life values" through the instrument of life insurance. After several years of wrangling, the NALU created the American College of Life Underwriters in 1927 to govern such an effort. This college gave examinations for the CLU certificate and thereby controlled the content of the training program. The college did not, however, conduct classes on this material, leaving that task primarily to the nation's business schools. Huebner, the first dean of this college, prepared an exacting curriculum that included training in finance and law as well as insurance. The program awarded its first 22 CLU's in the summer of 1928; within ten years there were 1,400; and, after half a century, fully 25,000. All were thoroughly trained in the principles and procedures of insurance underwriting and had taken the pledge written by Huebner:

In all my relations with clients I agree to observe the following rule of professional conduct: I shall, in the light of all the circumstances surrounding my client, which I shall make every conscientious effort to ascertain and to understand, give him that service which, had I been in the same circumstances, I would have applied to myself.

In many of the nation's finest insurance companies the CLU became part of the basic culture of the corporation, with status, income, and promotions hinging on the number of CLU courses passed or possession of the CLU certificate.[13]

Huebner's commitment to professionalization did not stop at life insurance. In 1942, after years of promotional activity, he and his associates at Wharton and in the industry organized the American Institute for Property and Liability Underwriters. Modeled on the American College of Life Underwriters, the institute offered no classes but provided syllabi and study outlines, and held examinations for the new Chartered Property and Liability Underwriter (CPLU) certificate. In 1943 the first six CPLU's passed their examinations and made a pledge of ethical professional conduct similar to that expressed in the CLU oath. Huebner, now over sixty, did not take on the deanship of the new institution, but he saw to it that his colleague at the Wharton School, Dr. Harry J. Loman, was appointed to that post. During a severe illness in the mid-1930s, Huebner also gave up the deanship of the American College of Life Underwriters. There, too, leadership remained at Wharton, with Huebner's longtime second in command, Dr. David McCahan, assuming responsibility over the educational program.[14]*

Aside from this success with insurance, Dean Johnson's program of mimicking the CPA and professionalizing the school's various specialties did not take hold. In areas such as finance the policy could have been pursued, but the faculty was simply not interested. In others, the fields themselves resisted such treatment. Such was the case, ironically, in Johnson's own specialty of transportation. The reasons for this are not hard to find. The transportation curriculum itself contained little to be learned aside from arbitrary business procedures or descriptive details of the industry — the field had none of that esoteric elegance or numerical clarity that distiguished accountancy or even insurance. In the entire industry of transportation, therefore, no large occupational class emerged comparable to public accountants and insurance agents — business people upon whom firms and the public depended for judgment, honesty, and analytical expertise. American railroads, the nation's largest transportation companies, had

*By this time Wharton clearly dominated the academic study of insurance. One out of three full-time collegiate teachers of the subject were on the Wharton faculty, and most of the rest had won their Ph.D.'s under Huebner at Penn. But a shortage of qualified instructors was becoming a serious bottleneck to the educational program in the industry. To relieve this pressure and to give homage to the "dean" of their profession, the nation's insurance community established at Wharton the S. S. Huebner Foundation for Insurance Education. At a huge gala at the Bellevue Stratford Hotel in 1940, twelve hundred leaders of the industry gathered to honor Huebner and make their presentation. There the three leading industry associations pledged twenty-five thousand dollars a year for five years for fellowships to train teachers of insurance at the Wharton School. The initial venture proved so successful that the foundation became a permanent institution at the university. By 1952, 100 insurance companies were contributing forty thousand dollars a year to the program, and by 1965 that figure had risen to one hundred thousand dollars. Helped along by the foundation, Wharton has continued as the preeminent educational center of the insurance industry.

clerks, not sophisticated independent agents, handle their business with the public and hired engineers, not business school
graduates, to fill entry-level executive positions. The transportation curriculum was thus not linked to significant professional
opportunities. Although Wharton offered more courses in transportation than all but one other institution in the nation, few
undergraduates signed up and the subject drew the smallest classes
at the school. Johnson thus never attempted a CPA-type project
in his own discipline.[15]*

The rapidly growing academic field of marketing also resisted
professionalization, despite the fact that in terms of employment
opportunities, student popularity, and academic vintage, it lay at
the opposite end of the curricular spectrum from transportation.
Mercantile pursuits, the oldest form of business, became the most
important source of livelihood for Wharton graduates in the 1920s,
as more than 1 out of 5 found work in the field of distribution.
While the nation's oldest large-scale enterprise, the railroad, passed
over Wharton's new breed of sons in the 1920s, the marketplace,
the ancient heart of the business system, yielded them sufficient
profit: Alumni in advertising and marketing earned among the
highest incomes, and of all managerial positions, those in sales
management were the best paid. Student course selection followed the lure of opportunity, and by 1930, undergraduate demand had made marketing the second-largest segment of the
curriculum. (Only finance offered more class-hours; transportation was third.) While transportation drew less than 3 percent of
those who followed one of Wharton's specialized curricula, marketing drew six times as many (second only to accounting). Students were shunning one of the school's oldest business programs
in favor of its newest.[16]

Undergraduate patronage did not produce a rigorous and
useful professional curriculum in marketing, and, in fact, its rapid
growth clearly hampered the development of such intellectual
sophistication. The continuous history of marketing at Wharton

---

*Transportation studies had somewhat greater success at the graduate level.
Johnson had taught several prominent Oriental transportation officials, including
the director-general of the Chinese National Railroad system and a director of the
Japanese government system, and these powerful gentlemen now sent a steady
stream of advanced students to study with their old mentor. This patronage
justified, to a degree, the continuation of course work in the area.

had begun only in 1909, with a course in advertising and sales-manship offered by Herbert Hess, and a "merchandising" depart-ment, chaired by Hess, quickly expanded to a faculty of ten by 1922-1923. Most of these new instructors, however, were recent Wharton graduates with only B.S. degrees in economics and neg-ligible practical experience; initially, at least, they brought neither scholarship nor savvy to their task. The whole affair of marketing, moreover, had few laws and standard procedures, let alone any necessary analytical frameworks that students needed to learn. So Wharton's merchandising professors returned to apprentice-ship patterns of instruction, giving their charges supervised ex-perience in the various branches of the business.[17]*

Over the course of the 1920s, observers of marketing studies became "impressed with a certain lack of coordination in the field" and its dearth of scholarship. As revealed in the title of his 1931 text, *Advertising, Its Economics, Philosophy, and Tech-nique*, Hess also felt the need for larger perspectives and a set of principles that could unify the field. He steadily added more and more psychological materials to his courses, and his 1931 book discussed issues such as crowd psychology, sense experience, instinct, memory, and attention. As an organizing principle Hess adopted what he called the "merchandising approach," the pro-cess of adjusting products to the desires of the consumer. He thought that by codifying a standard vocabulary for his merchan-dising approach, while somehow preserving the creativity that he believed to be essential in advertising and selling, he could help transform his field into a profession. For a time, he even required a course in symbolic logic of all merchandising majors. But so-phistication could not be manufactured in such fashion, and pro-fessionalization, the Holy Grail of business specialists, forever eluded Hess's efforts.[18]

---

*Hess's expertise lay in advertising, and he spent much of his early years initiating his students into the techniques of the field. By 1915 he had written a text, *Productive Advertising*, and had designed, as the culminating course in his program, a class on "The Construction of Advertising Campaigns" that had gotten students to do advertising. Hess's curriculum emphasized the practical concerns of typographic style, copy writing, and media selection. As enrollments climbed he added a course on "Market Research," in which he taught his students how to conduct those surveys that the leading advertising agencies now considered nec-essary for a successful campaign. His colleagues taught other practical courses on such topics as mail-order sales and retail store management.

Joseph Wharton, of course, did not have Emory Johnson's vision of professional specialization in mind when he first organized his school. The original plan had aimed at educating general business leaders, those who would control the major enterprises of the nation and would employ the various professionals that Johnson hoped to train. The heirs of the founder's ambitions, the faculty of industry in the Department of Geography and Industry (G & I), had not prospered during the great prewar speciation of business programs, but now, in the 1920s, managerial studies at Wharton throttled ahead. Joseph Willits, a student of J. Russell Smith who had specialized in industry, had replaced his mentor as chairman of G & I in 1919, and he quickly built up the offerings and faculty in his area of interest. The school's developing program in management, however, was schizophrenic. On the one hand, the faculty of industry prepared students for specialized technical careers, thereby proceeding according to the program of the dean. But professional specialization was not the chosen telos of Wharton's young doctors of industry. They saw themselves as involved in a much more grandiose enterprise, one that commanded the attention of all men of affairs. As one professor of industry put it,

Executives have come to talk management, periodicals have come to talk management, and the general public is beginning to realize that in the force of management lies the path to better understanding of industrial problems and through that to better community life. The test of the present industrial system is its ability to adjust itself to modern conditions. Management will largely determine whether or not it will meet that test.[19]

Wharton's program in management concentrated on the general area of factory production, an activity that had become a major concern of businessmen only since the industrial revolution. As yet there was no significant "business" approach to production, and the major figures in this field had been engineers. So Wharton's faculty of industry joined the movement to establish the "engineer as economist" of the new industrial age, a movement that had reached its first stage of maturity with the work of Frederick W. Taylor. Taylor and his colleagues had spearheaded American business's campaign to take control of the factory floor, pushing aside the powerful foremen, skilled workers, and occasional union chiefs who had formerly set the pace and pattern of industrial production. With such control, these engineers had then promised to make the productive process more fluid, efficient, and responsive to the needs of business. Such had been Joseph Wharton's experience with scientific management at the turn of the century. But it had been America's economic mobilization during the First World War that had led to the widespread adoption of Taylor's program. The crush of industrial novelty — new military products, skills, tasks, and procedures — had disrupted traditional patterns in American manufacturing, and the patriotic clamor for speed and efficiency had dramatically accelerated the movement toward scientific management. Richard H. Landsburgh, Wharton's prominent professor of industrial management, wrote that "the effect of the war in changing operating methods in American industry and causing a rapid growth in the management movement can hardly be over-estimated." Now, in the postwar period, Wharton's professors of industrial management hoped to prepare their students for either the specialized or the generalized careers that the scientific managers had defined: A Wharton graduate in industry could, following in the footsteps of Frederick Taylor, embark on a career as a management consultant; he could hope to find work as a full-time "works manager"; or he could aspire to become an "inside man," an employee with "no particular duties connected with the actual administrative work of the concern, but act[ing] entirely as a specialist in management." Beyond opening up such career opportunities, the industry faculty offered exposure to the new science that claimed to hold the key to organizational efficiency. Landsburgh promised to teach the "policies and principles" that made it possible for "good management to be looked upon as universally applicable."[20]

Despite Landsburgh's ambitious claim, his instruction in industrial management followed Taylor's emphasis on engineering and the problems of a "medium size factory." He discussed at great length "the physical side of the plant," from ventilation systems to power transmission. He emphasized the central lesson of the entire engineering approach to management — that standardization was "a primary management step" — and assured his students that organizing work into a parsimonious number of uniform components would soon improve efficiency. He taught

Taylor's and Frank Gilbreth's procedures for breaking worker time and motion into small, standard pieces that could be reorganized and controlled by the plant management. The class also explored the issue with which the modern scientific management literature had begun: how to design wage incentives to induce above-standard worker performance.[21]

At the conclusion of his course, Landsburgh discussed the problem of integrating the various elements and functions of an enterprise. Ever drawn to the engineering approach to organization, he told his classes that "the gears of policy in finance, sales, and productive organizations must mesh together as closely as the driving gears on the factory lathe." Although he detailed the various budgeting, routing, and inventory techniques that Taylor and his followers had developed for "controlling operations" in the *shop*, Landsburgh proved incapable of offering any universal solution to the complex problem of *business* integration. He outlined the common line and staff "military organization," with its clear channels of executive authority and responsibility. Ever attentive to Taylor's ideas, Landsburgh criticized the rigidity of this type of bureaucracy and its excessive reliance on the well-rounded abilities of those in command; he liked Taylor's functional foreman scheme — a "boss" for each aspect of worker performance — but recognized its abundant potential for conflict and confusion. Many firms were then turning to a committee system to help "mesh together" the "driving gears" of their organizations, and Landsburgh hoped that such contacts would soften the dilemma between specialization and unified authority.[22]

Although Landsburgh's industrial management courses drew larger enrollments, the young field of labor management became the main strength of the new G & I department. Like factory management, labor issues had not been a major concern of businessmen before the industrial revolution; only as entrepreneurs took control of the process of physical production did the recruitment, handling, and remuneration of a work force become an essential component of commercial life. As in the case of factory management, businessmen had not developed their own approach to labor relations, and they initially came to rely on the "science" of others. Known as the "Labor Problem," the general dependence of American livelihoods on the wage-labor system had occupied a central place in the work of numerous nineteenth-century reformers and social scientists. Their work provided the original impetus to the academic study of labor management, and endowed this branch of Wharton's industry faculty with its own tradition of addressing issues of general concern.[23]

Wharton's leading figure in labor was the young man who became chairman of G & I in 1919, Joseph Willits. The son of a Quaker farmer who later became Pennsylvania State Secretary of Agriculture, Willits had taken his undergraduate degree at nearby Swarthmore College, and had arrived at Penn as a graduate student in 1911. There he had studied social science with Simon Patten and Leo Rowe, and then specialized in industry under J. Russell Smith. Like many of his progressive colleagues at the time, the civic minded Willits had entered the service of Philadelphia's Blankenburg administration, where he had investigated "The Relation of the Municipality to the Problem of Unemployment." Using Wharton's standard social science procedure, Willits had surveyed the problem of joblessness in Philadelphia and had then presented a plan for reform: He proposed a network of municipal employment offices to help prospective employees and employers find each other.* As part of this project Willits had helped organize the Philadelphia Association for the Discussion of Employment Problems, a group of influential local manufacturers and corporate employment officers. There he had come to know the problems faced by industrial employers, and without abandoning his sympathy for labor, had decided to make an academic career studying this area of management. Like Wharton's pioneering business professors, Willits had used these business contacts to collect materials and organize knowledge in his specialty. The problem of labor turnover, in particular, occupied his attention. In 1916 he edited a special issue of the *Annals* entitled "Personnel and Employment Problems in Industrial Management," "the first comprehensive 'book' ever written on employment management" and "the early guidebook of the fledgling

*Willits's recommendations resembled Clyde King's proposal to assist local farmers in selling their produce to urban consumers. Both hoped to use municipal government to strengthen the market system and thereby promote the "community of equals." Willits, however, soon moved away from this interest in making markets.

personnel movement." But before the field of personnel had a chance to develop much further, world events changed the course of its history.[24]

America's entry into the European conflict thrust Willits and his colleagues into important positions of responsibility and exposed them to new problems and possibilities for their field. During the war Willits left academic life, became an employment manager at a naval aircraft factory, and won an enviable reputation for smoothly hiring, disciplining, training, and maintaining his work force. These tasks, like that of controlling production itself, had hitherto been largely in the hands of foremen, who as a class had acted more like subcontractors than employees of the manufacturer. But the severe wartime shortage of labor, coupled with the dramatic rise of scientific management, hastened the reduction of the foreman's place in American manufacturing. Where industrial engineers controlled the internal productive system, the new employment managers, like Willits, usually kept them supplied with a reliable and qualified labor force. This association encouraged personnel men to adopt a scientific-management approach for describing the various slots in the labor force, a procedure that they called "job analysis." Taking up where time and motion study left off, job analysis focused on the employee, rather than the task; it recognized that organizations needed various types of labor and it attempted to define the specific attributes needed by each worker to perform his specific duties. With such information and with means to test job applicants, personnel managers could hire a more suitable work force. The pioneering attempts at job analysis, including that of the famous Committee on Classification of Personnel in the Army, were not especially effective. But as the emerging profession of personnel administration entered the 1920s, job analysis and testing methods joined turnover studies as the crucial issues in the field.[25]

After Willits returned to the Wharton School and assumed the chairmanship of his G & I Department, the professional specialty of personnel management was recognized as a legitimate part of the business curriculum. The unsettled labor markets in the 1920s, moreover, created a large demand for personnel managers: A returning army of job-seekers and then the tremendous expansion of engineering-based industries — automobiles, chemicals, electrical equipment, and electronics — kept employment offices overworked. American manufacturers were also drafting personnel managers into their "American System" campaign against unions, strikes, and "Bolshevic" agitation, making them responsible for a broad array of welfare functions designed to keep workers happy and corporate enterprise humming.* With students drawn to personnel work because of this demand, and with the wealth of materials and experience from his work at the naval aircraft factory, Willits organized a new curricular specialty in personnel management and industrial relations. With support from philanthropic foundations and local businessmen, he set up Wharton's Industrial Research Department, and made it one of the leading personnel and labor research establishments in the nation.[26]†

Although establishing his field as a specialty, Willits never foresook his concern for the broad issues of democracy and social justice. He always insisted that the study of personnel management and labor relations provided the best means of addressing the great psychosomatic social crisis brought on by the wage-labor system. Accomodating the nation to the rigors of industrial work, he believed, comprised the central managerial task of the day. But Willits's program in labor, like Landsburgh's in production, did link up with rather specific entrepreneurial responsibilities. And these functional identifications, not their approach to general business leadership, gave each half of the industry group its primary definition at Wharton. Thus these programs in management also conformed to Emory Johnson's design for the school: they were two specialties among many.[27]‡

---

*So effective was this campaign that the 1920s were the first period of economic prosperity in the nation's history that saw union membership decline.

†Students specializing in personnel relations could also study with Lightner Witmer or Morris Viteles of Penn's Psychology Department, two of the nation's pioneers in industrial psychology.

‡Willits did offer a general management "capstone" course in "Industrial Policy." In this class, which was restricted to seniors, practicing executives presented a current problem; students wrote solutions; the businessman read the best papers, and then returned to discuss these proposals. At least one young student, Gordon Hattersley, got a job because the visitor, Lessing Rosenwald of Sears, Roebuck, liked his analysis. The course was quite popular, but had an enrollment limit of approximately twenty-five.

II

Dean Johnson's program of encouraging specialization, essentially a continuation of Edmund James's plan of of 1885, was largely successful. But his ambition to align Wharton's various business programs with certified professions was not. In accounting, of course, the CPA had served as the foundation of the profession for over a generation. Accountancy enjoyed an established intellectual content, regulated by the CPA examination, and practitioners who had won their certificate had thus demonstrated their competence to handle accounts and, significantly, to teach at Wharton. In 1919 no other business specialty had had such characteristics, and by 1929, only Huebner's program in insurance successfully negotiated a similar path of development. All of Wharton's professional programs, including insurance, continued to rely on the school's Ph.D. program and the leadership of their senior professors to develop their curricula and to produce a corps of qualified teachers.

Huebner had the energy and intelligence needed to lead Wharton's insurance program and to direct the construction of the CLU apparatus. But beyond his leadership, the basic reason for the great success of the insurance program — both with the CLU and among students at the Wharton School — was the able and dedicated faculty that Huebner had gathered. Huebner "did not tolerate compromise or mediocrity" among his colleagues, and his charismatic style attracted an excellent staff of instructors. He induced some of his best undergraduates to enter academic careers on his staff and also pilfered some of Wharton's best young graduate students who originally happened to be working in other areas. As a group, the insurance professoriate proved to be vigorous teachers, solid administrators, and thoroughly trained scholars. An extraordinarily high percentage of Huebner's 1932 faculty held Ph.D.'s: 11 out of 14 (79 percent), as compared with 40 percent for the entire Wharton School and 26 percent for business schools in general.[28]

The other chairmen, in whom Dean Johnson had placed full responsibility for faculty personnel matters, were clearly not so effective as Huebner in assembling their instructional staffs. In 1919 they all faced the same challenge: Enrollments had doubled from those of the previous year, from 1,100 to 2,100, and Johnson had given them carte blanche to recruit instructors from wherever they could be had. All business schools in the nation were then experiencing a similar explosion in their student populations, a situation that aggravated the chairmen's problems in finding professors. Indeed, they lost a significant portion of their faculty to the competition, and in September 1919 two out of three Wharton instructors were new. Most of the new men on the staff, however, had been at the school before: The chairmen found their most available supply of faculty among their recent undergraduate students and hired them in large numbers. So great was this postwar draft that only in the 1880s had more Wharton graduates entered academic life.[29]

Meeting the faculty shortage with untrained instructors merely substituted one problem for another, and in June 1921 Johnson and his ten department chairmen met to discuss how they could bring their young colleagues up to academic snuff. They decided to require all new, full-time instructors to take at least four hours of graduate instruction a year. They restricted assistant professorships to those with eighteen or more hours of such work, and professorships to those with the Ph.D.* As the new crop of instructors worked their way through the graduate program and into tenured slots on the staff, they became the largest professorial cohort. Since most had done both their undergraduate and graduate degrees at Wharton, they also formed the most ingrown faculty in the history of the school. The cohort that had succeeded Albert S. Bolles and Robert E. Thompson — James, Patten, and J. F. Johnson — had been Midwestern boys who had won their Ph.D.'s at Halle; then had come the group including Faulkner, Lindsay, and Rowe, Wharton graduates who had followed their mentors to Halle for Ph.D.'s; next came Kelsey, King, E. R. Johnson, Mead, Willits, and the Huebners, who had first arrived at Wharton as graduate students. But this group that joined the faculty in the 1920s had attended no educational institution other than Wharton since high school. And for the next thirty-five years this homogeneous group dominated the institution.[30]

The graduate education that they received at Wharton in the 1920s had severe limitations. The decade's huge horde of graduate

---

*Accounting's Moxey objected: The CPA certificate seemed a sufficient credential, while the Ph.D. was superfluous for a professional accountant.

and undergraduate students overwhelmed the senior faculty, denying them time to give close attention to individual members of the Ph.D. program. Moreover, the school had lost its prewar center, Patten's social science. The intellectual vigor, moral power, and theoretical acuity of the school's great economist had stimulated all who had passed through the Ph.D. course, even those who specialized in business areas. Now that he was gone, no one on the staff could replace him. Because of his hostility to exhaustive, in-depth dissertations, Patten had also left behind no institutionalized tradition of rigorous basic research.

Academic responsibility fell to the various department chairmen in the postwar era, and the graduate program thus came under a new kind of direction. Much like rugged entrepreneurs, these men had created their departments and had initiated their academic subjects: They had defined the areas, written the texts, and now hired their teaching staffs and trained them as well. As a result, these chairmen came to identify with their fields and faculty in a deeply personal way. More often than not this intimate acquaintance led them into idiosyncratic, albeit insightful views on their subjects. For the most part they themselves embarked on no research projects that would challenge their perspectives. Wharton's pioneer business professors, while often charismatic figures and great undergraduate lecturers, thus failed to initiate their graduate students into an innovative intellectual life or a broad-ranging research tradition.[31]

The main remnant of Patten's social science to survive and flourish after the war was sociology. Although the social work program was gone, the Wharton Sociology Department entered the 1920s led by Carl Kelsey and James P. Lichtenberger, who both maintained the prewar progressive vision and its commitment to reform. Like Patten, Kelsey assembled arguments against simplistic and reactionary biological models of society and highlighted the limitations in the Malthusian and social-Darwinian conceptions. He and Wharton's other sociologists emphasized the significance of human cooperation, made the common welfare the measure of policy, and concentrated their attention on correcting social problems. Kelsey and Lichtenberger both taught courses on race and immigration, which most Americans in the 1920s viewed as problems, and they soothed anxieties about the influx of foreign elements by emphasizing the virtues of diversity. Lichtenberger wrote that "our sociological generalization, which seems to stand unchallenged, is that heterogeneous populations, because of the diversity of their racial elements, tend towards progressiveness whereas homogeneous populations tend towards conservativism."[32]*

Sociology was not a major and satisfied practically no requirements at Wharton or in the College, and only the ability of its courses to attract large and diverse enrollments kept the program afloat. Aside from Wharton, the department drew students from the College (especially from the Department of Psychology), the School of Education, the Pennsylvania School of Social Work, and local theological seminaries. Only in 1924-25 did the department organize a sociology major, a program that never grew to large dimensions. The discipline survived, but became a peripheral issue to Wharton's economic and business programs. These faculties rarely required their students, especially their Ph.D. candidates, to take work in sociology, and as a result, this aspect of Patten's heritage failed to influence the new professoriate.[33]

Patten's Economics Department, the traditional heart of the Wharton School, had emerged from the war a shell of its former self. Ernest Minor Patterson, who had begun his career in finance, had been named professor of economics and Patten's replacement as chairman in 1919. The economics faculty, still smarting over Patten's forced exit, had at first resented Patterson, but he proved himself a responsible chairman and a capable, if not inspired, economist. He also assumed the presidency of the American

---

*Lichtenberger was referring to the mixture in the United States of the "Mediterranean" and "Nordic" races. He envisioned less amalgamation of the Caucasian and Negro races, observing instead a growing "equilibrium" between the two. These comments, as well as those on relations between native "Nordics" and immigrant "Mediterraneans" were intended to answer common reactionary complaints about the racial composition of the nation.

Maintaining prewar traditions, the department hired new instructors who worked on social problems. In 1920 James H. S. Bossard joined the faculty, took over a basic survey course, "American Social Problems," and taught how various education and welfare agencies could raise the "dependent and defective" classes up from their misery. Thorsten Sellin, who entered the Ph.D. program and worked as an instructor in 1920-21, chose criminology as his specialty. He studied abroad for several years before winning his degree at Penn and taking over the criminology courses in the curriculum. Sellin's work on the culture of crime soon won an international reputation, and his course became an undergraduate favorite.

Academy of Political and Social Science in 1930, when Rowe resigned, and kept the organization vigorous until he stepped down in 1953. As the department reconstituted itself in the years between the wars, however, a young economist, Raymond T. Bye, became the intellectual leader of the department and its foremost theorist.* Although Bye had studied with Patten, he championed the neoclassical tradition, and Alfred Marshall's *Principles*, not Patten's work, became the foundation of theoretical economic thinking at the Wharton School.[34]

Like most devotees of neoclassical theory, Wharton's economists stayed to themselves. They had little interest in practical business, nor did they respect the men without theoretical sophistication who specialized in such pursuits. Completing a Wharton Ph.D. still required courses in economic theory, and these theorists had no qualms about flunking deficient graduate business students—regardless of their standing or successes elsewhere. Of all courses in the doctoral program, the new business faculty had the most trouble with those in economic theory, and many prominent and not-so-prominent members of the faculty never got their Ph.D.'s because of their inability in economics. Such distance and antagonism, unfortunately, now characterized the relationship between the school's dismal scientists and its practical professoriate.[35]

The recession of social science theory from the center of the Wharton program never seemed to trouble Dean Johnson. His own success as a transportation expert, after all, owed little either to the heterodox theories of Patten and the Philadelphia School or to mainstream neoclassicism. Abstractions about "divisions of labor," "weak appetites," and "marginal costs" had had no influence on his work at the Panama Canal Commission or the National Transportation Conference. When setting the tolls on the canal, Johnson had merely extrapolated from preexisting rate schedules, especially those of the Suez Canal. His efforts for the Chamber of Commerce had demanded detailed empirical knowledge of the business interests associated with the nation's railroad

---

*Although Bye wrote an important economics text, neither he nor the department as a whole made a great reputation for theorizing. The interwar period, prior to the late thirties, was not a great era in the development of economic theory, and Wharton's economists did little to change the situation.

system. It was a mastery of factual and procedural detail, and not any theoretical virtuosity, that explained Johnson's prominence, and only by the loosest construction could he be called an "applied" economist.[36]

Johnson let the old unifying force of Patten's theory and ideology fall from the center of the Wharton program, and he gloried in Wharton's impressive array of specialties. But while encouraging the chairmen to develop their various interests, Johnson knew that he had to establish a new mechanism of order: The curriculum of specialties threatened to jumble up into a heap of repetitious and overly detailed courses; as large numbers of students now flocked to Wharton, they needed guides to help them through this maze of offerings and into business life; the persistent demands of the alumni also had to be addressed. According to Johnson, the pedagogy of professional specialization and Wharton's new size demanded reforms in the structure and administration of the school. The dean turned to address these internal problems, and when he did, he became an economist in the ancient Greek sense of the word — a manager of a household unit.[37]

To begin his program of administrative reform, Johnson organized various faculty committees to analyze "the specific needs of different groups and classes of students . . . and adjusting their work to these needs, also to establish a closer personal touch between such students and the faculty." Upon investigating their students, the professors found them to be a tremendously varied group. One-fourth of the freshman class was "tottering on the verge of illiteracy"; at the same time Wharton was admitting, as seniors, liberal arts college graduates who wanted business training. Students were designing programs by themselves, independently of the faculty, and at the end of four years many had accumulated a random series of courses, but not the required credits for graduation in any major.[38]

The surging demand for seats at Wharton gave Johnson the leverage he needed to correct these problems. In 1920 he exploited his new power by taking the "primary management step" of standarizing the student body. First the faculty eliminated the entire class of "special" students, the narrowly pragmatic group that took an abbreviated program of business courses and rarely sampled the arts and sciences of the college. (As recently as five years previous, such students had been the mainstay of the school's constituency, and this action clearly indicated Wharton's new market power.) After eliminating this least "liberal" element in the undergraduate population, the faculty then dealt with those at the other end of the spectrum, the liberal arts undergraduates that the school admitted as seniors. Johnson explained that these young men "cannot get a *technical equipment* at all equal to that of the regular Wharton School student" in just one year. So in 1921 the school removed these students from the undergraduate program and created for them a two-year graduate business course. Similar to Harvard's prestigious Graduate School of Business Administration, the new division awarded the Master of Business Administration degree. But unlike Harvard, which cultivated general leadership skill through the case method, Wharton's new venture offered a stepped-up version of its undergraduate program of specialization. M.B.A. students took 10 out of 28 courses and then wrote a thesis in their major field of study. They worked at a faster pace than the undergraduates, did more original research, and entered the business world with finer "technical equipment" in their specialty. Wharton produced fewer than 500 M.B.A.'s in the entire interwar period, but these college graduates were now much better served than they had been before 1921.[39]*

With the student population thus straightened out, Johnson moved on to the main task at hand, bringing order to the undergraduate program. The dean characterized his strategy as "individualizing" education. He intended this slogan to calm alumni anxieties over the university's supposed trend toward "mass education" — anxious graduates from yesteryear would hopefully recall long chats with mentors and the flowering of their characters. While Johnson shared these goals, he had another understanding of what "individualizing" education could accomplish. While the alumni conjured up visions of liberal cultivation, the dean was still pursuing his original strategy, and he intended his initiatives to help students exploit Wharton's unique opportuni-

---

*Between 1921 and 1932, the M.B.A. program was officially a part of Penn's graduate school and not of Wharton. Thereafter the school had *de jure* as well as *de facto* control of the course. For its own graduates who wanted advanced training and an M.B.A. degree, Wharton required only one year's study. Similar arrangements were usually worked out by graduates of other business or economics programs.

ties for specialized study. His means for achieving this "individualized" program also would have surprised those who would turn the university back into a small and cozy college: Johnson set up a new "administrative organization" to do modern "personnel" work among the students. Personnel offices had become quite fashionable in the world of affairs, but Wharton became the first academic institution with such an administration. The new apparatus was designed to shepherd each undergraduate into a specialty, enforce curricular standards for graduation, and then help the student into a business career. Like bureaucracies in big business, this one at Wharton was designed to facilitate a complex productive process that employed an extensive division of labor.[40]

Johnson's new organization began guiding the flow of students in 1920. Working closely with three young professors in the G & I Department — Chairman Willits, Alfred Williams, and William Hockenberry — the school then set up an "external" placement office called the Industrial Service Department. Johnson put the "internal" personnel work into the hands of a young instructor of accounting, Thomas Budd. Named school registrar in 1920 and rising to vice-dean in 1933, Budd enforced the school's dress code and its curricular standards for graduation; he also made up rosters, kept student records, and offered counsel on personal and academic problems. To facilitate this last function, Budd set up a reporting system similar to those used by scientific managers in industrial enterprises, with instructors sending him monthly reports on how each student was progressing. Thus Budd and his staff would soon know if anyone fell into trouble and could call the young man in for counseling.[41]*

Johnson's administrative reforms worked quite well. Because of these new personnel efforts and the exclusion of special students and liberal arts graduates, the great majority of undergraduates now completed the full four-year program in fine fashion. With the flow of students thus routinized, the departmental chairmen could confidently proceed with their various specialized programs. Johnson was satisfied, and he held up these adminis-

---

*Budd's department also collected general statistical information on the student body: In 1927, for example, Budd reported that the average Wharton student slept seven and one-half hours a day and each week spent twenty-seven hours at his studies and seven hours at extracurricular activities.

trative achievements as the most important contributions of his deanship.[42]

Contentment, however, was not universal, and several professors, especially those in the social sciences and in the G & I Department, took exception to the dean's program. They criticized Johnson's abdication of power to the departmental chairmen and argued that the school had become a collection of academic fiefs, all struggling against each other for students and faculty appointments. His associated emphasis on professional specialization also came under fire. Most business departments, the critics claimed, offered only one or two genuinely useful courses; the rest covered peripheral details or duplicated material taught in other parts of the school. These professors found most of their colleagues with narrow competencies and largely ignorant of work done outside of their fields of specialization. While not the best situation for students who would take jobs in their major fields of study, these reformers claimed that the program did a most serious disservice to graduates who would change careers or who would assume the general responsibilities of running a business enterprise. They supported Johnson's administrative innovations and the order that they brought to Wharton, but they argued that the school's academic program lay in pieces and that the faculty should now develop a more cohesive, integrated curriculum.[43]

The movement to limit specialization and to broaden business education at the school did not, of course, originate in the dean's office. It came from the faculty Curriculum Committee, led by Joseph Willits. In December 1924, Willits's Curriculum Committee issued a wide-ranging policy statement that became Wharton's basic blueprint for reform. It contained a long section that supported the personnel work then under way, and urged the faculty to strengthen and consolidate these efforts under a new "Department of Student Personnel." But its main focus was on the curriculum. The committee began its report by dividing the curriculum into three parts: a "'common core' of 'educational universals' essential to the well-rounded development of all men" and necessary "if business is to attain a more professional spirit"; a "'common core' of 'business fundamentals' which should represent the minumum vocational equipment of every business man"; and "specialization in a man's preferred field of business interest."

The committee thus acknowledged the value of the various technical business subjects, but it wanted to reduce their significance in the curriculum. A Wharton student could then graduate with fewer than 25 percent of his credits in liberal arts and most of the remainder in narrowly defined procedural study. The committee hoped to push the beginning of specialization out of the sophomore and into the junior year and to raise the overall number of required courses in "educational universals" and "business fundamentals." Like Joseph Wharton, Willits and his colleagues aimed at preparing students for general executive responsibilities, not specialized technical professions. Managerial preparation, they believed, ought to provide the center of the school's program, and their call for more education in liberal arts and general business skills likewise reiterated the two parts of the founder's original plan.[44]

Willits and his 1924 committee struck another chord reminiscent of Joseph Wharton's program by placing "science" at the center of their strategy for managerial education. The ironmaster had had great respect for social science, especially that of Henry C. Carey, while his colleagues at the American Social Science Association had had great hopes for such knowledge as a foundation for professional civil service. The Willits Committee followed in this tradition, but placed greater emphasis on hard natural science, and advocated methodological training for its own sake. Moreover, it believed that science *itself* could provide the key to general managerial vision and understanding.

To give entering freshmen "a sense of the relationships between different fields of knowledge [and] a sense of the unity of all knowledge," Willits and his colleagues proposed a new introductory course on the "History of Science and Scientific Ideas."* To the same end, the committee recommended a general reduction in textbook recitations, the favorite pedagogical technique among the business professoriate, in favor of more original student research. This, they hoped, would train Wharton students in the general

method of collection of materials, the recording of such materials in systematic, convenient form for effective use, the orderly arrangement of

*This course was modeled on one of the same title offered at Columbia University.

records and data, the inexorable requirement of ample data over a sufficiently broad range, as a basis of all conclusions, the distinction between primary and secondary sources, also the encouragement of resourcefulness and initiative in discovering new sources of information.

To support this expansion of student research activity, the committee urged the establishment of a large business library. Finally, Willits proposed a capstone "Theory of Business" course, in which seniors would gather together the general scientific principles that they had learned in their various courses and apply them to practical problems. The committee's program would thus establish science as a continuous theme running throughout the Wharton program.[45]

These Curriculum Committee suggestions would limit the influence of the separate departments and thereby the powers of the chairmen. They would push departmental control and specialized study out of the sophomore year; deemphasize the texts that were often written by the chairmen; and establish a general "Theory of Business" capstone course as an alternative to the detailed procedural courses that the chairmen offered as bridges into an occupational specialty. And the assault went further. The committee suggested that the school hire ten senior professors, "primarily for graduate work," to "aid" the chairmen "in the development of our instructors and graduate students who may some day become instructors." But most brazen was a plan to give the reformers control over the specialized curricula. The committee proposed that the school "make a careful inventory of the personal qualities and technical training and information that make for success in the various occupations into which our graduates go . . . [in order to] aid the Curriculum Committee" in designing a suitable program. Thus a "scientific" job analysis reviewed by the Curriculum Committee, and not the personal wisdom and experience of the chairmen, would stand as the final authority over the professional courses. Much like the foremen in industry, the chairmen were now challenged by scientific management; in the name of "science" and greater overall integration, the Willits committee would reduce the scope of their traditional power.[46]

Certain of the committee recommendations won swift approval. Within a few years, the school had a Department of Student Personnel, the Lippincott (business) Library, and an introductory course on the place of science in the modern world entitled "Physical Factors of Civilization." Further changes, however, came much more slowly. The chairmen considered themselves, quite correctly, as experts in their fields and in no need of job analysis to tell them what was important and what was not. With great personal investments in what they were doing, they fought any attempt to reduce the significance of their courses in the curriculum. (Solomon Huebner's biographer reports the frustrated snort of one reformer that "any curriculum is a good curriculum to Sol if it has enough insurance in it.") So the faculty never conducted the job analysis, and Johnson recalled that

the struggle through which we went in revising the Wharton School curriculum had sometimes reminded me of Grant's campaign to capture Richmond. The struggle began with a battle more or less in the Wilderness, and was followed by Spotsylvanias and Cold Harbors where there was bleeding at many wounds, but where no decision was reached. After that it was decided to approach the objective from a different angle, and a long siege followed during which it seemed that little was being accomplished.[47]

The "new angle" in Johnson's remarks referred to a major study of business education conducted between 1929 and 1931. Financed by Willits's Industrial Research Department and directed by two advocates of curricular reform, sociologist James H. S. Bossard and industry professor J. Frederick Dewhurst, the report on *University Education for Business* supported the party of change. The book was nevertheless an impressive piece of research and provided useful documentation for this position. Bossard and Dewhurst reviewed contemporary opinion and reported a strong national consensus favoring the general business curriculum and hostile to specialization. Their most impressive arguments, however came from an in-depth survey of the Wharton alumni. The school's graduates claimed that they had received the most long-run benefit from classes in English and more from general courses than from those in specialized business areas. Bossard and Dewhurst, moreover, found a tremendous amount of change over time in alumni "specialization." Only 1 out of 6 arrived at Wharton with a career in mind, majored in the same specialty, and then actually worked in the field. Only 1 in 3 actualized Dean Johnson's expectations by finding permanent careers in their undergraduate areas of concentration. As fewer Wharton graduates joined family businesses, alumni career patterns became even more fluid. Bossard and Dewhurst concluded, therefore, that "business *per se* constitutes sufficient specialization."[48]

Bossard, Dewhurst, and their colleagues associated the general business curriculum with a greater emphasis on academic values. Their program stressed the authority of "science," more liberal arts courses, and closer ties with the College. They scorned the intellectually trivial, "cookbook" quality of many of the existing courses on business practice. But the party of reform was not entirely academic in its orientation, and their appreciation of the traditional arts and sciences was often more practical than liberal. Specialization was the grand strategy of the university, and these Wharton reformers chose to scrap rather than rehabilitate it. Bossard and Dewhurst used the alumni course evaluations to attack specialization and to justify the general business curriculum, not to promote liberal education: The tremendous acclaim that the alumni had given to courses in English, the only College subject that Wharton students had taken in significant amount, led to no crusade for the humanities; the reformers *would* use alumni distaste for foreign language instruction to remove it as a requirement for a B.S. in Economics. Of all the College subjects, they prized only one, the natural sciences. That the alumni had found little value in their science courses, Bossard and Dewhurst dismissed as evidence of poor teaching or of the inevitable search for "gut" courses. They insisted that "the exploitation of natural resources by means of scientific knowledge is the most conspicuous feature in the history of civilization during the past two centuries. This exploitation of nature constitutes the basis of modern business." They therefore strongly endorsed courses in science for all business students — courses such as the "Physical Basis of Civilization" that had been recommended by the Willits Committee and was being taught by Bossard.[49]

Wharton's professors of the 1920s had a somewhat different understanding of science from the one we have today. The science that they championed had little regard for deductive theory, hypothesis falsification, or mathematical subtlety; it recognized "naught save the suzerainty of fact" and emphasized the collection and correlation of data. This definition of science came in part from engineers like Frederick Taylor and his "scientific" management movement; in part it reflected the stripped-down pragmatism that was then so much in vogue. Coming under these influences, it is not suprising that science became a search for control, not for knowledge per se. Bossard explained that

modern man, applying rigidly the law of cause and effect, evolving control out of understanding and *honoring the latter only as it facilitates the former*, holds himself responsible both for the shaping of his present and the directions of his future. And this is the dominating philosophy of the modern world.

Bossard appropriately concluded his course with a set of lectures on the scientific method entitled "Man's Method of Mastery."[50]

Patten and his fellow progressive reformers had had a similar instrumental vision of science, and the Wharton School's understanding of the subject in the 1920s owed something to the influence of its great prewar economist. But there were differences. Aside from Patten's great regard for deductive theory, he had a powerful, engaged vision of history. Willits, Bossard, Dewhurst, and their colleagues shared many of Patten's values, but they cultivated a "tough-minded" view of affairs and would not allow themselves to embrace Patten's enthusiasms. In fact, they distanced themselves from the "loose thinking and easy generalizations which have characterized the social sciences," preferring instead the example of the engineer who "can be depended upon to work with such precision as to bring two and two together and dovetail them perfectly into four." They would not speculate on the course of history or fashion a "progressive" science; instead they focused on the facts and aimed at some simple adaptation to, and control over, an ever-changing material environment.[51]

Patten's "science" had clearly relied on irrational faith as much as it had on reason. But if Bossard and Dewhurst had been less pragmatic, they might have avoided an embarrassing indignity that grew out of their alumni survey. Their investigation showed that power and income, two excellent indicators of "adaptation" in the business world, came more readily to students who had done poorly in their work at Wharton than to those who had done well. Academic achievement, the survey seemed to be saying, mattered little. So Bossard and Dewhurst, two accomplished scholars, urged their colleagues in the university to stop emphasizing intellect and start giving their students the real tools of success.[52]

In business education circles, a consensus had grown up that "personality" now held the key to successful adaptation in business. Rather than any lack of intelligence or skill, it was the "defects in the attitudes, habits, and traits of college and university graduates which business most frequently emphasizes." For careers in corporate management and marketing, executives needed a "socially effective" personality, one with the ability to control, cooperate, or communicate with people as the situation demanded. Bossard and Dewhurst accepted these propositions, and cultivating personality, along with intellect, became the final core of their program for general business education. The new focus on personality could justify their advocacy of scientific education, because their brand of science was primarily a matter of orderly habits, a new version of the "businesslike" disposition. They also believed that the pedagogy of personality supported more hours in the College and a broader business education, for what could be a better training for all-around "social effectiveness?"[53]*

Curiously enough, viewing general business effectiveness as largely a matter of personality and general intellectual facility helped to reunite the school. The business faculty had always appreciated the value of personal skills in the world of affairs, supported the Department of Student Personnel, and were ready for more work along the same lines. They made great use of class recitations in part because they, like classics professors in the nineteenth-century college, believed that such education built character — the nineteenth-century predecessor of personality which emphasized ego strength, mental discipline and systematic habits. Members of the business faculty also appreciated the need to cultivate flexibility and initiative, and viewed research inves-

*This emphasis on personality also allowed Bossard and Dewhurst to address alumni concerns over the "increasing heterogeneity" of Penn's population. They pointed out that personality was associated with racial background and that Wharton should weigh its admissions policy toward racial types suitable for corporate sales and managerial careers. The school, they added, should also help its other students adjust their personalities to the new corporate dispensation.

tigations as a fine instrument for this pedagogical purpose. Emory Johnson's only intrusion into the curriculum was to revive senior research. Solomon Huebner oversaw the program and, in language reminiscent of Edmund James, wrote that

the spirit of inquiry and the method of approach and realization . . . does more than anything else to make of us creative individuals in thought and action — leaders if you please — instead of floaters on the dead line of routine. It keeps us refreshed in *our business calling*, and helps us to understand that our *particular business* is a growing institution and that we ourselves, by utilizing facts of *our calling* creatively, constitute the power that forces that growth. The power of university graduates to research in the facts . . . is the greatest single power that we can acquire for vocational usefulness and happiness.[54]

General agreement on the centrality of personality and intellect finally facilitated the adoption of a new curriculum. Both reformers and traditionalists concurred that the curriculum needed to instill more discipline and more initiative, and, according to Dean Johnson, such a consensus "prepared the way for ultimate success and genuine peace." On 9 February 1932, the Wharton faculty unanimously voted to standardize the sophomore year, to add some optional work in statistics, to allow students to satisfy their language requirement by examination, and to permit them to choose more freely from among the courses in their majors. The faculty also added four credit hours to the curriculum and restricted the addition of new majors to the program. These were all victories for the reformers. But clearly, little was changed, and the movement for reform was in large measure defeated: The specialized programs remained the basic elements of the Wharton curriculum.[55]*

With the curricular feud now put to rest, Johnson stepped down as dean in 1933. He had been at Wharton for forty years,

*Dean Johnson's role in the curricular struggle cannot be fully fathomed. While clearly committed to the pedagogy of specialization, he presented himself in his autobiography as searching for a compromise between the two factions. However, two members of the current Wharton faculty heard tales of a huge showdown meeting (probably in 1931) that voted for reform by a one-vote margin. Supposedly Johnson then rose and announced that surely the faculty had no intention of denying him his vote simply because he had chaired the meeting. He turned the chair over to the university provost and voted against change. The provost, however, then announced that surely he, in turn, was not to be denied his vote simply because he held the chair. He supposedly cast the deciding ballot for reform, and Johnson thereupon resigned. Unfortunately, the faculty minutes for that year have not been preserved. There was a tie vote on the curriculum in 1931, but contrary to this faculty folktale, Johnson resigned two years later.

since the time of Edmund James, and in one more year he became emeritus. In his own mind he had successfully adapted James's program of specialization to the new conditions in the 1920s. To assume Johnson's responsibilities for the 1930s, however, the university administration decided on a different tack: to lead the school forward, it appointed as dean the major figure in the movement for curricular reform, Joseph Willits.

Source Notes

1. James H. S. Bossard and J. Frederick Dewhurst, *University Education for Business* (Philadelphia: University of Pennsylvania Press, 1931), 283.

2. Emory R. Johnson, *The Life of a University Professor* (Philadelphia: privately printed, 1943), 148–72.

3. George J. Stigler, *Trends in Employment in the Service Industry*, National Bureau of Economic Research Study no. 59 (Princeton: Princeton University Press, 1956), 7, 140; Bossard and Dewhurst, *Education for Business*, 254; Minutes of the Wharton Faculty, 7 May 1917, 7 Jan. 1918.

4. Bossard and Dewhurst, *Education for Business*, 257, 177, 187, 200–201; records of the Wharton Evening School of Accounts and Finance.

5. Edward P. Cheyney, *History of the University of Pennsylvania* (Philadelphia: University of Pennsylvania Press, 1940), 387, 382–88; Who's Who, s.v. "Joseph Wharton Lippincott" and "Bertram H. Lippincott."

6. Reprint from the *Journal of the National Institute of the Social Sciences*, quoted in Thomas L. Haskell, *The Emergence of Professional Social Science* (Urbana: University of Illinois Press, 1977), 233 n. 64; Johnson, *University Professor*, 141, 131–47.

7. Johnson, *University Professor*, 151–52, 154, 161–62; Emory R. Johnson, "Recent Developments of the Wharton School," *Proceedings of the First Annual Conference of the Wharton School* (Philadelphia: Alumni of the Wharton School, 1926), "Wharton School File," Archives, 13; L. B. Hopkins, "Individualizing Education," ibid., 15–20; Thomas A. Budd, "The Department of Student Personnel," ibid., 21–25; Solomon S. Huebner, "Senior Research," ibid., 27–30; Emory R. Johnson, "Undergraduate and Graduate Education in Business at the University of Pennsylvania," ibid., 39–46.

8. Johnson, "Wharton School," 8–9; Emory R. Johnson, "The Wharton School," Minutes of the Wharton Faculty, 5 June 1939, 12; Minutes of the Wharton Faculty, 30 May 1916.

9. Johnson, *University Professor*, 153; Emory R. Johnson, "The Wharton School: 1919–1933," 28 Jan. 1933, "Wharton School File," Archives, 23; interviews with Joseph Willits, Joseph Rose, and Richard Gordon; [Oliver Nelson?], "A History of the Accounting Department of the Wharton School of Finance and Commerce," mimeographed, 1939, files of the Accounting Department, Wharton School; 1980 alumni survey, conducted by the author.

10. Mildred F. Stone, *The Teacher Who Changed an Industry* (Homewood, Ill.: Richard D. Irwin, 1960); [Solomon S. Huebner?], "Insurance and the Insurance Department," typescript, 4 Apr. 1932, "History of the Insurance Department File," files of the Insurance Department, Wharton School; Johnson, *University Professor*, 167–68.

11. Stone, *Teacher*, 124–44.

12. Ibid., 145, 146, 150, 147, 146, 146–47.

13. Ibid., 190, 154–79; interview with Dan M. McGill.

14. Ibid., 172–73, 190, 194–216.

15. Johnson, *University Professor*, 249; Bossard and Dewhurst, *Education for Business*, 45–46, 233, 288, 446–49; Joseph R. Rose, "The Department of Transportation and Public Utilities," mimeographed, 1973.

16. Bossard and Dewhurst, *Education for Business*, 168, 171, 191–93, 205, 211, 212, 285–87.

17. *Catalog of the University of Pennsylvania (1915–16)*, 160, 179; Herbert W. Hess, *Productive Advertising* (Philadelphia: J. B. Lippincott, 1915).

18. Bossard and Dewhurst, *Education for Business*, 418; Herbert W. Hess, *Advertising, Its Economics, Philosophy, and Technique* (Philadelphia: J. B. Lippincott, 1931); Herbert W. Hess, foreword to Herbert W. Hess, ed., "Scientific Distribution — Selling, a Wealth Producing Force," *Annals* 115 (1924):v–viii; Herbert W. Hess, "Selling Distribution and Its New Economics," ibid., 1–7, esp. 5–6; interviews with Reavis Cox and Thomas Cowan.

19. Richard H. Landsburgh, *Industrial Management* (New York: John Wiley & Sons, 1923), 2.

20. Henry R. Towne, "The Engineer as Economist," *Transactions of the American Society of Mechanical Engineers* 7 (1886):428–32; Landsburgh, *Industrial Management*, 32, iii, 34, iii, 20–36; Bossard and Dewhurst, *Education for Business*, 285–87; Daniel Wren, *The Evolution of Management Thought* (New York: Ronald Press, 1972), 86–88, 118–19, 128–33.

21. Ibid., iii, 101, 101–70.

22. Ibid., 21, 37–100, 171–478.

23. Cyril C. Ling, *The Management of Personnel Relations* (Homewood, Ill.: Richard D. Irwin, 1965).

24. Morris L. Cooke, *Our Cities Awake* (New York: Doubleday, Page, 1916), 226; *Dictionary of American Biography*, s.v. "Joseph H. Willits"; Joseph H. Willits, *Steadying Employment* (Philadelphia: American Academy of Political and Social Science, 1916), iii, iv–v, and passim; Ling, *Personnel Relations*, 339, 273–338; Meyer Bloomfield and Joseph H. Willits, eds., "Personnel and Employment Problems in Industrial Management," *Annals* 65 (1916); interviews with Willits and Rodger Evans.

25. Interview with Willits.

26. Landsburgh, *Industrial Management*, 22; Ling, *Personnel Relations*, 350–54, 383; Former Members of the Staff [of the Industrial Research Department], "A Research Program in Retrospect: A Review of the Work of the Industrial Research Department, 1921–1953," mimeographed (Philadelphia: University of Pennsylvania, 1955).

27. Bossard and Dewhurst, *Education for Business*, 512–13; interview with William Hockenberry.

28. Memorial Minute on the Death of Solomon S. Huebner, Minutes of the Wharton Faculty, 5 Oct. 1964; Johnson, "Recent Developments," 9; [Huebner?], "Insurance Department"; Bossard and Dewhurst, *Education for Business*, 523, 526.

29. Bossard and Dewhurst, *Education for Business*, 201, 250; Johnson, *University Professor*, 153; Johnson, "Recent Developments," 9.

30. Minutes of the Wharton Faculty, 2 June 1921.

31. Interview with Simon Kuznets; Bossard and Dewhurst, *Education for Business*, 455–57.

32. James P. Lichtenberger, "The Race-Making Process in the United States" in *University Lectures, 1912–1913* (Philadelphia: University of Pennsylvania Press, 1914); James P. Lichtenberger, *The Development of Social Theory* (New York: Century, 1923); Carl Kelsey, "The Importance of the Physical Basis in the Teaching of Sociology," *Publications of the American Sociological Society* 21 (1927):128–37; *Catalog (1921–22)*, 63; James H. S. Bossard, *The Problems of Social Well-Being* (New York), 4–6. Bossard, along with the profession in general, became uncomfortable with a definition of society's

problem people as "dependent, defective and delinquent." By 1927 he had moved to the vague notion of those who suffered from "social ill-being." Ibid., 6; "James H. S. Bossard File," "Thorsten Sellin File," Archives; James H. S. Bossard, "A History of Sociology at the University of Pennsylvania," *General Magazine and Historical Chronicle* 33 (1930 – 31):420, 508 – 10, 514ff.

33. Bossard, "History of Sociology," 505 – 7; *Catalog* (1924 – 25).

34. Rexford G. Tugwell, "To the Lesser Heights of Morningside," MS memoir, 134, 156; "Ernst Minor Patterson File," "Raymond T. Bye File," Archives; Raymond T. Bye, *Principles of Economics* (New York: F. S. Crofts, 1924); interviews with Hockenberry and Irving Kravis.

35. Interview with Hockenberry.

36. Johnson, *University Professor*, 91 – 92, 109 – 30.

37. Ibid., 148 – 54; see Minutes of the Wharton Faculty, 4 Mar. 1910, for an earlier administrative reform: the organization of standing faculty committees.

38. Minutes of the Wharton Faculty, 20 June 1920, 1 Dec. 1919.

39. Landsburgh, *Industrial Management*, 84; "Recommendations of the Special Committee as to the Curriculum and Degrees for the Graduate Course in Commerce and Finance," Minutes of the Wharton Faculty, 19 Oct. 1920; Johnson, "Recent Developments," 9 – 13; Johnson, *University Professor*, 156.

40. Johnson, "Recent Developments," 10; Hopkins, "Individualizing Education"; Budd, "Department of Student Personnel"; Huebner, "Senior Research"; Johnson, *University Professor*, 155ff; J. A. Livingston and Beverley M. Bowie, "An Outside Look at Wharton," reprinted from *Pennsylvania Gazette* (Jan. 1947):1, 2.

41. Johnson, "Recent Developments," 9 – 14; Budd, "Department of Student Personnel," 21 – 25; Johnson, *University Professor*, 154 – 58; "Thomas A. Budd File," Archives; "Report of the Department of Student Personnel for the Year ended December 1, 1927," "Thomas A. Budd File," Archives.

42. Minutes of the Wharton Faculty, 3 Mar. 1924, 19 Dec. 1924.

43. Bossard and Dewhurst, *Education for Business*, 48 – 49, 108 – 13, 289 – 321, 451 – 57, 463 – 76, 530 – 35.

44. Joseph H. Willits, "Recommendations of the Curriculum Committee," Minutes of the Wharton Faculty, 19 Dec. 1924.

45. Ibid.; Bossard and Dewhurst, *Education for Business*, 491, 512 – 13; Minutes of the Wharton Faculty, 2 Feb. 1925; "The Wharton School in 1925: Reported by the Dean to the President of the University," "Wharton School File," Archives, n.p.

46. Willits, "Recommendations."

47. Stone, *Teacher*, 80 – 81; Emory R. Johnson, "The Wharton School: 1919 – 1933," paper presented at a dinner given by Wharton Faculty, 28 Jan. 1933, to Johnson and Willits, 16, "Wharton School File," Archives; Johnson, *University Professor*, 158 – 61.

48. Bossard and Dewhurst, *Education for Business*, 101 – 10, 171, 225 – 26, 313, vii, 12 – 18; Johnson, *University Professor*, 164.

49. Bossard and Dewhurst, *Education for Business*, 354, 341 – 44; Minutes of the Wharton Faculty, 4 June 1934.

50. James H. S. Bossard, ed., *Man and His World* (Harper & Brothers, 1932), 25, 24, 3 – 28, 673ff.

51. Memorial Minute for Alfred H. Williams, Minutes of the Wharton Faculty, 24 Sept. 1974; Bossard and Dewhurst, *Education for Business*, 469.

52. Ibid., 217.

53. Ibid., 375, 563, 370 – 76, 563 – 67.

54. Solomon Huebner, "Senior Research," 27 – 28; Livingston and Bowie, "Wharton School," 1; Minutes of the Wharton Faculty, 17 Feb. 1922; Bossard

and Dewhurst, *Education for Business*, 370–76; Johnson, *University Professor*, 161.

55. Johnson, "The Wharton School: 1919 – 1933," 15; Minutes of the Wharton Faculty, 9 Feb. 1932; Johnson, *University Professor*, 165, 170; interviews with Richard Clelland and Gordon Keith.

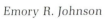

Emory R. Johnson

Ernest M. Patterson

Raymond T. Bye

Carl Kelsey

James P. Lichtenberger

James H. S. Bossard

Edward P. Moxey, Jr.

George A. MacFarland

Herbert W. Hess

Thomas Conway, Jr.

Grover G. Huebner

G. Lloyd Wilson

Solomon S. Huebner

Archives of the University of Pennsylvania

LIFE INSURANCE

A TEXTBOOK

BY

SOLOMON S. HUEBNER, Ph.D.

PROFESSOR OF INSURANCE AND COMMERCE, WHARTON SCHOOL OF FINANCE
AND COMMERCE, UNIVERSITY OF PENNSYLVANIA

*ENDORSED BY THE EDUCATION AND CONSERVATION BUREAU
THE NATIONAL ASSOCIATION OF LIFE UNDERWRITERS*

NEW YORK AND LONDON
D. APPLETON AND COMPANY
1921

CONTENTS

PART I

THE NATURE AND USES OF LIFE INSURANCE

ix

Wharton Insurance Faculty, ca. 1931

HOW THE LIFE-INSURANCE SALESMAN SHOULD VIEW HIS
PROFESSION [1]

An address delivered by the Author before the Annual Meeting of
the Baltimore Life Underwriters Association on February 20,
1915, and before the New York Life Underwriters Association
on February 24, 1915.

Life-insurance "salesmanship" and "profession" are entirely compatible terms; in fact, they should be synonymous.
The time is rapidly drawing near when the cardinal idea underlying every business and vocation shall be service to the
customer or client. On every hand — among physicians, lawyers, teachers, bankers, investment houses, credit men, ex-
porters, brokers and many other groups — there is noticeable a
distinct tendency to organize the component members within
the group into associations with a view to standardizing the
calling and elevating its ethical and utility phases. This is
as it should be and constitutes true progress. It is therefore
with pleasure that I have been following the concerted efforts of life-insurance salesmen to take stock of the standing
of their group in the community and to combat the temptations and meet the problems which are so peculiar to their
calling. During the past year I have had my attention called
to at least a score of able addresses on this subject delivered
by leaders of your vocation. Throughout all I note the same
general line of thought — the advocacy of a high standard of
honor and service. Many speak with a frankness that is perfectly amazing. All refer to the "professional aspects" of
the business. All want it to have the status of a profession
and not that of a mere occupation as regards both the methods
pursued and the quality of service rendered. Practically all,
too, assume that in this way alone can the calling command

[1] This address is based upon the subject matter discussed in the
preceding chapters, and is reprinted to illustrate the way in which
life-insurance salesmen should pursue their profession.
427

Solomon S. Huebner, *Life Insurance,*
title page, first page of contents, first page
of Appendix I

Logan Hall Classroom

Terrace between Logan Hall, Houston Hall, and College Hall

Thomas A. Budd

Lippincott Library, fourth floor, Logan Hall

*Emory R. Johnson handing the office of the dean
to Joseph H. Willits, 30 June 1933*

7

The Institutions of
Industrial Research

When Joseph Willits became dean of the Wharton School in 1933, America's brief age of normalcy had already crumbled into the Great Depression of the 1930s. Dust storms and bankruptcy had swept over the prairies; one of every four workers had no job; and only Franklin Roosevelt's emergency "bank holiday" had saved the financial system from total collapse. With no profit in the land and business enterprise circling its wagons in self-defense, the promise of financial success no longer inspired the nation. Far from providing a guide to the Wharton curriculum, the business system now needed the school to help chart a path to survival, to devise new tools, perspectives, and government policies. But in 1933 the Wharton School had little capacity for generating innovations. Its faculty concentrated on the current practices of business and conjured up few new programs to deal with the catastrophe at hand. Viewing Wharton as a potential physician for the nation's economic ills, Joseph Willits shifted the school's emphasis away from clinical business training and returned to the older academic traditions of Patten and James. These earlier leaders had fashioned social studies into pragmatic sciences through a program of engaged academic scholarship and research. Willits hoped to do the same for the business fields by making academic research in economics "central to our work." Even though the Depression limited his resources, Willits did succeed in raising the level of scholarship in nearly all departments and made the school, in many ways, an institution of applied economics. As a result the Wharton School made important contributions to the management of the American economy and helped bring academic research into the fabric of business affairs.[1]

The Depression's most immediate impact on Wharton was a sharp fall in the student population. In 1934, the school enrolled only 1,669 undergraduates, compared with the norm of 2,200 established in the previous decade. The less affluent high school graduates, as could be expected, felt the impact of the Depression most directly and had to find work, rather than a place in the university. Compared with the previous decade, a greater proportion of Wharton's students in the 1930s joined family firms upon graduation and contributed little or nothing to the cost of their education through part-time work. To fill their emptying classes, the faculty accepted far more applicants who had graduated in the lower half of their high school class, and when many of these students later encountered academic difficulty, the professors showed them unusual tolerance. Enrollments turned up in 1935, and the faculty stiffened admissions requirements to the school in 1937. But the decade as a whole was one of retrenchment, a trying period in which to develop ambitious new programs.[2]

In the university as a whole, the general financial crisis precipitated a dramatic strengthening of the central administration. Even before the onslaught of the Depression, a multiplying complex of administrative offices had given Penn an ill-contrived and unwieldy bureaucratic structure, and many thought that the institution needed more forceful management than it was getting from the Board of Trustees and a soft-spoken academic provost. By 1930 the university's fortunes had turned so sour that the trustees sought out a strong executive to control the affairs of the institution. They created an office of president of the university, upon which they discharged "all executive duties," and gave the job to Thomas S. Gates. A dignified and forceful gentleman, Gates was not an academic, but a Wharton graduate (class of '93) and E. T. Stotesbury's heir at Drexel & Co., the Philadelphia affiliate of J. P. Morgan & Co. The new president so improved the operating efficiency of the institution that the faculty suffered only modest declines in salary, and all parts of the university, including the Wharton School, continued to function.*

Without question, Gates gave Penn its most effective executive leadership since the provostship of Charles C. Harrison. Like Joseph Wharton when he took control of the zinc works, Gates achieved a unity of purpose unattainable as long as a board of directors and other interested parties controlled crucial aspects of the enterprise.[3]

Gates's leadership combined personal charisma with great skill in handling accounts and finance — skills that he had first learned at the Wharton School. Willits, however, believed that "the facts of this depression have stupendous significance to those who are formulating the educational and scientific programs" of the school, and had little interest in training students in such business practices. Although a Wharton Ph.D., Willits himself had never taken courses in finance, accounting, transportation, insurance, or marketing; aside from industry, all of his graduate training had been in social science, especially in economics. As the leader of Wharton's 1920s reformers, Willits had championed the place of science in the business curriculum, and he not surprisingly thought that academic economic science now held the key to solving the nation's crisis. Willits's brand of scientific economics held prewar, progressive moral zeal at arm's length, and took a hard-boiled, matter-of-fact attitude toward affairs. What it offered was a sober view of the external environment of an enterprise — the patterns of price, output, technical change, and the like. Now that the whole economy lay in a wreck, Willits was convinced that the nation's business and political leaders desperately needed such accurate pictures of their surroundings; they could otherwise not proceed. Men who had worked with Willits in Wharton's industry faculty — Rexford Tugwell, Leon Henderson, and Richard Landsburgh — had gone to Washington, D.C.,

---

*While serving as a leader of the alumni, Gates had supported the dismissal of Scott Nearing and had voiced concern over Penn's movement toward "mass education." But as university president, Gates concentrated on financial and administrative matters and his initiatives saved Penn many hundreds of thousands of dollars over the course of the Depression: He consolidated mortgages, improved investments, and took the athletic program out of the hands of free-spending alumni, who had heretofore used it for their private sport. He enforced some "painfully rigid economies" and slowed the pace of academic promotions and appointments. One year he even held back 10 percent of faculty salaries until June, when he saw that the university had sufficient funds to pay its professors.

with Franklin Roosevelt to develop such scientific information on the economy and see to it that it entered the plans of business and government. As for Wharton, Willits believed that

> the world demands . . . that we step up the quality of our understanding of the complex and changing phenomena with which we deal so that the basis for a more stable and better planned society may be present. . . . The quality of product which was adequate before 1929 will not be adequate for the future. Business education should emphasize relationships ahead of mere technical information in order that broad comprehension of our entire economic process shall characterize our graduates. . . . Our scientific contribution to economic understanding must be rated as of major importance.[4]

The Wharton School was far from united behind the new dean and his ambitions. The senior members of the business faculty were inherently conservative men, suspicious of innovation and social science intrusions into business affairs. Because most blamed the economic crisis on loose-minded speculation, the Depression actually strengthened their belief in sober business practice. Many saw Willits and his program for reform as another dangerous speculation, and they resented his attacks on their traditions at the school. The new dean, however, did have his supporters on the faculty. In the year that Willits took office, 1933, seven of his closest allies in the battles over curricular reform* issued an important manifesto on "The Future of Business Education" that marked out the school's new direction.[5]

Continuing Bossard and Dewhurst's complaint, Willits's allies attacked Wharton's specialized programs with unusually strong language. They claimed that "our excessive training in specialized techniques may handicap a man for all but routine work" and that such material "can be learned with greater facility at a trade school." They then sharply accused the proponents of specialization of being "dogmatically certain of the validity of their own opinions, . . . apt to be impatient when differences of opinion arise," and having "a predeliction for political subterfuge" and an

---

*Alfred H. Williams and C. Canby Balderston of industry, Clarence N. Callender of law; C. Arthur Kulp and Harry J. Loman of insurance, and W. C. Schluter and F. Cyril James of finance. All of these men became leaders of the school during Willits's regime; Williams, Balderston, and Kulp succeeded Willits as dean and together the four men occupied the office for the twenty-four years between 1933 and 1957.

"attitude in regard to business problems . . . of complete amorality." Despite this obvious continuation of old conflicts, the authors of the "Future of Business Education" now concentrated primarily on bolstering Willits in his new embrace of the academy. Willits and his "generalist" party had always been closer to the university than the advocates of specialization, but they now quit justifying academic values on the narrow grounds of their professional utility. They explicitly differentiated the business school from the world of business, and announced that "it is precisely because teachers are not businessmen that they have created the enduring and priceless traditions of this and every other great institution of learning." Business education, the seven claimed, should stand as

the direct descendant of the finest traditions of education in the past . . . [which] attempt to orient the student to the environment in which his life would be cast. . . . [I]n a world so dominated by economic and social problems as that in which we live, business education, properly conceived, represents a far more satisfactory adaptation of the individual to his environment than that which is offered either by training in the liberal arts or in the physical sciences.

Willits and his supporters thus viewed education pragmatically, as a help in adaptation to the surrounding conditions of life. But they insisted that business education "is emphatically not a trade school routine." Similar to the education offered in the liberal arts college, they proposed a brand of business education "in which a preponderant part of the student's time is spent in developing an understanding of the economic and social structure of the world, in attaining an appreciation of the functions of business activity and the implications of current economic ideals." From this perspective, the most serious charge that the reformers now laid at the door of their opponents was that they lacked "sympathy with and appreciation of a liberal education."[6]

When he was serving as chairman of the Curriculum Committee in the 1920s, Willits's major goal had been to standardize the curriculum and to prepare students for careers as general business executives. As dean of the school, Willits now embarked on a vigorous program to enhance Wharton's level of academic achievement, emphasizing the cultivation of knowledge rather than preparing students for future employment. He told the faculty that "the confusions of the last two decades in our national life and in the world of affairs have stressed once more the importance of the person capable and worthy of *intellectual* leadership, whether in business, government, or academic circles." Believing that Wharton ought to develop special programs for academically talented students, the dean set up a committee, headed by F. Cyril James, to design a new honors course. This committee proposed a program of advanced training in economics and a series of honors seminars, but conservative members of the faculty objected to the additional work in social science and the apparent independence of this course from the rest of the school. Willits assured the faculty that the honors program would not begin until "new money" appeared to support it, that no such resources were on the horizon, and that only a small number of students would ever participate. With Willits's explanations, the faculty approved the program in a secret ballot and sent the dean shopping for funds at the Carnegie and Rockefeller Foundations.[7]

Willits's emphasis on academics made the professoriate the crucial issue, and aside from establishing this honors program the dean concentrated on improving the Wharton faculty. He had far less interest in curriculum, student "personality," and administrative control — the major focus of the 1920s. As "The Future of Business Education" declared,

an educational institution, unlike many other types of enterprise, cannot by means of a hierarchy of authority, create and maintain control over the quality of its output. Administrative machinery is, of course, necessary but it possesses no value apart from the purpose it serves — to facilitate teaching and scholarship. . . . Teachers are the only permanent university, and without their devotion to duty, their love of learning, their desire to transmit learning, the university resolves itself into nothing other than a group of more or less picturesque buildings.

In evaluating the quality of faculty members, Willits placed special emphasis on those "nonteaching" activities that kept the school's professors alive to the development and application of knowledge in their fields. He thought government and business experience quite valuable, especially in certain areas of study. But the most important activity of modern faculty members, he wrote, was "in improving scholarly mastery of their fields or in contributing to the advance of scientific knowledge." The central theme of Willits's tenure as dean was to make such pursuits the foundation of the institution.[8]

Joseph Wharton had not originally seen the production of knowledge as an essential function of his new school. He had defined its role as that of teaching business skills and social science, leaving Edmund James to introduce research to the school when he redesigned Wharton along German lines. Under Simon Patten, the school developed a successful Ph.D. program, one that required each graduate to produce an original piece of research. But as a professional school, utility, not idle curiosity, motivated Wharton's scholarship; the school cultivated a specific brand of knowledge — the kind that helped solve practical problems. This necessary association with the world of affairs had always presented researchers at Wharton with several serious difficulties. Political conflicts and vested economic interests surrounded their objects of study and intruded on the objectivity of their investigations. The continuous press of problems to be solved, whether child labor or confusion and failure in the railroad industry, allowed little time for careful exploration and debate. Moreover, the basic subject matter of the school, the institutions and practices of business and government, were in continual change, with neither telos nor equilibrium in view. Patten's response to these dilemmas was to encourage his colleagues to focus on the affairs of the day and conduct investigations of immediate public value. Responsibility for basic social science research he referred to large, well-staffed organizations independent of universities, such as the New York Bureau of Municipal Research.

During its first half-century, the Wharton School's major contributions to business and social understanding were its textbooks, not its research publications. These texts provided useful overviews and compendia of current practice; they were never vehicles for communicating basic research. Wharton's professors periodically revised their texts, but new editions reflected changes in the world of business and politics more than any advance in understanding. The very importance of textbook writing and revising at Wharton, in fact, illustrated the passive role of scholarship in the development of new policies and techniques: The methods and institutions of businessmen and politicians changed without much reliance on academic research, and the basic function of the Wharton School was to help students understand this independently evolving environment and to train them in its latest procedures.

When Willits became dean in 1933, the faculty of the Wharton School did hardly any basic research. Half kept up with current business practices by consulting or by operating businesses of their own, but only 1 out of 6 pursued scholarly investigations. The man who made the greatest career out of the business of research, in fact, was Joseph Willits himself. In 1921 he and Ann Bezanson, a young Harvard Ph.D. in economic history, had organized at Wharton a research institute known as the Industrial Research Department. Both had worked as personnel officers during the turbulent years of the First World War, had been appalled at the turnover, instability, and general confusion in American labor markets, and had resolved that the nation should never again enter such a crisis with so little understanding of how its economy works. The two founders of the IRD had also brought to their program a moral commitment to ameliorative social change. Willits and Bezanson had believed that working out a mutually acceptable relationship between industrial labor and industrial management was "the greatest experiment in government" then facing the nation. They had then designed an ambitious program of research to both illuminate and help civilize the conditions of industrial work. Various philanthropic foundations, especially the Rockefeller, had given their new department its initial backing, and business, labor groups, government, and the university soon added their support. So successful was the IRD that by 1929 it had a budget of over $110,000, larger than either the Wharton evening or extension programs. The organization that Willits and Bezanson had established thus resembled those large, independent research organizations that Patten had so admired. As the director of such an impressive enterprise, Willits had by then also become a national spokesman for academic business research.[9]

During the 1920s, fully half of the nation's leading business schools had established "bureaus of business research." Most of these, however, were much smaller affairs than the IRD and, following the lead of Harvard's Bureau of Business Research, limited themselves to collecting case studies for teaching purposes. At an important meeting of business educators in 1926,

Willits frankly accused these bureaus of engaging in "kinds of fact-gathering which are hardly to be called research at all." He told the assembly that

just as a medical school, or any other professional school worth the name, is not performing its full function unless it is contributing to thorough-going research on the fundamental problems in the field of medicine, so should a . . . school of business aim to contribute its share toward the solution of the fundamental problems of business.

Quite naturally, Willits suggested that Wharton's sister institutions found research organizations like the IRD. He believed that "the solution of the fundamental problems of business" lay in "group thinking," and that

the day is not past, but it is certainly very rapidly passing when the major contribution to research in this field will be made by lone workers working within the limitations of experience and capacity, if not the resources, of single individuals. Such research tends to partake too much of opinion and too little of fact. The "research philosophy" of the IRD was that fundamental research in the social sciences . . . can best be performed by establishing a center for a small community of research scholars who engage in continuous work in depth over a period of years within relatively narrow but significant research areas . . . [and that] research should be the major professional activity of the staff, who should work together in a center administered independently of the teaching departments.

As it had come in commodity production, Willits would bring "industrialization" to the process of academic discovery. The IRD, he believed, could support and organize effort so complex and intensive that it far surpassed the capabilities of any individual.[10]

The future dean earned a reputation at the IRD as a research manager, not as an investigator. Although Willits did some research, his major activities after seeing the department established were to find funds and projects, to organize its activities, and to advise its investigators on the course of their work. But being a very busy man, who also taught courses and chaired the Wharton Curriculum Committee and the Geography and Industry Department, Willits placed much of the actual management of the IRD on the shoulders of Ann Bezanson, its codirector. She proved to be an efficient researcher as well as a fine administrator. In the early part of the 1920s she produced an important series of studies on the traditional issues in personnel — turnover, worker amenities, and accident prevention. Later in the decade she began a massive, two-decade undertaking that in the end produced one of the foundation-pieces of modern scholarship in economic history: her five-volume history of prices in Philadelphia between 1720 and 1896.[11]

While working on her price history, Bezanson also guided a series of industry studies which became the major program of the IRD in the 1920s. She and Willits believed that "topical research [on issues such as turnover or unemployment] had major shortcomings if divorced from an economic complex and that a new perspective could only be obtained by using the *industry* as a focus for research." Industries seemed to capture a well-defined economic "whole," satisfying Willits's general managerial taste; as the immediate external environment of the firm, industries were also the meat and potatoes of institutional economics. By dividing the labor of research along industry lines, the IRD was thus able to reap the benefits of specialization without abandoning the perspective of either the generalist or the economist. So Willits and Bezanson assigned the major research responsibilities in each industry to one investigator who, with Bezanson's supervision, surveyed labor conditions, capital equipment, physical output, and final demand.[12]*

*The industries that they chose, or that came to the IRD, were all fiercely competitive, labor intensive, and geographically concentrated in or near Philadelphia. These were the local trades with the most serious economic and labor difficulties, and the ones least able to deal with them effectively: In 1922 the U.S. Coal Commission "drafted" Willits, Bezanson, Waldo Fisher, and three other members of the IRD staff to study the bitter industrial relations in the industry. They wrote seven chapters in the commission's final report, *What the Coal Commission Found*, and in the process became experts on the problems of the industry. Fisher continued to specialize in this area and authored additional studies on costs, sales, price fixing, and labor conditions. In 1926 a group of hard-fisted entrepreneurs, the Philadelphia Metal Manufacturers Association, cooperated with the IRD on a series of studies on its labor market. Members of the staff produced statistical surveys of turnover, wages, job classification, and output in the Philadelphia metal trades, but never developed a close working relationship with the industry. The IRD did develop such a relationship with the woolen textile industry, where Hiram S. Davis studied the trade for over a decade and authored or coauthored over a dozen publications. He focused primarily on output and equipment, rather than the IRD's traditional concern with labor issues, and when the National Association of Wool Manufacturers established a department to collect trade statistics, they proceeded on the foundation that Davis had established.

The most significant industrial work done at the IRD was that of George W. Taylor on the full-fashion hosiery (women's silk stocking) trade. The nephew of a manufacturer from the Kensington section of Philadelphia, Taylor had graduated from Wharton with a B.S. in 1923 and then entered the school's Ph.D. program. He wrote his dissertation on the full-fashion hosiery industry, then Philadelphia's largest and fastest-growing employer: The annual production of the industry had increased 250 percent between 1919 and 1928, and well over half its capacity was located in Philadelphia and nearby Reading. But this trade, like other textile manufacturing, rapidly began moving south, and when the Depression arrived, the Philadelphia industry faced a major crisis. In his dissertation and other publications, Taylor charted the course of the industry, its stock of equipment, inventories, seasonality, and output. But like most of his colleagues at the IRD he was primarily interested in its labor relations, and he explored the gyrations of the hosiery trade because he shared the philosophy of the department that

individual industrial conditions are a part of a "total situation" that is changing constantly. The status of employee earnings, for instance, can be understood only if the production tendencies and the price situation are comprehended, as well as numerous other factors that make up the "total situation" of the hosiery industry.[13]

Taylor's major concern, throughout his career, was the challenge that industrialization presented to peace and democracy in the United States. Born into a manufacturer's family, he had witnessed as a child a good deal of violence between labor and management; like Willits, he had also come to see industrial relations as the great arena of political experimentation in the United States. Taylor believed in private enterprise as the foundation of freedom and democracy. However, he thought that wageworkers in large manufacturing plants had lost a crucial measure of control over their livelihood, and thereby their independent social standing and human dignity. The militant posture of American business in the 1920s — breaking up independent unions and substituting company organizations in their stead — only aggravated the precarious political situation in industry. Taylor was convinced that workers had a basic right to organize independent unions and to strike to protect their interests. He also believed that labor and management shared the fundamental goals of stability and prosperity in their trade, and that these common interests provided the basic conditions for an accomodation. He believed that legitimate economic differences could be harmonized peacefully in America, because unlike other societies, America was "fundamentally a meeting of the minds civilization." The ultimate purpose of Taylor's research and his later activities was to support a "meeting of the minds" in industry.[14]

Taylor himself soon became actively involved in establishing such a collective bargaining process in the hosiery trade. In 1929 hosiery became the first national industry to follow the example of the New York needle trades and set up a collective bargaining procedure with an "impartial chairman" to arbitrate grievances. Taylor's research supported the vital "fact-finding" process of such arbitration, and in 1931 he himself became the "impartial chairman" of the industry. Economic conditions in the hosiery trade were already quite critical in 1931, with a bloody strike under way at the nearby Aberle Hosiery Mills. Taylor helped end this strike, the first of more than two thousand he would help settle, and worked hard to find a way to keep the industry operating in the face of the huge falloff in demand. In some cases he facilitated a reduction in wages that allowed plants to continue in production; in others he failed to find an accommodation, workers struck, and companies shut down. His experience, however, convinced Taylor of the practical value of the IRD philosophy: that only long-term, in-depth study of the economics of a particular industry provided the knowledge essential for understanding labor conditions. To insure this close familiarity with material conditions in the industry, Taylor advocated a policy of continuous communication between labor and management, even after a contract had been signed. The impartial chairman could thereby facilitate a real meeting of the minds in industry, and not just pass judgment on disputes over contractual provisions. As he wrote,

ad hoc arbitration should be looked upon, at best, as a transitory method and as entailing disadvantages that outweigh its advantages to labor, management, and arbitrators. As a support for industrial relations stability, a permanent arbitrator is a prime requisite. Out of a continuing relationship, consistent policy and mutually acceptable procedures can gradually be evolved.

Teaching these principles to his students at Wharton, Taylor became the fountainhead of a major American collective bargaining tradition.[15]

The Industrial Research Department had thus served the interests of scholarship and the public far better than any other part of the Wharton School. It had given Dean Willits valuable experience in research, research administration, and in the uses of scholarly investigation in the world of affairs. But Willits could not rely on the IRD to raise Wharton's general level of academic achievement, because the organization had not developed close ties with the rest of the school. The department viewed economic research as a full-time occupation, and most of its workers did no teaching. Nor did they see many Wharton Ph.D. students, since the department chairmen ran their own graduate programs. Aside from its important connection with the Department of Geography and Industry, the IRD "was not successful in imparting knowledge of research methods on a broader scale."[16]

The basic problem that Willits faced as dean in the 1930s was that the school's young faculty and their chairmen-mentors placed little value on scholarship and research. And since Emory Johnson had long ago granted the chairmen control over hiring and promotion, Willits inherited no "handle" with which to do some remedial "personnel work" among the faculty. At the time that Willits became dean, however, the powerful Educational Council of the university was also quite anxious about the quality of the university's professoriate. In November 1933, after a period of deliberation, the council called on all schools in the university to establish new "standards of faculty personnel." The council urged each school to define minimum qualifications for each rank, and to set up

a committee . . . to consider any appointment or promotion. . . . That more care be exercised in recruiting. . . . That the dangers of excessive inbreeding be guarded against. . . . That whenever necessary departments be strengthened by the addition of able men from outside. . . . That unsatisfactory members of the faculty below the rank of full professors be systematically eliminated from the staff.

The authors of "The Future of Business Education" joined this chorus "for defining and raising the standards of faculty selection, promotion, and retirement." With such support, Willits proceeded to change the old rules of faculty tenure, and equipped himself with the means of reforming the faculty.[17]

In October 1933, even before the Educational Council of the university had issued its final report, Willits won faculty approval at the Wharton School for a new Committee on Faculty Personnel. Willits appointed Harry Loman chairman of this committee, and by the spring of 1934 it had devised a new set of "rules and procedures of the Wharton School . . . for appointments, promotions and advancements of members of its staff." When compared to the regulations that the school had adopted in 1921, the new standards appeared especially striking. Loman's committee made "a Ph.D. degree or its equivalent . . . and . . . promise of continued progress and intellectual growth" necessary for appointment as an assistant professor; an associate needed "distinction in his chosen field"; and a full professor had to show "exceptional ability." In 1921 only a full professor had needed the Ph.D. The 1934 regulations, moreover, stipulated that the dean of the school and the Committee on Faculty Personnel review all appointments and promotion before they were sent on for approval to the final university authorities. This combination of stiffer academic requirements and careful review marked an important shift in the conditions of faculty success, taking a great deal of discretion out of the hands of the department chairmen. Although the committee rarely objected to proposed appointments and promotions, the chairmen now rarely nominated unqualified candidates. Looking back on his tenure as dean, Willits was as proud of establishing this Faculty Personnel Committee as Johnson had been of setting up the Department of Student Personnel.[18]

As important as the Committee on Faculty Personnel in improving the academic quality of the school were the new faculty members that Willits himself was able to hire. The school had few openings during the Depression decade, but when they occurred Willits often broke with Wharton's recent wont of hiring its own, went outside the university, and hired the excellent scholars then available in the academic marketplace. Clearly the greatest hiring coup of Willits's tenure was securing Simon Kuznets, the great economic statistician associated with the National Bureau of Economic Research (NBER) in New York. A Jew born in Russia in 1901, Kuznets had come to the United States early in life and had been educated at Columbia University. Earning his Ph.D. in economics under Wesley C. Mitchell in 1926, he had immediately thereafter joined his mentor at the NBER. Kuznets had also begun teaching at Wharton on a part-time basis in the final years of the Johnson regime. Stuart Rice, Wharton's well-connected sociologist and promoter of statistical research, had arranged for Kuznets to commute from New York and teach some courses in the school's floundering new statistics program. Johnson had given him a series of one-year contracts and, offering him a bit of well-intentioned advice, urged him to emulate the career of Solomon Huebner.[19]

Kuznets, however, was a creature of the NBER and had no particular interest in uplifting the business professions. His ambitions were more in line with those of Joseph Willits — to do research in order to establish a clearer picture of the American economy. Kuznets's area of research was the entire national economy, and what IRD researchers had done for their various industries, he did for the whole system. He created reliable statistical data on national output, prices, investment, and capital stock; he also measured the seasonality, cycles, and secular trends of these phenomena. In his *National Income and Its Composition, 1919-1938* and in his preliminary reports, Kuznets laid out what became the standard procedures for defining, measuring, and subdividing "Gross National Product." He presented estimates of current G.N.P. and for the national output over the past twenty years; by 1946 he had pushed back his measurements to 1869 and then led an international effort, the International Association for Research in Income and Wealth, to devise reliable statistical information on all national economies in the world. For this enormously consequential contribution, Kuznets was awarded the Nobel Prize in economics in 1971.[20]

Willits, who served as president of the NBER in 1933 and as chairman of its board and its executive director between 1936 and 1939, had an opportunity to see and appreciate firsthand the work that Kuznets was doing. Upon becoming dean, he immediately gave Kuznets a three-year contract at Wharton and quickly promoted him from assistant to full professor, all the while allowing him to continue his work at the NBER in New York. At Wharton, Kuznets taught only graduate students, the first member of the faculty to do so. Serious students sought out his classes and, because he spoke with a gentle voice, they fought for seats at the front of the room so as to make out his words. They battled for a place because there, more than anywhere else at the Wharton School, master's and doctoral candidates could learn sophisticated research methods. Kuznets also trained an important corps of economic statisticians, including J. Parker Bursk, Morris Hamburg, and Richard Easterlin, who remained at Wharton with Kuznets and became fixtures at the school. In the 1890s, when Roland Post Faulkner had been on the faculty, Wharton had been one of the nation's leading university centers for statistical work on the economy; the addition of Kuznets restored the school to this position.[21]

Willits's greatest success in reforming existing conditions at Wharton came in the field of marketing, the area at the school with the least claim to academic respectability. Herbert Hess and his colleagues in merchandising were enthusiastic and popular teachers. But with little scholarly research or sophisticated procedure to pass on to their students, they primarily gave instruction in the "how-to-do-it" of advertising and retail selling. As in the case of Kuznets, Willits went to Columbia University, an outside institution, to find a new leader for the field at Wharton. Roswell McCrea, now the de facto dean of Columbia's business school, recommended a young man named Reavis Cox for the job. Cox had originally gone to New York to become a journalist, had then specialized in business reporting, and to advance his career had entered Columbia's School of Business. There, however, he had become enamored of the study of economics and had decided on an academic life. Cox wrote a dissertation on "Competition in the American Tobacco Industry, 1911-1932," and joined Columbia's instructional staff. His thesis was just the type of long-term, detailed research on an industry that Willits and his IRD held in great esteem. With these research interests and a strong letter from Roswell McCrea, Cox became Willits's clear choice to redirect the school's work in marketing.[22]

When Cox arrived at Wharton in 1935, he was made chairman of a specially created "Marketing" Department. His new unit absorbed Hess's merchandising operation and included two "commerce" professors from Johnson's old Department of Commerce and Transportation. The appointment of a man only thirty-five years of age and without reputation to a position of such extensive authority made many people unhappy. Cox had just finished a dissertation that was not even in the field of marketing; he had taught just a few courses in the subject at Columbia, where he had held the lowly rank of instructor; and he had been hired only because the dean wanted to bring an economist's perspective and a researcher's interest to the field, qualities neither shared nor admired by the existing group in merchandising. Making matters more difficult, Cox's department included Hess, now demoted from the rank of chairman, and the "personnel" problems that Willits hoped to soon see eliminated. The bitter economic situation in the country prevented any wholesale firings, but the new guidelines for promotion limited the avenues for advancement for the less academically inclined. Members of the faculty, many of whom were quite able at merchandising, soon found better opportunities in local businesses, and Cox accepted resignations as quickly as they were offered.[23]

One Wharton professor in the new Marketing Department, Ralph F. Breyer, did have a serious academic approach to his subject. One of the refugees from the Commerce and Transportation Department, Breyer had earned his Ph.D. at Penn and then had gone on to produce some of the most innovative economic research on the marketing process. Like Cox, Kuznets, and the members of the IRD, Breyer was an institutional economist who dispensed with neoclassical economic theory and concentrated on developing clear pictures of complex economic structures. He chose as his focus of research marketing "channels," or the succession of agents that handled the flow of goods from the raw material producer to the final consumer. Devoting tremendous archival research to his task, Breyer had produced a series of fundamental studies of the marketing channels of different commodities. But despite these academic achievements, Breyer could not have been Willits's man to take administrative control of marketing studies. Soon after he had begun his career he had suddenly gone deaf, a disability that had destroyed his interpersonal effectiveness. On a more academic plane, however, he had a decisive leadership role and his "channels" approach became the mainstay of marketing studies at Wharton. Cox's subsequent output, including his important studies of installment buying, the marketing of house-building materials, and his major work on *Distribution in a High-Level Economy*, all followed Breyer's lead and investigated the actual channels of economic flow. Many of Wharton's finest doctoral students in marketing also did their dissertation research on commercial channels.[24]

As the Depression eased in the late 1930s and enrollments grew, Willits bolstered more business departments, hiring other scholars with academic economic orientations. Of all the professional faculty, aside from his own colleagues in G & I, Willits had been happiest with certain members of the Department of Finance. F. Cyril James, Wharton's noted financial historian and expert on the economics of money and credit, offered what Willits considered exemplary instruction. James, however, left Wharton at the end of the Depression decade, and to replace him Willits helped hire C. Ray Whittlesey from Princeton University. A bright, enthusiastic, and well-trained economist, Whittlesey was committed to academic research and learning and he quickly became a leader of his department. Other faculty added during Willits's regime included Joseph Rose, who had entered Wharton's graduate school while working with the state Public Service Commission. A fine economist, Rose became the school's able professor of public utilities in its new Department of Transportation and Foreign Commerce (the rump of Emory Johnson's old unit after the creation of the Department of Marketing). Bernard Cataldo, son of a South Philadelphia businessman and graduate of the university's law school, joined the business law faculty in 1936. Charming and erudite, he soon became the favorite of both faculty and students alike. Only the Insurance Department, with its powerful chairman and able faculty, and Accounting, the essential practice-oriented program at the school, were not strengthened during the 1930s with the addition of such academically inclined faculty.[25]

Despite the Depression, Willits was thus able to change the nature of Wharton's "faculty personnel" and had some success in making economics "central to our work." As previously mentioned, he also believed that the school, with its growing strength in applied economics, had a great contribution to make in dealing with the economic crisis. Faculty with a commitment to empirical research could develop reliable pictures of the nation's economic situation, information that Willits considered absolutely essential to those responsible for forming policy. Because of their experience in handling statistical and institutional data, Wharton's faculty and students were also equipped to make policy on a large scale. In his first year as dean, 1933-34, Willits thus began several programs designed to bring the resources of the Wharton School to bear on the problems of the nation. Quite naturally, these programs were intended to strengthen ties between Wharton and government. The Depression was clearly a systemic crisis, within the responsibilities of the state. The catastrophe, moreover, had drastically reduced the ability of business enterprises and voluntary organizations to influence events, and only government remained with any significant freedom of action.

When Willits became dean, the school no longer enjoyed the close engagement with public issues that it had had during the James and Patten eras. The American Academy still served as a bridge between academics and the world of affairs, and members of the Wharton faculty still monopolized its leadership positions. But during the interwar period, the academy no longer occupied an important place in the affairs of the school. The Political Science Department, which had been so active in state and local affairs before the war, had lost much of its former vitality. Professor of Municipal Government Leo Rowe had resigned in 1920; the energetic Clyde King had spent much of the decade in distinguished public service, but away from the university. Upon becoming dean, Willits made it a goal of his administration to reestablish close ties with government. It was "obvious" to him that "the public service is not only expanding as a professional opportunity but is also destined to play a very much more influential part in our economic and social affairs."[26]

In October 1933, the faculty approved Willits's plan for monthly assemblies where the entire school would gather and hear prominent statesmen address the problems of the nation. Willits scheduled these assemblies in Irvine Auditorium, the university's mammoth new hall, and insured a large attendance by holding these meetings in the middle of the day and cancelling all competing classes. Typically, 1,500 to 2,500 auditors turned out while some of the most respected actors on the national stage, especially those involved in designing Franklin Roosevelt's New Deal, responded to Wharton's invitation to come and explain their programs. At the first "Wharton Assembly," held on 12 December 1933, the general counsel for the National Recovery Administration, Donald Richberg, explained Roosevelt's controversial scheme for cartelizing the economy. In the years that followed, speakers such as Adolph Berle, Harold Ickes, Ralph Flanders, James Warburg, and Chester Barnard presented their policy ideas before the school. During the 1934 electoral campaign the Assembly hosted a debate on the New Deal, which the chairman of the Columbia Broadcasting System, Wharton alumnus William Paley, carried on his radio network. Willits was justifiably proud of this nationally recognized program. He believed that it brought serious public issues before the school, provided a common basis of discussion, and gave insight into the direction of economic society. In the 1930s these "Wharton Assemblies" came to have a position in the life of the school akin to that of the chapel services led by Robert Ellis Thompson, James's American Academy meetings, Patten's seminar, or Scott Nearing's survey course. It housed Wharton's commitment to moral economic leadership, now in a time of reconstruction rather than in the initial organization of America's urban, industrial economy.[27]*

In addition to the Wharton Assembly program, which helped push public issues to a central position at the school, Willits attempted to get the Wharton School directly involved in the public policymaking process. He appointed a committee "to study and report upon the University's obligation, both educational and scientific, to the public service and the most effective methods of discharging that obligation." This committee proposed that the school develop a strong curriculum and a research institute in state and local government operations, Wharton's forte in the days of James, Rowe, and the National Municipal League. Lack of funds and a cautious attitude on the part of the Curriculum Com-

---

*A Mrs. Howard Crawley endowed the Assemblies in 1938 and they were thereafter known as the "Crawley Lectures."

mittee, however, produced an austere Bureau of Public Affairs. Funded at a modest $2,500 a year, this bureau merely placed students in government internships, announced public information on employment and research opportunities, and explored the possibility of offering advanced training to government officials. The effort, however, bore some fruit, since a total of thirty-four members of the Wharton faculty were working on state, local, and federal government projects by the end of the 1934-35 academic year.[28]

Still seeking to establish a significant program in state and local government, Willits soon found the ear of Philadelphia's wealthy soap manufacturer and philanthropist, Samuel S. Fels. Fels believed quite strongly that efficient local government, with thoroughly trained civil servants, was essential for the survival of American democracy. He had been an original member of Philadelphia's prestigious civic reform organization, the Committee of Seventy, a founder and director of the city's Bureau of Municipal Research, and an officer of the National Municipal League. Assured of Fels's interest, Willits organized a series of conferences in the early part of 1936 to work out an academic program in state and local government. The dean then drew up a proposal for a multifaceted enterprise, offering a variety of educational, research, consulting, and conferencing services. The philanthropist liked the design, and his Samuel S. Fels Fund anonymously gave the Wharton School forty thousand dollars a year for six years to support an Institute for Local and State Government.* Pleased with its success after six years, Fels increased his support; when he died in 1950, the organization became the Fels Institute of Local and State Government and it inherited its sponsor's spacious house at Thirty-ninth and Walnut Streets. The Fels Fund continued to increase the Institute's substantial subsidy, and by 1966 provided $240,000 out of a total annual budget of $268,500.[29]

---

*From the opening of the Institute in 1937, and for the next thirty years, Stephen Binnington Sweeney directed the Fels Institute. Sweeney had finished his Wharton B.S. in Economics in 1922, his Ph.D. in 1927, and stayed on as a regular member of Solomon Huebner's insurance faculty. Sweeney had then left the university, becoming the first director of Pennsylvania's workman's compensation program and then working as assistant state administrator of the Works Progress Administration. With roots in both the Wharton School and local government, Sweeney proved to be an excellent choice for director of the Institute. In time, he made it one of the leading university programs of its type in the nation.

Eventually the institute would operate in all areas that Willits originally proposed (research, education, consulting, and conferencing), but at first it concentrated on placing research skills at the service of civic leaders. In 1937 both Samuel Fels and university president Thomas S. Gates sat on the Philadelphia City Charter Commission, and they employed the new organization to investigate city-state relationships. Gates also chaired the Philadelphia Advisory Finance Commission, charged with the task of sorting out why Philadelphia's bonds were then selling at a significant discount. The institute again provided research services, producing a financial history of the city and an analysis of its various operating departments and revenue sources. Although criticizing Philadelphia's methods of tax collecting, debt structure, and control over expenses, the Wharton group also noted the stability of the city's industrial base and proposed a series of fiscal reforms. Apparently as a result of their reports, the price of Philadelphia's bonds rose, relieving the city's anxious creditors and reducing the burden of interest payments on its new obligations.[30]

Although successful in strengthening ties between the Wharton School and government and raising the efficiency of local and state administrations, the Fels Institute had little impact on the major crisis at hand — the national economic emergency. The Wharton faculty did address this critical public problem, and, as in the case of the Fels Institute, they did so primarily as academic researchers. Again this was just as Willits had planned. As befitted the dean's vision of research, the school's professors also conducted their most significant investigations through organizations. These included those large institutes independent of a university that Patten had favored; university-affiliated establishments such as the Industrial Research Department and the Fels Institute, and new decentralized arrangements combining the efforts of faculty at many different campuses. But unlike the National Municipal League, the American Academy or the old Social Science Association, where men of affairs were active participants, these groups were exclusively academic. Some focused entirely on basic research, while others became involved in policy prescription and practical management problems. But in all cases, academic research constituted their primary purpose.

Of all independent research establishments in the United States, the Wharton faculty had its most significant relationship with the National Bureau of Economic Research in New York. Simon Kuznets did all of his research at the NBER, and at the end of the decade various members of the Finance and Economics Departments, including Ralph Young, William Carson, and Gordon Keith, did valuable work there as well. Among the members of the Wharton faculty at the NBER, Kuznets was clearly the star; his work on national income accounts, in fact, gave society its single most basic instrument for examining its material affairs. But despite such success at combining academic excellence and worldy practicality, work at such bureaus never became a major part of academic life at Wharton. The demands of time, travel, and research commitment always limited the number of professors who could take part in such intensive organization.[31]

As the full force of the Depression struck the nation, the men and women associated with the Industrial Research Department were the members of the Wharton faculty most prominently engaged in fighting the catastrophe. During Herbert Hoover's administration Willits served on the President's Emergency Committee for Employment, where he advocated a national employment service similar to the one that he had designed for Morris Cooke in 1915. When Franklin Roosevelt assumed the presidency in 1933 and set up the National Recovery Administration, George Taylor and several colleagues helped design "NRA Codes" in their industries. (These codes gave each firm some share of the market and guaranteed the right of labor to bargain collectively.) In the face of the crisis, the IRD decided to abandon its patient industry-by-industry research strategy and embarked on a series of major studies of the unemployment problem. Ann Bezanson, J. Frederick Dewhurst, and Gladys L. Palmer authored a large number of studies that measured the social and economic characteristics of unemployment in Philadelphia, issues such as the incidence of joblessness, the transferability of skills, what jobs existed, and how workers found them. Gladys Palmer, a 1924 Wharton Ph.D., became especially expert at gathering and interpreting these labor statistics during the Depression decade, and various agencies of the federal government, including the Bureau of the Census and the Bureau of the Budget, came to regard her work very highly. These agencies and the Rockefeller Foundation funded Palmer's work, and it soon formed the bulk of the IRD's activity. By the end of the interwar period, Palmer had become a widely recognized leader on the collection of labor statistics, an important consultant on the subject, and head of a federal inter-agency committee on labor-force and occupational statistics. Her methods for investigating labor conditions became the national standard, and her empirical studies helped policymakers to get a much sharper view of the magnitude and composition of the unemployment problem that they faced.[32]

Everyone clearly recognized the importance of the contributions of the NBER and IRD. But as mechanisms for engaging the faculty of the school in policy-oriented research, these formal institutes had a limited potential. Most professors, after all, were not interested in the specific subjects or types of research pursued by the Fels Institute, the NBER, or the IRD, nor could they afford the large and continuous stretches of time that even the on-campus enterprises required. As a result, relatively few Wharton professors worked with these institutes. Another research organization, the Social Science Research Council, offered those faculty interested in policy-oriented research a much broader and more flexible range of opportunities. Officially made up of the various national academic societies in the social sciences and supported by the Rockefeller philanthropies, the SSRC operated through a series of subordinate committees that investigated specific topics in social science and policy. These committees designed programs of investigation and then farmed out the actual research chores to faculty members on campuses across the nation. This "putting-out" system of research organization could not match the concentrated effort achieved by the more "industrial" institutes. But the SSRC generated a greater variety of programs and, because it gave the faculty significant flexibility in how they would contribute their time, induced far more participation. In the 1930s the Rockefeller Foundation, which also supported the NBER, the IRD, and other such institutes, shifted its emphasis away from those large, expensive, and high-overhead establishments and toward the smaller-scale operations of the SSRC. Encouraged by Dean Willits, as well as Rockefeller dollars, the Wharton faculty joined SSRC programs in growing numbers throughout the decade.[33]

Willits himself took an active role in the affairs of the SSRC, serving as chairman of its Advisory Committee on Population Redistribution and as a member of its Committee on Economic Security. Willits brought Columbia economic historian Carter Goodrich to Wharton on a part-time basis as head of the population study; he helped appoint Wharton insurance professor C. Arthur Kulp as senior economic consultant to the economic security committee. In 1929 Kulp had taught what may have been the nation's first collegiate course on "Social Insurance," and in the early 1930s he had served on various state commissions on unemployment insurance and workmen's compensation. While on the SSRC Committee, between 1935 and 1938, he traveled abroad to study European methods of social insurance firsthand and helped organize the unemployment insurance systems of Pennsylvania, New York, New Hampshire, and Massachusetts. His committee made a series of recommendations on how the United States ought to set up a social security system, and many of these suggestions, including several offered by Kulp, found their way into the 1937 Social Security Act. In that year Kulp left the SSRC committee and became a consultant to the new Social Security Administration.[34]

Perhaps Wharton's most active participants in SSRC projects were its sociologists. Stuart Rice, the man who had first brought Simon Kuznets to Wharton, served on the SSRC Committee on Scientific Method in the Social Sciences, and under its auspices he edited his well-known compendium *Methods in Social Science: A Case Book*. Rice's volume emphasized statistical procedures, the bread and butter of the NBER and the IRD, and argued that these numerical forms of data collection and analysis had become the essential mode of understanding and communication in social research. In 1935 Thorsten Sellin, Wharton's great criminologist, chaired an SSRC subcommittee on delinquency and wrote its final report, *Culture Conflict and Crime*. Sellin emphasized the essentially statistical, probabilistic nature of knowledge in the field and then used this "scientific" approach to trace the cause of crime to conflicting cultural norms. *Culture Conflict and Crime* and Rice's book on *Methods* were primarily intended to encourage and facilitate research work among academics; Kulp's studies of social security were directly involved in policymaking.

But in either case, the SSRC helped bring the resources of members of the Wharton School to bear on widely recognized social problems.[35]

By the end of the Depression decade, Wharton was a noticeably more scholarly institution. Economic research enjoyed far greater prestige at the school than it had in 1933 and occupied a more central position. This change had not gone unnoticed in the outside world. In 1939 Willits was offered, and took, one of the most important academic jobs in the United States, the directorship of the Social Science Division of the Rockefeller Foundation. The Rockefeller Foundation was the leading sponsor of social science research in the nation — witness its backing of the SSRC, the NBER, and the IRD — and Willits was now in charge of its policy in this area. The deanship at Wharton was then passed on to Alfred H. Williams, Willits's close friend and colleague, who had quite literally followed in Willits's footsteps; he had chaired the Geography and Industry Department and the Wharton School Curriculum Committee before rising to the deanship. By all accounts, Williams was extremely able and would have made a fine dean. But before he had much of a chance to make a mark on Wharton, after only two years as dean, Williams left academic life to become president of the Philadelphia Federal Reserve Bank. He handed the deanship on to his own successor as chairman of G & I, C. Canby Balderston. By then, however, the nation was busily preparing itself for war. Professors, as well, left the school's employ and found their way into a great variety of useful positions with the federal government. Wharton, in fact, all but adjourned for the duration of the conflict, and the number of its full-time faculty, which had recently totalled 165, fell to 39 by 1944.

The entire Wharton faculty did their part in the war effort with honor and distinction. But among the most important contributions were those made by two professors who had gathered extensive experience in economic research and its practical application in the 1930s — George W. Taylor and Simon Kuznets. As vice-chairman and then chairman of the War Labor Board, Taylor was given the power to regulate wages in all industries and the responsibility to prevent inflation, solve labor disputes, and keep the nation's workers on the job. In the interest of both efficiency and justice, he tried to find flexible solutions to labor-management conflicts and to requests from workers and their labor-starved employers to increase wages, change job classifications, award bonuses and promotions, or otherwise enhance the conditions of employment. Relying on his IRD experience, Taylor developed a close relationship with the Bureau of Labor Statistics, which collected data on work and wages. He then became "deeply involved in the area of employee relations," encouraging the parties to form a consensus. Taylor's board settled all but 300 of the 21,000 disputes that it handled, and, through the Little Steel Formula and other agreements,

changed the complexion of modern wage administration. Not only did the board rigidly constrain wage decisions during the war, but it also created or nurtured concepts that have become a permanent part of wage administration, namely the cost-of-living criterion, wage surveys, and consistent internal wage structures based on job evaluation. The WLB also contributed materially to the growth of the employee services function: its wage stabilization program caused unions and employers to greatly expand the area of fringe benefits in order to circumvent wage controls.[37]

In 1942 Simon Kuznets went to work for his former student Robert Nathan as the associate director of the Bureau of Planning and Statistics at the War Production Board. When Kuznets arrived, Nathan and his colleagues at the WPB were making "big, basic plans for producing planes, guns, ships, tanks, and other munitions." But these plans were so ambitious that military purchase orders soon generated a maze of bottlenecks all through the economy. Huge piles of semifinished goods sat in inventory: "tanks without motors, planes without propellers, merchant ships without turbines." Obviously, the WPB had devised its plans without knowing how the demand for tanks, planes, and ships created demand for motors, propellers, and turbines. Lacking information on these "derived demands" and the capacities of subsidiary industries, WPB planners could not really gauge the nation's ability to produce arms. Kuznets gave them this vital information through a massive "input-output" survey of the economy. He divided the nation's industries into five hundred different categories and then showed where the output of each industry went and from whence it got its supplies. Now planners could estimate the demand generated by war production in each industry, and could thereby marshall the national economy far more effectively. Kuznets's study showed that procurement projections had to be scaled down, but by so doing America could actually produce more finished guns and uniforms. Nathan convinced War Production Board chairman Donald M. Nelson and Army procurement chief General Brehon Somervell that Kuznets's information was reliable. They then lowered production schedules and saw a greatly expanded flow of materiel pass into the nation's arsenal.[38]

As shown by the great exodus from the Wharton School during the war and by the specific contributions of Taylor and Kuznets, Wharton was far more capable of contributing to this emergency than it had been during the original onslaught of the Depression or in the mobilization for the First World War. To no small extent, the school's new effectiveness was the result of the experience in economic research and application fostered by Joseph Willits. As in Taylor's work in labor relations and Kuznets's in national income accounting and production planning, a host of managerial tasks in the wartime economy critically depended on the availability of reliable information and on the ability to use it in a reasonable and innovative fashion. The school continued to train large numbers of students in traditional business subjects, such as accounting, finance, and insurance, and professors and graduates in these areas also found themselves drafted into responsible positions during the war. Solomon Huebner, for example, served on the Insurance Advisory Committee to the War Department and was insurance consultant to the Civil Aeronautics Board. But their expertise in standard business procedure had limited value in reorganizing the basic productive machinery of the nation, the crucial economic tasks of the 1930s and 1940s. By demonstrating its great practical value in modern economic management, empirical economic research became an integral part of the school's professional program.[39]

Source Notes

1. Joseph H. Willits, "Some Suggestions to the Wharton School for 1934–35," Minutes of the Wharton Faculty, 8 Oct. 1934, 5.

2. Minutes of the Wharton Faculty, 7 Mar. 1932, 7 Nov. 1932, 18 Dec. 1935, 2 Mar. 1936, 11 Jan. 1937; unpublished data from the 1980 Wharton alumni survey, conducted under the direction of the author.

3. Edward P. Cheyney, *History of the University of Pennsylvania* (Phila-

delphia: University of Pennsylvania Press, 1940), 415, 420, 433, 414–24; interviews with Willits and William Hockenberry; E. Digby Baltzell, *Puritan Boston and Quaker Philadelphia* (New York: Free Press, 1979), 235.

4. Willits to Judge Horace Stern, 26 Oct. 1933, in Minutes of the Wharton Faculty, 6 Nov. 1933; interview with Willits.

5. C. Canby Balderston, Clarence N. Callender, F. Cyril James, C. Arthur Kulp, Harry J. Loman, W. C. Schluter, and Alfred H. Williams, "The Future of Business Education," mimeographed, 1933, "C. Arthur Kulp File," Archives, 17, 11–12, 12, 16; interview with Dan McGill.

6. Balderston et al., "Business Education," 13, 7, 6, 15.

7. Willits, "Some Suggestions," 5, my italics; Minutes of the Wharton Faculty, 5 June 1935, 1 June 1936; Minutes of the Board of Business Education, 28 Oct. 1936.

8. Balderston et al., "Business Education," 13; Willits to Loman, 27 Oct. 1933, in Minutes of the Wharton Faculty, 6 Nov. 1933.

9. Interview with Willits; Former Members of the Staff [of the Industrial Research Department], "A Research Program in Retrospect: A Review of the Work of the Industrial Research Department, 1921 – 1953," mimeographed (Philadelphia: University of Pennsylvania, 1955), 6, 7, 50–59; Joseph H. Willits, "Research in a Graduate School of Business," in *Stanford Conference on Business Education* (Palo Alto, Calif.: Stanford University Press, 1926), 102 – 9; Minutes of the Board of Business Education, 1 May 1929; James H. S. Bossard and J. Frederick Dewhurst, *University Education for Business* (Philadelphia: University of Pennsylvania Press), 526.

10. Willits, "Research in a Graduate School," 10, 3, 105–6; Members of the Staff, "Research Program," 1, 3, 4; Bossard and Dewhurst, *Education for Business*, 473–74.

11. Members of the Staff, "Research Program," 4, 6 – 10, 14 – 18, 31–32, 51–52; Willits, "Research in a Graduate School," 105; Anne Bezanson et al., *Prices in Colonial America* (Philadelphia: University of Pennsylvania Press, 1935), *Prices and Inflation during the American Revolution in Pennsylvania, 1770 – 1779* (Philadelphia: University of Pennsylvania Press, 1951), *Wholesale Prices in Philadelphia, 1784 – 1861* (Philadelphia: University of Pennsylvania Press, 1936–37), and *Wholesale Prices in Philadelphia, 1852 – 1896* (Philadelphia: University of Pennsylvania Press, 1954); interview with Rodger Evans.

12. Members of the Staff, "Research Program," 18, 8, 20, 25–29, 50–52, 54; E. E. Hunt, F. G. Tyron, and J. H. Willits, *What the Coal Commission Found* (Baltimore: Williams and Wilkens, 1925).

13. George W. Taylor, *The Full-Fashion Hosiery Worker: His Changing Economic Status*, Industrial Research Department Research Studies no. 13 (Philadelphia: University of Pennsylvania Press, 1931), 1; George W. Taylor, *Significant Post-War Changes in the Full-Fashion Hosiery Industry*, Industrial Research Department Research Studies no. 4 (Philadelphia: University of Pennsylvania Press, 1929), 1, 6; Edward B. Shils, Introduction, in *Industrial Peace-maker: George W. Taylor's Contribution to Collective Bargaining*, ed. Edward B. Shils (Philadelphia: University of Pennsylvania Press, 1979), 1–2.

14. William Weinberg, "Accommodation and Mediation," in Shils, ed., *Industrial Peacemaker*, 75; Shils, ed., *Industrial Peacemaker*, passim.

15. George W. Taylor, quoted by Walter J. Gershenfeld, "Early Years: Grievance Arbitration," in Shils, ed., *Industrial Peacemaker*, 47, 32–33; Shils, Introduction, 3; Irving Bernstein, *The Lean Years* (Boston: Houghton, Mifflin, 1960), 277–79, 303, 335–36; Members of the Staff, "Research Program," 22.

16. Members of the Staff, "Research Program," 8 – 14, 20, 21, 26, 36, 40, 55–57; interview with Ann R. Miller.

17. "Educational Council: November 21, 1933," in Minutes of the Wharton Faculty, 12 Dec. 1933; Balderston et al., "Business Education," 14.

18. Minutes of the Wharton Faculty, 23 Apr. 1934, 6 Nov. 1933; Minutes of the Board of Business Education, 25 Oct. 1933; interviews with Willits, Hockenberry, and Reavis Cox.

19. *American Men of Science* (hereafter *AMS*), s.v. "Simon Kuznets"; Minutes of the Board of Business Education, 3 June 1931, 25 Oct. 1933; interview with Kuznets.

20. Simon Kuznets, *National Income and Its Composition, 1919–1938* (New York: National Bureau of Economic Research, 1941); Simon Kuznets, *National Product since 1869* (New York: National Bureau of Economic Research, 1946); Simon Kuznets, ed., *Income and Wealth*, International Association for Research in Income and Wealth (Cambridge, England: Bowes & Bowes, 1951–).

21. *AMS*, s.v. "Simon Kuznets" and "Joseph H. Willits"; interviews with Kuznets and Nancy Schneer.

22. Reavis Cox, *Competition in the American Tobacco Industry, 1911–1932* (New York: Columbia University Press, 1933); interviews with Cox and Willits.

23. Interview with Cox.

24. Ralph F. Breyer, *The Marketing Institution* (New York: McGraw Hill, 1934); interview with Cox.

25. Interviews with Willits, Whittlesey, and Cataldo; *AMS*, s.v. "Charles Ray Whittlesey," "F. Cyril James," and "Joseph R. Rose."

26. Willits, "Some Suggestions," 12; *AMS*, s.v. "Leo S. Rowe," "Ernest Minor Patterson," and "Clyde L. King."

27. Willits, "Some Suggestions," 7–9; Minutes of the Wharton Faculty, 9 Oct. 1933, 4 Dec. 1933, 23 Apr. 1934, 8 Oct. 1934; Minutes of the Board of Business Education, 27 Mar. 1935; Emory R. Johnson, "The Wharton School," Minutes of the Wharton Faculty, 5 June 1939; interview with Willits.

28. Willits, "Some Suggestions," 12; Minutes of the Wharton Faculty, 11 Feb. 1935, 27 May 1935; Minutes of the Board of Business Education, 4 Feb. 1934, 20 Nov. 1934.

29. Dale Phalen, *Samuel Fels of Philadelphia* (Philadelphia: Samuel S. Fels Fund, 1969), 24–25, 37, 70–72; Graham W. Watt, "Education for Public Service — Executives or Technicians?" *Wharton Quarterly* 6 (Summer 1972):39; "Memorandum from Lloyd M. Short to Willis Winn, 23 Aug. 1966," in "Fels Institute of Local and State Government: Background Materials for Director Selection Committee, 1966," files of Charles Beale, School of Public and Urban Policy, University of Pennsylvania, 1, 24; Stephen B. Sweeney, "Strengthening Democracy at the Roots," reprinted from the *[University of Pennsylvania] Library Chronicle*, (June 1943):8–9 in "Background Materials"; "School of Public and Urban Policy," promotional pamphlet, n.p., n.d., 2, files of the School of Public and Urban Policy; "The Plans for and the Organization of the Institute in State and Local Government," Minutes of the Wharton Faculty, 1 Nov. 1937; "Towards a Better Life Through Training in Government," *Philadelphia Bulletin*, 14 May 1967, sec. 2:6.

30. "Graduate Program in Local and State Governmental Administration" and "The Fels Institute," Minutes of the Wharton Faculty, 2 Nov. 1964; J. A. Livingston and Beverly M. Bowie, "An Outsider Looks at Wharton," reprinted from the *Pennsylvania Gazette*, 1 Jan. 1947, 7; "Memorandum from Short," 17–18; "Towards a Better Life," 6; "Plans for the Institute."

31. *AMS*, s.v. "William J. Carson," "E. Gordon Keith"; interview with E. Gordon Keith.

32. Members of the Staff, "Research Program," 25–29, 50–52, 54; *AMS*, s.v. "Gladys L. Palmer."

33. Robert E. Kohler, "A Policy for the Advancement of Science: The Rockefeller Foundation, 1924–1929," *Minerva* 16 (1978):480–515.

34. Minutes of the Wharton Faculty, 25 Apr. 1934, 18 Dec. 1935; AMS, s.v. "Carter Goodrich"; "C. A. Kulp," dated 27 Jan. 1953, and "[C. Arthur Kulp]," dated 3 May 1955, "C. Arthur Kulp File," Archives.

35. Stuart A. Rice, ed., *Method in Social Science: A Case Book* (Chicago: University of Chicago Press, 1931); Thorsten Sellin, *Culture Conflict and Crime*, Report of the Subcommittee on Delinquency of the Committee on Personality and Culture (New York: Social Science Research Council, 1938).

36. "Alfred H. Williams File," Archives; AMS, s.v. "Joseph H. Willits"; "Report of the Dean of the Wharton School of Finance and Commerce, 1942–1943 and 1943–1944," files of the Dean's Office, Wharton School.

37. Cyril Curtis Ling, *The Management of Personnel Relations* (Homewood, Ill.: Richard D. Irwin, 1965), 476, 481; Shils, Introduction, 4; Edward B. Shils, "Regulation and Public Policy: Government Regulation of Wages," in Shils, ed., *Industrial Peacemaker*, 131–60.

38. Livingston and Bowie, "Look at Wharton," 3.

39. Mildred F. Stone, *The Teacher Who Changed an Industry* (Homewood, Ill.: Richard D. Irwin, 1960), 206–7.

Joseph H. Willits

Stuart A. Rice

Clarence Callender

Thorsten Sellin

Reavis Cox

Alfred H. Williams

F. Cyril James

Thomas Sovereign Gates

Samuel S. Fels

Simon Kuznets in class, lecturing to (left to right),
Edward Brink (future professor of marketing, Wharton),
Morris Hamburg (future professor of statistics, Wharton),
Bertram Zumeta (future executive vice-president, First Pennsylvania Bank),
Edward Du Bois (future professor of business administration, Fort Lewis College),
and Hyman Menduke (future professor of biostatistics, Jefferson Medical College)

Irvine Auditorium

Simon Kuznets, *National Income and Its Composition, 1919–1938,*
title page and first page of contents

National Income

and Its Composition, 1919·1938

by Simon Kuznets

assisted by Lillian Epstein

and Elizabeth Jenks

VOLUME I

National Bureau of Economic Research

NEW YORK · 1941

Contents

vii

George W. Taylor

8

Taking Stock

After the victory over fascism in World War II, the nation embarked on a tremendous wave of economic expansion. Real G.N.P. surged 40 percent between 1946 and 1955, with a booming outpouring of planes, cars, chemicals, plastics, children, and suburbs spreading thick layers of success across America. New diversified and decentralized managerial structures sprang up in the business landscape, and faith in a revitalized capitalism banished depression and wartime visions of a government-managed economy. During this period, American social science also enjoyed a time of unusually healthy development. Led by scholars such as Paul Samuelson in economics and Talcott Parsons in sociology, the postwar generation enormously strengthened the mathematical and theoretical sophistication of these disciplines. But as the worlds of affairs and ideas rushed headlong into the future, the Wharton School resumed its prewar routines. The Huebner brothers, Thomas Budd, George Taylor, Simon Kuznets, Raymond Bye, Gladys Palmer, Reavis Cox, George MacFarland, Thorstin Sellin, Ray Whittlesey, and most of the other major figures on the faculty returned to their old posts; C. Canby Balderston continued as dean. Like most other American business schools, Wharton found few new opportunities in the rejuvenated private sector and made little capital out of contemporary advances in social theory. The school, moreover, lost some of its distinctive impetus toward

233

economic research, and several of Willits's initiatives came undone. By the mid-1950s a swarm of critics had descended on the school and on collegiate business education in general, insisting that Wharton and her sister institutions respond to the recent developments in management and academe. The old battles over the curriculum sprang up once again and became the primary focus of faculty attention. The process, however, proved invigorating. After various manueverings and long readjustments, the school launched another campaign to pump up the academic content of its program and to prepare its students for general managerial responsibilities.[1]

Wharton's dean in the postwar decade, C. Canby Balderston, spent his entire academic career at the Wharton School. He took his B.S. in 1921, his Ph.D. in 1928, and became a full professor of geography and industry three years later. Like most of his colleagues in G & I, Balderston had concentrated on the field of labor management. He had worked in the Industrial Research Department, authoring a survey on innovative industrial relations programs and a volume on *Wages* written with Morris Leeds, Philadelphia's prominent and progressive Quaker manufacturer. During the curricular feuds of the twenties and thirties, Balderston had been a partisan of Willits's party of reform and had signed the "Future of Business Education" manifesto. But Balderston was by nature a conservative man; the passage of time and his assumption of administrative responsibility only accentuated this trait. During his thirteen years as dean, 1941 to 1954, his basic goal was to maintain the traditions of the school.[2]

Canby Balderston considered the construction of a new building for the school the greatest success of his deanship. Joseph Wharton had promised the school a home of its own and in 1904 had donated for this purpose a large triangular plot of land on the southeast corner of Thirty-Seventh and Locust Streets. But expectations of commodious accommodations had been frustrated after the founder had had his tiff with the trustees and had removed the building funds from his will. For forty-five years, therefore, the school had sat crowded in Logan Hall (and then in the adjacent Hare Hall). In 1941, after the Depression but before Pearl Harbor, Balderston and his faculty had begun a campaign to raise funds for new quarters and by the end of the 1940s had gathered $2.3 million from alumni and faculty. In September 1952, Wharton finally occupied its new building, the first erected at the university after the war. Two brothers, alumni H. Richard and Daniel W. Dietrich, contributed the largest sum of money, and the hall was named in honor of their uncle, D. Wellington Dietrich.[3]

With over three hundred rooms, Dietrich Hall finally provided Wharton with ample accommodations. So eager was the school for room, however, that it spent the bulk of its funds for space, not stylistic flair. Dietrich's plain facade, dark hallways, and spartan appointments, as a result, recalled a public high school more than it did the stately old Pennsylvania campus. This "underbuilding" of Dietrich Hall owed much to the university's bias against spending money on its business program. Balderston was not an aggressive soul, and according to general opinion, he could not overcome this prejudice and command anything close to a "fair share" at the university trough. Forced to rely on its own resources, Wharton even came up short on the much coveted matter of space. Dietrich's faculty offices were half the size of the university average, and plans for a new wing to house the Lippincott Library were never funded. The university, meanwhile, invested its own brick and mortar in dormitories, administrative offices, and its other schools, and in the years after 1952 put up buildings of great architectural distinction. An elegant new campus materialized, leaving Dietrich's austerity an ever more apparent statement of the Wharton School's second-class status in the university.[4]

As to student body and educational program, the decade after 1945 much resembled the return to normalcy that followed World War I. Enrollments swelled as returning veterans, financed by the G.I. Bill, filled all Wharton programs. As early as 1946, 2,416 undergraduates crowded into Logan Hall. Of these, a quarter were destined to join firms owned by or affiliated with their families, a figure that remained amazingly stable during the four decades between 1920 and 1960. Fraternities also continued as a major part of student life, attracting more than 60 percent of Wharton undergraduates. These postwar students, like their predecessors, were also said to be "significantly below the [academic] quality of those entering elsewhere in the University of Pennsylvania." Many, however, now had little patience for the traditional Wharton formalities, ignoring the tie and jacket dress code, and smoking in class. What they wanted was training in practical business skills. And under Dean Balderston, as during the regime of Emory Johnson, the departmental chairmen took on major responsibility for providing such specific preparation for the world of affairs. In each department the proliferation of courses began all over again, with students especially enamored of a new assortment of narrowly focused, two-credit short courses. An in-depth study of the school led by F. Cyril James, former professor of finance and later vice-chancellor and principal of McGill University, found that Wharton "has gone farther in this direction than most schools and in fact offers a greater degree of specialization in some fields than do most of the other collegiate schools of business . . . Specialization at Wharton may have gone too far."[5]

Students needed 144 credit hours to graduate, and to meet this steep total they often crammed eight or even ten different courses into one semester's schedule. Such loads, of course, left little time for reading or preparation outside the classroom. So in 1954, in the hope that students would approach their education with more patience and maturity, the faculty cut the credits needed for graduation to 128. The new curriculum, however, resulted in students taking an even greater percentage of their programs in specialized business subjects and less in the humanities. Non-Wharton requirements (neither business nor social science) dropped from 24 percent to 19 percent of the curriculum, and at any given time fewer than 1 percent of the undergraduates studied mathematics, natural science, or foreign language; fewer than 3 percent studied history. "In the face of this evidence," the James panel concluded, "the traditional Wharton claim to providing a broad liberal education, along with business training, is not at present being achieved."[6]

In the great explosion of enrollments during World War I, Emory Johnson's basic task had been to find enough faculty members to staff the classrooms. Canby Balderston now faced a similar problem, but it grew less from a shortage of qualified teachers, as was the case in the 1920s, than from a shortage of cash. Salaries at Wharton were shockingly low. They were not only lower than those in other parts of the university, but below the national average for collegiate schools of business. The effort begun under

Willits to hire "non-Pennsylvania" professors and to diversify the staff therefore came to a halt. Inbreeding, in fact, increased during this period, and by the mid-1950s Wharton men constituted 80 percent of the full-time professoriate. Unable to lure outside scholars, the various departments again pressed graduate students into service as instructors, as was done in the 1920s. On the undergraduate teaching staff, these graduate instructors soon out-numbered full-time professors by a margin of two to one.[7]

Low salaries led the faculty to supplement their incomes in traditional ways. Half taught in the evening and extension pro-grams, increasing their incomes 17 percent but raising their course loads above the maximum established by the American Associa-tion of Collegiate Schools of Business. By the 1950s, consulting had become "a part of the Wharton way of life." Although con-sulting could offer valuable experience and opportunities for re-search, fees were the primary incentive, and the James Committee termed much of this work "routine, repetitive, and enervating." That panel found the Wharton faculty skilled and highly moti-vated, and it sympathized with their financial straits. But it was "shocked" at these remedies and claimed that the situation cre-ated "a climate of indifference to real scholarly pursuits and ac-counts for a lesser outpouring of significant research than might be expected for the faculty of a school such as Wharton." Other investigators agreed that "the Wharton School isn't alive. A feel-ing of dullness prevails."[8]

These criticisms, although clearly excesssive, reflected justi-fiable anxiety about the intellectual life of the Wharton School. The overall amount of economic research did not decline in the postwar decade, and Wharton maintained its relative standing among the nation's business schools. Faculty in various fields of study launched truly impressive investigations between 1945 and 1960, with professors in the business specialties developing an important new research vehicle — Wharton-based research cen-ters financed primarily by private corporations. But setbacks in long-established areas offset these achievements. And these highly visible problems, combined with the sparkling example of vitality elsewhere in the academic world, raised the alarm among much of the school's faculty and its visiting critics.

Wharton's postwar years were not without scholarly achievement. In the social sciences, for example, the field of demography then became an important new area of economic research. The subject had first arrived at the school in the 1930s as a Social Science Research Council project: Joseph Willits had been chairman of the SSRC Committee on Population Redistribution and Economic Growth and had brought economic historian Carter Goodrich to Wharton as director of this study. After Goodrich left the school, the Wharton Sociology Department adopted the subject and in 1944 even made population the focus of its introductory survey course. The real development of the field, however, awaited the appointment of Dorothy S. Thomas, Wharton's first tenured woman professor, as director of the study in 1948. Although a member of the Sociology Department, Thomas, like Goodrich, was trained as an economist and conducted a program of economic rather than sociological research. She worked quite closely with Simon Kuznets, and between 1957 and 1964 the two put out an extensive three-volume report on their work, *Population Redistribution and Economic Growth: United States, 1870-1950*. In this and in their preliminary publications, Wharton's demographers laid down basic statistical descriptions of American population movements and illuminated the tremendous impact of sheer geographic mobility on the rise in national per capita income. This project also prepared the way for two new Ph.D. programs at Penn, one in demography (only the second in the nation) and the other in economic history.[9]

Nowhere during this period did the adoption of a program of economic research effect a more dramatic change than in the field of finance. Until the retirement of Edward Mead in 1944, Wharton's efforts in the area had consisted primarily of training students in the laws, accounts, and practices of various funding businesses. A dozen years later, economists dominated the department, and a new "Securities Research Unit" conducted long-term empirical investigations on policy questions in the finance industry.

Despite the long hegemony of the procedural orientation in finance, the potential for movement toward economics had always existed. Debates over banking and credit had been a constant point of contact between businessmen and scientific writers, and

Joseph Wharton, in his original design of the school, had specified general instruction "upon . . . the meaning, history, and functions of money and currency." Albert Bolles had offered such courses, as well as training in "practical banking," and throughout its history Wharton continued to offer instruction on the economics of financial systems. During the interwar period F. Cyril James, a 1924 Wharton Ph.D., coauthor of "The Future of Business Education," and good friend of Joseph Willits, gave courses in "money and currency."* James's courses and textbook, *The Economics of Money, Credit and Banking*, discussed topics such as the determination of interest rates, the causes of inflation, and the nature of financial crises; his research on the history of banking, especially his two-volume *Rise of Chicago Banks*, won him an enviable academic reputation. James, however, had little influence on his colleagues. When he left Wharton in 1939, the professors of professional practice remained in firm control of the finance curriculum.[10]

The transformation of finance at Wharton originated with Cyril James's successor C. Ray Whittlesey, a 1928 Princeton Ph.D. in economics who began teaching in the department in 1939. Already a prominent monetary economist, Whittlesey arrived in Philadelphia known as one of the first Americans to defend the exotic new Keynesian theories. In two publications, *International Monetary Issues* and *Golden Avalanche*, he presented highly readable arguments, using perspectives drawn from the English theorist, against the prevailing rigidities of the gold standard. Although Joseph Wharton would have been aghast at such teachings,

Whittlesey quickly established himself as a provocative and inspiring teacher, hesitant and desultory in method, but carrying his students along by his own enthusiasm for the subject matter. This was reinforced by his interest in and sympathy with his students, a remarkable number of whom became life-long friends and correspondents. Through this rapport

---

*Between 1933 and 1943, Hans Neisser, a sophisticated international monetary theorist and refugee from Germany, also taught graduate courses in the Department of Finance. But Neisser held an irregular appointment with outside benefactors, Samuel S. Fels and the Dietrich brothers among them, paying his salary. He was barely accepted by his colleagues, and when he finally came up for tenure, the department turned him down. As could be expected, Neisser had little impact on the course of financial instruction at the school.

with students and his well-written publications, Whittlesey single-hand-edly made Keynesian analysis a legitimate enterprise at Penn.[11]*

Although a solid academician, Whittlesey made a greater contribution to the department as a promoter of scholarship. He assumed the chairmanship of the Finance Department one year after Mead resigned, in 1945, and championed a new emphasis on economic analysis and research. Surprisingly, Whittlesey en-countered little opposition from the older, practice-oriented mem-bers of the faculty. His charm and his success in pacifying many of the peeves and bickerings that inevitably find their way into a chairman's office won their personal friendship. The senior fi-nance faculty, moreover, had little investment in graduate training and even less desire to staff a department with like-minded jun-iors. They considered themselves to be economists, and recog-nized that Whittlesey and his theoretical bent represented the future of their discipline. They therefore allowed the new chair-man a free hand in charting the future course of the department. Joining Whittlesey as the nucleus of a new program were E. Gor-don Keith, the Harvard-trained economist recruited in 1939, and a young Wharton graduate student then finishing his Ph.D., Willis Winn. Both men had spent the war years doing policy-oriented research, Keith with the Treasury Department and Winn with the National Bureau of Economic Research, and had returned to Phil-adelphia with the notion of continuing such work.[12]

In 1948 Whittlesey used his charm and connections to organ-ize the Securities Research Unit (SRU), which became the focus of financial research at the school. The Merrill Foundation for the Advancement of Financial Knowledge, a charity associated with the Merrill, Lynch brokerage house, funded the chairman's

---

*Julius Grodinsky, Mead's protege and successor as chief man on the cor-porate side of the department, also journeyed beyond the procedural tradition. His *Ebb and Flow of Investment Values* (nominally coauthored by Mead) "de-parted from accepted methods of investment analysis" by looking outside the firm to identify "the influences which produce changes in corporate profits." His conclusion, that the "changes come largely from fluctuations in demand," proved quite sensational in 1940. For this and for his keen insight into stock market gyrations, Grodinsky was a favorite among brokers around town. Any conference that Wharton put on for these gentlemen scheduled Grodinsky at the end, to insure attendance throughout the event. Like Bolles and Cyril James, Grodinsky also wrote history; his books included a two-volume biography of Jay Gould (a buccaneering contemporary of Joseph Wharton's) and a fine study of *The Iowa Pool*, an early attempt to "stabilize" the railroad industry.

enterprise because it wanted an in-depth study made of the "over-the-counter" securities markets.* Although Whittlesey sat on the advisory committee of the SRU and Willis Winn served as senior staff member, G. Wright Hoffman, an insurance professor, became the first director of the unit. Ever since Solomon Huebner had taught the world's first collegiate course on security and commodity exchanges, in 1904, Wharton's expertise in the subject had been under the jurisdiction of his department. But when Hoffman left the country in 1954 and Winn succeeded him as director of the unit, the SRU and the O-T-C study fell predominantly under the influence of the Finance Department.[13]

The ultimate success of the O-T-C study and the rising influence of Wharton's Finance Department owed much to the arrival of an exciting new professor whom Whittlesey recruited in 1953, Irwin Friend.† Bringing exceptionally high standards of scholarship, analytical skill, and plain hard work, the new professor immediately established himself as the intellectual force on the O-T-C study and in the department in general. With Friend's leadership, the SRU succeeded in providing

for the first time a comprehensive picture of the magnitude, structure, and operation of . . . the over-the-counter markets. . . . These studies have been widely used by Congressional committees, Federal and state regulatory agencies, various securities associations, and numerous academic groups. In fact, it has been stated that a large part of practically all of the data available on the over-the-counter markets was developed by the Securities Research Unit.

So successful was this venture that a variety of new research and consulting opportunities opened up for Wharton's investigators, and the SRU survived the completion of the O-T-C project. Whittlesey's advisory committee, which gained access to private records and maintained communications between Wharton's scholars and the New York financial community, also continued. It expanded its jurisdiction to the entire department and became a

---

*The O-T-C markets were, in fact, a variety of institutional arrangements for transferring securities without the services of a central exchange. Although less well known than the New York, American, and other exchanges, the O-T-C markets actually handled the bulk of all stock and bond trading in the nation.

†Prior to this appointment, Friend had been with the United States Department of Commerce, as head of its Business Structure Division.

permanent fixture, known as the Finance Department Advisory Committee.[14]

Following closely behind the O-T-C study, the SRU, led by Irwin Friend, launched an investigation of the mutual fund industry. Like the unit's former project, this one also charted a little-studied but extremely important area of finance. Friend and his colleagues again provided "the first extensive description and analysis of the growth of the mutual fund industry to its present important position in the financial structure of the country." Their investigation dismissed certain allegations leveled against the industry, including claims that these funds controlled the management of American corporations or manipulated security prices. But they did identify a number of serious problems. They found, for example, that the performance of these "professionally" managed funds "did not differ appreciably from what would have been achieved by an unmanaged portfolio." The study also criticized the practice of paying a closely associated "external" advisor unusually steep fees. The charges of these advisors, absorbing one dollar for every six paid out to investors, were "substantially higher than those charged by the same advisors to the aggregate of their clients other than investment companies. Nevertheless, it was found that the expenses involved in advising mutual funds were less." The report also questioned "whether there may be a conflict of interest between a mutual fund's shareholders and the fund's investment advisor as regards the effort that should be devoted to selling shares." Increased sales "automatically produce increases in the dollar amounts of management fees . . . and . . . brokerage business to distribute," with no benefit to investors. As could be expected, the study generated enormous controversies. But the quality of the research soon won wide recognition, and the SRU report led to various reforms in the industry.[15]

The success of Friend and the SRU brought the study of securities markets under the jurisdiction of the Wharton Finance Department. As if to compensate for the loss of this business, another research center, the Pension Research Center, sprang up in Wharton's Insurance Department in 1952. This unit studied the rapidly growing corporate practice of providing retirement benefits as part of an employee's wage package, an arrangement that had only recently become important in collective bargaining negotiations. George Taylor and his War Labor Board, in fact, had accelerated the growth of this practice when they allowed employers to "pay" workers these promises of future income while vetoing inflationary hikes in cash wages. During the postwar prosperity, pension plans took on a tremendous popularity, and a host of banks and insurance companies competed vigorously for contracts to organize, manage, and underwrite these retirement programs. But the whole business was brand new. Even at Wharton, advanced life insurance courses devoted just one week's time to private pension plans, and hardly any literature approached the subject from a professional or scientific perspective. As could be expected, few could agree as to which funding scheme or operational procedure was best. To clear the air, and especially to resolve the heated controversy between advocates of group plans and those of individual contracts, Ben S. McGiveran, a Chicago agent for the Northwestern Mutual Life Insurance Company, induced Wharton to set up the Pension Research Center.[16]

To direct the PRC, Dean Balderston and Solomon Huebner hired Dan M. McGill, a Wharton Ph.D. then teaching insurance at the University of North Carolina. They could not have made a better choice. Combining intelligence, grace, good humor, and organizational skill, McGill soon became the undisputed "dean" of the pension industry. In many ways the task before him resembled that of Wharton's pioneer business professors—to bring light to a contentious business and to establish acceptable standards of performance. As in the case of his predecessors, McGill's first chore was to write a textbook on the subject, his *Fundamentals of Private Pensions*. Under his direction the PRC then sponsored several more studies of pension and retirement issues in the mid-1950s, and these investigations raised serious questions about the soundness of many of the nation's private pension programs. Like Emory Johnson and Solomon Huebner of Wharton's pioneering generation of business professors (and his contemporary colleagues investigating the mutual fund industry), McGill therefore became actively involved in reform.[17]

In 1958, with the financial support of the Metropolitan Life Insurance Company, McGill organized an ambitious "Inquiry Into the Security behind Pension Fund Expectations."* McGill divided the labor of participants of this "Inquiry" along traditional lines: Wharton's original business program of the 1880s specified courses in law, accounting, and "practice"; the pioneering professors in the business specialties defined curricula covering the laws, accounts, and practices of their particular fields of study; so McGill assigned research teams to the law of private pensions, to the actuarial (similar to the "accounting") aspects of the problem, and to "the functions associated with the establishment and operation of a private pension plan and the various agencies which perform one or more of these functions" (practice). McGill's division of responsibility and the work of his research teams proved quite effective. In their individual reports and in McGill's "capstone" work, *Fulfilling Pension Expectations*, the PRC outlined a series of rather outrageous legal and financial problems and recommended various reforms that could put the whole business on a sounder footing. Congress and a presidential commission, which employed McGill as its consultant, then looked into the matter. They agreed with the PRC's findings and wrote many of its recommendations into the landmark Employee Retirement Income Security Act of 1974, commonly known as ERISA.[18]†

No one, not even McGill, was satisfied with all details of the ERISA legislation. Nevertheless, his PRC, the SRU, and Dorothy Thomas's demography center made indisputable contributions to social understanding and the management of practical affairs. But while these scholarly projects took root in the decade after 1945, other research efforts at Wharton fell away. The Fels Institute of

---

*The Metropolitan Life Insurance Company not only financed the "Inquiry," but at the same time created the Frederick H. Ecker Chair of Life Insurance at the Wharton School. Ecker was Metropolitan Life's retired chairman; the endowed professorship in life insurance was the first in the world; and McGill became the first Ecker Professor.

†In 1946 George Taylor established the Labor Relations Council at Wharton. Like the PRC and the SRU, corporate contributions financed this enterprise, and its activities had great relevance to the practical problems faced by those supporting firms. Under Taylor's leadership, the council sponsored one series of research projects on industry-wide collective bargaining and another on labor arbitration. But academic investigations were never the chief focus of the LRC. Its "prime thrust" was "to sponsor an interchange of ideas between executives in the personnel and labor relations field and faculty members who teach in this field, and to expose both executives and faculty members to a variety of ideas and opinions in their general field of interest."

Local and State Government, for example, had spent most of its early years conducting investigations. In the postwar era, however, the institute came to emphasize instruction. Its graduate training program, leading to a Master's of Government Administration degree,* was distinct from that of the traditional Wharton M.B.A. and far more practice-minded. Fels students sat through one semester of courses on the "objectives," "practices," and "problems" of state and local government administration; in their next semester they served supervised "apprenticeships" in various government agencies; finally, they took six-month "internships" in the field. Even the relatively brief period of classroom instruction focused on procedural detail. As Fels director Stephen B. Sweeney explained,

the Institute strives to make its academic program as serviceable as possible. This is done by building the training in government administration on a broad foundation of technical courses. The reason for this is that the demand in public service, especially at lower levels of government, is primarily for technicians or technicians with administrative training rather than for persons with administrative training alone.[19]†

The School's primary research institution, the Industrial Research Department, came upon hard financial times in the postwar period and suffered accordingly. Willits had been an excellent

*The institute at first awarded a "Master's of Business Administration in Government" and changed to the M.G.A. in 1947.

†Although scholarly ambitions found little encouragement at Fels, its M.G.A. program was quite successful and its graduates highly regarded. The institute paid the tuition of its full-time graduate students, thereby attracting a fine pool of applicants. By the mid-1960s Fels turned out approximately twenty-five M.G.A.'s a year, and an estimated 85 percent of its 500 graduates held "responsible positions in, or related to, the public service." By using the institute as an educational and conferencing center in the 1950s, Sweeney further contributed to the professionalizing of public service careers. The institute hosted numerous conclaves of city managers and public administrators and provided secretarial and administrative service to professional associations in these areas. Perhaps inspired by his old mentor, Solomon Huebner, Sweeney set up an "in-service" educational program somewhat akin to the C.L.U. effort: the institute offered a five-course curriculum on public administration, awarding a "plaque" to those who completed the entire series and a "certificate" to those who passed any one course. Just as insurance companies valued the C.L.U., many governments in the region valued these Fels commendations when making appointments and promotions. By the mid-1960s, 300 civil servants held the Fels plaque and approximately 250 students were enrolled in its "in-service" courses.

fund raiser for the IRD as its director and as dean of the school, and had continued to support its work from his position as social science chief of the Rockefeller Foundation. In 1945, for example, he had given the department one hundred seventy-five thousand dollars to support its operations through the end of the decade. But no one replaced Willits at the IRD, and as he approached his retirement at Rockefeller, the department was left without friends who could command similar resources: Its annual budget fell from seventy thousand dollars in the 1930s to forty thousand dollars in the inflationary postwar period. It finally collapsed in 1953, when its final Rockefeller grant ran out. Gladys Palmer, still funded as an individual researcher by the Rockefeller Foundation, became a research professor of industry and director of an "Industrial Research Unit." Three women researchers from the old staff also continued with IRU. But when they and Professor Palmer died, fell sick, or moved on, no replacements were hired, and even this "unit" fell into decay.[20]

The departure of Simon Kuznets, however, provided the clearest symptom of Wharton's intellectual distress. The school's great economic statistician, the personification of Willits's academic program, accepted a very attractive offer from the Johns Hopkins University in the year following the demise of the IRD. Although he had never felt totally at ease at the Wharton School, Kuznets had enjoyed his life in Philadelphia and had no real desire to move to Baltimore. He was comfortably engaged in a number of important projects and could easily take the train up to New York and the National Bureau of Economic Research. As is customary in academe, when he received the offer from John Hopkins, Kuznets went to the dean with the expectation that Wharton would match the Hopkins offer. But lacking both money and a real interest in promoting the school as a research center, Balderston refused to bid for the economist's services. All the dean could manage was, "Why congratulations, Simon!" and Kuznets went to Hopkins. Needless to say, there was much embarrassment in Philadelphia and glee in Baltimore when the American Economic Association immediately elected Kuznets as its next president.[21]

The death of the IRD and the departure of Simon Kuznets signalled the crisis in the academic life of the Wharton School. With the best work of the demography group, the Securities Research Unit, and the Pension Research Center still in the future,

the faculty grew increasingly anxious about the intellectual validity of their corporate enterprise. Everyone understood that Wharton provided excellent occupational training, but according to a
James Committee survey, only 20 percent of the faculty considered this "very important." The professors defined their primary
educational responsibility as teaching students to think and solve
problems, and they thought the Wharton program unsuccessful
at that. The faculty also faulted their school for failing to cultivate
morality, contemplative habits, or intellectual curiosity. Whether
or not facts could justify these sentiments, the James Committee
"surveys of Wharton faculty opinion . . . disclosed a general concern for the improvement of the scholastic atmosphere, even if
that involves the disaccommodation of personal interests."[22]

This "general concern" at Wharton was, in fact, part of the
general mood of the Pennsylvania professoriate in the mid-1950s.
For twenty of the twenty-five years since 1930, nonacademics
had controlled the institution, and they had not turned in especially impressive performances. The Gates regime brought administrative efficiency, but little interest in or attention to scholarship.
In 1948, Harold Stassen, a Republican politician of national
standing, had taken over the presidency. He and his proper Philadelphia friends had seen the job as a resting spot on his road to
the White House, not a suitable nor permanent focus for his
energies. But after a few years on the job, Stassen found himself
embroiled in embarrassing spats with the faculty. The professors
pressed his administration for higher salaries and improvements
in the "scholastic atmosphere." They raised an especially vehe-
ment protest against a proposed state law demanding loyalty oaths
of all instructors in state-funded universities. To strengthen the
voice of the faculty, politically active professors, including Wharton's Reavis Cox, Bernard Cataldo, and Clarence Callender, organized a Faculty Senate in 1952. In time, this senate assumed
constitutional stature in university affairs; it became the "lower
house" of the university, representing the interests of the academics before the administration and the "upper house" of the trustees. With the faculty thus acting up — asserting its interests and
demanding new powers — Stassen grew conscious of the political
perils of university management. He resigned in 1953, going else-

where to await the Republican presidential nomination. Power at the university then passed into the hands of academic reformers.[23]*

As the next president of the university the trustees chose Dr. Gaylord P. Harnwell, a well-respected physicist on the Pennsylvania faculty. Firmly committed to raising the level of scholarship, Harnwell and his supporters on the board quickly embarked on a vigorous campaign to transform the university into a premier academic institution. Harnwell rejected once and for all the plan to move the university to Valley Forge, and instead launched the huge construction program that raised Penn's magnificent new campus in West Philadelphia. The word went out that the university would no longer look first to its own Ph.D.'s when hiring new faculty, and that antisemitism, a real factor in faculty recruitment in the past, would no longer be tolerated. Research, the vital element in academic life, thenceforth ranked as the primary criterion in faculty personnel decisions.[24]

Harnwell's campaign for reform did not bypass Wharton. The president and his colleagues made every effort to keep Simon Kuznets at Penn, offering the economist a generous financial package and painting rosy horizons in the university's future. But it was too late; the die had been cast, and Kuznets went to Baltimore. More successful were Harnwell's efforts to engage the faculty's "general concern" to improve the "scholastic atmosphere" at their school. In 1954, after Dean Balderston resigned to become a governor of the Federal Reserve System, Harnwell brought Wharton's professors into the process of choosing their new dean. The faculty had never before participated in this decision, but the president's reliance on professorial input was quite consistent with the recent creation of the Faculty Senate at the university level. Harnwell's injunction that they make academic leadership the main consideration in their deliberations also agreed with the current climate of reform.[25]

In 1955, Professor of Insurance C. Arthur Kulp became the first Wharton dean named with the participation of the faculty. A well-known researcher and writer on social insurance, Kulp had worked in the IRD and had been among the pioneer designers

---

*An old saw explains the squalid nature of academic politics by the smallness of the stakes. For a man such as Stassen, who had set his ambitions on grand affairs of state, the bickerings at Penn must have been a trial.

of the nation's social security system. He had coauthored "The Future of Business Education" manifesto and, upon assuming office, announced that the document still reflected his views. He had the general respect of the faculty and the potential to become a great dean. However, he died in August 1957, just two years into his administration. After another search in which the Wharton faculty played a key role, the university administration named Willis Winn as Kulp's successor in 1958. Winn, of course, was an active researcher with the school's Security Research Unit. In addition, he had shown administrative abilities as director of the SRU, as Kulp's vice-dean, and then as acting dean during the 1957-58 academic year. As could be expected, Winn's ambitions for the school were quite similar to those of the university's new president, and they cooperated to raise Wharton's academic standards.[26]

An intensive five-year "Educational Survey" of the university provided the centerpiece of Harnwell's program for academic revival. To direct this investigation Harnwell secured none other than Joseph Willits, recently departed from the Rockefeller Foundation. The Willits Survey had a mandate to review all parts of the institution, from the Board of Trustees down to the various departments of the Wharton School, and issued a series of lengthy reports proposing a variety of sharp reforms. Among its central recommendations the survey called for a much stronger university president, with strict limits on the influence of the trustees. The trustees, also caught up in the mood for revival, agreed and formally transferred many of their administrative prerogatives to the office of the president.* The investigation of the Wharton School came to no less radical conclusions.[27]

With Willits as head of the Educational Survey of the entire university, the investigation of the Wharton School naturally found its way into trustworthy hands. F. Cyril James, Willits's old as-

---

*These changes thus finally institutionalized Charles Stillé's nineteenth-century ambitions for strong administrative leadership of the university, pushing the trustees out of the daily operation of the institution. University President Thomas S. Gates and Provost Charles C. Harrison had commanded enormous influence over the course of the institution, but in both cases their power grew out of charismatic personality, prestige in the Philadelphia business and social world, and command over financial resources. Both, as well, were leading members of the university trustees. Harnwell had no such basis of support, and to be effective he needed formal grants of authority to the office of university president.

sociate from Wharton's Finance Department, now vice-chancellor and principal of McGill University, chaired the Wharton study and was joined by a distinguished panel of educators and businessmen.* The James committee met in three-day sessions every month or two for more than three years. As director of research it appointed Waldo Fisher, formerly of the IRD, and used his twenty-eight detailed studies of conditions and opinions at Wharton as the foundation of its deliberations. The committee also benefited from a series of candid discussions with faculty, both at Wharton and in the university, about their perceptions and ambitions for business education. The panel thus based its recommendations on a thorough survey of the institution.[28]

In April 1958, the James Committee issued its final report. After praising the integrity of the faculty, the document proceeded to the tough business of criticism. The great pioneering tradition of the school, of course, provided a key point of reference. The James Committee claimed that "what was once the outstanding program in the entire nation seems now to be running grave risks of becoming more 'run-of-the-mill' than most," and that "the Wharton School of Finance and Commerce has not been an inspirational leader in the field of business education for at least a generation." The panel was perhaps most dissatisfied with the academic quality of the undergraduates, claiming that "a predominance of mediocre students lowers the level of performance throughout the school, producing a deadening effect upon the students and faculty." It then faulted Wharton's low faculty salaries and the excess teaching and consulting that they entailed. To get better "inputs" into the educational process, the committee urged the school to stiffen student admission standards, raise faculty pay, and put the professoriate on an "up or out policy."[29]

The primary reform proposed by the James Committee, however, was curricular: that the school move its entire educational program to a new five-year course leading to the M.B.A. It specified that Wharton use the additional year to expand nonbusiness

---

*The other members of the Wharton Survey were John S. Keir, who began his career with Willits in Wharton's G & I Department before World War I and then left academic life for a long and distinguished career with the Dennison Manufacturing Company; Albert J. Hettinger, partner of Lazard Freres and Company, investment bankers; Maurice W. Lee, dean of the University of North Carolina business school; and William H. Newman, a former Wharton professor of business administration, now at Columbia University.

"general education" from the equivalent of two to three academic years. The committee would also concentrate all business courses in the final two years of the proposed five-year course, returning to the original "elective system" plan of offering specialized education only after a general core of liberal studies. In these final two years of professional education, they would also drop Wharton's traditional emphasis on specialized programs and provide instead general management training. In this critical sense, the James Committee stood as the direct descendant of Joseph Willits's Curriculum Committee of the 1920s. Both believed that a thorough foundation in the humanities and a general business education would prepare Wharton graduates for positions of business leadership.[30]

In and of itself the James report would have received a serious hearing. It was thorough, intelligent, and compiled by a well-respected panel. As part of the Educational Survey, moreover, the document carried the imprimatur of Willits, Harnwell, and the cause of academic reform. The entire James effort, however, soon found itself caught up in a much larger assault on the entire field of American business education. At the same time that Cyril James and his colleagues issued their report, two independent investigations of business education, one financed by the Carnegie Institution and the other by the Ford Foundation, also appeared in print. The Carnegie investigation, directed by Frank C. Pierson,* and the Ford Foundation study, led by Robert A. Gordon and James E. Howell, reached the same general conclusions about American business education that the James Report had about the Wharton program, albeit in less delicate language. Both utterly disparaged the typical specialized undergraduate program, with Pierson warning that training for "callings which require relatively brief and elementary academic preparation pose[s] a serious threat to an institution's standards. . . . The central problem confronting this branch of higher education," he insisted, "is that academic standards need to be materially increased."[31]

---

*Pierson taught economics at nearby Swarthmore College and spent a good deal of time at Wharton. Three members of the Wharton staff consulted with Pierson — Robert G. Cox, Martin Estey, and James E. McNulty — and Cox even wrote the section on accounting in the final report. Pierson had also collaborated with George Taylor in the recent past, coediting a book on *New Concepts in Wage Determination*.

Impressive in research and rhetoric, these reports exerted a profound influence on collegiate business education. Indeed, they have been called the most important documents in American higher education since the Flexner study, which revolutionized the nation's system of training physicians. Their criticism caused most schools of business to expand the liberal arts content of their programs and led some of the most prestigious private universities to eliminate undergraduate business education altogether. With such pressure all around, the Wharton School was now forced to come to terms with its destiny.

The school's first response in its long process of self-examination came from an eight-member "Wharton Survey Advisory Committee." Dean Kulp had established this group to assist James and his colleagues and to insure that their work had an impact on the faculty. Known as the "Horlacher Committee" after its chairman, political scientist Perry Horlacher, it prepared its own "positive program" for the school. Caution marked the committee's report, which began with the conservative observation that in

reviewing the course of American higher education over the past fifty years, one is struck by its almost fad-like quality. . . . In some colleges and universities adoption of a fad has led to the wholesale revamping of the business curriculum — sometimes with unsatisfactory results. In other cases, the effects have been more salutory.

The Horlacher Committee agreed that the school's academic atmosphere needed improvement, and it proposed a stiffening of humanities requirements, "more liberal and humanistic orientation of the business courses," and an emphasis on general management at the M.B.A. level. This spirit of reform faded quickly, however, and the committee staunchly defended Wharton's basic undergraduate program, the central focus of attack. It sanctioned undergraduate specialization, devoting between 40 and 50 percent of the curriculum to business subjects, and maintaining the school's traditional mixture of liberal and professional courses throughout all four years. But as a hedge against the future, the Horlacher report also recommended adding a new five-year program leading to the M.B.A., similar to that proposed by the James Committee. Although they would mix liberal arts and business courses throughout all five years, it was agreed that the M.B.A. program should emphasize general management rather than preparation for one of the business specialties. Unwilling to burn any bridges, they counseled their colleagues that

it is perhaps too early to tell whether the future path of business education lies in the direction of graduate training emphasis, or whether such emphasis is part of a more or less temporary phenomenon in educational circles. In this sense, our Five-Year Program is proposed as a systematic attempt to explore and support the graduate training movement without being definitively forced to put all our eggs in one basket.[32]

But the issue would not rest with such an accommodation. The Wharton School's enrollments were on the decline, and many of its best applicants ultimately chose to go elsewhere. The foundations clamored for change and dangled financial sweeteners to lure Wharton toward a program emphasizing the humanities. President Harnwell joined the chorus, writing in his annual report that "it is probably safe to say that in no segment of our American higher educational system is dissatisfaction with the existing practice as widespread and as deep as in the area of collegiate business education." Harnwell, however, expressed no interest in dissolving Wharton or its undergraduate course: It was the only school at the university then covering costs, and its alumni made "very strong" contributions to the university treasury. But the administration privately told key members of the faculty that it would "act" if the school did not develop an ambitious program for reform.[33]

As in the 1920s, the Wharton Curriculum Committee took the lead in the party for change. This committee, chaired by Reavis Cox and including many of the most prominent men at the school, presented the faculty with a truly radical proposal in November 1959. While favoring the continuation of the four-year undergraduate program, and agnostic as to the merits of "emphasizing management in general rather than management of particular functions in business," the committee urged a drastic cut in the amount of business courses that a student needed for graduation. Their proposal called for a 70:30 split between nonbusiness and business courses, slashing the market for the professional departments by 40 percent. Undergraduates would take 12 rather than 20 courses in business: 1 each in accounting, law, finance, marketing, and management; a 4-course major; and 3 business electives. The place of statistics and social science would probably decline somewhat, depending upon student choice of electives, while education outside of the Wharton School would double, to between 35 percent and 50 percent of an undergraduate program. Only by such radical action, the committee concluded, could the Wharton School "once again assume the leadership in education for business."[34]

These November 1959 proposals, needless to say, generated huge excitement. On seven consecutive working days, from 30 November to 8 December, the Wharton School faculty met to debate the committee recommendations. Between these meetings professors pursued each other through Dietrich Hall's corridors and offices, making points, striking deals, and gathering information. Six wrote carefully worded statements that they distributed to their colleagues and one—Joseph Rose—wrote two. The social scientists had little to lose and generally supported the Curriculum Committee, while those in the "applied departments" tended to object. As one young professor of management candidly admitted, the proposal "scares hell out of us."[35]*

The gregarious chairman of the Statistics Department, J. Parker Bursk, led the conservative faction defending the status quo. A powerful personality, who "looked like a somewhat enlarged Ernest Hemingway," Bursk ran his department in the traditional manner. He hired his instructors on the basis of personal judgement and controlled the curriculum in similar fashion. Himself with little scholarly interest in developing the science of statistics, Bursk defined the central (albeit not the only) mission of his department as training business students in the fundamentals of statistical technique. In the late 1940s, when the school required all undergraduates to take a course in statistics and the size of his department had grown quite rapidly, Bursk had great freedom to plan its future. He then recruited a faculty primarily on the basis of teaching ability, assembling an exceptionally fine corps of instructors. The rigors of a Ph.D. program, however, lay outside his concerns, and Kuznets had supervised all dissertations in the department. (After Kuznets had left and before the younger faculty members could assume such duties, Irwin Friend, the Fi-

---

*The large number of expendable graduate students then serving as instructors, however, ensured that the proposed curriculum would not result in a loss of faculty livelihoods.

nance Department's able economic statistician, took on this responsibility.) Bursk evaluated the work of his department, and of the Wharton School as a whole, primarily by its contribution to professional training, and he was satisfied with the existing program. As Bursk explained,

the public at large has differences in tastes and the Wharton School offers an excellent education for business for those whose intellect will be stimulated more by a study of business than by a study of the liberal arts. The responsibility of the Wharton School is to offer business education to those whose interests, tastes and aptitudes lie in that direction.[36]

With his quick wit, sharp logic, and deep bass voice, Bursk championed the traditional program with some effect. He sharply accused the proposed curriculum of threatening the very existence of the Wharton School as an independent undergraduate institution: "We might as well abandon the undergraduate Wharton School. Business simply becomes a major in the College." The College, he continued, had never really taught courses relevant to a business program, and its responsibilities in the Wharton curriculum ought not to be expanded. Many professors also agreed with Bursk that the school could not offer a reasonable education in the various functional areas with only one-semester surveys, as recommended by the Curriculum Committee. He thus convinced his colleagues that the committee's insistence on a maximum of twelve business courses represented an arbitrarily inflexible position. At the end of the week's acrimonious debate, the Curriculum Committee acceded to this last complaint, declaring the 70:30 figures open to negotiation. "The basic issue before the faculty," Reavis Cox now insisted, was not a specific ratio, but merely "one of accepting or rejecting the idea that substantial changes are necessary in the curriculum."[37]

Joseph R. Rose, the school's feisty professor of transportation, offered a defense of an extensive business program, but shared little with Bursk's argument for tradition. The committee's report, Rose claimed, grew out of the genteel notion that only the liberal arts offered a true education. Such a conservative opinion, he continued, disparaged all forms of professional education as mundane exercises, as mere training for the world of work that in no way prepared students for the life of the mind. Rose found this position both pretentious and foolish. Indeed, he saw practicality as the spur, rather than the barrier, to intellectual development. Although justifying professional business education, Rose differed from Bursk in that he held no brief for the current quality of education at Wharton. He found the proliferation of descriptive and procedural courses especially disturbing. As an economist with a strong taste for theory, Rose thought that the faculty should embark on a major effort to bring "rigour and precision to business education." He would emphasize "the basic disciplines applicable to all fields of business study such as economics, statistics, and accounting; and perhaps . . . introduce some of the newer techniques such as linear programming." But Rose found the Curriculum Committee overawed by the genteel argument for the humanities and uninterested in his line of discourse. With obvious annoyance, he remarked that "the committee has evidently chosen virtually to abandon business education and not to improve it."[38]

After a thorough airing of views, the faculty had to decide. Dean Winn spoke on the last of these consecutive days of debate, and he placed his prestige behind the committee proposals. He referred to facts now known by all: the decline of student interest in the Wharton School, the criticisms of the Educational Survey and the foundation reports, and the anxious concern of business leaders. Winn told the faculty that "there is a need for defining the purpose of the school" and that "the risks [of acceptance] are less than the risks of alternative action; the chances of success are great. . . . The important thing is for the Wharton School to rise again to the apex of excellence in business education." When the votes were counted, they showed that the faculty had agreed, approving the proposals by an overwhelming margin of 100 to 41.[39]

The Curriculum Committee immediately began redesigning the school's program in earnest. Instead of 12, it allowed 15 courses for business, with all three additions assigned to the general business core. Less radical than the committee's original proposal, this revision still cut the former levels of professional preparation by a significant 25 percent. In "This is Wharton," a promotional pamphlet issued in 1964, the school emphasized its social science and humanities orientation, claiming that "the important role which liberal arts can play in the training of business executives is today more widely recognized than ever before." The brochure explained that "vocationally oriented work was not emphasized in Joseph Wharton's design for business education, nor is it given much emphasis in the present Wharton curriculum."[40]

As well as pruning Wharton's business curriculum, the school also took up Joseph Rose's charge to improve it through liberalization. Although the debates had focused on the 70:30 split and the faculty had never sanctioned Rose's proposals, it was his program that had the greater impact on business education at Wharton. After 1965, in fact, the school allowed its undergraduates to take over 40 percent of their credits in professional subjects, a figure comparable to that existing before the entire curricular fuss. What remained from this great period of self-examination were improvements in "imparting a liberal education in all matters concerning Finance and Economy." Dean Winn set the tone of the new campaign in his 1959-60 annual report. There he echoed Rose's contentions, writing that

in modern industrial society, there are new areas of education which belong to the liberal tradition. This assumes that "liberal education" is interpreted in its original dynamic sense rather than as a new orthodoxy seeking to replace the earlier orthodoxy of "classical" education. Courses in general business education, while required of future Wharton School students, will be designed so as to be attractive and worthwhile offerings for liberal arts students as well.[41]

With leadership from Winn and the Curriculum Committee and with support from the Harnwell administration and the Ford Foundation, Wharton quickly upgraded the academic content of its entire professional program. The school expanded oppportunities for academically aggressive students to take "enriched" sections in certain required courses, elect honors programs in several majors, and by the mid-1960s it allowed Dean's List students to take waiver examinations in two business core subjects at the end of their sophomore year. The Curriculum Committee oversaw the development and introduction of new courses in sociology and political science. For the first time in its eighty-year history, Wharton required all students to take mathematics—a freshman course in calculus. This, in turn, led faculty in areas such as economics and statistics to upgrade the level of their instruction. Parker Bursk's Statistics Department, for example, had hitherto "emphasized 'logic', not mathematics," and had required from its students no more preparation than high school algebra. But with the arrival of calculus (and strong pressure from the James Committee), Wharton's program moved decisively into the exotic new world of mathematical statistics.[42]

In its practical subject areas, Wharton also attempted to provide a more "liberal" form of instruction. According to the 1964 promotional pamphlet, for example, the school's new "Introduction to Law" course presented law "as an expanding social institution," not as a compendium of rights and procedures. It likewise claimed for the revised survey of "Risk and Insurance" a focus on principles, rather than a review of contracts and policies. The brochure insisted that

Wharton's basic accounting course, prior to the adoption of the new curriculum, had been developed primarily as the first course in a series for accounting majors. Although it was not a course in "bookkeeping," it did place a considerable emphasis on periodical procedures and the preparation of financial statements, and it gave greater attention to professional accounting than to management uses of accounting data. Under the new curriculum, the basic accounting course which students take as part of their general business education has been designed to instill in the student an understanding of the uses and limitations of accounting information, an awareness of the reasons behind current practices, a realization of the defects and inconsistencies existing in published financial statements, and similar managerial and financial uses of accounting data.[43]

"This is Wharton," in its exuberance, exaggerated the difference between the old and the new forms of instruction. Solomon Huebner had made a great career for himself by teaching the principles of insurance, while Wharton's business law professors had always offered broad and often brilliant perspectives on their subject. A certain amount of procedural detail, moreover, remained an essential part of professional education. But the new program did move in the direction advertised. The introduction of the calculus requirement alone marked a critical juncture in collegiate business education. In addition, the revised curriculum clearly installed general business education as the leading purpose of the school. In the past, survey courses in the various functional specialties had been introductions to a further series of courses on the subject. The Curriculum Committee now bent these surveys into components of a general business core. It also limited departmental "concentration" requirements to four courses, thus making business in general as much a Wharton student's major as such subjects as finance or marketing.[44]*

Wharton thus parted company with the pedagogy of professional specialization, its basic strategy since the days of Edmund James. This specialization, easily overdone, had consistently been a major cause of criticism. But now, with barely a third of all students who graduated with Wharton B.S. degrees taking jobs upon graduation, vocational preparation no longer seemed so compelling; most students went on to get their "technical equipment" in graduate professional schools. The Wharton School could thus comfortably aim its undergraduate program at providing a general, liberal preparation for the world of affairs.[45]

The Wharton School finished this basic redesign of its undergraduate curriculum by the mid-1960s, and it could not have chosen a more propitious time to launch an ambitious new enterprise. With the postwar baby boom generation then arriving at the nation's colleges, the school's supply of well-qualified applicants increased automatically. Wharton, in fact, chose to take only the most promising students, and reduced undergraduate admissions far below former levels, to 1,400 in 1967. This policy led to a dramatic 200-point increase in entering freshman S.A.T. scores between 1957 and 1967. With the Harnwell administration and the major foundations both extremely solicitous of the health of business education, Wharton also inaugurated a whole new era in faculty renumeration. Average salaries for full professors rose from seven thousand dollars in 1954, to eighteen thousand dollars in 1967. These salaries, along with the retirement of many of the professors recruited in the 1920s, led to a much stronger faculty. Very few appointments now went to Wharton Ph.D.'s. Joseph Willits, writing to the members of the James Panel eight years after they issued their report, wrote that "the filling of any new [faculty] post is now viewed as a sacred opportunity and approached with the greatest of care." Their efforts had been successful, Willits continued, and the "undergraduate Wharton School

---

*For students especially interested in accounting, the school opened a "Fifth-Year Program" leading to an M.S. in Accounting in 1962. With six courses in accounting, one in mathematics, and three business electives, the program provided a thorough preparation for a professional accounting career.

is again an educational institution" of the first rank. Indeed, an impartial survey taken on the eve of Wharton's centennial, in 1981, declared that the school then offered the finest undergraduate business education in the nation. By that time, Wharton stood as the University of Pennsylvania's most prestigious and sought-after undergraduate program, a radical reversal of its traditional status in the institution.[46]

Wharton thus embarked on a new and clearly more academic path. The school drew closer to the university by "liberalizing" its curriculum, by shifting toward a discussion of principles and away from a rehearsal of procedures. But whatever the criticisms made of it by the foundation reports and the James Panel, Wharton's old program did achieve a certain measure of success. Even if the world of academic research passed many of them by, the faculty of the 1950s had gathered a great deal of practical experience, and on the whole they were excellent teachers. The undergraduates of the 1950s did give up two hundred S.A.T. points to Wharton students a decade later, and they entered the world of affairs without the benefit of courses in calculus. Nevertheless, they managed to turn their education to good account. A 1980 survey of earned income, a crude measure, perhaps, of business success, showed that 1 out of 4 graduates from that decade were then earning more than one hundred thousand dollars a year. Their successors, however, would receive a different preparation.[47]

Source Notes

1. U.S. Bureau of the Census, *Historical Statistics of the United States, Colonial Times to 1957* (Washington, D.C.: United States Government Printing Office, 1960), 139; Alfred D. Chandler, Jr., *Strategy and Structure* (Cambridge, Mass.: M.I.T. Press, 1962).

2. "C. Canby Balderston File,"Archives; C. Canby Balderston, *Executive Guidance of Industrial Relations: An Analysis of the Experience of Twenty-Five Companies*, Industrial Research Department Research Studies no. 25 (Philadelphia: University of Pennsylvania Press, 1935); C. Canby Balderston and Morris E. Leeds, *Wages: A Means of Testing Their Adequacy*, Industrial Research Department Research Studies no. 11 (Philadelphia: University of Pennsylvania Press, 1931).

3. Minutes of the Wharton Faculty, 6 Jan. 1941, 3 Nov. 1947, 5 Jan. 1948, 10 May 1949, 5 May 1952; Minutes of the Board of Business Education, 12 Nov. 1940, 30 Nov. 1950; Marty Kramer, "C. Canby Balderston," *Daily Pennsylvanian* 66 (1952); n.a., "A New Building for the Wharton School of Finance and Commerce, University of Pennsylvania," 28 Oct. 1950, mimeographed, "Alfred H. Williams File," Archives.

4. Interviews with Richard Clelland, Erwin Miller, Ernest Browne, and Eric van Merkensteijn; private communication, E. Gordon Keith to author, 26 Aug. 1980.

5. F. Cyril James, John S. Keir, Albert J. Hettinger, Maurice W. Lee, and William H. Newman, "The Wharton School of Finance and Commerce, The Report of the Board of Consultants," mimeographed (Philadelphia: Educational Survey of the University of Pennsylvania, 1958), 53, 19, 19−20; Minutes of the Bureau of Business Education, 24 Oct. 1946, 20 Nov. 1947, 30 Nov. 1950, 22 Jan. 1953; Keith to author, 26 Aug. 1980; Thomas A. Budd to Gaylord P. Harnwell, 13 Jan. 1955, "Annual Report File," files of the Dean of the Wharton School, 13; 1980 Wharton Alumni Survey, conducted by the author; interview with William Hockenberry.

6. James et al., "Report", 25; Minutes of the Board of Business Education, 22 Jan. 1953; "Report of the Curriculum Committee," Minutes of the Wharton Faculty, 6 May 1954, 17.

7. James et al., "Report", 82, 92; Budd to Harnwell, 13 Jan. 1955, 3, 5−6; C. Arthur Kulp to Jonathan E. Rhodes, 15 Apr. 1956, "Annual Report File," files of the Dean of the Wharton School.

8. James et al., "Report," xii, 87, 84, ix−xiii, 21−22, 84−85; "Minutes of the Wharton Advisory Council," 12 Dec. 1951, Minutes of the Wharton Faculty, 7 Jan. 1952.

9. Minutes of the Wharton Faculty, 18 Sept. 1944; AMS, s.v. "Carter Goodrich" and "Dorothy S. Thomas"; Simon S. Kuznets and Dorothy S. Thomas, *Population Redistribution and Economic Growth: United States, 1870−1950*, 3 vols. (Philadelphia: American Philosophical Society, 1957−64); interview with William Whitney; Annual Report of the Dean of the Wharton School (1965−66), files of the Dean of the Wharton School.

10. Interviews with Keith and Miller; AMS, s.v. "Frank Cyril James" and "Hans P. Neisser"; F. Cyril James, *Rise of Chicago Banks* (New York: Harper Brothers, 1938); F. Cyril James, *The Economics of Money, Credit, and Banking* (New York: Ronald Press, 1930.)

11. [E. Gordon Keith?], Minute in Memoriam [for C. Ray Whittlesey], files of Prof. Jean Crockett; Edward Mead and Julius Grodinsky, *The Ebb and Flow of Investment Values* (New York: Appleton−Century, 1939), vii; Julius Grodinsky, *The Iowa Pool* (Chicago: University of Chicago Press, 1950) and *Jay Gould, His Business Career, 1867−1892* (Philadelphia: University of Pennsylvania Press, 1957); interview with Keith; C. Ray Whittlesey, *International Monetary Issues* (New York: McGraw-Hill, 1937); C. Ray Whittlesey and Frank D. Graham, *Golden Avalanche* (Princeton, N.J.: Princeton University Press, 1940).

12. Interview with Keith and Jean Crockett; AMS, s.v. "Willis J. Winn" and "Edward Gordon Keith."

13. Interview with Whittlesey; Minutes of the Wharton Faculty, 6 Dec. 1948.

14. Irwin Friend, G. Wright Hoffman, and Willis J. Winn, *The Over-the-Counter Securities Markets* (New York: McGraw-Hill, 1958), v, v−vi; interviews with Whittlesey and Winn; AMS, s.v. "Irwin Friend."

15. Irwin Friend, F. E. Brown, Edward S. Herman, and Douglas Vickers, *A Study of Mutual Funds* (Washington, D.C.: Government Printing Office, 1962), ix−x, xii−xiii, xiii.

16. Interview with Dan M. McGill.

17. Ibid.; Dan M. McGill, *The Fundamentals of Private Pensions* (Homewood, Ill.: Richard D. Irwin, 1955).

18. Industrial Research Unit, *Report on Progress* (Philadelphia: Industrial Research Unit, 1978), #57,70−71; Dan M. McGill, *Fulfilling Pension Expec-*

tations (Homewood, Ill.: Richard D. Irwin, 1962), xxi, xxii, xix–xxiii; interview with McGill.

19. "Towards a Better Life through Training in Government," *Philadelphia Bulletin*, 14 May 1967, sec. 2:6; "School of Public and Urban Policy," promotional pamphlet, n.p., 2; Thomas J. Davy, "Formal Educational Activities of the Fels Institute," Outline of Remarks, Minutes of the Wharton Faculty, 2 Nov. 1964; Stephen B. Sweeney, "Strengthening Democracy at the Roots," reprinted from the *[University of Pennsylvania] Library Chronical*, June 1943; "Memorandum from Lloyd M. Short to Willis J. Winn, 23 Aug. 1966," 13–14, files of the School of Public and Urban Policy, University of Pennsylvania.

20. Minutes of the Board of Business Education, 31 May 1945; Former Members of the Staff, "A Research Program in Retrospect," mimeographed, 1955, 40–41, 47.

21. Interview with Simon Kuznets.

22. James et al., "Report," 29, xiii, 28–29.

23. Interviews with Cataldo, Kuznets, Joseph Rose, and Cox; Martin Meyerson and Dilys P. Winegrad, *Gladly Learn and Gladly Teach* (Philadelphia: University of Pennsylvania Press, 1978), 215, 238, 242; Minutes of the Wharton Faculty, 3 Dec. 1945, 12 Dec. 1950, 9 Apr. 1951, 3 Dec. 1951, 12 Feb. 1952, 22 Feb. 1952.

24. Meyerson and Winegrad, 215; interviews with Kuznets and Willits.

25. Interview with Kuznets; Minutes of the Wharton Faculty, 11 Nov. 1954, 8 Dec. 1959; Minutes of the Board of Business Education, 24 Feb. 1955.

26. "Dr. Clarence A. Kulp Dies," *Philadelphia Bulletin*, 21 Aug. 1957; news release, University of Pennsylvania News Bureau, 3 May 1955, "C. Arthur Kulp File," Archives; news release, 11 June 1971, University of Pennsylvania News Bureau, "Willis J. Winn File," Archives.

27. Interviews with Willits and Kuznets.

28. James et al., "Report," front cover, 3–5.

29. Ibid., 21–22, 100, vi, xi, 32–43.

30. Ibid., 24–45.

31. Frank C. Pierson et al., *The Education of American Businessmen* (New York: McGraw-Hill, 1959), 26, ix, xvii; Robert A. Gordon and James E. Howell, *Higher Education for Business* (New York: Columbia University Press, 1959); George W. Taylor and Frank C. Pierson, eds., *New Conceptions in Wage Determination* (New York: McGraw–Hill, 1957).

32. John P. Horlacher et al., "A Program for the Wharton School," mimeographed, Nov. 1957, 37, 26, 16–21, 30, 49.

33. Statements by E. Orin Burley, Minutes of the Wharton Faculty, 3 Dec. 1959, and Willis Winn, Minutes of the Wharton Faculty, 4 Dec. 1959.

34. "A Recommendation to the Faculty of the Wharton School of Finance and Commerce, 16 Nov. 1959," Minutes of the Wharton Faculty, 30 Nov. 1959, 4, 10–13.

35. John F. Lubin, as reported in Minutes of the Wharton Faculty, 7 Dec. 1959.

36. Reminiscences of Nancy Schnerr, in *The Story of Statistics*, offset, ed. Nancy Schnerr (Philadelphia: Wharton School, 1981); J. Parker Bursk, as reported in Minutes of the Wharton Faculty, 1 Dec. 1959; reminiscences of Schnerr, Don Murray, John de Cani, and Morris Hamburg, in Schnerr, ed., *The Story of Statistics*; interview with Nancy Schnerr.

37. J. Parker Bursk, as reported in Minutes of the Wharton Faculty, 7 Dec. 1959; Reavis Cox, as reported in Minutes of the Wharton Faculty, 4 Dec. 1959; statement by E. Orin Burley, Minutes of the Wharton Faculty, 3 Dec. 1959; Minutes of the Wharton Faculty, 30 Nov. 1959 to 8 Dec. 1959, 15 Dec. 1959; interview with Clelland.

38. Statement by Joseph Rose, Minutes of the Wharton Faculty, 1 Dec. 1959; interviews with Clelland and Rose.

39. Willis J. Winn, as reported in Minutes of the Wharton Faculty, 8 Dec. 1959; Minutes of the Wharton Faculty, 4 Jan. 1960.

40. "This is Wharton," promotional pamphlet attached to Minutes of the Wharton Faculty, 5 Oct. 1964, 4; Annual Report of the Dean of the Wharton School (1960–61), files of the Dean of the Wharton School, 1.

41. Joseph Wharton, "Project"; Minutes of the University Trustees, 24 Mar. 1881; Annual Report of the Dean of the Wharton School (1959–60), files of the Dean of the Wharton School, 2; Minutes of the Wharton Faculty, 1 Feb. 1965; "This is Wharton," 8.

42. "This is Wharton," 9; reminiscence of John de Cani, in Schnerr, ed., *The Story of Statistics*; Annual Report of the Dean of the Wharton School (1963 – 64), files of the Dean of the Wharton School, 1 – 2; interviews with Clelland and Schnerr.

43. "This is Wharton," 6, 6–7.

44. *Ibid.*, 13; Minutes of the Wharton Faculty, 7 May 1962.

45. Joseph Willits, "Some Comments to the 'James' Panel on The Wharton School of the University of Pennsylvania in 1967," in the author's possession.

46. Willits, "Some Comments," 2, 3, 1–3; Annual Report of the Dean of the Wharton School (1957 – 58), files of the Dean of the Wharton School, 3, (1958–59), 5; "Penn's Undergraduate Business Program Rated Best," *Chronicle of Higher Education*, 30 June 1980, 8.

47. 1980 Wharton Alumni Survey, conducted by the author.

C. Canby Balderston

Calculating room, Dietrich Hall, 1952

Student lounge, Dietrich Hall

Wharton students

Houston Hall cafeteria

Dietrich Hall, rear elevation and front façade

Harold Stassen

Gaylord P. Harnwell

Bernard Cataldo

Dorothy S. Thomas

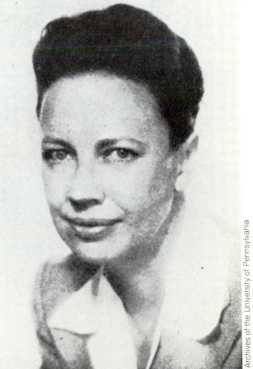

Dan McGill

C. Ray Whittlesey

Irwin Friend

Julius Grodinsky

G. Wright Hoffman

E. Gordon Keith

C. Arthur Kulp

Willis J. Winn

Irving B. Kravis

J. Parker Bursk

Joseph R. Rose

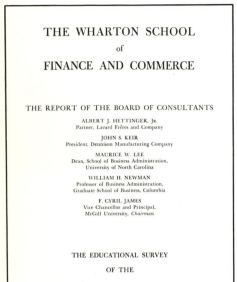

THE WHARTON SCHOOL

of

FINANCE AND COMMERCE

THE REPORT OF THE BOARD OF CONSULTANTS

ALBERT J. HETTINGER, Jr.
Partner, Lazard Frères and Company

JOHN S. KEIR
President, Dennison Manufacturing Company

MAURICE W. LEE
Dean, School of Business Administration,
University of North Carolina

WILLIAM H. NEWMAN
Professor of Business Administration,
Graduate School of Business, Columbia

F. CYRIL JAMES
Vice Chancellor and Principal,
McGill University, *Chairman*

THE EDUCATIONAL SURVEY

OF THE

UNIVERSITY of PENNSYLVANIA

April 1958

SUMMARY

The full report of the Board of Consultants including its findings and recommendations runs to some one hundred pages. The Research Studies done under the direction of the Director of Research runs to some thousands of pages. The present summary is designed to provide an over-view of the whole.

Matters Considered by the Board

1. Implications and impact of the changing setting in which business, government, and social affairs are conducted.

2. Performance of the Wharton School, graduate and undergraduate.

3. Factors limiting its achievement and potential.

4. Strengths at Wharton upon which to build for the future.

5. Design for the future.

6. Transition from the present to the future.

Background and Setting

The Wharton School is the oldest collegiate school of business in this country. And much of the evolutionary path of collegiate education in this field may be traced to the pioneering work of members of the Wharton School faculty. From this early beginning when Wharton towered alone in the field, the passing decades have witnessed a phenomenal growth of similar institutions. Today more than 200 separate schools and departments of business administration and more than 600 colleges and universities offer some work in such fields in the United States.

Survey of the Wharton School, cover and first page of text

9

Models, Mathematics, and the Apotheosis of Economic Theory

The Wharton School emerged from the curricular controversies of the 1950s with a new commitment to academic values. At no time since the establishment of the school's practical business programs at the turn of the century had it been so enamored of the university. And as it happened, the times were especially inviting for such proximity. A group of ambitious academics were then creating a sophisticated genre of social science disciplines carrying great promise for the Wharton School. At once liberal and practical, these "policy sciences" provided men of affairs new means of analyzing their situations, predicting the future, and optimizing performance. Once Wharton integrated these new disciplines into its program, the school embarked on a period of tremendous vitality and usefulness. This success, however, had its frictions. So practical were the new policy sciences that they usurped several fields of study from the older procedural tradition of business education; so liberal were they that pressure built up to pull them out of Wharton and into a new enlarged "faculty of arts and sciences." Despite these tensions, however, the policy science disciplines brought Wharton to a new level of intellectual sophistication, and they constituted the school's most distinctive intellectual contribution to the world of affairs to date.

Only once before had such a collection of new disciplines established themselves at Wharton — when the school developed its original business programs at the turn of the century. At that time, courses of study in the procedures and institutions of transportation, commerce, insurance, finance, financial accounting, and management all found niches in the curriculum. From a sociological point of view, these two "speciations" of academic disciplines had much in common. Both occurred quite rapidly, with the new genres of academe winning places at Wharton within a decade. In the most successful cases in either period, one entrepreneurial professor provided strong intellectual and organizational leadership. In both the 1900s and 1960s, the new species of academic life shared common intellectual foundations, while being differentiated primarily by their specific problem areas. These root subjects had previously been taught at Wharton, but in somewhat restricted fashion. With the spawning of the new fields, each specialty absorbed the parts of the foundation subjects germane to its problem area and developed them with far greater sophistication than had hitherto been the case. The turn-of-the-century business disciplines grew out of accounting, law, and "mercantile practice," with each new field specializing in the laws, accounts, and practices of a specific trade. Wharton's policy sciences of the 1960s shared a common concern with economic theory (either the theory of market systems or the theory of household management)* and mathematics (including the statistics and techniques for using the recently invented electronic computing machines). These common foundations facilitated communication, cooperation, and even transfers of personnel among sister disciplines. Because of such flows, both traditions supported extensive divisions of labor. Work could proceed on numerous topics and, given a reasonable amount of time, initiates of the tradition had access to contributions made in any component field.

The speciation of business disciplines in the 1960s, like that of the 1900s, grew out of changes in both the university and its environment. The establishment of a viable Ph.D. program at the turn of the century had given Wharton the capacity to generate new fields of study; the burgeoning growth of specialized business occupations and a sudden rush of college students seeking vocational training at that time had created hearty appetites for

---

*The policy sciences growing out of theories of household management will be discussed in the next chapter.

such education. The 1960s also saw the supply and demand for business education increase. The children of the postwar baby boom then came of college age, and the rising level of academic aptitude among Wharton's student body, as reflected by their S.A.T. scores, facilitated the expansion of business education toward the university. "Supply-side" considerations, however, played a far greater role in this second speciation.

The modern source of academic innovations, in 1960 as in 1900, were entrepreneurial scholars and vigorous Ph.D. programs. In the 1950s, neither were especially prominent at Wharton. However, Dean Willis Winn and his associate dean, Irving Kravis, quickly devised a successful strategy of academic development. Winn and Kravis made it the policy of the school to recruit ambitious senior scholars and to give them the freedom and resources that they needed to develop their own programs of teaching, research, and doctoral training. Such leaders, they reasoned, would attract and then stimulate junior faculty and Ph.D. students; these young people would then contribute a stream of research that would make Wharton a major center of creative scholarship.

The success of Wharton's new strategy was made possible by the great bull market for graduate programs and academic research that continued throughout the 1960s. The national need to educate the baby boom generation led to a disproportionate increase in doctoral programs, which now had to construct whole new faculties, not just replace retiring professors. Replacement demand in undergraduate business faculties, moreover, was especially high, as the large cohort of business instructors turned out in the 1920s was then leaving the work force. The 1957 Soviet launch of Sputnik, in addition, generated a national commitment to research that included generous support for all types of doctoral students and social science investigations.

Despite the similarity of circumstance, the new policy sciences that flourished at Wharton during the 1960s were far more academic than the business practice disciplines that had grown up at the turn of the century. Members of the new tradition, from the senior scholars with national reputations to their recently graduated Ph.D. students, all went through a far more rigorous doctoral program than their predecessors. Doctoral students typically took three to six years to win their degrees, not one to two;

requirements in mathematics, theory, and research also bore little resemblance to those of 1900. Wharton's pioneer business professors, as could be expected, had found most of their curricular materials in the business world, not in the university. Despite their energy and enthusiasm, their scholarship had essentially been an extended form of business journalism. The new policy scientists, however, took their basic materials from academe. They substituted theoretical models for institutional description; behavioral theories for legal prescription; and abstract rationality for standard procedure. In doing so, they created whole fields of knowledge and practice that were new to the business scene. But since these policy sciences proved themselves to be potent managerial instruments, they quickly found a place in the world of affairs.

When Wharton went looking to intensify the academic content of its professional program, after the curricular debates, the school turned first to the social sciences. These disciplines had always been the most scholarly at Wharton and had provided the most significant academic input into business education. During the prosperity that followed World War II, moreover, these subject areas had experienced one of their greatest eras of growth and development. Economics had always been the most rigorous and sophisticated social science — the "physics" of the group — and throughout this creative period the dismal science only enhanced its preeminence. At Wharton the stature of economics grew even more quickly, completely overshadowing its sister sciences by the end of the 1960s. Sociology and political science had some measure of success after World War II, but not nearly to the same degree as economics. Nor did they exert a comparable influence on the large course of the Wharton School.

Wharton never developed a strong academic program in political science during the postwar period. In large part that was due to the fact that two semiindependent institutes — the Fels Institute and a new Foreign Policy Research Institute (FPRI) — dominated work in political science at the school and neither generated a significant amount of scientific research. Each had a budget larger than that of the Political Science Department itself, and thereby exerted a decided influence over faculty hiring and graduate education. Because of the Fels influence, public administration occupied the attention of most members of the department, and in the mid-1960s "only one of the senior people [specializing] in American politics . . . was clearly identified with national politics." The legacy of Edmund James thus controlled this half of the Political Science Department eighty years after his arrival in Philadelphia.* The study of international affairs, the department's major postwar departure, developed under the auspices of the FPRI and its director, Robert Strausz-Hupé. A European emigre with a 1946 Wharton Ph.D., Strausz-Hupé and his operation had unusually close ties with the U.S. Departments of State and Defense. He argued a tough, cold-war line in his well-attended lectures and in books such as *Forward Strategy for America* and *Building the Atlantic World*. As director of the FPRI, he had the funds to "persuade the Department to hire certain kinds of faculty" — other hard-line anti-Communists with military or emigre pasts. Control over certain university fellowships and a strong influence in the Ph.D.-granting Graduate Group in International Relations also gave the FPRI a dominant position in the Ph.D. program. Strausz-Hupé and his colleagues, however, focused on a rather narrow line of research, and the department assumed not so much an academic as an ideological identity. Because the FPRI and the Fels Institute loomed so large, the department "failed to reflect the changes in the discipline"; while Strausz-Hupé's group in international affairs broadened the horizons of political science at Wharton, the school could no longer boast one of the leading political science programs in the nation.[1]

Wharton's postwar sociologists expanded the scope of their interests and caught the new vitality in American social science far more effectively than did their colleagues in political science. The department maintained its traditional interest in social problems, but issues of reform no longer constituted its unifying theme. Marvin E. Wolfgang, who succeeded his mentor Thorsten Sellin as the school's professor of criminology, best maintained Wharton's connection with its past.† But from the beginning of the postwar era, the department added first-class scholars with altogether different interests. In the mid-1940s, the department es-

---

*James C. Charlesworth, educational director of the institute, also served as president of James's American Academy of Political and Social Science between 1953 and 1970.

†Wolfgang also became president of the American Academy, in 1972.

tablished its strong group in demography. E. Digby Baltzell, who arrived with a Columbia Ph.D. in 1947, studied social elites, and wrote impressive sociological studies of the upper classes of the United States and his native Philadelphia. In 1961, the department hired Philip Reiff, who held a degree in sociology from the University of Chicago. Reiff was then publishing his seminal work *Freud, the Mind of the Moralist*, and, as both author and editor, soon established himself as one of the foremost authorities on the theory and sociology of psychoanalysis. During the 1960s, therefore, sociologists at Wharton successfully developed various new lines of scholarship. But unlike earlier work in the department, no common purpose or intellectual tradition unified the faculty. Reiff leaned toward psychology, the demographers toward economics, and no one had much to do with attempts by Harvard sociologist Talcott Parsons to establish a common theoretical framework for the discipline. Certain aspects of Wharton's work in sociology had a bearing on the school's professional purposes, but since the department lacked a unified voice, these relationships were neither as apparent nor as powerful as those emerging from economics.[2]

Since the very beginning of the school, in the founder's "Project," economics had been Wharton's primary link with the liberal arts of the college. Inasmuch as Wharton's subsequent business program had any foundation in the academy, it had been in economics: The school had always required the subject of its students, and nearly all members of the faculty had graduate training in the field. These professors had taken some courses in theory, but had concentrated on the descriptive, "institutional" brand of economics; it was Joseph Willits's strategy, in fact, to ground all Wharton programs in this descriptive tradition. Since the creation of the modern American university, the economic theorists and institutionalists had uneasily shared control over their discipline. After 1945, however, the theorists had grown steadily more powerful and had relentlessly pushed the institutionalists to the periphery. Since Wharton had found its primary academic moorings in this declining tradition, the upheaval in economics promised radical changes in the future of the school.

Alfred Marshall's neoclassical theory of markets had formed the center of the Wharton Economics Department during the years between the wars. As a group, the school's economists of the period had been cool to the practical, descriptive thrust of Wharton's business programs and had had little interest in the managerial arts and sciences that were taught in those parts of the school: Their neoclassicism had been a jealous god, one that would not allow the details of business to obstruct its own elegant symmetries. This faculty's primary concern was to teach the marginalist analysis of market price and output, and Raymond Bye's *Principles of Economics*, first published in 1924, presented the standard Marshallian system. He cautiously included the contributions of his contemporaries in revised editions, but remained quite conservative with his theory: Only slowly did he accept the work of Keynes, the major revolutionary of the century; so powerful was his attachment to Marshall that he "gave a very subordinate position" to a promising alternative to traditional marginalist methods of modeling production functions and consumer preferences — indifference curves.* Such conservatism had a legitimate place in textbook writing, and Bye's texts won a wide audience. But neither he nor his colleagues at the university made significant contributions to theoretical economics or to its application to managerial problems. Aside from the recruitment of Sidney Weintraub, a wide-ranging scholar and noted Keynesian, this remained the case throughout the entire decade after World War II.[3]

Things began to change rapidly as the University Survey and the Foundation reports created an atmosphere at Wharton quite favorable to the social sciences in general and to economics in particular. Beyond this change of air, the school's Economics Department had the benefit of a new and exceedingly energetic chairman, Irving Kravis. Kravis had joined the faculty in 1947, after winning his Wharton Ph.D. in international economics, and soon became active in academic administration. When C. Arthur Kulp became dean in 1955, Kravis became chairman of the Economics Department; in 1958, Dean Winn named Kravis associate dean for budget and personnel. Kravis worked tremendously hard as associate dean—people still commented on his energy in office twenty years after he left that post. But Kravis attached himself

---

*Advocates of the indifference apparatus claimed that it avoided marginalism's sticky assumption that consumers measure utilities. Bye thought this "a dubious claim" and that "both the terminology and the mechanics of the indifference theory are more awkward than the marginal utility explanation."

primarily to the Economics Department. He served as associate dean for only two years, but chaired Economics for seven of the eleven years following 1955. Overriding all other ambitions was his hope to make Wharton's department one of the best in the world, and he fought the innumerable battles necessary to get the money and personnel he wanted. Dean Winn and Provost Jonathan Rhodes, themselves convinced that a strong business school needed a strong program in economics, generally gave him their support. Kravis, in turn, promised them a world-class assembly of economists, and by 1960 had hired Walter Isard, Lawrence Klein, Arthur Bloomfield, and Dorothy Brady.[4]

Kravis's major coup was the hiring of Lawrence Klein in 1958. The son of clerical workers in Omaha, Nebraska, Klein had studied economics at MIT, under the brilliant Paul Samuelson. His dissertation, later published as the *The Keynesian Revolution*, had provided the first complete, formal mathematical statement of the new macroeconomics. The Keynesian theory, as Klein explained it, had argued that industrial capitalism could settle into a stable "equilibrium" with millions of workers unemployed and thousands of factories idle. These English notions, however, had generated little enthusiasm on the Western shores of the Atlantic where mainstream American economists had continued to regard full employment as the only natural condition of free market economies despite the Depression of the 1930s. Conservatives, in particular, feared Keynes because he advocated government management of the economy and justified increased social service expenditures to compensate for a supposed decay of private investment opportunities. While Klein's volume did not dispell this political distaste, it clarified many of Keynes's arguments and convinced most theorists of the cogency of the new economics.[5]

Putting Keynes's arguments into mathematical form served as the catalyst, rather than the culmination, of Klein's career. Klein could have remained in the world of theory, as did his mentor Paul Samuelson. But he recognized that mathematical modeling opened an exciting new opportunity to yoke theory with empirical measurement, and Klein chose to work with facts as well as concepts. Hitherto most economists had either spun theories or studied data, and bridges between the two camps had been scarce and flimsy. Wesley Clair Mitchell of the National

Bureau of Economic Research, one of the great empiricists of the interwar period, had not based his measurements on any deductive theory at all; Wharton's Simon Kuznets, Mitchell's student and the other great empiricist of the era, used an accounting-type theory that presupposed no causal connection between the behavior of one variable and that of another. But econometrics, as the new combination of theory and empirical research was called, derived from traditional predictive economics. Econometricians took theories — such as Keynesian macroeconomics or Ricardo's analysis of how growing populations cause rents to rise — and put them into well-defined, quantifiable mathematical terms. They then attempted to test the validity and measure the strength of the indicated causal relationships. Once such causal connections were known, and present conditions suitably defined, econometricians could speak of the future. They could predict the course of rents from population statistics; data on investment could indicate next year's level of employment. Although still in its embryonic form, econometrics promised to give the discipline rigorous new means of testing its theories and powerful new tools of prediction.

In his first public prognostication, Klein used a simple six-equation model to predict a booming postwar prosperity. Since most pundits had warned of renewed depression, the return of good times validated both Keynesian theory and the new econometric technology. But Klein's work had just begun. To construct more complex and more accurate models, he and his fellow econometricians had to develop quantitative techniques never before used in the discipline. Earlier economic statisticians, such as Mitchell and Kuznets, had worked up a great deal of expertise in finding data to fit categories and in fashioning statistical measures of economic phenomena. Econometricians, of course, profited from these contributions. But the study of causal relationships demanded new procedures, such as accounting for lags between cause and effect; handling measurement-error terms while manipulating variables mathematically; and reducing a mass of empirical readings to simple, clear equations. Klein contributed to the solution of some of these technical issues, and by 1955 he and a graduate student with whom he worked closely, Arthur J. Goldberger, felt confident enough to construct the world's first modern econometric model of the United States economy. So successful were their forecasts that by the early 1950s, business firms soon made regular use of their results when designing strategic plans.[6]

To Klein, then at the University of Michigan, his work seemed to be progressing quite well. But when the econometrician came up for tenure, the university authorities denied him a permanent spot on the faculty. Klein, it seemed, had been a Communist. Although he had gotten "bored" with Marxism and soon left the party, Senator Joseph McCarthy learned of Klein's indiscretion and was in no mood to take chances with the future of the republic. Neither was the University of Michigan in any mood to take chances with the senator from Wisconsin. Hurt and disgusted by this ignorant rejection, Klein left the country and joined the faculty of Oxford University. There Kravis found him, and with strong promises of academic freedom and a voice in designing the future of the department, brought him to the University of Pennsylvania in 1958.[7]

Once at Wharton, Klein and his econometrics flourished magnificently. He immediately went to work training graduate students and constructing a new and more ambitious model of the national economy. Economists from several major industrial corporations, whose job it was to fathom the future, soon came to the university to have Klein build forecasting models of their particular environments. In 1963 he combined five corporate clients into a consortium to fund an "Economic Forecasting Unit" at Wharton; this unit would then supply the corporations with even more sophisticated data. Sponsorship of the EFU quickly increased to 20 organizations, totaled 150 after a decade, and reached 300 by 1980. Rather than use this patronage to enrich himself, neither an unknown nor illegitimate purpose at the Wharton School, Klein invested in econometrics. He used the growing stream of revenues to support scores of graduate students and several faculty members. As it turned out, the times were especially propitious for such an investment. Affordable electronic computers were arriving on the scene, providing tremendous efficiency in econometric work. Klein had made some use of these new machines while at Michigan, and knew their advantages over the original technical equipment used at the EFU — paper files and hand calculators. Computers could take much tedium out of empirical research, and they labored with such speed and precision that they could greatly multiply the power of econometric analysis. The graduate students in economics who came to the Wharton School and the EFU in the 1960s "were very much computer-oriented," and, with Klein and his colleagues, they "developed almost all the major first-generation programs for econometric analysis." The Wharton group soon had the machines estimating complex equations, managing vast stores of data, and simulating highly detailed scenarios.[8]

By 1969, the EFU had grown into a million-dollar operation, and its needs for space, office machinery, and secretarial support had completely overwhelmed the capacity of the Economics Department. So the bulk of the operation then moved into new quarters at 4025 Chestnut Street, and the EFU became the Wharton Econometric Forecasting Associates, an independent, not-for-profit corporation organized under the trustees of the university. With more room and independence, the econometric enterprise again expanded. WEFA added time-sharing computer services that allowed its clients to run their own experiments and test out different strategies on the Wharton model. To make five-, ten-, and even twenty-five-year projections, Klein integrated input-output analysis with his traditional Keynesian macroeconomics and constructed a mammoth two-thousand-equation simulation of the United States economy. WEFA either built or advised in the construction of models for thirty-seven different nations, large and small regional economies, and for international markets in various commodities and currencies. At the end of the 1970s, Klein and his group were at work on the capstone project of the entire econometric movement — Project LINK. Headquartered at WEFA, LINK brought together econometricians from all parts of the world, Communist and third-world nations as well as those in the developed West, to work on a model of the world economy and the economic interactions among nations. Just as Simon Kuznets's International Association for Research in Income and Wealth spread national income accounting across the world, so did LINK transport Klein's techniques of macroeconomic modeling. By 1980, "The craft of econometric model building and application, first developed by Lawrence Klein, [had] become the basis for economic planning and policy management all over the world."[9]

In the best tradition of the Wharton School, Klein's work excelled as both a scientific achievement and as a tool of practical management. So practical did his science become that econometric forecasting became a highly valued service bought and sold on the open market. A host of competitors sprang up, and the industry reached one hundred million dollars in sales by 1980. By that time, however, the business had become so demanding that a university operation could no longer afford to finance and operate an enterprise in the field. Compared to the other firms, WEFA had underinvested in customer service, and the Wharton model became relatively difficult for most users to comprehend and manipulate. So in 1980 the university sold WEFA, with the services of Klein and his staff, to the Ziff-Davis publishing house. Ziff-Davis invested in software improvements and field marketing, making WEFA "a viable enterprise in an increasingly competitive market." The publisher, in turn, financed a research unit in the university's Economics Department with one million dollars in cash and a 20 percent interest in WEFA through 1985. With Ziff-Davis handling the business, Klein could concentrate on the WEFA model of the U.S. economy, project LINK, and his other scientific interests. And it was his scientific contributions, not the financial success of WEFA, that made Klein the "father of econometrics" and moved Paul Samuelson to label the post-World War II era in economics the "Age of Klein." As if to justify this new division of labor, the Royal Swedish Academy of Sciences awarded Klein the 1980 Nobel Prize in economics six months after the sale of WEFA.[10]

As the world's master econometrician, Klein was the premier exemplar of the new policy scientist. More than anyone, he showed how the combination of mathematics and economic theory could identify causal factors, simulate (and thus test) various policy scenarios, optimize preestablished goals, and thereby improve the management of affairs. Adding Klein to the faculty brought Wharton's Economics Department tremendous prestige and greatly facilitated Kravis's recruiting program. Over the course of the 1960s, he attracted a dozen first-class faculty members and scores of fine graduate students. Econometrics, of course, drew a disproportionate share of the graduate students. Several other professors, including F. Gerard Adams, Albert Ando, and Robert Summers, also did econometric work. But Klein had few imperialistic instincts, and neither he nor anyone else attempted to make macroeconomic modeling the exclusive focus of the Wharton Economics Department. Indeed, the department went out of its way to build strength in a variety of fields and established powerful groups in the specialized areas of labor, international economics, industrial organization, economic history, and theory.[11]

In each area that Wharton developed, its economists turned out important streams of research and well-trained Ph.D.'s. Some contributions were essentially descriptive and resembled the fine empirical work done by the Industrial Research Department and Simon Kuznets. Kravis, Summers, and Alan W. Heston, for example, revised the basic technique for comparing the levels of income among nations. Rather than measure national income in the standard manner and then use foreign exchange rates to convert these figures into comparable quantities, they constructed "world prices" for each commodity and then used these new values to compute the levels of income in each country. Edwin Mansfield, upon measuring the sources of technical innovation, presented startling evidence that big business was *not* the leading font of industrial progress. He also found time to continue the tradition established by Raymond Bye, and produced a widely used textbook in economics. Much of the department's work in economic history followed Klein's lead into econometrics and attempted to specify causal relations in the long-term record of economic activity. Richard Easterlin and Michael and Susan Wachter, for example, modeled the historical interplay between fertility and economic conditions, showing the relationship to be far more complex than had been imagined by Malthus and Ricardo. Among Wharton's theorists, Oliver E. Williamson fashioned a strikingly innovative analysis of business organization based on the concept of "transaction cost": He developed a system for classifying costs involved in economic exchange, pointed out the relative efficiencies of different organizational forms in handling various transaction situations, and then illuminated the rationales behind much of the institutional structure of the economy. The department also assembled a group of theorists somewhat more in the mainstream of the discipline, including Karl Shell and Robert Pollak. These men worked on many branches of theory, including problems of allocation, indexing, investment, and macroeconomic dynamics. Employing innovative mathematical techniques, from the calculus of variations and game theory to differential topology, they soon gave the University of Pennsylvania a new reputation as a leader in mathematical economics.[12]

Although Wharton's economists had embarked on a variety of academic enterprises, they all shared the literature of theoretical economics as a common tradition. As graduate students they had learned the classical, neoclassical, and Keynesian texts, and now as teachers, they passed them on to the next generation. All research in the department grew out of the two great branches of economic science — the microeconomics of markets and firms and the macroeconomics of systemic phenomena; the basic variables and forces that they investigated all derived from these two sources. The mathematics useful in economics — calculus, statistics, and linear algebra — provided another common resource. Because of the shared understandings provided by economic theory and mathematics, economists from all over the world, not just at the Wharton School, could communicate efficiently and build on each other's work.

The hegemony of theory and number had a potent effect on the organization of the discipline. Its precision gave economic genius an ideal material in which to work, quickened the recognition of such talent, and facilitated the development of its new ideas by lesser lights. Journal articles — short pieces of brilliance, comment, and extension — best capitalized on this theoretical and mathematical common ground and quickly became the standard genre of the discipline. This periodical literature, with its short message units, sped communications among members of the field and brought many minds into the process of developing new knowledge.* Because of its universalistic intellectual framework and the effective new mode of communications that it allowed, economics clearly became the strongest and most potent social science at Wharton by the end of the 1960s.[13]

---

*In time, various members of the Economics Department would serve their colleagues by editing important journals in their fields: Oliver Williamson edited the *Bell Journal of Economics*; Karl Shell the *Journal of Economic Theory*; Lawrence Klein and Robert Pollak the *International Economic Review*.

By 1970, the authority of economic *theory* at Wharton extended far beyond the confines of the official department, and the discipline exerted an influence over the school that had been equaled only during the days of Simon Patten. Many older members of the Wharton faculty had considered themselves as economists of the institutional stamp. Their younger colleagues, however, tended to think of themselves as theoretical economists, and they conceptualized their problems as problems of applied economic theory. As such, they posited an economy composed of rational decision makers and explicit schedules of supply and demand; they specified the alternative "opportunity costs" of any economic action and paid strict attention to activity on the "margin." Using mathematics, they then proceeded to derive ingenious solutions to a host of theoretically defined problems. This new mode of scholarship clarified certain knotty controversies, facilitated communication and cooperation, and led to better ways of handling a variety of practical issues. As best illustrated by the work of Lawrence Klein, economics in the postwar period became more than the institutional science that described the environment of business; it became a basic framework for decision making. In many fields at Wharton, in fact, economics and mathematics challenged the original trilogy of accounting, law, and practice as the foundations of professional business education. In some of these fields, they became the core of entirely new disciplines that actually replaced the older approaches to the subject.

Nowhere was the transition more complete than in J. Russell Smith's discipline of geography. Although Simon Patten thought the subject the natural foundation of a business education, its importance at Wharton had steadily declined in the half century between the 1900s and the 1950s. Wharton's geography faculty in the period did boast Lester Klimm, one of the most productive geographers of his generation, and student favorite Michael Dorizas, the mild-mannered world traveler, Olympic champion, and self-proclaimed "strongest man in the world." But aside from the geographers themselves, no one any longer saw an essential connection between their largely descriptive surveys of the economic landscape and the educational mission of the school. With Klimm soon to retire, and Dorizas dying in 1957, little remained of Wharton's dwindling geography program at the time that Willis Winn became dean. Rather than revive the traditional discipline or bury the subject altogether, the dean turned responsibility for the area over to the school's new Department of Regional Science.[14]

Before the establishment of the Wharton department in 1958, Regional Science had never been recognized as an independent academic discipline. Walter Isard, the department's young chairman, had been trained neither as a geographer nor "regional scientist" but as an economist under Wassily Leontieff at Harvard. Isard, however, had specialized in the theory of industrial location and had written fine historical essays on the economic geography of the American iron and steel industry. The young economist soon grew restless with such empirical work, and he set out for more abstract territory. With the publication of his 1956 volume *Location and Space Economy*, he successfully established himself as a major figure in the theory of economic geography. Isard pulled together the various strands of locational analysis, combined them with elements taken from the economics of international trade, and reached a "more general theory of the shaping of the space economy." By this time Isard had become quite ambitious, envisioning regional analysis as a major division of economics, if not as a separate discipline altogether. His colleagues at Harvard, however, and then at M.I.T., were not so enthusiastic. Locational problems had never been a prominent part of the American discipline — the Germans had done most of the major work in the area — and Isard's ambitions found no support in Cambridge. But Irving Kravis and Willis Winn in Philadelphia were looking for just such aggressive academic entrepreneurs. In 1956 they brought Isard to the university as professor of economics and within two years gave him what he really wanted: his own department.[15]

Isard proved to be a ferocious worker, master organizer, and inspiring intellectual leader. With his Wharton department as a base, he created a new discipline, practically single-handedly. Isard became the "moving spirit" behind various journals, including the *Journal of Regional Science*, *Regional Science and Urban Economics*, and *International Regional Science Review*. In 1954 he founded the Regional Science Association and built it into an international body with more than twenty-five hundred members by 1967. All new academic fields need an introductory text, and the collaborative volume that he put together in 1960, *Methods of Regional Analysis: An Introduction to Regional Science*, provided such a survey. It offered, as well, "the most comprehensive review of this literature and the most exhaustive bibliography published to date (or likely to be published for some time to come)." Isard also raised money, a necessary ingredient for any such enterprise. Regional Science was fertilized by funds he squeezed out of Wharton and general university budgets and by grants he won from outside agencies such as the National Aeronautics and Space Administration and the Resources for the Future foundation. Isard used these resources and the research that they funded to create intellectual substance and skilled "personnel" in his discipline — he hired an exceptional faculty of productive young "regional scientists," primarily quantitative economists fresh out of Ph.D. programs, and set up a vigorous doctoral program at Penn.[16]

Isard followed the basic strategy of Wharton's other new sciences. He emphasized policy issues, built the foundations of graduate training in regional science on economic theory and applied mathematics, and taught both within his own department. The program's required courses in economics made "special reference to spatial interaction." Its instruction in quantitative methods, which included surveys of statistics, input-output analysis, and programming techniques, was presented with specific applications to regional problems. By 1980 the program had produced eighty Ph.D.'s, with approximately half entering academic life and many of the others finding positions in governmental planning agencies. This output of doctors and dissertations assured the future of the discipline and established Wharton as a major center of intellectual vitality in regional studies. Isard's group also joined an indigenous movement among geographers, centered at Washington University, to make quantification and econometric analysis the most exciting salient in that discipline as well. So successful was the new scientific program that when the last professor of transportation and public utilities retired, in 1970, the Regional Science Department also absorbed its remaining responsibilities. Like geography, transportation had originally been the responsibility of Emory Johnson, Wharton's first commercial specialist. When Regional Science inherited these subject areas, the school's first professional tradition, based on descriptions of particular environments and of laws, accounts, and practice, gave way to its newest, one grounded in mathematics and applied economics.[17]

A more striking display of the power of the new policy-science paradigm came in the transformation of the Fels Institute from a facility for training state and local administrators into a center for applied economic analysis. Isard's enterprise had replaced two disciplines—transportation and geography—that had lost their drive and direction in the postwar era. But the institute had operated a robust program, highly regarded by the region's institutions of state and local government. Although successful in the world of affairs, Fels had its problems in academe. Strausz-Hupé and his foreign policy crowd looked down on the men of the institute, creating a certain "lack of intimacy" between the two major parts of the Political Science Department. The Wharton administration also felt uneasy about the academic content of the M.G.A. curriculum, and especially its part-time, in-service program. So with Fels director Sweeney set to retire in 1967, Dean Winn ordered an investigation of the institute and its future. After receiving a variety of proposals, from continuing the current format to establishing an independent Department of Public Administration, Winn decided to organize an entirely new program in the science of government policy.[18]

As in each enterprise that Winn promoted, he found an established leader in the field to take charge of the new program. For Fels, he found Julius Margolis, a premier theoretician of the new economics of government policy formation. Margolis had build up an international reputation through his skillful analyses of the proper response to "market failure" and of which level of government — federal, state, or local — could best handle various communal services. As with Winn's other investments, he gave Margolis the freedom and resources to build up a program as he saw fit. The economist immediately set up a new Ph.D. program that emphasized the parts of economic theory relevant to government policy formation (including new economic analyses of political behavior) and the quantitative skills needed to model problems and derive solutions. Margolis, however, had no interest in the mechanics of public administration, the traditional concern at Fels, and as quickly as he set up the new Ph.D. program he scrapped the M.G.A. Much to the dismay of local government managers, the old Fels Institute vanished overnight, and in its place stood a radically different, impeccably academic program in policy formation.[19]*

Among Wharton's traditional business areas, the policy science paradigm had its greatest impact on the field of finance. In the mid-1950s, on the eve of the policy-science revolution, Wharton's Finance Department stood better prepared to participate in the coming upheaval than any other professional unit at the school. Led by Irwin Friend, economists with active interests in both theory and research dominated the faculty and were quick to recognize useful new developments in theory. Since the days of Cyril James the department had offered its own courses in macroeconomics, paying special attention to the structure and behavior of the banking system. Because of Bye's conservatism and Whittlesey's precocity, Keynesian theory had even come to this branch of the finance curriculum before it found sponsors among Wharton's official economists. Finance also had a flourishing research center — the Securities Research Unit — and it was staffed by theoretically and quantitatively skilled investigators. But aside from courses in macroeconomics, most instruction in finance remained in the procedural or institutional economics tradition. The early 1960s, however, saw the emergence of a new economic theory of financial policy. A few of Wharton's finance professors participated in this process of defining theory for their subject, but most devoted their creative energies to empirical investigations; economists at other institutions did the significant work in developing the economic theory of finance. Wharton's department, however, was well equipped for the new era, and members of the existing faculty, not outsiders installed by the dean, quickly brought the new approach to the school. So successful were they, that Wharton soon boasted perhaps the finest program of modern financial education and research in the world.[20]

*Margolis had an exceptional degree of control over the future of the Fels Institute. He enjoyed the full confidence of the dean and had few money problems, since the Fels Fund continued to support the operation, and other foundations added to this income. Most important, the institute had few obligations to retain current members of its academic staff, as all senior personnel held tenure in the Political Science Department, not at Fels.

The new economic science of finance provided analytical frameworks for dealing with a host of traditional issues of financial policy. It offered, for example, methods for determining the optimal financial structure of a firm and for choosing from among various investment opportunities. These, of course, were important contributions to the management of business affairs. But by far the most sophisticated contribution of economics came in analyzing the value of equity holdings. In traditional financial analysis, accounting measures of variables such as earnings, dividends, and liquidity provided the essential elements of stock price evaluation. The new financial science, however, concentrated on the relationship between total return (dividends plus capital gains) and the risk involved in holding an asset (measured by the volatility of the price of the asset). By concentrating on these two variables, the "capital asset pricing model" (CAPM) claimed to explain the value of equity shares. CAPM quickly became the foundation of the new science of finance, and it made the pricing of assets under uncertainty the central theoretical issue in the field. In addition, "finance" became that area of economic theory that concentrated on general problems of valuation under conditions of risk and uncertainty, and specialists in the area developed particular skills in the mathematics of stochastic processes—the mathematics of risk and uncertainty.[21]

CAPM, with its component element, portfolio theory, proved amazingly fertile. Portfolio theory provided a theoretical proof of the value of diversification, showing that such a policy could reduce risk without cutting into expected rates of return.* Using the indifference-curve apparatus, which Bye had disparaged, CAPM showed quite precisely the value of debt instruments in an investment strategy: Investors could increase their returns, without increasing risk, either by buying bonds and medium-risk equities (a low-risk strategy) or by borrowing money to invest more funds in the same medium-risk stocks (a high-risk strategy). As the investment community adopted these "mixed" portfolio strategies (and it would, if it were rational), CAPM would provide a theoretical derivation of the size of "risk premiums," the addi-

---

*Portfolio theory offered a different defense of variety from that found in the works of Adam Smith and Henry C. Carey. Joseph Wharton, we can be sure, would have been pleased with the new doctrine and undoubtedly would have found ways to use it in the defense of the tariff.

tional returns accorded to volatile assets. According to the model, the risk premium ought to be a direct linear function of one specific type of risk — the volatility that cannot be diversified away through the construction of an efficient portfolio. In the most common specification, this risk was measured by the co-variance of the price of the asset with the value of the stock market as a whole, a measure known as the "beta" coefficient of the security. The traditional variables of financial analysis, earnings, dividends, liquidity, and the like, continued to provide some measure of explanation of equity prices and remained the major guides in individual stock selection. But the new economic theories of finance provided analytical frameworks for predicting the behavior of financial markets and for designing overall investment strategies. They were especially useful to the large institutions that increasingly took over the business of managing investments in corporate securities. Although Wharton's Finance Department maintained its traditional strength in procedural training and in-stitutional studies, by the mid-1960s it became primarily a center of applied economic theory. Its instruction concentrated on the new analytical techniques for making financial policy and spent far less time than in the past on analyzing financial statements or describing financial markets and institutions.[22]

The New York investment bankers who sat on Wharton's Finance Department Advisory Committee found the CAPM and other work done at the school quite useful in their businesses. So valuable did they consider the work of the department that they raised funds for a new research center to "accelerate the flow of applied and theoretical research to the business and academic communities." The fruit of their labor, the Rodney L. White Center for Financial Research, opened its doors in 1969, with Irwin Friend as director. Although Wharton had little to do with the initial development of the CAPM, the Rodney White Center made perhaps the greatest contribution to the acceptance of the CAPM by the financial community and to its practical value in guiding investment strategies. Central to this success was the ability of Friend and his close associate, Marshall Blume, to employ elec-tronic data processing in conducting sophisticated empirical re-search and in providing a variety of services to the "member" firms of their center; as in the case of macroeconomic forecasting, the arrival of the computer rendered theoretically grounded policy analysis far more powerful and infinitely more practical than it had been in the past. The Rodney White Center provided its subscribers with the raw material of CAPM analysis — beta coefficients computed in various ways and for thousands of different companies; it carried out exhaustive empirical tests of the model, pointing out limitations and qualifying conditions of its predictive power; the center also distributed working papers and monographs on current research and held periodic roundtables, workshops, and seminars on the lastest theoretical and empirical insights into the behavior of securities markets. While pursuing this pragmatic research, the department trained a group of Ph.D.'s in the sophisticated techniques of modern financial analysis. Many of these joined finance faculties across the nation. As was the case in other policy sciences, others went to work in the world of affairs. Among the latter, a significant portion found their particular arena on Wall Street, with the same investment banking houses that financed the Rodney White Center.[23]

The success of the Rodney White Center and of theoretical instruction in finance, as well as Julius Margolis's transformation of the Fels Institute, Walter Isard's new Regional Science Department, Lawrence Klein's WEFA, and the various activities of Klein's colleagues in the Department of Economics, brought new vigor and enthusiasm to the Wharton School. These ambitious economists, armed with mathematics and computers, believed themselves to be at the genesis of a new age of scientific policymaking. Governments from John F. Kennedy's New Frontier to Richardson Dilworth's reform administration in Philadelphia, major corporations including the Ford Motor Company and AT&T, and the New York banking establishment all concurred. These responsible parties gave Wharton's scholars piles of money for research and consultations and lured perhaps half of their Ph.D. students out of academic careers and into policymaking. Wharton's entrepreneurial professors had indeed fashioned new "technostructures" that now claimed authority over significant areas of social and economic decision. Their confidence and excitement inspired junior colleagues and graduate students, and filled the classrooms and corridors of Dietrich Hall with a lively exchange of ideas. Neither Joseph Wharton in 1881 nor Willis Winn, Irving Kravis,

Reavis Cox, and Joseph Rose in 1959 could have hoped for a more fruitful integration of scholarship and affairs.[24]

This close and vibrant connection between economic theory and practical policy that characterized Wharton in the 1960s did not continue into the 1970s. The doctoral programs, which had spawned so much commitment and research, shrank as the national demand for new faculty evaporated. A nasty war in Vietnam steadily drew resources away from social and economic research, confounded the policies of the country, and dragged down the general reputation of the "technostructure." But Wharton's future hinged more on events at the Pennsylvania campus than on these general considerations. The first and, to some observers, the greatest divide came in 1970. In that year the Departments of Economics, Sociology, and Regional Science moved into McNeil Hall, a separate new facility built with funds mostly provided by the National Science Foundation. Although less than a city block from Dietrich Hall, members of these departments now fell out of daily contact with their other colleagues at Wharton. McNeil Hall, moreover, anointed the social sciences with gracious offices and distinctive public spaces; the structure had all the architectural flair that the builders of Dietrich Hall had not been able to afford in 1950. Because of the physical separation of the two parts of the school and the dramatic new difference in amenities, interaction became more the exception than the rule.[25]

The move to McNeil, however, was only the first presage of the final departure of the social sciences from the Wharton School. Several leading members of the Economics Department had been dissatisfied with their affiliation with Wharton for some time. Young theorists with mathematical interests, in particular, preferred the company of philosophers, historians, and physicists to that of experts in management or marketing. Irving Kravis, who wanted to recruit and retain economists with precisely such tastes, led the forces of secession in his department.* Dean Winn, however, vigorously rejected the idea, and because of his objections this unrest among the economists could never have gotten very

---

*Spats between the Economics and Finance Departments over turf and personnel added tensions to the relationship between the economists and the school. Kravis himself was involved in one particularly tough jurisdictional battle with the Finance Department over a course in international finance. In a vote of the entire Wharton faculty, the economist lost.

far on its own. The insurgents, however, soon found powerful allies in the central administration of the university.

In the late 1960s and early 1970s, a powerful institutional consensus emerged which called for a dramatic strengthening of the university's liberal arts core. Hitherto, Penn's professional schools had dominated its humanities faculties, often bending "liberal" speculation to practical concerns. The emphasis that Wharton's Political Science Department had long placed on public administration provided a perfect illustration. But now university president Gaylord Harnwell, Harnwell's successor in 1970, Martin Meyerson, and an influential faculty Task Force on University Governance resolved to bolster the position of the liberal arts at Penn. Explaining the rationale behind the policy, Meyerson located the greatest danger to the modern university, and especially to Penn, in the possibility

that education may become — or has become — too narrow and too applied, with the arts and sciences relegated to the periphery as insufficiently productive of the tangible results demanded by a modern world. It is to achieve a more tempered balance at the University of Pennsylvania, that a central focus for these disciplines was brought about by the creation of a Faculty of Arts and Sciences. This core division of the University gathers together what were formerly the College, College for Women, Graduate School of Arts and Sciences, as well as the social science departments of the Wharton School.

The institutional consensus concluded that the social sciences were now sufficiently liberal for admission into the heart of scholarship; it determined that it was in the best interest of the university, if not of the Wharton School, to unite the various social science departments with those of the liberal arts and sciences.[27]

The creation of a Faculty of Arts and Sciences thus formed the cornerstone of the university's educational program. After Willis Winn resigned as Wharton dean in 1971 to become president of the Federal Reserve Bank of Cleveland, the major figure opposing the division of the school left the scene. The ambitions of the intellectually ambitious economists to stand among the humanists therefore found fulfillment. There was, of course, a series of votes in the various social science departments. But the outcome was clear, and only a major revolt against the new arrangements could have preserved the traditional structure of the Wharton School.[28]

In 1974 all formalities were completed and the Wharton School was split. The Departments of Economics, Sociology, Political Science, and Regional Science joined the new "core division" of the university; the Fels Institute became the nucleus of a new School of Public and Urban Policy. The University of Pennsylvania thus joined the ranks of typical American universities with strong faculties of arts and sciences, while Wharton assumed the composition of a typical American school of business. Its old arrangement, combining social science and professional departments, had for some time been one of Wharton's archaic idiosyncrasies. Ironically, this marriage proved most fruitful immediately before the separation. With the emergence of the new policy sciences in the 1960s, no final divorce, in fact, seemed possible between studies of business and studies of economy and society. The economists in Wharton's Finance Department, for example, continued to operate the most powerful and popular program at the school. But after 1974, the relationship at Wharton of social science theory and business training would be decidedly less direct.

Source Notes

1. Henry Teune, "The History of the Department of Political Science of the University of Pennsylvania: 1888–1979," mimeographed, 1979, files of the University of Pennsylvania Department of Political Science; Robert Strausz-Hupé et al., *Forward Strategy for America* (New York: Harper, 1961) and *Building the Atlantic World* (New York: Harper and Row, 1963); memorandum from Lloyd M. Short to Winn, 23 Aug. 1966, from "Fels Institute of Local and State Government: Background Materials for Director Selection Committee, 1966," files of Charles Beale, School of Public and Urban Policy, University of Pennsylvania 28; *AMS*, s.v. "James Clyde Charlesworth."

2. *AMS*, s.v. "Marvin Eugene Wolfgang," "E. Digby Baltzell," and "Philip Rieff"; see Marvin E. Wolfgang, *Patterns of Criminal Homicide* (Philadelphia: University of Pennsylvania Press, 1958), E. Digby Baltzell, *Puritan Boston and Quaker Philadelphia* (New York: Free Press, 1979), and Philip Reiff, *Freud, the Mind of the Moralist* (New York: Doubleday, 1961).

3. Raymond T. Bye, *Principles of Economics*, 5th ed. (New York: Appleton-Century-Crofts, 1956 [1924]), vi, 344, 345; also see Paul F. Gemmill, *Fundamentals of Economics* (New York: Harper Brothers, 1930). Gemmill's text was more elementary and was used in freshman courses; interviews with Joseph R. Rose, C. Ray Whittlesey, and Edward S. Herman.

4. *AMS*, s.v. "Irving Kravis," "Arthur Irving Bloomfield," "Dorothy Brady," "Walter Isard," and "Lawrence R. Klein"; interviews with Irving Kravis, Willis Winn, Richard Clelland, and E. Gordon Keith.

5. Lawrence R. Klein, *The Keynesian Revolution* (New York: MacMillan, 1947); Thomas H. Maugh II, "The 1980 Nobel Memorial Prize in Economics,"

Science 210 (1980):758 – 59; F. Gerard Adams, "The Work of Lawrence R. Klein," *[University of Pennsylvania] Almanac* 27(28 Oct. 1980):12.

6. Maugh, "Nobel Prize"; Adams, "Work of Klein."

7. Maugh, "Nobel Prize."

8. Robert A. Federico, "An Uninflated View: An Informal Discussion with Dr. Lawrence Klein," *Wharton Account* 14 (Dec. – Jan. 1974 – 75):18, 17 – 18; Maugh, "Nobel Prize"; "Economics at Penn," FAS Reports, *[University of Pennsylvania] Almanac* 26 (1980):2s.

9. Adams, "Work of Klein"; "WEFA: Before and After the Sale," *[University of Pennsylvania] Almanac* 27 (3 Mar. 1981):1; Maugh, "Nobel Prize"; Federico, "Discussion with Klein," 18 – 21.

10. "WEFA: Before and After the Sale;" Adams, "Work of Klein"; "Economics at Penn"; Maugh, "Nobel Prize."

11. Interviews with Michael Wachter and William Whitney; *AMS*, s.v. "Albert K. Ando," "F. Gerard Adams," "Herbert S. Levine," and "Robert Summers."

12. "Economics at Penn"; interviews with Wachter, Oliver Williamson, Karl Shell, and Robert Pollak.

13. Interviews with Williamson, Shell, and Pollak.

14. "Lester Klimm File" and "Michael Dorizas File," Archives; private communication, Keith to author, 26 Aug. 1980.

15. Harvey S. Perloff and Lowdon Wingo, Jr., Introduction to *Issues in Urban Economics*, ed. Perloff and Wingo (Baltimore: Johns Hopkins University Press, 1968), 5, 3; Eric E. Lampard, "The Evolving System of Cities in the United Statess: Urbanization and Economic Development," in Perloff and Wingo, eds., *Issues*, 83; Walter Isard, "Some Locational Factors in the Iron and Steel Industry in the Early Nineteenth Century," *Journal of Political Economy* 56 (1948):203 – 17 and *Location and Space Economy* (Cambridge: MIT. Press, 1956); interviews with Stephen Gale, Ronald Miller, and Thomas Reiner.

16. Harvey S. Perloff, *Founder's Medal, Walter Isard* reprinted from *Papers of the Regional Science Association* (1978); Walter Thompson, *Preface to Urban Economics* (Baltimore: Johns Hopkins University Press, 1965); interviews with Miller and Reiner.

17. Annual Report of the Dean of the Wharton School (1958 – 59), Files of the Dean of the Wharton School, 4; Rose to Jeannette Nichols, 2 Oct. 1973, files of Joseph R. Rose; interview with Gale.

18. Interviews with Charles Beale, Ada Katz, Louis Taylor, and David J. Wynne; "Towards a Better Life through Training in Government," *Philadelphia Bulletin*, 14 May 1967; memorandum from Short to Winn, 24 Aug. 1966.

19. "School of Public and Urban Policy," promotional pamphlet, n.d., files of Ada Katz, School of Public and Urban Policy, 2; "Fellowships in Public Policy Analysis," promotional pamphlet, n.d., files of Ada Katz; interviews with Beale, Katz, Anita Summers, Taylor, and Wynne.

20. Interviews with Marshall Blume, Edward Herman, and Richard Startz; see Douglas Vickers, *The Theory of the Firm* (New York: McGraw-Hill, 1968).

21. See Haim Levy and Marshall Sarnat, *Capital Investments and Financial Decisions* (London: Prentice-Hall International, 1978), the text used in Wharton's introductory M.B.A. finance courses.

22. Ibid., 155 – 86; interview with Blume.

23. "Rodney L. White Center for Financial Research," promotional pamphlet, n.d. [1974?] n.p., ; interviews with Blume, Whittlesey, Friend, and Startz.

24. John Kenneth Galbraith, *The New Industrial State* (Boston: Houghton Mifflin, 1967), 71; interviews with Clelland, Gale, and Jamshed Ghandi.

25. Interviews with Gale and Ghandi.

26. Interviews with Clelland, Kravis, Shell, and Winn; Minutes of the Wharton Faculty, 7 May 1974.

27. Martin Meyerson and Dilys P. Winegrad, *Gladly Learn and Gladly Teach* (Philadelphia: University of Pennsylvania Press, 1978), 231, 238.

28. News release, 11 June 1971, University of Pennsylvania News Bureau, "Willis J. Winn File," Archives; interviews with Clelland, Gale, Wachter, and Winn.

Willis J. Winn

Robert Strausz-Hupé

Stephen B. Sweeney

Lester E. Klimm

Michael Dorizas, with students

E. Digby Baltzell

Marvin Wolfgang

Philip Rieff

Lawrence Klein

JOURNAL OF
Economic
Theory

EDITOR: Karl Shell

ASSOCIATE EDITORS:

Kenneth J. Arrow · Harold W. Kuhn
A. B. Atkinson · Edmond Malinvaud
David Cass · Roy Radner
Peter A. Diamond · Amartya Sen
David Gale · Robert M. Solow
Koichi Hamada · Joseph E. Stiglitz
Leif Johansen · Carl Christian von Weizsäcker
Sidney G. Winter, Jr.

Volume 1, 1969

ACADEMIC PRESS
New York and London

Contents of Volume I

Journal of Economic Theory, volume 1, number 1, cover and contents

Irving B. Kravis

Arthur Bloomfield

Dorothy Brady

Sidney Weintraub

Richard Easterlin

Oliver E. Williamson

Karl Shell

Edwin Mansfield

Walter Isard

Julius Margolis

School of Public and Urban Policy

Irwin Friend

Marshall Blume

Jean Crockett, *professor of finance*

Jack Guttentag, *professor of finance*

Paul Smith, *professor of finance*

Douglas Vickers, *professor of finance*

McNeil Building, center court

Locust Walk, with Dietrich Hall
in the near middleground,
McNeil in the
far middleground,
and the High-Rise dormitories
in the background

10

Masters of Business Administration

I

Joseph Wharton established the Wharton School with one clear purpose in mind: to prepare the nation's "young men of inherited intellect, means, and refinement" to assume the leadership of America's industrial economy. It was the ironmaster's genius to understand, twenty years before his contemporaries, both the tremendous new managerial tasks that faced American men of affairs and the absence of any means of preparing the next generation to assume such responsibilities. By constructing huge new economic organizations, Wharton and his fellow industrial entrepreneurs had reversed the centuries-old expansion of the market system. They had usurped the "invisible hand" of the market and placed ever-larger portions of the economy under the "visible hand" of their own management. These businessmen then divided labor of society far more extensively than ever before, and equipped workers with tools vastly more powerful than would otherwise have been available. To capitalize on the promise of industrial enterprise, Wharton and his colleagues had employed the traditional business skills — finance, law, accounting, and economic analysis; each of these tools they then adapted to corporate organization and industrial production. Radically new tasks also came with industrial ventures. Businessmen now maintained discipline and effort among vast armies of laborers, established

293

efficient work processes, and protected their industrial complexes from the storms of competition. Wharton would have all these managerial skills passed on. He therefore struck his bargain with the University of Pennsylvania, which in exchange for a one hundred thousand dollar endowment, agreed to raise future generations of business leaders.

As we have seen, the task assigned to the new Wharton School proved far more elusive than the ironmaster had imagined in 1881. Throughout the remaining two decades of the nineteenth century, vigorous programs in social science completely overwhelmed the school's meagre offerings in "mercantile" law, accounting, and practice. During the first third of the next century, the institution established a host of sophisticated training courses in various business specialties, but made no concentrated effort to equip young men to operate an entire enterprise. Despite this diffusion of purpose, the founder's ambition had not expired. Beginning in the mid-1920s and continuing for thirty-five years, Joseph Willits directed his campaign for a schoolwide emphasis on managerial preparation. During the late 1950s this internal party of reform united with the new authorities at the University of Pennsylvania and the major foundations to finally break the domination of the various functional specialties. While the economics-based policy sciences mushroomed up at Wharton in the invigorated 1960s, general management became the school's focal professional program. With Dean Willis Winn's resignation in 1971 and the subsequent departure of the social sciences, educating future managers emerged as Wharton's central concern. As it approached the end of its first century of existence, the school thus faced the task established by Joseph Wharton with hitherto unmatched simplicity.

The man who replaced Willis Winn as dean in 1972,* Donald C. Carroll, accepted Joseph Wharton's vision for the school with uncanny relish. A product of twentieth-century corporate society, not the market and family-dominated nineteenth, Carroll nevertheless came closer to the model established by the founder than had any previous dean of the school. Like Joseph Wharton, he had come from a prominent business background: Although

---

*Professor of Statistics and Associate Dean Richard Clelland served as Acting Dean during the 1971-72 academic year.

not descended from patrician merchants and owners of substantial estates, Carroll's father, Dudley DeWitt, had founded the University of North Carolina School of Business Administration in 1918 and had served as its dean until 1950. Like Wharton, the younger Carroll had combined technical education with training in "inside" business practice and had used these skills to create a thriving commercial enterprise. The nineteenth-century ironmaster had learned chemistry from tutors, and accounting at Waln and Leaming; Donald Carroll had gone to school, studying mathematics at the University of North Carolina and management at the Massachusetts Institute of Technology. At MIT he had become a *doctus* of the latter subject, joined the faculty, and rose to become head of its management science group. Carroll, several colleagues, and the institute had organized the TMI Systems Corporation, a designer of computerized information systems, to serve as a research and consulting vehicle. In time the corporation had split free from the school and, even if not so profitable as Joseph Wharton's Bethlehem Steel Company, was nevertheless quite successful. Upon coming to Philadelphia, the new dean announced his purpose as making "Wharton the best school of management in the world and further, to [have it] be *known* as the best." In Carroll's day, alma mater had already replaced family as the foundation of social standing, and corporations, not family firms, held the keys to success; but by upbringing, education, experience, and even temperament, the new dean thus carried with him the spirit of the founder.[1]

The dean fell heir to a substantial "managerial" legacy from Wharton's recent past. The debates of 1959 had officially inaugurated management as the professional telos of the school's curriculum, and especially of its M.B.A. course. During the mid-1960s, the faculty had revamped this graduate program, built up its general management "core," and, following a national trend in business education, made postgraduate management training the heart of the school's educational effort. Dean Winn had overseen the construction of a dramatic new building to house "Wharton Grad," Vance Hall,* with the structure reaching completion as

---

*Henry Thomas Vance, graduate of Wharton's Class of 1927 and university trustee, had enjoyed a long and extremely successful career managing mutual funds. He donated one million dollars to the building fund, and, as a result, the edifice bore his name.

Carroll arrived in 1972. The new space allowed M.B.A. enrollments to expand to 1,350 (up from 1,050 in 1972 and a mere 388 in 1949), and its huge "greenhouse" wall and modular brick and concrete construction gave "the Graduate Program . . . its own physical identity" and enhanced its prestige at Wharton, at the university, and in the wider society.[2]

During the deanship of Willis Winn, the school had also laid new foundations in managerial scholarship. Before the debates of 1959, as we have seen, managerial studies at Wharton had found their home in the Department of Geography and Industry. But as indicated by the name *industry*, the special problems of manufacturing, and not the general operation of an enterprise, had formed the basic concern of this group. In the years before 1960, the department's emphasis on industrial engineering, the original "scientific" approach to management, had grown, rather than decreased. Robert P. Brecht, the chairman of G & I for much of the 1940s and 1950s, had taught the "Industrial Management" survey (a course introduced into the Wharton curriculum by Edward Mead in 1901), had authored its text, and had continued its traditional emphasis on "scientific management." During the Second World War the department had set up a "Management Laboratory," "fully equipped with the layout tables, photographic equipment, projectors, and stop watches needed for the intensive training of advanced management subjects." With these facilities Wharton had trained students to "solve [such] problems as: Should the workman insert the sheet metal into the stamping machine with his left hand or his right? Or, where should the raw material be placed in relation to the machine?" With financial support from Frederick Taylor's widow, the laboratory had become an integral part of the regular Wharton program in 1949 and was named in honor of her late husband.* As late as 1960, a professor of industry observed that the prominence of the unit "reflects the

---

*Mrs. Taylor used the funds from the sale of "Boxley," her husband's famous Philadelphia estate, to support the laboratory, which Wharton used in its normal undergraduate and graduate programs and for an intensive two-week summer course on "Time Study and the Development of Work Measurements" for managers already in the field.

department's close contacts with the early pioneers in the field of scientific management."[3]*

Like most of their colleagues, Wharton's faculty of industry had traditionally grounded their instruction in actual business practice. These professors had spent their time outside the classroom in business—as consultants or arbitrators—not at academic research, and their income and even their academic standing had depended primarily on their success "in the field." This close proximity to the world of affairs, largely in the role of outside "expert," had pushed the faculty into one type of special competence or another. These extracurricular careers then conspired with the practical concerns of job-conscious students to frustrate Joseph Wharton's broad intentions. Although some members of the faculty shared the founder's interest in the problems of general management, the pedagogy of professional specialization controlled the industry curriculum, as it did the Wharton School as a whole.[4]†

*Industrial engineering had comprised the primary, but not the sole focus of Wharton's program in industry during the 1940s and 1950s. The G & I Department had also offered the concentration in "Labor and Industrial Relations" that Joseph Willits and his colleagues had established in the 1920s and 1930s. George Taylor had returned to the faculty after World War II, but devoted most of his attention to outside arbitration and taught only on a part-time basis. So John Abersold, a lawyer who had formerly taught in the Business Law Department, had headed Wharton's curriculum in "labor." Abersold had developed a special competence in industrial relations as labor advisor to Douglas MacArthur in occupied Japan and as the author of Pennsylvania's first labor arbitration law. Befitting his professional background, he had developed a more legalistic and judicial style than had George Taylor, with his "meeting of the minds" approach. Nevertheless, Wharton had continued to provide a thorough preparation for careers in personnel and industrial relations.

†The G & I Department had offered several elective courses that addressed the problems of general management. It had continued Joseph Willits's old class on "Industrial Policy," in which business executives presented current problems and students offered solutions. Chairman Brecht had a genuine interest in the administration of large-scale enterprises and taught a course on "The Principles of Organization." As a founder and early president of the Academy of Management, a largely academic professional association, Brecht had kept in contact with current thinking on the subject and had introduced his students to the administrative theories of businessmen Henri Fayol and Chester Barnard, and to the analyses of industrial "human relations" presented by the Harvard social psychologists Elton Mayo and F. J. Roethlisberger. Brecht had also taught a course on "The Development of Management Thought," the least pragmatic of management studies but one that often touched on the general problems of operating an enterprise. After World War II, American business had also shown a new interest in education for general managerial responsibilities. As firms had expanded in the postwar prosperity and as they had adopted "decentralized" organizations, they had found themselves in need of greater supplies of general managerial talent. This corporate concern, however, had not been to hire "managers" fresh out of

With the transformation of the entire school in the years following 1960, this situation changed dramatically. Preparing students for general managerial responsibilities then became Wharton's manifest purpose, while defining the essence of modern management emerged as the Holy Grail of American business scholarship. At the time of Wharton's transition, however, managerial studies in the United States lay in a state of advanced confusion. The old "scientific management" had never really addressed the problem of overall enterprise management, and it rapidly fell into eclipse. With the old approach in retreat and the stakes of the game dramatically upgraded, various groups of scholars appeared on the scene to press claims of succession. A 1962 conference of the nation's leading new theorists, convened in order to define their common ground, only managed to display the discipline as a squawk of contentious factions and incompatible approaches.[5]

Then committed to no one strategy, the Wharton School successfully avoided the difficult chore of choosing from among these contending schools of management. Blessed with size, a high rate of faculty retirements, and a flush treasury, it enjoyed the luxury of sampling various programs. Each arrived on campus full of fiery ambition, eager to unlock the secrets of successful management. But mutual competition and the sheer elusiveness of the managerial essence frustrated all claims to the Grail. The parade of managerial programs in the 1960s recapitulated much of the history of scholarship in the field, and in time each would find some accommodation in the Wharton curriculum. The resulting assembly formed an essential new branch of the school's general program and would present Dean Carroll with an impressive array of managerial talent.

With Robert Brecht ill and soon to retire, and with management assuming new importance at the school, Willis Winn, at the very beginning of his tenure as dean, went to George Taylor for advice on the future of the G & I Department. Impressed by the

the university, but to remedy a serious shortage of competent senior officials. In 1950, at the instigation of the Johnson & Johnson company, Abersold had established a two-week summer course for experienced executives on "Coordination and Policy Formation." The program proved successful and continued throughout the 1950s.

new mood at Wharton, Taylor hinted rather broadly that he himself would like to return to the university on a full-time basis and
assume the chairmanship. The dean quickly offered him the position and the opportunity to develop his institutionalist approach to the subject. Taylor's tutelage under Joseph Willits and
his own experience with collective bargaining had convinced him
that the problems of modern management were essentially political: that the future of American civilization depended on its
ability to establish a just system of corporate authority. Taylor's
program in management studies grew out of these commitments.
The new chairman defined the constitution of corporate power
and adjudication as the basic subject matter of the department,
with the conditions of industrial justice and equity as its essential
concerns. He intended to make the study of collective bargaining
—in his eyes the basic mechanism of industrial democracy—the
foundation for the study of management in general.[6]

To develop his program, Taylor added faculty to the "labor"
side of the department and continued to lead his own renowned
seminar in collective bargaining. For the "management" side he
hired William Gomberg, a longtime industrial engineer and theoretician with the International Ladies Garment Workers Union
and pioneer in the use of scientific management as a tool for
collective bargaining. Gomberg set up a seminar in "Managerial
Philosophy" and took charge of the department's new M.B.A.
survey course on general corporate "administration," B.A. 803.*
The chairman and his new professor of management were both
institutionalists and campaigners for democracy; Gomberg, in fact,
had come from the New York City garment trades, whose experiments in industrial government had exerted a powerful influence
on the young George Taylor. Like the chairman, Industry's new
professor believed that "the leading problem of our time is how
[to] structure a managerial model for the modern corporation that
will combine the pursuit of efficiency with the protective con-

---

*This course had just joined, and would soon replace, the ancient engineer-
ing-based "Industrial Management" as the department's basic introductory class.
By directing the departmental survey, required of all M.B.A. students, and by
offering of upper-level instruction on management theory, Gomberg's role in Taylor's scheme of instruction was analogous to that played by Robert Brecht in the
1950s.

straints of due process against arbitrariness for all members of the corporate family." Collective bargaining, of course, was Gomberg's primary solution.[7]*

George Taylor taught at Wharton throughout the 1960s, while Gomberg stayed for nearly a quarter-century, joining Taylor as a fixture at the school. The two articulated the institutionalist approach with vigor and panache, but their program never got off the ground. They understood that their study of contemporary management needed to expand beyond its initial base in labor. On that level, the program had lost its central historic urgency as far back as 1937, when the Supreme Court had declared the Wagner Act constitutional, thereby establishing the basic legitimacy of independent labor organizations in the United States. Gomberg pressed the claim that the collective bargaining apparatus had relevance to general constitutional and judicial issues in modern management, not just to labor problems. But such extensions never became significant in either theory or practice. In fact, so close did Gomberg himself remain to labor issues that when Taylor retired, Gomberg took over his courses on collective bargaining and on the American labor movement. There were attempts to appoint other, more broadly based institutionalists and thereby achieve a "critical mass" for management studies at Wharton. But these plans failed to work out.[8]†

*For intellectual justification, Gomberg relied most heavily on the writings of the great American institutionalist, John R. Commons. He taught Commons's assertion that hierarchy was the essential reality in modern industrial relations, and that the legal and political institutions of contemporary enterprise ought not be based on an assumption of equality between labor and management. Gomberg thus rejected the classical economic model of the labor market, which assumed such equal status; he also scorned socialist alternatives because they obfuscated the inescapable political fact of modern industry — the need for some central authority to coordinate the productive process. The key issue, he claimed, was to protect subordinates from arbitrary uses of managerial power. Gomberg concluded that this could only be accomplished through reliance on mechanisms of redress independent of the managerial apparatus — through independent unions and collective bargaining procedures.

†In 1958-59, the same year in which Taylor appointed Gomberg, he also hired Selig Perlman, the author of the classic *A Theory of the Labor Movement*. But Perlman, then seventy years old, died over the summer and never taught at Wharton. Peter Drucker, author of the fine study of *The Concept of the Corporation* and a leading interpreter of modern management, came as a visiting professor in 1959 with the possibility of staying on as a permanent member of the faculty. There were some personal frictions, however, and Drucker left at the end of his appointment. Wharton did succeed in bringing Ernest Dale to the industry faculty in 1965. A prolific author and careful observer of modern management, Dale promised to make a major contribution to Wharton's institutionalist pro-

In 1961 Taylor succeeded in bringing Herbert Northrup into the department. Far more conservative than either Taylor or Gomberg, Northrup appealed to the chairman as a clear foil to his new professor of management: After earning his Ph.D. at Harvard, Northrup had worked for major American corporations for a dozen years, and his long experience with industry counterbalanced Gomberg's with the unions. At Wharton, he would present the position of the corporate industrial relations officer, defending the often "unpleasant" chores necessary to preserve the company's "rights" to manage its labor and assets.* Northrup had also authored an important text in the field and expressed interest in doing research. The industry faculty, once a leader in business research, had become sorely deficient in the area, and Northrup promised to redress this weakness. Finally, Taylor was already tiring of his duties as chairman, and Northrup, with corporate administrative experience, promised future relief. In 1964, when Taylor did step down, Northrup succeeded him. The new chairman, however, ran the department in a style far too "industrial" for many of his colleagues. Enough friction resulted so that Northrup took a leave of absence in 1968 and resigned a year later. While in office, however, he had discovered the nearly moribund Industrial Research Unit, with only Gladys Palmer, then ill and at the very end of her life, housed in the remnants of the old IRD. Eager for a research vehicle, Northrup revived the unit, with himself as director. After resigning as chairman of the Department of Industry, he devoted his abundant energies to resurrecting the IRU.[9]

Northrup provided the leadership that the IRD/IRU had lacked in the postwar era. He raised large sums of money from governments, foundations, and business corporations, and supported the research of several Wharton professors and large numbers of M.B.A. and Ph.D. students. The Ford Foundation and the federal government financed the new IRU's first major project, a study of the

gram. He had barely arrived, however, before a serious stroke afflicted him, severely limiting his participation in the activities of the school.

*Northrup, more than Gomberg or Taylor, carried out Joseph Wharton's instructions that the school "teach . . . the necessity, for modern industry, of organizing under single leaders or employers great amounts of capital and great numbers of laborers, and of maintaining discipline among the latter; [and] the nature and prevention of 'strikes.'"

status of black workers in America, and the unit produced "the most complete, thorough, and detailed analysis of the Negro in industry and of industrial race relations in existence." After 1968, Northrup turned to the traditional issues of industrial relations, collective bargaining, and labor-management conflict. Here, however, the unit ventured into far more controversial waters, and financial support from the federal government and the mainstream foundations fell sharply. Northrup's consistently pro-management studies, however, found new funding with corporations and politically conservative philanthropies.* In 1974, after the IRU expanded its labor relations research to cover the entire world, Northrup organized a corporate research advisory group to finance his unit's investigations; in return for their support, member firms would receive IRU reports on multinational unionism and the labor climate in numerous nations. Northrup's sensitivity to the problems and interests of corporate America thus kept research on industrial relations flourishing at Wharton at a time when the area fell into general academic eclipse. So successful was Northrup's enterprise that the IRU actually became "the largest academic publisher of books in the broad manpower and industrial relations field."[10]

Northrup's IRU shared many characteristics with the various other research centers that sprang up at Wharton in the 1960s and 1970s. It relied on external funding, including subscription payments from private businesses; Ph.D. students found dissertation topics, financial support, and collegial interaction at the unit and then entered careers in both academe and industry. But unlike many other centers, the IRU did not become the vanguard of its discipline; the area of labor relations, although of undoubted significance, was simply not the central problem in contemporary managerial scholarship or practice. Nor was research at the IRU

---

*The Unit's investigation of *The Impact of OSHA* (Occupational Safety and Health Act), for example, found "little improvements in safety records resulting from the law, but considerable cost and organizational impact and some impact on labor relations, with possibly more in the future." "Few studies have been so widely quoted, . . . or praised or damned as much" as the IRU report on *Welfare and Strikes*, which connected public welfare payments to strikers with longer work stoppages and costlier settlements. The unit's report on labor relations in the Philadelphia public school system argued that the unions held a "veto over management actions" and recommended a "complete restructuring of the Philadelphia Board of Education's approach and staffing of its employee relations function."

grounded in one of the policy sciences that were the rage in the 1960s; it offered no predictions of the future based on economic theory and sophisticated quantitative analysis. Northrup's program, in fact, was far closer to the institutionalist empiricism of the old IRD. It researched the legal environment of labor relations and provided statistical descriptions of current industrial structure and behavior. Northrup's IRU joined Taylor's and Gomberg's seminars as important parts of the school's program in management, but new approaches growing out of the policy science paradigm soon made far stronger claims than either on the future course of managerial studies at Wharton.

By 1960 a new "management science," analogous in many ways to econometrics, had dramatically arrived on the national scene. Like the advanced areas of economic science, this new form of business learning brought contributions from some of the more arcane mathematical and theoretical branches of the university to the service of the nation's managers. Pioneering practitioners of this management science, found most often in the business departments of leading engineering schools, had been quietly at work for twenty years and had assembled an impressive store of managerial models, quantitative procedures, and conceptual frameworks. In the 1960s, with radical reforms under way at the nation's business schools, with the great expansion of graduate education, and with the spread of computing machinery throughout society, the demand for management science, as well as its supply, now reached substantial levels. The members of the movement thus entered the 1960s with a tremendous flush of confidence in themselves and in the future of theoretical science in the world of affairs. Herbert A. Simon of the Carnegie Institute of Technology, a leading guru, struck the tone of optimism common among his colleagues when he declared himself "positively exhilarated by the progress we have made . . . toward creating a viable science of management and an art based on that science."[11]

At Wharton, these management policy sciences arrived and developed along lines similar to the new sciences based on economic theory. Both began their intensive growth during the deanship of Willis Winn and shared the same organizational forms and sources of financial support. As in economics, forceful individuals with powerful ambitions played a critical role in introducing these disciplines into the curriculum. These academic entrepreneurs raised huge piles of cash from corporations, governments, and philanthropies; they assembled faculties, set up Ph.D. programs, organized thriving research centers, and thereby fostered new types of scholars and scholarship. Such personal dynamism, and that of the management science movement in general, could not be contained within the jurisdiction of the old faculty of industry. Like the economics-based policy sciences, management science "speciated" into various new units—some within the Industry Department and some not. But all shared common commitments to mathematical modeling, empirical research, and a theoretical approach to the problems of management.

Systems theory, a new conceptual framework with particular application to the issues of management, provided Wharton with its central paradigm for scientific management study in the 1960s and 1970s. This systems approach had emerged as an independent intellectual exercise in the 1940s, growing out of the convergence of speculations in a wide variety of fields: biology, engineering, institutional economics, sociology, Pragmatic philosophy, and the work of the prewar writers on administration. These various strands of intellectual history had all championed the organic integrity of living creatures, social institutions, and complex technical systems; they abhorred theories, including neoclassical economics, that attempted to reduce such integrated organizations to the interactions of component parts. Some intelligence and control apparatus, they claimed, had to coordinate the diverse elements of all such systems to insure their survival in an often hostile environment and guide them toward the achievement of some common purpose. This intelligence and control apparatus constituted the essence of the system, and it provided theorists with their primary object of investigation. Since it was the function of management to serve as the intelligence and control apparatus of an enterprise—to integrate its parts, make adjustments to external changes, and give direction to the common activity—systems theory provided a logical framework for constructing theories of management.[12]*

*The most important theoretical work in post-World War II American sociology and social psychology was quite similar to systems theory in its concern for organizational structure, goal orientations, and system-environment interac-

Systems theory was essentially a conceptual framework, not an engine of analysis and prediction like neoclassical economics. It offered a general approach to organizational problems, such as understanding and improving corporate structures and information flows; it itself, however, owned no quantifiable, schematic models that could resolve otherwise obscure issues. One important set of analytical instruments grew up in management science, however, that was compatible with and to some degree inspired by systems theory. Known as "operations research" (OR), this advance in scientific management practice originated with English attempts to construct an effective air defense system during World War II. The Royal Air Force had developed radar and the Hurricane fighter plane as the central pillars of their defensive strategy, but they had quickly discovered that "combining them into an effective system could not be left to improvisation." By rigorously studying and measuring the interaction of the two components, a team of British scientists had integrated the weapons system, with excellent "operational" results. Bolstered by this success, the operational research program of scientific modeling and testing spread throughout the British and American military and, following the war, into industry. The apparatus of mathematical optimization then entered operations research.* After thousands of modeling and optimizing procedures, researchers discovered the continual recurrence of a few basic operational problems, such as queuing, replacement, and search. With models of these common concerns as a foundation, leaders of the new field announced that "the structure of operating organizations does constitute a unitary field for study and . . . is sufficiently distinct to merit a separate classification as a subject for specialized scientific study."[13]

As the traditional seat of management studies at Wharton, the Industry Department would have seemed to be the logical

---

tions. And with such new modes of analysis, sociologists and psychologists created significant bodies of literature on the problems of management and won important appointments on business school faculties. At Wharton, however, such social sciences exerted an important, but ultimately a secondary influence.

*Like their fellow policy scientists, the econometricians, operations researchers employed mathematical statistics, computers, and calculus. They also developed an impressive new set of models and solution techniques, often derived from linear algebra, to help managers design productive systems.

sponsor of the new scientific approaches to the subject. A few of the younger faculty in operations management did have some background in engineering and had followed the development of management science at schools such as the Massachusetts, Carnegie, and Case Institutes of Technology and the university's own Moore School of Electrical Engineering. Operations research techniques did find their way into industrial management courses, and the department offered instruction on computerized information systems, a subject especially suited to the new systems perspective.* But the department's leadership in the early 1960s had neither the inclination nor the resources to build an aggressive program in management science. George Taylor viewed operations research as little more than a collection of useful gadgets. Gomberg liked it even less, and contemptuously dismissed the bulk of systems theory and much of managerial social science as charlatan nonsense.[14]

Herbert Northrup and his 1969 successor as chairman of the department, Edward Shils, showed more sympathy and hired several young practitioners in these fields. Northrup went "outside" to hire George Parks, with a doctorate from the University of California, and James Emery, fresh out of MIT's Ph.D. program, and gave them authority to build up Industry's nucleus in operations research and management information systems. Parks and Emery proceeded to assemble a clatch of fine young professors, all of whom carried the modern trappings of theory and advanced mathematics. The psychology and sociology of business organizations were also coming under intense scientific scrutiny in the 1960s, and the department hired several scholars who could teach in these areas. Ross Webber, a young Columbia-trained specialist in the social psychology of managerial organizations, also took

---

*Adrian McDonough, Industry's instructor in the area of business information systems and a director of the Taylor Laboratory, made the school's most important contribution to management science during this early period. He wrote a significant book on *Information Economics and Management Systems* and later authored a pioneering text on the subject. Intelligent and useful, McDonough's work and that of his colleagues were nevertheless far from the cutting edge of the field. McDonough, in fact, took Frederick W. Taylor as his model and attempted to apply the old "scientific management" to modern information systems. He broke business communications into linguistic components, which he compiled into a "directory of management vocabulary," and would then have executives design neat and efficient business information systems out of these elements.

over the department's M.B.A. core course, B.A. 803, from William Gomberg. Industry thereby shifted its introductory survey from an institutional to a "scientific" basis: Where Gomberg had raised questions of justice and social philosophy, Webber emphasized scientific theories of managerial behavior and applications useful in operating an enterprise.[15]

Despite this movement, however, neither chairman, Northrup or Shils, was himself active in developing the new managerial sciences. Unlike the situation in the Economics Department, in fact, the senior faculty in industry, as a whole, had little interest in these new scientific initiatives. Nor did they rush to hire someone with the stature of Lawrence Klein, a scholar who could create a vigorous theoretical group and lead the department in a dramatic new direction. Things in industry therefore changed at a rather leisurely pace. But the tides of business scholarship in the 1960s flowed strongly in the direction of "science," and neither operations research nor systems theory had to wait patiently at the door of the Wharton School for a proper invitation from the industry faculty. Wharton's earliest and strongest advocates of these sciences sprang up in other parts of the school. Management studies, as a result, lost their close identification with the Industry Department and began to diffuse across the entire curriculum.

At the end of the 1950s, quantitatively oriented professors in various Wharton departments were eager to exercise their talents in the emerging area of operations research. The nationwide campaign to upgrade the mathematical component of business education led by the major foundations, and the addition of calculus to Wharton's curriculum, clearly encouraged such ambitions. So Morris Hamburg, Richard Clelland, and John DeCani of Statistics, John Lubin and Adrian McDonough from Industry, and Benjamin Stevens from Regional Science took the initiative to promote an independent program in operations research. They worked closely with the Graduate Division Curriculum Committee, conveniently chaired by Morris Hamburg, and set up a four-course M.B.A. "OR option" in 1961; two years later they added an M.B.A. major in the field. This group did not attempt to build a school-wide general management program on this mathematical foundation, an admittedly radical step for Wharton but one perhaps suggested by the newly declared commitment to the general management M.B.A. An interest in things quantitative united these various professors, and mathematics, not operations management applications, dominated their curricula. They and their colleagues on the faculty took the traditional Wharton route and pushed operations research into collaboration with the various departments: They required all OR students to major in one of the several business areas as well. Such deference to the departments certainly facilitated the acceptance of operations research and helped spread mathematics to more fields at the school. And by this original design Wharton deflected its operations research program away from any grandiose scheme of establishing a single, unified program in general management.[16]*

The companion to operations research, systems theory, came to Wharton without any sponsorship whatsoever from the faculty of the Industry Department. This mode of analysis arrived on campus in 1959, when Wroe Alderson left his flourishing downtown consulting practice to join the school's Department of Marketing. Alderson had suffered a severe heart attack and retired to the groves of academe on doctor's orders, to pursue a more leisurely pace of life. But he was an incorrigible dynamo, and despite his physicians' instructions, Alderson became the school's vigorous champion of management science in general and systems theory in particular.

Although he had never won a Ph.D. nor held a full-time academic appointment, Alderson had been marketing's leading theoretician for over a decade. In 1948, he and Wharton's Reavis Cox had written a pioneering essay, "Towards a Theory of Marketing," and two years later they had edited an anthology on the subject. But unlike Cox, who had always considered himself an economist, Alderson had consumed literature from all parts of the social sciences. He had been quick to draw implications for

---

*The school, for example, could have constructed courses in "applied" OR that would have drawn examples from a variety of business situations or from problems confronting top-level executives. The Curriculum Committee explained, however, that "the fundamental assumption on which this proposal is based is that it is desirable for the student to acquire some of the content of a *specific* business field together with work in mathematical and statistical knowledge." The faculty nevertheless had reason to be pleased with their new program, and the dean reported that it had "attracted to the Wharton School many excellent students with strong backgrounds in mathematics and statistics, the physical sciences and engineering."

marketing practice from this material, and his consulting firm's newsletter, the *Cost and Profit Outlook*, served as the major vehicle for bringing useful social science theories to the attention of his colleagues. Alderson had found time to organize his ideas into a book only after his heart attack, and while still in bed recuperating he dictated *Marketing Behavior and Executive Action*. Reflecting his reading of thinkers such as John Dewey, William James, John R. Commons, Thorstein Veblen, Talcott Parsons, Julien Steward, Carl Rogers, and the Gestalt psychologists, Alderson's book had presented a systems-theoretical analysis of marketing; traditional economic theory, by contrast, appeared only as a negative point of reference. Arguing in a fashion reminiscent of Simon Patten, Alderson had claimed that rich heterogeneity, not bland homogeneity, characterized the modern world of supply and demand. According to Alderson, sophisticated businessmen, not Patten's educated consumers nor the simple neoclassical interaction of buyers and sellers, "made the market." Such middlemen gathered information on consumer desires and productive possibilities and then matched particular needs with specific bundles of goods and services. Alderson had insisted that this process, which he called "sorting," constituted the essence of modern marketing. He also had claimed that the information thus processed by such businessmen, and not the price adjustments studied by economists, ultimately "cleared" the nation's markets.[17]

Alderson died in the summer of 1965, but during his six years as Marketing's apostle of "management" he brought a radical new direction to the department's program. As developed by Reavis Cox and Ralph Breyer, marketing studies at Wharton had been a branch of institutional economics. Although painting fine descriptions of complex distribution systems, the research of these institutionalists had actually said little about how to manage a marketing operation; Herbert Hess and his old group in merchandising had had much more to offer on such practical matters. Wroe Alderson returned to the problems of marketing practice, but with a professional, scientific apparatus that Hess had searched for in the 1920s but could never find. Using mathematical models and quantitative techniques, Alderson would attack such problems as how to analyze consumer tastes, "how much to spend on advertising, how big a sales force to maintain, how to allocate salesmen to accounts, and how to apportion marketing messages across the media." To enhance the scientific rigor of his program, he brought onto the faculty young scholars who were superbly trained and extremely talented in things quantitative.[18]

Alderson then took a leaf from his days as a consultant, when he had successfully integrated scholarship with the practical problems of business, and opened a Management Science Center at Wharton in February 1962. With his able collaborator Paul Green,* Alderson quickly made the center an important part of his M.B.A. course in Marketing Management, giving his students a chance to act as consultants and to practice their various new techniques on real-world problems. Beyond these connections with marketing, the center also became

an integral part of the School's expanding program in the applications of quantitative methods to business problems, . . . able to provide both opportunities and support for faculty members and graduate students whose research interests lie in the areas of operations research and management science.

As a fitting symbol of its transition from the old "scientific management" to the new management science, the Wharton School housed Alderson's center in space appropriated from its Frederick W. Taylor Laboratory.[19]

Wharton's program in management science took a quantum leap forward in 1964, when Wroe Alderson, Professor of City Planning Robert B. Mitchell, and Willis Winn brought Russell L. Ackoff to the campus. One of the premier thinkers in operations research and systems theory, Ackoff was also an academic entrepreneur of the most ambitious and charismatic variety. He had coauthored a pioneering text in operations research, had cofounded the world's first academic program in the field (at the Case Institute of Technology), and had been a leader in the transition of operations research from military to industrial applications. Over the years Ackoff had also developed an outstanding reputation as a consultant. Just as Lawrence Klein had invested

*A brilliant statistician, Green had just won his Ph.D. in the subject under Morris Hamburg at Wharton and had been offered a teaching position in the Statistics Department. But Alderson, and the more promising opportunities in marketing, convinced him to change fields.

in econometrics, Ackoff had used business contracts, along with foundation grants, to set up an impressive OR research establishment at Case. Beyond problem-solving genius and this commitment to his field, Ackoff had a compelling personality that had attracted a swarm of disciples. When he and the Case Institute came to their parting of the ways, his entire operations research group, faculty and students, resigned and followed their guru to Philadelphia. Ackoff thus arrived with a complete Ph.D. program and thriving research center in train. Wroe Alderson, a good friend and supporter, gladly turned over to Ackoff and his much larger research group control of the Management Science Center. Dean Winn also anointed Ackoff chairman of a new Department of Statistics and Operations Research, with significant authority over the school's quantitative programs. As an historian of operations research has observed, "While Wharton's interest in operations research antedates the arrival of Russ Ackoff on the scene there, it was certainly when he and his team came to Wharton that the School found its major place on the OR map."[20]

Despite Ackoff's arrival and the growth in numbers and influence of management scientists in other parts of the school, the late 1960s were difficult days for Wharton's professors of operations research, management information systems, and managerial social science. Those who were in the Industry Department felt constrained by the preexisting curriculum and the traditionalist leadership, which, they felt, had never allowed them enough resources to create vigorous, concentrated programs. They came to resent Industry's tempestuous internal politics and rather authoritarian management style; several young left-leaning management scientists also found themselves embroiled in nasty personal feuds with some of their Nixon-Republican seniors. As could be expected, digesting the strong-willed Ackoff gave rise to additional discomfort. The two groups of specialists in Wharton's new Department of Statistics and Operations Research soon realized that they viewed the world through quite different glasses, and conflicts between personalities as well as professional purposes kept the members of the department continually on edge. After a few years of turmoil, Willis Winn had to dissolve this over-hasty union.[21]

More troublesome than administrative squabbles, however, were tensions arising from a crisis in management science itself, and especially in operations research. By the late 1960s, problems in operations research applications had begun to crop up around the nation with disturbing frequency: Errors in modeling, measurement, or computation had led to serious blunders, and "in some cases the results were unequivocally disastrous." Ambitious attempts to proceed to grander arenas — to the broader fields of corporate and public policy — tripped rather badly over the problem of defining the goals of an enterprise.* The nightmarish war in Vietnam, going badly and supposedly under the management of quantitative "whiz kids," provided a nagging public symbol of OR's distress. For practitioners, a special anxiety derived from the fact that the once heady pace of mathematical discovery had suddenly slowed, raising fears that little excitement remained for the future. Moreover, the accumulated body of models and techniques, the legacy of the recent heroic past, had grown so large that the mere task of mastering and transmitting this literature now required a substantial commitment of time and resources. Operations research thus showed signs of "routinization" — of becoming just another academic discipline and middle-management skill. Its audacious pioneering days, when ambitious and brilliant interdisciplinary teams went out to solve whatever problems there were, seemed numbered. Ackoff, ever the adventurous

---

*Establishing proper evaluative criteria had long been a difficult task in OR. In 1960 Ackoff wrote, for example, that he had

> not yet seen a good single consolidated measure proposed for the performance of an aircraft. Nor is there sufficient knowledge to relate any of the less perfect available measures of performance to the large number of design variables of such craft. As a consequence, design is currently accomplished by a combination of scientific analysis, intuition, and aesthetic considerations.

But in 1960 Ackoff had faith that "current design procedures are only an evolutionary stage which will be replaced as rapidly as possible by effective modelling and the extraction of solutions from the resulting models." For a time there was a vogue in OR for "Pareto optimality," a neoclassical economics decision criterion which compared the marginal net benefits of a program with those of alternative projects. While this procedure offered useful enlightenment on certain important issues, it begged the question on problems such as measuring the value of an aircraft and in general obscured the "systemic" properties of industrial production. But it was when OR tried its hand at politically sensitive issues, with various interest groups and ideologies competing for recognition, that it encountered its most serious difficulties. In the late 1960s, in a society seriously upset over war and racial unrest, the problem of defining a social utility function became a practical impossibility.

radical, wanted to push forward into realms of broad corporate and social policy. To negotiate this transformation he would scuttle much of the mathematical baggage that the field had gathered, emphasize systems theory as a conceptual framework, and strengthen links with behavioral scientists.* He was, however, unable to convince his colleagues at Wharton to accept such an irregular proposition.[22]

II

It was at this point that Willis Winn stepped down as dean, the social sciences began packing their bags in earnest, and the optimistic Donald Carroll arrived in Philadelphia. Carroll took office in the fall of 1972 and, despite the disarray in the more sophisticated reaches of management science, there was never a better moment in Wharton's history to make the school "the best school of management in the world." After a decade of experience, corporate America had a newfound appreciation for the quantitative and theoretical educational and research services available at American business schools. It now stood eager to receive a huge expansion in the supply of M.B.A.'s and business research. In the 1970s the children of the postwar baby boom would also reach professional-school age. Upon discovering the low cash value of their college B.A.'s, and finding traditional career opportunities such as medicine highly restricted, law crowded, and college teaching utterly depressed, they turned to business in droves. The annual outpouring of M.B.A.'s grew sevenfold in the decade, and Wharton, with its solid, prestigious program and ambitious new dean, floated on the top of this tidal expansion.[23]

The M.B.A. boom of the 1970s blessed Wharton with the most capable, mature, and diverse student body in its history. The average Graduate Management Aptitude Test scores of incoming students shot up from the eighty-second to the ninety-second percentile between 1972 and 1977. Eager matriculants arrived from a great variety of job experiences, educational backgrounds, and socioeconomic origins, and many had demonstrated some managerial accomplishment in the world of work before gaining

---

*To bolster his unit's grasp on problems of organized human behavior, he hired Eric Trist, the well-known theorist of "sociotechnical systems," and changed the name of his research unit to the Management and Behavioral Science Center.

admission to the program. Seeing management becoming an increasingly international affair, Dean Carroll went out to recruit a substantial number of foreign M.B.A. students, raising their numbers to a healthy 1 out of 4 by 1981.* While not the result of an explicit policy, the enrollment of women also exploded in the 1970s, growing from 4 percent to 25 percent of the class. Women in that decade claimed a place in society's managerial apparatus, hitherto a male domain, and a Wharton M.B.A. provided them with a first-class ticket of admission.[24]

As Wharton's M.B.A. program boosted its admission standards and expanded its applicant pool, the school finally scrapped its original assignment of educating the heirs of family enterprise. Whereas 1 of 6 undergraduates in the 1960s had still entered the world of affairs through a family connection, that was the case for a mere 3 percent of M.B.A.'s in the 1970s.† The Wharton graduate school's new cohort of students were nevertheless more "aristocratic" in their tastes than their predecessors. All intended to do well in their careers, and they worked hard to prepare themselves for pecuniary success and corporate advancement. But they also appreciated art and science, delighted in fine food and clothing, and hoped to devote considerable time to family life. They likewise looked forward to positions of general responsibility and diverse challenges, not some single-minded application of a specialty. Joseph Wharton himself had been a man of such varied sensibility: Although an ascetic in matters of sensual pleasure, he had cultivated science, verse, art, politics, and family relations; he had mastered several business skills and had settled for nothing less than general executive authority. The new M.B.A.'s lacked "family," in the traditional social sense of the word, but had nevertheless acquired that acuity and genteel polish that the founder had expected from Philadelphia's "young men of inherited intellect, means, and refinement." Upon graduation, "Wharton" would become their surrogate surname, their nom d' affaires.[25]

---

*Wharton was also quite active in expanding the international scope of collegiate business education through assistance and exchange programs with foreign universities. The school first entered this arena in 1954, when it helped the University of Karachi establish its School of Public and Business Administration. By 1981, Wharton had formal arrangements with ten foreign institutions, in both developed and developing nations.

†The trend among undergraduates was toward this M.B.A. model: The percentages of first jobs secured through family connections dropped from 25 percent between 1920 and 1960, to 17 percent in the sixties, to 9 percent in the seventies.

The Wharton School had successfully absorbed the new mathematical and theoretical policy sciences in the 1960s and now provided its students with a strong intellectual preparation for managerial careers. To this academic framework Carroll added in the 1970s an aggressive program of practical engagement with the world of affairs. At the core of the dean's policy was his vision of both the modern manager and the ideal Wharton professor as variants of single type: the "sophisticated problem solver." He would do his best to recruit such pragmatic scholars, to facilitate their work, and to promote them as "role models" for Wharton students. Carroll believed that the time was then ripe for all purveyors of practical learning to boldly enter the commercial arena, and his vision encouraged contact with business rather than contact with scholarship. There they would become experienced in implementing existing techniques, learn how to temper managerial science with managerial art, and at the same time find fresh new problems to be solved. As a businessman who had sold advanced management information systems to some of the largest firms in the nation, the dean knew firsthand of corporate America's lusty demand for academic services and of the professional development to be gained through such practical activity. "Never," Carroll exuberantly declared, have "the opportunities for mutual backscratching been so numerous or so attractive," and he vigorously promoted all manner of contact between Wharton and the world.[26]

Carroll was able to pursue his program of engagement with unusual vigor because he fell heir to a new administrative organization at the University of Pennsylvania — responsibility accounting. This system required the deans of the various schools to operate within their incomes or else go hat explicitly in hand to the central authorities; conversely, it greatly enhanced their power to raise and dispense money. As head of the university's most solvent school, Carroll thus enjoyed significant managerial freedom, which he used to advance his policy.* He freely encouraged the practice of consulting, believing that the school suffered

---

*Responsibility accounting revealed, for the first time, the tremendous profit that the university had garnered from its business school. Despite low costs and a good supply of cash customers, a full realization of the value of this asset had somehow eluded past administrations. Provost Charles C. Harrison, an otherwise shrewd businessman, had in fact accused Wharton of not even living within its income.

from too little, rather than too much, of such business. To advertise Wharton as the best school of management in the nation, Carroll established a strong public relations office, commissioned a full-length, scholarly history of the institution, and created the *Wharton Magazine* as a prestigious, general-circulation business periodical. Carroll financed the expansion of Wharton's student placement service, under the vigorous direction of Arthur Letcher, into a highly sophisticated marketing agency for the school's esoteric and perishable products. The dean's most ambitious initiative along these lines was a major eighteen-million-dollar renovation of Dietrich Hall that would raise Wharton's entire physical plant to "world-class" status. To facilitate his policy of engagement, Carroll set up the "Wharton Partnership," whereby large corporations exchanged substantial contributions to the school in return for "a first look at promising graduates and a chance . . . to learn from Wharton faculty."[27]

The dean's major program in expanding and intensifying interaction between faculty and management involved a huge development of corporate-sponsored research and "executive education" (continuing education for executives). Both initiatives provided opportunities for professors to see how their ideas fit various "real time" situations, to quickly address new gaps in the knowledge market, and to reconnoiter emerging areas of concern. During Carroll's administration, sponsored research, of the type conducted by the Rodney White Center and the Management Science Center and funded by private business firms rather than government or philanthropic foundations, became a defining characteristic of the institution. Much of this activity had originated in the 1960s, and some even earlier; corporate-financed research also became more common at all American business schools in the 1970s. But under Carroll, sponsored research revenues grew by a factor of 10, and Wharton soon held contracts for such investigations totalling four to five times the value of those held by its nearest competitors.[28]

During Carroll's deanship, executive education grew by a factor of 40, and by 1981 the school came to dominate the market for executive education "short courses." This program opened a great new market for Wharton instruction: practicing business people of some responsibility. Its short-course format fit neatly into the schedules of these busy executives, while its curriculum conveyed useful and rather specific information of the type most often supplied by sophisticated consultants. The pressures of business life tended to frustrate powers of generalization, but in the vacationlike atmosphere of an executive education course, businesspeople could gather new perspectives and instruments with which to approach their work. Such instruction proved so valuable that corporations bought whole courses for their employees, and professors were soon conducting seminars all across the country and in Canada and Europe as well. A recent survey of the Wharton alumni confirmed the utility of executive education, showing that those who had attended such sessions earned significantly more money than those who did not.[29]*

Financial considerations were as significant for Carroll's strategic thinking as his belief in the professional benefits of faculty management interaction. Under the responsibility accounting system, the dean had become manager of Wharton's business affairs, answerable for the bills of the school. The university, moreover, had fallen into financial difficulties in the 1970s and took increasingly large "overhead" charges from Wharton's revenues. Carroll foresaw the coming national decline in university

---

*In 1975 the school opened its doors to a far more ambitious executive education course, the Wharton Executive M.B.A. Program. Meeting on alternate Fridays and Saturdays and for four week-long sessions, the two-year course put highly successful businesspeople through the entire M.B.A. curriculum. (The 1980 class averaged twelve years of business experience and salaries of forty thousand dollars.) Successful from the start, WEMBA was soon drawing its targeted number of 40 to 45 students in each class.

These executive education programs represented not something brand new, but the latest effort of "outreach" education, a tradition which had begun at Wharton with Edmund James's work of "uplift" with the university extension movement. Wharton's great program of this type had been Edward Mead's far more pragmatic Evening School. Although terminating its classes in outlying cities in 1965, the Evening School continued its operations into the 1980s and added a bachelor's degree program in 1972. Significant numbers of the city's less advantaged population, especially blacks and women in the 1970s, took this route to new opportunities in business occupations. In 1970 the school set up a new "extension" effort: the Community Wharton Education Program (CWEP). Relying on volunteer instructors from the Wharton faculty and graduate student body, CWEP prepared capable but undereducated blacks for the Evening School and even the regular day program. Believing that "there is still a vast reserve of management potential among minorities that has not begun to be tapped," CWEP recalled the original spirit of uplift and the vision of unexploited resources that had inspired James's original university extension movement.

enrollments, as the baby boom generation passed through its college years, and interpreted the phenomenon as a serious threat to Wharton's financial position. By greasing the wheels of sponsored research and executive education, the dean eased the school into lush new markets and product lines. Both turned out to be cashbox bonanzas, with the two ventures together generating over 40 percent of Wharton's total revenues by the end of the decade. This substantial new stream of income, which came to the faculty as well as the institution, reinforced the academic rationale for engagement and fueled a pervasive entrepreneurial ethos among the professoriate. Programs that succeeded in the marketplace, and met academic standards, would thrive. Wharton's academic feuds likewise subsided as the various contentious groups found eager customers in the corporate community and dutifully attended to their own expanding external affairs. And behind this pragmatic peace and prosperity stood the dean and his staff, ready to help "sophisticated problem-solvers" get contracts, students, and freedom from academic politics.[30]

By opening professional opportunities and bringing new resources to the school, the policy of engagement refreshed all of Wharton's various divisions. The decade of the 1970s witnessed the efflorescence of the Rodney White Center and the continued productivity of the Pension Research Council. But the strategy benefited the emerging efforts in management far more than the school's well-established specialties. As the management sector grew under the impetus of engagement, it divided into a host of new and expanded programs: By the end of the decade, 15 research centers, 6 academic departments and teaching units, and 15 M.B.A. majors concerned with management populated Wharton. Most of these outfits, of course, specialized in one managerial activity or one area of application, making no pretense at overall understanding. Not all were in robust health in 1981, and some were actually quite frail. Nevertheless, the sheer number and variety of managerial programs at Wharton were impressive and marked a sharp contrast to the situation twenty or even ten years earlier.[31]

The only field at Wharton to become less managerial under the aegis of engagement in the 1970s was marketing. As the practical disappointments with modeling had surfaced at the end of the 1960s, marketing practitioners had come to believe that "*less* rigorous modeling approaches are often needed to maintain adequate realism and [to] provide a basis for empirical testing of marketing strategies." Of far greater significance in the decline of the managerial perspective, however, was the fact that the discipline found a more compelling identity in market research. New "psychometric" techniques for measuring consumer tastes and econometric methods for segmenting markets emerged around 1970 and quickly became the salient interests in the field. Expertise in analyzing the composition of demand now gave marketing professionals a clear field of jurisdiction, one not to be confused as a stray branch of applied operations research. Encouraging this differentiation were powerful incentives from the consulting market, stimuli liberally accommodated by the school's administration. Sales was one of the most lucrative fields of business, and establishing a successful specialization in the area guaranteed a fine return for one's labors. No Wharton faculty consulted with greater zest or satisfaction than marketing, and consulting contracts blazed a clear trail to market research.[32]

Success in market research demanded the same quantitative skills needed for management science, and Alderson's program thus prepared Wharton for marketing in the 1970s. The young professors whom he recruited were so well prepared, in fact, that they actually led the field into the more sophisticated reaches of market research. Paul Green, Alderson's principal collaborator at the Management Research Center, pioneered in using conjoint analysis in marketing applications. As this psychometric technique developed into the discipline's most powerful tool for analyzing consumer taste, Green became marketing's most frequently cited author. Ronald Frank, who joined the faculty in the early 1960s, would become a master of market segmentation, a prominent student of the effects of television, and the third most frequently cited scholar in the field. In 1965, Green and Frank took charge of recruitment for the department, and over the years they hired an outstanding faculty with similar quantitative skills and expertise in consumer behavior, people such as Yoram Wind, Thomas Robertson, Scott Ward, and Leonard Lodish. Within a decade, Wharton's Marketing Department boasted great strength in statistical technique and psychometrics; economics, marketing's former "mother discipline," was now a secondary influence;

operations research mattered even less; and systems theory was practically irrelevant. From the standpoint of 1981, Alderson's genius served as a catalyst in the introduction of advanced quantitative methods and the return of marketing to a practical, technical orientation. In its most sophisticated and rigorous expression, the field became a policy science much like finance — analyzing and predicting social behavior external to the enterprise; but as a *science*, the discipline again had little to say on how to manage a store or a sales organization.[33]

The business sciences of finance and marketing both flourished in Wharton's engaged atmosphere in the 1970s. Professors in each field then intensified their interaction with business firms, while refining their theoretical and mathematical instruments. Throughout the decade they formed the most powerful and respected specialties in the institution, with faculty, students, businesspeople, and outside academics all acknowledging the growing value of their sciences. But management was the shibboleth of the day, and management nevertheless remained the special beneficiary of the dean's initiatives.

To the scientific faculty in Wharton's Department of Industry, and especially to its young professors of operations research and management information systems, the policy of engagement brought a new age of freedom and expansion. By the time that Carroll had assumed office, this management science group had grown significantly in size, sophistication, and confidence, and chafed quite openly at its constraints in Industry. The tension came to a head in 1973, when the senior faculty denied early promotions to four members of the group. A disgruntled assembly marched to the dean, who knew several of these professors extremely well from his days at MIT. Carroll concluded that the group could best fulfill its promise without the assistance of the other members of the industry faculty, and he decided to give them their own Department of "Decision Sciences."[34]

Once housed in their independent establishment, Wharton's management scientists developed their subject quite rapidly. Led by a succession of able chairmen — James Emery, E. Gerald Hurst, Howard Kunreuther, and Paul Kleindorfer — the department garnered significant funds from grants, research contracts, and executive education. And it had no dearth of projects to pursue.

The department absorbed much of Industry's responsibilities for operations research and management information systems, and spent a good deal of time working in these areas. But a vision of integrating the two fields possessed the entire Decision Sciences faculty, a vision largely inspired by Professor Herbert A. Simon of the Carnegie Institute. Simon had argued that the process of making decisions in an enterprise ought to form the primary focus of management studies, and once his overarching concern for the decision process had been accepted as a focus, research on operating procedures and internal information systems fell together quite nicely: Mathematical decision models defined information needs, while information resources controlled the potential for operational planning.* This emphasis on decision processes pointed out various shortcomings in traditional management science and led to remedial research. The psychology of decision making, for example, became a major area of investigation and an important consideration in otherwise standard studies in operations research or management information systems. As the early confidence in modeling declined, Wharton's decision scientists were among the leaders in "heuristics," an important computer-based, information-intensive alternative: By substituting data processing for mathematical manipulation and settling for something less than an optimal decision, heuristics provided managers with workable solutions to a large variety of difficult problems. Through work such as this, the new department established itself as one of the outstanding academic groups in the entire field of management science, with a strong and growing reputation in both business and educational circles.[35]

The second group of management scientists in the Industry Department studied organizations. Since the mid-1960s they had controlled B.A. 803, the core course in management, and after the departure of the decision scientists they took undisputed possession of the center of the department. As everyone understood, these professors explored a phenomenon of primary significance in the modern world of affairs. With the rise of big business and the division of entrepreneurial authority, organizations had re-

---

*This relationship between OR models and computerized information paralleled the close connection in Frederick W. Taylor's scientific management between planning schemes and cost accounting.

placed individuals as the managers of the capitalist economy. These organizations were themselves in need of management, and that was the interest of this faculty group. They studied the division of enterprises into administrative and staff units, their relationships with their various environments, the resulting performance of entrepreneurial work, and the psychology and sociology of those modern businesspeople who toiled within these leviathans.

Despite its clear importance in the world of modern affairs, the Wharton School never developed a vigorous, original program in organizational studies. The faculty in this area took advantage of their opportunities in consulting, executive education, and sponsored research, but too much individual success, as much as any other factor, limited the development of the area. In the 1960s, no one at Wharton had the combination of interest, energy, and commitment necessary to develop a major research effort in organizational studies. Only in the early 1970s, with the arrival of the amazingly energetic Jay R. Galbraith, did a program show signs of emerging. Primarily interested in practical organizational design, Galbraith approached his topic with an interest in systems theory and information flows. His research and writing concentrated on "matrix" organizations, an interesting new design specifically geared to projects of the "research and development" type.* Galbraith's ideas and enthusiasms created considerable excitement both at Wharton and in the outside business world. However, his reception by the corporations was so warm and his consulting opportunities so lucrative and interesting that Galbraith decided to leave Wharton and pursue them full-time.[36]

---

*Galbraith's matrices divided authority over an individual worker between his project boss, who directed his labors, and his home divisional boss, who took care of bureaucratic paperwork and long-term human resource development. This type of organization thus resembled Frederick Taylor's functional-foremen scheme in that both violated the old "unity of command" managerial axiom. But the matrix departure from traditional doctrine and its affinity with Taylorism went further: Although the project boss had nominal control over the work process, he would actually exert little authority over his subordinates. The "workers" in an R & D-type matrix were skilled professionals, much like Taylor's eight specialized foremen, and in both systems their particular knowledge justified a high degree of independence. The actual work program would be determined through some voluntary meeting of minds. Galbraith and the illustrious founder of scientific management thus minimized the difficulty of integrating the work of such white-collar, entrepreneurial specialists, and they expected overall coordination to be established without benefit of the general executive power of the enterprise.

A somewhat similar fate awaited Andrew H. Van de Ven, who set up shop at the school in 1975. Methodologically sophisticated, and doggedly persistent in his scholarship, Van de Ven provided academic leadership to Wharton's organizational studies group through the last half of the 1970s. With financial help from the dean and then from major American corporations, he and economist Oliver Williamson set up a Center for the Study of Organizational Innovation. Under the auspices of the center, Van de Ven launched an "audacious" attempt to model the interconnections among organizational environment, structure, and performance. But Van de Ven's academic enterprise, like Galbraith's success in consulting, led to his departure from Wharton. In 1981, after only six years at the school, he accepted a professorial chair at the University of Minnesota. Since Van de Ven was Wharton's prime mover in organizational studies, his departure meant that the school's program would have to find still another framework.[37]

Whatever their ultimate scientific value, however, it had become clear by the mid-1970s that disciplines such as decision sciences and organizational behavior were not about to unlock the essence of managerial success. They offered solutions to only certain pieces of the puzzle, and their students found employment as staff specialists, with no special claim to general executive positions. Although unmistakably "managerial," these sciences came no closer to fulfilling Joseph Wharton's or Donald Carroll's guiding ambitions than did the old curricula in industrial engineering or labor relations. During the 1970s, however, new programs sprang up to train students to operate an enterprise as a whole. Although not scientific in the traditional sense of the word, these programs had the virtue of addressing head-on the school's announced purpose of training professional managers. The dean therefore gave these efforts his full encouragement. So did the American business community, which, through research contracts and executive education tuition payments, supplied these new Wharton initiatives with a rich flow of cash.

Edward Shils, who had succeeded Northrup as chairman of the Industry Department in 1969, was among those who developed a new program in general management. A Wharton professor of the traditional variety, Shils had earned both his B.S. and Ph.D. at the school and had then constructed a career in the staid and rather technical specialty of personnel management. The 1970s, however, found him with a new and more innovative spirit. He changed the name of the department from "Industry" to "Management" and, more to the point, established a center and a course of study in general "entrepreneurship."* Small business formed the primary, although not exclusive focus of the program: Shils got major grants to help little companies make their way in the marketplace, and courses in entrepreneurship appealed primarily to students interested in operating their own businesses. In small business, the traditional capitalist firm, all entrepreneurial chores fell on the shoulders of one person. It was for this type of enterprise that Joseph Wharton had been trained at the Waln and Leaming dry-goods house and, like the education that the founder had received there, Shils's program in entrepreneurship emphasized apprenticeship, a "departure from the traditional approach to education at Wharton." Courses relied on "live case studies and field experience, . . . extensively supplemented with input and lectures by leaders in the business community." Although light on the academic side of the ledger, the new entrepreneurial program gave Wharton a valuable clinic where it could train and give support to this, the traditional class of businesspeople.[38]

Corporate America, however, not the family firm, now formed Wharton's primary clientele. To the dean, management meant policy-making for large-scale enterprise, and he made it a major priority to develop a program in the area of overall corporate strategy and policy. Carroll's chief ally in this was John F. Lubin, associate dean of the school and, in 1976, Shils's successor as chairman of the Management Department. A Wharton Ph.D. with twenty years' experience teaching industrial relations and industrial engineering, Lubin had been among the first on the industry faculty to teach a course on general corporate management — his 1970 course on strategic planning. After Lubin became chairman of the Management Department, a one-semester policy and plan-

---

*"The entrepreneur," Shils later explained, is "someone who integrates the functions of marketing, accounting, finance and management and creates something out of nothing. I thought the future of the country depended on our developing business leaders who had the entrepreneurial instincts, who had the ability to actually plan growth and make decisions about growth." The dean liked the idea and gave the enterprise its initial funds. This investment provided an ample return, as Shils raised substantial endowments for his program in entrepreneurship and generated overhead revenues for the school through gifts, contracts, and executive education tuition fees.

ning requirement was added for all M.B.A. students, and the department's program began to grow. Lubin assembled a new faculty, including strategy-minded professors from other Wharton departments. This group concentrated on mechanisms for forward planning in an enterprise and on schemes for "scanning" the changing environment of the firm; unlike Joseph Willits and his colleagues, who had taught strategy courses from an industrial perspective, this "corporate" group was not especially interested in manufacturing or in the integration of internal operations. In other respects, however, the new program remained loosely defined. Strategy was an enormously difficult subject to isolate, and the new faculty, who came from a great variety of backgrounds, filled their courses with an eclectic array of case studies, institutional economics (especially from the industrial economics tradition), theoretical models (especially from organizational studies), computer simulations, and live presentations by visiting corporate executives. Research was also problematic: Major enterprises preferred to keep their innermost plans to themselves, and, as Joseph Wharton had recognized in 1881, executives caught up in such machinations had little time for academic activities. For these various reasons, the business policy group was slow to exploit the professional and financial opportunities of engagement—consulting, executive education, and sponsored research. In due time this, the newest and most ambitious part of the Management Department, may firm up and indeed become the sought-after capstone of the entire Wharton program. Its history, however, awaits the school's second hundred years.[39]*

No one attacked the problem of overall management or took to Carroll's program of engagement with more gusto than the "independent," Russell Ackoff. Just when the new dean arrived at Wharton, in 1972, Ackoff's frustration with the narrowing scope of traditional operations research had reached its limit. He and several associates had resigned from Wharton's operations

*The old Industry Department had offered two ancient courses, vintage 1902, that provided clinical education and long-term strategic insights: "Field Work in Industry" and "Manufacturing Industries of the United States." Field Work, however, never joined the graduate curriculum. At the undergraduate level, it was subsumed into a survey course in the early 1960s, then died out altogether a few years later because of logistical difficulties. "Manufacturing Industries," now known as "Industrial Structure and Policy," survived by changing its format and becoming essentially a course in the economics of industrial organization. It originally, but no longer, satisfied the policy and planning requirement.

research group and had begun searching about for a new and more ambitious academic watering hole.* As a consulting wizard, Ackoff had no trouble finding sponsors who would support his activities in the university; he needed only official academic approval of his new initiatives in "sophisticated problem solving," which the new dean was eager to arrange. Beyond the simple convenience afforded by Carroll's strategy, Ackoff himself had always espoused a grand engagement of the university with the world of affairs. He had never thought of operations research merely as mathematical modeling, but as the leading edge of a new, overarching integration of science and purposeful human activity. Ackoff had come to this vision in the 1940s, while a graduate student in philosophy at Penn, under the university's great master of pragmatism, Professor E. A. Singer, Jr. During the years that Ackoff had sat in his seminar, Singer was setting out, from a systems-theoretical perspective, a logical analysis of the interconnections between scientific inquiry and "functional, goal-seeking, and purposeful behavior." Ackoff saw his entire career as an extension of Singer's program of "applied philosophy," as the search for what he called "the philosophy that could bake bread."[40]

To bring the instruments of philosophy and science to bear on practical problems, Ackoff and C. West Churchman, his close friend and fellow Singer student, had set up an Institute of Experimental Method at the university in 1946. There they had looked for their practical philosophy within the general-purpose "unified science" movement, the academic analogue to Joseph Willits's program of "general management," and had found it wanting. While working on a practical investigation of *The Measurement of Consumer Interest*, they had decided, instead, that "interdisciplinary research" offered the strategy best suited to addressing real-world problems. As Ackoff later explained, it

was already clear that the problems most pressing mankind could no longer be fruitfully treated by specialists. A synthesis of scientific disciplines was inevitable. The effort to create scientific generalists was doomed to failure because it acquired breadth at the cost of depth. Research by interdisciplinary teams was the only feasible alternative.

The various participants of such teams would each have particular competences, sharing only the most abstract elements of the

---

*Shiv Gupta and John Cozzolino, two able operations research professors, remained behind and continued to operate the school's "unit" in OR.

"experimental method": mathematical sophistication and a philosophical appreciation of the nature of scientific method. Ackoff and Churchman soon had recognized the program of English operational research as fundamentally the same as their own: It was explicitly interdisciplinary, systemic, scientific, and normative. They had then joined forces with this larger movement, becoming recognized as leaders in American operations research. As academic life after World War II had gone off in a sharply different direction, toward increasing disciplinary specialization and esoteric abstraction, Singer's "children" had kept their faith in their interdisciplinary, problem-oriented inheritance. They had abandoned philosophy when it, like economics in Simon Patten's day, had turned away from broader problems and speculations, and had grown into a more narrowly defined, analytical exercise. When operations research had threatened to settle into a similarly "bankrupt" state, they left it as well.[41]*

In 1973, Ackoff and his followers organized a new academic enterprise called "Social Systems Science," or "S³" for short. Ackoff's ambitions for S³ were quite a bit more grandiose than

---

*In the 1940s, Ackoff and Churchman had come into contact with Wroe Alderson, himself a great devotee of Singer's. This, perhaps, explains their choice of a marketing problem, the measurement of consumer interests, as the focus of investigation for their Institute of Experimental Method. Alderson, then scrounging around for theory, had also gotten Churchman to pen the lead article in the *Theory of Marketing* anthology. Ackoff, Churchman, and Alderson were all developing an interdisciplinary, systems-theoretical perspective, and the three became colleagues and good friends. In academic life, however, things were rarely so serendipitous. Ackoff and Churchman's program, which so audaciously overflowed the banks of disciplinary channels, rudely conflicted with the departmental structure of American universities. The young systems scientists, therefore, rarely found stable faculty positions and remained unusually dependent on the favor of academic administrators. At Penn, Ackoff and Churchman's Institute originally had had the support of President George W. McClelland, who had succeeded Thomas Gates in 1944. But when administrations changed, and the new university authorities had little interest in the experimental method project, Ackoff and Churchman moved on to Wayne State University. In due time, however, the chairman of the Wayne State Philosophy Department became quite convinced that philosophers ought not to bake bread, and the two continued to the Case Institute. Churchman later left for the University of California at Berkeley, but Ackoff stayed at Case until a new president arrived who revoked the blessings of the central administration. Ackoff then came to the Wharton School. He arrived through the office of the dean, not any existing department, and the dean remained the major support of his academic position. When asked why he stayed in universities despite such turmoil and his abundant opportunities as a consultant, Ackoff listed the questioning students, the few exceptional minds to be found on almost any faculty, and the freedom of academic life. Quite characteristically, he made no mention of the access the university provided to various disciplines and specialists.

routine scholarship, and he specifically chose this awkward, amorphous name to "undefine" the new program and to avoid any possible confusion with the standard university disciplines. Managers and management scientists trained in the traditional academic fashion, he argued, had failed to understand that organizations were parts of still larger systems, and that they employed people who had purposes of their own. Ackoff had seen numerous operations research experts and technically skilled managers ignore these simple truths of systems theory and, like hyperskilled surgeons who knew nothing of anatomy, consistently proceed with the right operation on the wrong organ. To help mankind get back on track, S^3 prescribed booster shots of engagement and systems theory, a remedy that Ackoff called "interactive planning." In his prospectus for Social Systems Science, an enthusiastic Ackoff announced that the enterprise "may not only be able to assure man a future, but it may also enable him to gain control of it," that S^3 could lead man out of industrial civilization into a new era that "may well come to be known as the *Resurrection*."[42]

At the core of Ackoff's systems philosophy lay the idea of purpose, and the problem of specifying the purpose of an enterprise became the focal point of his interactive planning program. No longer interested in condensing the aims of an enterprise into a single, quantitative measure, the S^3 strategy would have organizations paint concrete "idealized futures" for themselves. According to Ackoff, management and representatives of all interested "stakeholders" should devote considerable energy to defining this telos and to laying strategy for getting from here to there. This cooperative planning process, Ackoff was convinced, was far more effective than operations research type problem solving in dealing with major strategic issues. Interactive planning had tremendous "informal" benefits as well: By inducing the participation of subordinates and "environmental" groups, and by harnessing their creativity, it formed a powerful consensus behind the collectively determined program. On a more exalted, historico-philosophical level, Ackoff believed that the process of interactive planning "*reveals that the largest obstruction between man and the future that he most desires is man himself.*" What could be more satisfying to Ackoff than this final truth, this vision of resurrection through pragmatic process?[43]

"reveals that the largest obstruction between man and the future that he most desires is man himself." What could be more
satisfying to Ackoff than this final truth, this vision of resurrection through pragmatic process?[43]

The S[3] program grew vigorously through the 1970s and became the closest thing to a Wharton approach to corporate management. The unit won so many research contracts that it could
support more Ph.D. candidates than any other program at the
school and boasted its largest aggregate research effort. Ackoff
organized a new and highly successful research center—the Busch
Center — while his students remained in charge of the Management and Behavioral Science Center. They also assumed direction
of the Wharton Applied Research Center, organized in 1976 as
"the clinical arm of the Wharton School." By offering some of the
most popular courses at Wharton, Ackoff and his associates helped
give the entire student body a distinctive, "systems-wise" managerial *Weltanschauung*. S[3]'s blueprint for social resurrection
(stakeholder representation and interactive planning with the
idealized-future technique) also won wide currency at Wharton
as an ethic for modern corporate society. Its participatory politics,
paralleled in such popular schemes as matrix organizational design and interdisciplinary research, satisfied the democratic pro-
clivities of a large portion of Wharton's young professional
managers. Within its first decade of operation, therefore, S[3] won
a significant following among the school's major constituents —
its students and its research sponsors.[44]

S[3]'s audacity, however, created a good deal of suspicion among
the Wharton faculty. Ackoff's disparagement of the traditional
scholarly disciplines and good old "reductionist" science sat none
too well with the professoriate. Some, in turn, scorned Ackoff's
new activities as mere guru hocus-pocus. Nor could many relish
his refusal to specify a curriculum for S[3] or his claim that self-
directed, interdisciplinary "learning cells" and "research cells"
did the job of education much better than the pedagogical techniques currently used at the Wharton School. Ackoff tried to
explain to his colleagues that academic departments

do not organize knowledge; they organize teachers and disorganize
knowledge. Disciplinary departments and bounded subjects are antithe-
tical to Systems Age education. A curriculum is a solution to a problem
that does not exist. Even if it did exist, its solution would change rapidly

with respect to time and place. Curricula as now conceived are a denial of the rapid rate of cultural and technological change.[45]

Disciplines, "bounded subjects," and curricula, however, were the essential twelfth-century innovations that had created the Western university, and the Wharton faculty was not quite ready to abandon them. Many professors also found Ackoff's notions of the "idealized future" and "stakeholder" representation confusing as well as a bit naive: Most economists assumed that making money, and the more the better, was the primary purpose of engaging in business, and the notion that an enterprise could pursue some idealized state struck dismal scientists as rather utopian. They assumed that markets and laws, not corporate conclaves, provided the fundamental means for sorting out arrangements among firms, their employees, and their larger environments. Inasmuch as modern managers operated in the capitalist world — in the same basic economy that had begun growing in twelfth-century Europe — Ackoff's principles made little sense. For these reasons, as well as the normal bad rubs of personality and fears of competition, the faculty gave S^3 a difficult time. Ackoff and his colleagues wanted to transform their unit into a separate Wharton department and to offer an S^3 major in the M.B.A. program. At first the faculty turned them down. But in 1981, after some serious lobbying from the dean, S^3 did get what it wanted.[46]

Of decisive importance to Ackoff's success was the fact that contemporary economic society was indeed decidedly different from that capitalism which had emerged in twelfth-century Europe. Of critical import for the entire Wharton School was the fact that management was in the ascendancy in society as a whole, with influence far beyond its original provinces in manufacturing and transportation enterprises. In the 1970s, Wharton relentlessly followed this expansion: Not only did the school develop strong programs in various managerial functions and in general management itself, but it also accommodated courses of study specific to the new territories of managerial colonization. The most important of these extensions, in fact, prepared student managers to enter the jurisdictions of the two great twelfth-century classes — independent professional practice and international trade.

Joseph Wharton's nineteenth-century colleagues in the United States Sanitary Commission and the American Social Science

Association had already brought professionals and men of affairs together to address the organized delivery of health, justice, education, and welfare services. But only at the end of its first century of activity did the Wharton School energetically combine its academic program in business administration with those of other professional schools. In the 1970s Wharton organized joint M.B.A. programs with the university's law school, its School of Engineering and Applied Science, and the School of Social Work, and it resuscitated a "public management" curriculum. A major effort in health care administration, established in 1967, flourished magnificently in the 1970s as Wharton became the federal government's National Health Care Management Center. With leadership from Robert Eilers, Samuel Martin, and William Pierskalla, the school developed exemplary research and training programs in health care administration. Using a research organization of the matrix type, Wharton's Leonard Davis Institute of Health Economics brought professors from various parts of the university together to examine the nation's increasingly complicated and hierarchical system of medical care. The Leonard Davis Institute, for example, encouraged Wharton scholars in marketing and insurance to bring important new insights into health services delivery problems and provided an opportunity for Gregory Prastacos, of the Decision Sciences Department, to design a prize-winning scheme of blood bank management. In various professional fields, and especially in medicine, Wharton took the initiative in developing scientific programs of administration. It thus accelerated the expansion of management's visible hand into the hitherto private realms of independent professional practice.[47]

The international import-export trade, capitalism's cradle, had been for centuries the meat and potatoes of business elites, and the field had long been taught at Wharton as part of its program in commerce and marketing. After World War II, however, managers of multinational corporations took control of the international flow of goods, technology, and investment. In response, the school's old program in import-export became a very small rump of the Marketing Department, while professors in other disciplines, especially management, gained interest in the area. In 1971, the school therefore created an independent Multinational Enterprise Unit, headed by Professor of Management and devotee of the systems approach, Howard Perlmutter. Ten years later the unit was absorbed into the Management Department itself, reflecting the control of modern management over international exchange.[48]*

Traditional Wharton programs, which prepared students for specialized professional careers or to do business in the marketplace, also felt the new influence of management in the 1970s. In that decade both accounting, the school's quintessential professional specialty, and finance, its most popular discipline and the one most closely associated with neoclassical economic theory, saw remarkable changes in their educational roles. They had hitherto prepared students to process information and handle transactions in the nation's financial markets. The wave of corporate decentralization and diversification after World War II and the subsequent efflorescence of corporate planning, however, had created vast "internal markets" for capital and information. Business once transacted in the open market by independent agents and brokers now became private affairs of the firm. Demand for Wharton M.B.A.'s expert in handling these new corporate activities shot up smartly in the 1970s, while demand for M.B.A.'s with market-oriented finance and accounting skills declined dramatically. Although the 1970s saw tremendous growth in the professional apparatus of financial accounting, a movement centering on the newly established Financial Accounting Standards Board, and although Wharton's accounting faculty, led by Professor David Solomons, was quite active in this process of professional articulation, Wharton M.B.A.'s steadily moved in a different direction: While 12 percent of Wharton's 1972 class of M.B.A.'s chose careers as accountants, a meager 4 percent did so in 1980.[49]

Instruction offered by the Finance Department remained the central pillar of a Wharton education throughout the 1970s. But both the department advisory committee and Dean Carroll continually encouraged the school's faculty to build strength in the

*Fields of study such as multinational enterprise and health care management were not formal disciplines, and their faculties created academic programs out of apprenticeships, case studies, and interdisciplinary research. At its best, as at the Leonard Davis Institute, this approach led to significant cross-fertilization. At its worst, however, these programs ran afoul of the prerogatives of the school's existing departments, which naturally insisted on controlling courses and tenure decisions in their areas of responsibility. These difficulties put a crimp, in particular, in the ambitions of the independent Multinational Enterprise Unit.

new area of managerial finance, a funding operation quite different from that found in commercial banks or in the stock and bond exchanges. Although this subject had little direct connection with neoclassical theory, the department's scholarly homeland, the faculty did make some adjustments in this direction. The students, over half of whom majored in finance during the decade, made even more: Between 1972 and 1980, the proportion of Wharton M.B.A.'s entering careers in corporate finance rose 70 percent, from 16 percent to 27 percent of the graduating class. The figures for recruitment into the other two financial fields, commercial banking and investments (stocks and bonds), were nearly the reverse, falling from 26 percent to 17 percent. Finance and accounting, the core of a traditional Wharton education and the most rigorous of business disciplines, remained critical components of the school's educational program. But they now found their curricular niches challenged by the new corporate dispensation.[50]*

The influence of management on the Wharton School was thus pervasive, with nearly all of its various curricula more managerial in 1981 than they had been in 1972. No one course of study, however, succeeded in capturing the essence of modern management. Fields such as corporate finance, health care administration, and multinational enterprise management were all particular by definition. Decision sciences and organizational studies, although originally organized with grander ambitions, had evolved into specialized academic fields of study and middle-manage-

---

*The business of insurance, and the Wharton Insurance Department with it, also adjusted to the new world of management. Corporations were purchasing ever-larger amounts of insurance for their employees as part of the wage bargain, and the task of contracting for pension plans, health, and even life insurance policies became functions of the firm. A new occupational class expert in handling these and other "fringe" benefits emerged in corporate administrations, and in the late 1970s the Wharton Insurance Department, together with the International Foundation of Employee Benefit Plans, decided to put the business on a more professional footing. With Professor of Insurance Jerry S. Rosenbloom as academic director, they established a "Certified Employee Benefit Specialist" program for these corporate officials, analogous to Solomon Huebner's CLU and CPLU arrangements for independent insurance agents.

The Marketing Department, which had clearly downgraded operations research approaches in favor of market research, also developed an interest in marketing management in the second half of the 1970s. Consistent with trends at the school, "strategic" rather than "operational" issues, and the case method, not rigorous modeling and testing, constituted the basic pedagogical technique in this new area of concern.

ment staff specialties. The very legitimacy of each of the school's various programs in general management, those in managerial institutions, entrepreneurship, business policy, and social systems science, indicated that the others failed to comprehend the whole. Wharton's central program in management education, as it turned out, was not to be found in one of these various curricula, but in its M.B.A. program in its entirety.

Known as the "Wharton Experience," the M.B.A. program of 1981 passed the student body through a largely common course of study with managerial careers as its clearly indicated telos. The curriculum specified a basic set of seven required courses, more than that allowed for any one major and amounting to nearly 40 percent of all M.B.A. course work. The mandated material included a survey of managerial topics: the policy and planning requirement, introductions to operations research and organizational behavior, and "Statistical Analysis for Management." Recognizing that the ability to do business in the marketplace remained essential to managerial success, the faculty still specified one semester of accounting and two of economics for all M.B.A.'s. The school also asked these students to demonstrate proficiency in computer programming and oral and written communications; valuable for all men (and now women) of affairs, these skills were essential for modern executives. Wharton's size and variety, classic strengths of the school, had often been viewed as barriers to a general managerial emphasis. But in the new M.B.A. program they constituted hidden strengths. The departments of statistics, law, and accounting boasted some of the finest teachers on the faculty and gave Wharton M.B.A.'s a solid grounding in these various managerial instruments. The curriculum discouraged students from pursuing any highly specialized program, but the continuing abundance of interests cultivated at Wharton still filled the school air with sophisticated analyses of arcane dealings and subtle interconnections among business functions and industries. Diversity continued to enrich business education at the school, while the strengthened core prepared M.B.A.'s for general executive careers.[51]*

---

*The managerial rewards that accrued to the specialized program — good teaching in technical areas and synergistic effects among fields of study — were, of course, traditionally present at Wharton. This perhaps explains why the school's

Energizing the atmosphere of Vance Hall and providing the central theme of the "Wharton Experience" was a powerful cult of executive leadership. Wharton's excellent students and hard-working professors eagerly embraced this managerial spirit, while Vance's striking architecture provided them with a suitably dramatic setting. But it was the dean and his staff that filled the school with this ambitious air. Urbane, experienced, and technically skilled, the dean himself stood as a prime example of managerial success. Despite his indirect leadership style, which encouraged joint ventures with other schools at the university and promoted matrix organizations to conduct interdisciplinary sponsored research, the dean never lost sight of the fact that creating "hard core, committed future business managers" was the primary function of "the best school of management in the world." Carroll systematically tied the school to the national culture of executive authority and in all his public appearances, through both his bearing and words, he conjured the image of the general executive as the object of education at Wharton. The dean saw to it that a seemingly endless parade of high corporate officials traveled to West Philadelphia to eat, speak, and rub up against the student body. At Carroll's invitation, Wharton alumnus and General Electric board chairman Reginald Jones led an impressive collection of his colleagues into active involvement with the school's activities.* When Carroll became the first occupant of the Reliance Professorship/Deanship of Management and Private Enterprise, in 1980, the chair suited him well.[52]†

older emphasis on specialized professional training had so little effect, with alumni changing their occupations so readily, and why these alumni were nevertheless quite successful.

*In honor of its retiring chairman, the General Electric Company endowed the Reginald Jones Professorship of Corporate Management at Wharton in 1981. Several key members of the dean's office hoped that this chair, and its associated Center for Management, Policy, Strategy, and Organization, would provide the school's long-sought focal point for studies in corporate management.

†The endowment of the Reliance chair, to be occupied by the dean of the school, was donated by Wharton alumnus and chairman of the Reliance Group, Saul P. Steinberg. The contribution, however, created quite a stir among the university faculty. The agreement between Steinberg and the university originally called for the dean to be "an outstanding business statesman" and a "spokesman . . . for the business . . . community" (presumably with a rather conservative repertoire of expressions). Joseph Wharton, no doubt, would have approved of the document, perhaps faulting it for lack of specificity. But the university professoriate cried foul and succeeded in deleting language that appeared to restrict the academic freedom of future deans. However, the apparently controversial words

In the 1970s the Wharton School thus took up its founder's ambition that it prepare a class of national leaders. Clearly, the decade presented the institution with its best opportunity to achieve that ambition since its original creation in the previous century: The school had lost touch with the American genteel elite when it had adopted the specialized educational strategy of the German university and had embarked on its crusade for progressive reform. Other educational institutions had then attracted the heirs of the national establishment, becoming their preparatory schools for leadership: the liberal arts colleges of Harvard, Yale, and Princeton, the Ivy League law schools (including that of the University of Pennsylvania), and the Harvard Business School. For over a half a century these institutions successfully facilitated the transfer of power from upper class fathers to their sons. But the traumas of the Great Depression and the Second World War, the tremendous growth of corporate complexity, and the development of sophisticated new policy sciences gave Wharton its new opportunity. In the post–World War II era, corporate America decisively outgrew the influence of its founding entrepreneurial families and came to rely on sophisticated social science and managerial instruments to handle its affairs. Because they offered training in these new tools of leadership, a few schools of business were clearly in line to provide professional preparation for a national managerial elite. Wharton seized this chance.[53]

The success of the Wharton M.B.A. stood, perhaps, as the culmination, perhaps, of the school's century-old effort to raise a leadership class for industrial society. More thoroughly and harmoniously than in its past, the program amalgamated the three classic Western leadership types—the professional, the aristocrat, and the businessman — into a new social persona. Like their fellow university-trained professionals, Wharton M.B.A.'s grounded their authority in special knowledge, not inherited status or wealth. Positions of general responsibility stood as their goal: Wharton

"private enterprise" remained in the title of the professorship. The faculty recognized either that the business of the Wharton School was private enterprise; that such a business was not controversial; or that legitimate compromise was possible when $1.5 million was involved. Pleased with the school's progress, Steinberg then donated $4 million toward the renovation of Dietrich Hall in 1981. This contribution assured his family's name a place on the revitalized structure, thus joining Wharton, Dietrich, Vance, Lippincott (the school library), and Mayer as families memorialized by the institution.

M.B.A.'s aspired to be the ones who integrated that tremendous diversity of economic activities and divisions of labor found in modern corporations. To this aristocratic function they brought the businessman's discipline — the contract, the income statement, and the balance sheet. This M.B.A. synthesis, however, may prove transient. Chameleonlike change and adaptation have always been Wharton's central characteristics. By its very nature, the school is caught between the world of affairs and that of scholarship, and the school will surely transform itself again as those two unsynchronized spheres spin out of their current alignment. But for the moment, at any rate, Joseph Wharton's project has come full term.

Source Notes

1. Joseph Wharton, "Is a College Education Advantageous to a Business Man?" (Philadelphia: Wharton School Association, 1890), 9; Donald C. Carroll, *Wharton: State of the School*, offset (Philadelphia: Wharton School, 1977), Carroll's italics; "Wharton News: Donald Cary Carroll," information sheet dated 15 May 1981, files of Dean Donald C. Carroll.

2. "Wharton Graduate Annual Report (1972 – 1973)," 3, 17; "Henry T. Vance File," Archives; Carroll, *Wharton*; Thomas A. Budd to Gaylord P. Harnwell, 13 Jan. 1955, files of the Dean of the Wharton School, 16.

3. Annual Report of the Dean of the Wharton School (1941 – 42), files of the Dean of the Wharton School, 8; J. A. Livingston and Beverley M. Bowie, "An Outside Look at Wharton," reprinted from *Pennsylvania Gazette* (Jan. 1947):6; Edward B. Shils, "A Reunion of Seven Men Who Made a Department," *Pennsylvania Gazette* (Nov. 1960): 19, 17 – 20; C. Canby Balderston, Robert P. Brecht et al., *Management of an Enterprise*, 2d ed. (New York: Prentice Hall, 1949 [1935]); *University of Pennsylvania Bulletin (1958 – 59): Graduate Studies*, 55, 62 – 63; *University of Pennsylvania Bulletin (1957 – 58): Undergraduate Studies*, 92, 94; Minutes of the Board of Business Education, 17 Nov. 1949; Minutes of the Wharton Faculty, 30 Mar. 1950; interviews with Adrian McDonough and Wayne Howard.

4. *University of Pennsylvania Bulletin (1958 – 59): Graduate Studies*, 63; Minutes of the Board of Business Education, 3 Mar. 1950; interview with Howard; Alfred D. Chandler, Jr., *Strategy and Structure* (Cambridge, Mass.: M.I.T. Press, 1962), 324 – 82.

5. Daniel Wren, *The Evolution of Managerial Thought* (New York: Roland Press, 1972), 246ff.; Harold Koontz, ed., *Toward a Unified Theory of Management* (New York: McGraw-Hill, 1964).

6. Interviews with Willis Winn and William Gomberg.

7. William Gomberg, "Enterprise in the Critical Society," reprinted from *Bedriften i/det kritiske samfunn, Foredrag ved, Hostkonferansen 1971, Norges Handelshoyskole*, Bergen, 2 – 4 Nov., 39; Annual Report of the Dean of the Wharton School (1958 – 59), files of the Dean of the Wharton School, 2; interview with Gomberg.

8. Interview with Gomberg; Selig Perlman, *A Theory of the Labor Movement* (New York: MacMillan, 1928); Peter F. Drucker, *The Concept of the*

Corporation (New York: John Day, 1946); Ernest Dale, *The Great Organizers* (New York: McGraw-Hill, 1960).

9. Joseph Wharton, "Project," Minutes of the University Trustees, 24 Mar. 1881; interviews with Northrup, William Evan, Gomberg, Howard, Mc-Donough, and Bernard Samoff; Gordon F. Bloom and Herbert R. Northrup, *Economics of Labor Relations* (Homewood, Ill.: Richard D. Irwin, 1950); Annual Report of the Dean of the Wharton School (1960–61), files of the Dean of the Wharton School, 2; *The Industrial Research Unit, 1921–1978, The Labor Relations Council, 1946–1978: Report on Progress* (Philadelphia: Industrial Research Unit, 1978), 4–5; *Industrial Research Unit: History and Current Research, 1921–1969*, mimeographed (Philadelphia: Industrial Research Unit, 1969), 3.

10. *Industrial Research Unit, 1921–1969*, 6; *Industrial Research Unit, 1921–1978*, 27, 29, 27, 29, 54, 8–21, 27–49; "Industrial Research Unit: Annual Status of Projects, Fiscal Year July 1, 1978–June 30, 1979," mimeographed, Industrial Research Unit, 4–6.

11. Herbert A. Simon in Koontz, ed., *Unified Theory*, 79, quoted in Wren, *Management Thought*, 427.

12. F. E. Emery, ed., *Systems Thinking* (Harmondsworth, England: Penguin Books, 1969), passim, and Introduction, 7–13; also see Edmund J. James, "Factory Laws," quoted in Richard A. Swanson, "Edmund J. James, 1885–1925: A 'Conservative Progressive' in American Higher Education" (Ph.D. diss., University of Illinois, 1966), 41; Wren, *Management Thought*, 446–68; see Talcott Parsons, *The Structure of Social Action* (New York: McGraw-Hill, 1937), *The Social System* (Glencoe, Ill.: Free Press, 1951), and, especially, *Economy and Society* (Glencoe, Ill.: Free Press, 1956).

13. Hugh J. Miser, "Operations Research and Systems Analysis," *Science* 209 (1980):139, 139–46; P. M. Morse, "OR Is Also Research," *Proceedings of the First International Conference on OR* (Baltimore: Operations Research Society of America, 1957), 5; Russell L. Ackoff and Patrick Rivett, *A Manager's Guide to Operations Research* (New York: John Wiley & Sons, 1963).

14. Adrian M. McDonough, *Information Economics and Management Systems* (New York: McGraw-Hill, 1963) ix; Adrian M. McDonough, *Centralized Systems Planning and Control* (Wayne, Pa.: Thompson Book Company, 1969); Adrian M. McDonough and Leonard J. Garrett, *Management Systems: Working Concepts and Practices* (Homewood, Ill.: Richard D. Irwin, 1965); interviews with McDonough, Ross Webber, James Emery, Gomberg, Northrup, and Edward Shils.

15. Interviews with Gomberg, Webber, Emery, and Northrup.

16. Minutes of the Wharton Faculty, 4 Oct. 1961, my italics; Annual Report of the Dean of the Wharton School (1963–64), files of the Dean of the Wharton School, 3; (1962–63), 2; Minutes of the Wharton Faculty, 9 Jan. 1961, 8 May 1963; interviews with Richard Clelland and Morris Hamburg; *AMS*, s.v. "Morris Hamburg."

17. Jon E. Friedman, "Alderson's Impact on Marketing" (independent study research paper, University of Pennsylvania Management Department, May 1980); Wroe Alderson and Reavis Cox, "Towards a Theory of Marketing," *Journal of Marketing* 13 (1948):137–52; Reavis Cox and Wroe Alderson, eds., *Theory in Marketing* (Homewood, Ill.: Richard D. Irwin, 1950); Wroe Alderson, *Marketing Behavior and Executive Action* (Homewood, Ill.: Richard D. Irwin, 1957); interviews with Cox, Charles Goodman, Ronald Frank, and Yoram Wind.

18. Paul Green, "The Future Marketing Researcher," xerox of typescript, files of Paul Green, n.p., n.d.

19. Annual Report of the Dean of the Wharton School, (1963–64), files of the Dean of the Wharton School, 3; (1962–63), 4, 4–5; (1963–64), 3–4; *University of Pennsylvania Bulletin, (1962–63): Graduate Studies*, 44; Fried-

man,"Alderson's Impact"; interviews with Green, Hamburg, and Clelland; *AMS*, s.v. "Edward Loren Brink."

20. Private communication, Hugh J. Miser to author, 19 Mar. 1981; interviews with Ackoff, Wladimir Sachs, Emery, and John Cozzolino; Ackoff and Rivett, *Manager's Guide*, 9.

21. Interviews with Paul Kleindorfer, Emery, Ackoff, and Nancy Schnerr; reminiscences of Nancy Schnerr, in *The Story of Statistics: Nineteen Thirty-one – Nineteen Eighty-one*, offset, ed. Nancy Schnerr, (Philadelphia: Wharton School, 1981).

22. Green, "Marketing Researcher"; Russell L. Ackoff, "Systems, Organizations, and Interdisciplinary Research," *General Systems Yearbook* 5 (1960), reprinted in F. E. Emery, *Systems Thinking*, 341; Giandomenico Majone, "Applied Systems Analysis: A Genetic Approach," working draft, Apr. 1980; Russell L. Ackoff, "The Future of Operational Research Is Past," *Journal of the Operational Research Society* 30 (1979):103 – 4; interview with Ackoff.

23. Carroll, *State of the School*.

24. Carroll, *State of the School*; private communication, Norman N. Palmer to author, 28 Aug. 1981; Roger Strong, "Wharton Continues To Draw Top Students," *Wharton Journal* 17 Sep. 1981, 1; "International Fact Sheet, 1981 – 82," files of the Dean of the Wharton School, 6.

25. 1980 Wharton Alumni Survey, conducted by author; Strong, "Top Students"; Michael F. Eleey, Mary Hawryshkiw, and Anand Desa, *The Wharton MBA Panel: Preliminary Report* (Philadelphia: Department of Decision Sciences, Wharton School, University of Pennsylvania, 1980).

26. Carroll, *State of the School*; "Wharton's Master of Growth," *New York Times*, 21 Nov. 1976; interview with Carroll and Eric van Merkensteijn.

27. Carroll, *State of the School*; "Wharton's Master of Growth"; Charles C. Harrison, "Autobiography of Charles Custis Harrison, 1844 – 1929" (Philadelphia: typescript, n.d.), Archives; "The Baby Boom and the Baby Bust: A Conversation with Dean Donald C. Carroll," *Anvil* (Wharton Graduate Alumni Magazine) 4 (Winter, 1980):2, 5 – 7; interviews with Carroll, Frank, van Merkensteijn, and Cozzolino.

28. Carroll, *State of the School*; "Baby Boom," 2, 5 – 7; interview with Carroll.

29. Carroll, *State of the School*; "Baby Boom," 5 – 7; Minutes of the Wharton Faculty, 3 May 1965, 9 June 1972; 1980 Wharton Alumni Survey, conducted by the author; Executive Education Annual Report (1976 – 77, 1977 – 78, 1978 – 79), files of the Office of Executive Education, Wharton School; "Executive MBA Program," promotional pamphlet (1981?): 1, 7; "Wharton Executive MBA" (1980?): clipping in the files of the Wharton Executive M.B.A. office; "The Community – Wharton Education Program: An Evaluation" (1976?): files of the Community – Wharton Education Program office.

30. Carroll, *State of the School*; "Baby Boom," 2 – 4, 7; interviews with Carroll and van Merkensteijn.

31. "Organization of the Wharton School," mimeographed, dated Sept. 1979.

32. Green, "Market Researcher"; Paul Green and V. Srinivasan, "Conjoint Analysis in Consumer Research: Issues and Outlook," *Journal of Consumer Research* 5 (1978):103; Paul Green and Yoram Wind, *Multiattribute Decisions in Marketing* (Hinsdale, Ill.: Dryden Press, 1973); Ronald E. Frank, William F. Massy, and Yoram Wind, *Market Segmentation* (Englewood Cliffs, N.J.: Prentice-Hall, 1972); interviews with Frank, Green, and Wind.

33. Interviews with Frank, Green, and Wind.

34. Interviews with Carroll, Emery, Kleindorfer, Shils, Howard Kunreuther, and Cozzolino.

35. Interviews with Michael Eleey, Kleindorfer, Kunreuther and Cozzolino; Herbert A. Simon, *Administrative Behavior* (Toronto: Collier – Macmil-

lan, 1945); "Decision Sciences at the Wharton School, University of Pennsylvania," promotional pamphlet (1980?).

36. Jay R. Galbraith, "Matrix Designs," *Business Horizons* 14 (1971):29 – 40; Jay R. Galbraith, ed., *Matrix Organizations: Organization Design for High Technology* (Cambridge, Mass.: M.I.T. Press, 1971); Ross A. Webber, *Management: Basic Elements of Managing Organizations* (Homewood, Ill.: Richard D. Irwin, 1975), 421 – 24; Wren, *Management Thought*, 123 – 26.

37. Comments by Charles E. Lindblom and Courtlandt Cammann, Conference on Organization Design and Performance, sponsored by the Wharton Center for the Study of Organizational Innovation, Philadelphia, 12 Apr. 1981; Andrew H. Van de Ven, "The Organization Assessment Research Program," draft of paper presented at Conference on Organization Design and Performance, Philadelphia, 12 Apr. 1981; Andrew H. Van de Ven, "Early Planning, Implementation, and Performance of New Organizations," in *The Organizational Life Cycle*, ed. John R. Kimberly, Robert H. Miles et al. (San Francisco: Jossey-Bass, 1980): 83 – 134; Andrew H. Van de Ven and Diane L. Ferry, *Measuring and Assessing Organizations* (New York: Wiley Interscience, 1980); Oliver E. Williamson, "Center for the Study of Organizational Innovation Report for the Calendar Year 1977," dated Feb. 1978, and "for Calendar Year 1980," dated Mar. 1981. The center supported a thriving program in industrial organization, led by Williamson, in addition to Van de Ven's group organization behavior. The two sections of CSOI, however, conducted their affairs independently of each other. Interview with Oliver E. Williamson.

38. Stuart Cantor, "Wharton Entrepreneurial Center," *Wharton Account* (Spring, 1980):3; "Beautiful Business Butterflies Come from Academic Cocoons," reprinted from *Pennsylvania Gazette* (Mar. 1974); "The Wharton Entrepreneurial Center Annual Report (1978 – 79)" and "(1975 – 76)"; interviews with Shils and William Zucker.

39. Interviews with Carroll, Lubin, and Peter Lorange; Joseph Wharton, "Project"; *Wharton Graduate Division Course Guide (1979 – 1980)*, 10, 119, 123 – 25; interviews with Ross Webber and Howard.

40. Interviews with Ackoff and Thomas Cowan.

41. Russell Ackoff, "Science in the Systems Age," *Wharton Quarterly* 7 (Winter, 1973):10; Russell L. Ackoff, "The Meaning, Scope, and Methods of Operations Research," in *Progress in Operations Research, Volume 1* (New York: John Wiley & Sons, 1961), ed. Ackoff, 25; interviews with Ackoff, Thomas Cowan, and Sachs; Ackoff, "Systems," 331, 342–43, 345–46; Russell L. Ackoff, "The Future of Operational Research Is Past," *Journal of the Operational Research Society* 30 (1979):93 – 104; Russell L. Ackoff, "Resurrecting the Future of Operational Research," *Journal of the Operational Research Society* 30 (1979):189 – 99; Ackoff, "Meaning, Scope, and Methods," 15, 17 – 18, 30; C. West Churchman and Russell Ackoff, "Psychologistics," mimeographed (Philadelphia: University of Pennsylvania Research Fund, 1947); C. West Churchman and Russell Ackoff, "Varieties of Unification," *Philosophy of Science* 13 (1948):287 – 300; C. West Churchman, Russell L. Ackoff, and M. Wax, eds., *Measurement of Consumer Interest* (Philadelphia: University of Pennsylvania Press, 1946); C. West Churchman, "Basic Research in Marketing," in *Theory in Marketing*, ed. Reavis Cox and Wroe Alderson, 3–17.

42. Ackoff, "Science in the Systems Age," 8, Ackoff's italics; Ackoff, "Resurrecting the Future"; Russell L. Ackoff, *Redesigning the Future* (New York: John Wiley & Sons, 1974); Russell L. Ackoff and F. E. Emery, *On Purposeful Systems* (Chicago: Aldine–Atherton, 1972); Ackoff, "Resurrecting the Future," 189 – 93; see Giandomenico Majone, "Applied Systems Analysis," 40–42.

43. Ackoff, "Resurrecting the Future," 193, Ackoff's italics.

44. "Wharton ARC," information letter, n.d.; "Wharton ARC," promotional pamphlet (1977?), files of the Wharton Applied Research Center; interviews with van Merkensteijn and Sachs.

45. Ackoff, *Redesigning the Future*, 92.

46. Minutes of the Wharton Faculty, 6 May 1980; Hasan Ozbekhan, "Social Systems Science Unit: Report to the Wharton Faculty Regarding the Establishment of an MBA Major," Adrian McDonough to Edward Lusk, 29 Mar. 1979, and Edward J. Lusk, "Curriculum Committee Report to the Faculty," 19 July 1979, in Minutes of the Wharton Faculty, 23 Oct. 1979.

47. Interviews with Anita Summers, Martin, and Thomas Dunfee; Minutes of the Wharton Faculty, 17 Feb. 1967, 20 Oct. 1970, 16 Oct. 1973; Annual Report of the Department of Decision Sciences, 1978–79, files of the Department of Decision Sciences, 1.

48. Interviews with Franklin Root, Perlmutter, Gordon Keith, Jean Crockett, and Frank; Minutes of the Wharton Faculty, 27 Oct. 1970, 19 Oct. 1971.

49. Office of Career Planning and Placement, Wharton School, *M.B.A. Placement Survey 1980*, 2; Carroll, *State of the School*; David Weinstein, "A History of Managerial Accounting and Managerial Finance at the Wharton School" (independent study research paper, University of Pennsylvania Management Department, December 1980); interview with Carroll.

50. Office of Career Planning and Placement, *M.B.A. Placement Survey 1980*, 2; Carroll, *State of the School*; Weinstein, "Managerial Accounting and Finance"; interview with Dan M. McGill; *Wharton Notes*, Feb. 1980.

51. *Wharton Graduate Division Course Guide (1981–1982)*, 8–12, 44–49; Minutes of the Wharton Faculty, 24 Sept. 1974, 19 Nov. 1974; Carroll, *State of the School*; interviews with Webber and Everett Keech; 1980 Wharton Alumni Survey, conducted by the author.

52. Carroll, *State of the School*; "Wharton Guest Speakers, 1979–80," *Anvil* (1980):10–12; interviews with Carroll, Lubin, and Keech; "Documents Relating to the Endowment of the Reliance Professorship/Deanship," *Almanac [of the University of Pennsylvania]*, 27 Jan. 1981:3–6.

53. Interviews with Carroll and Keech.

Donald Cary Carroll

Wharton School

Robert Brecht

Wharton School

William Gomberg

Herbert Northrup

Wharton School

Edward B. Shils

Wharton School

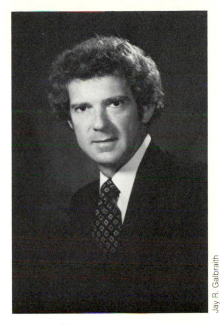

Ross A. Weber

Jay R. Galbraith

Andrew Van de Ven

Wroe Alderson, with Paul Green

Russell L. Ackoff

Edgar A. Singer, Jr.

Morris Hamburg

Shiv Gupta, professor of
operations research

James Emery

Paul R. Kleindorfer

Paul E. Green

Ronald E. Frank

Yoram Wind

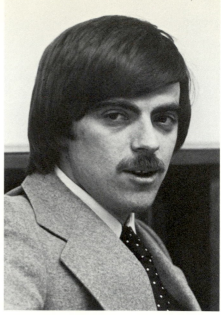

Thomas Robertson

William Pierskalla, professor of
decision sciences and executive
director of the Leonard Davis Institute

Jerry S. Rosenbloom

Thomas W. Dunfee, professor of legal studies

Howard Perlmutter

David Solomons

Frederick G. Kempin, professor of legal studies

Student at the computer,
Vance Hall

Wharton School

Students in discussion, Vance Hall Lounge

Wharton School

Wharton Magazine,
volume 5, number 2,
cover and contents

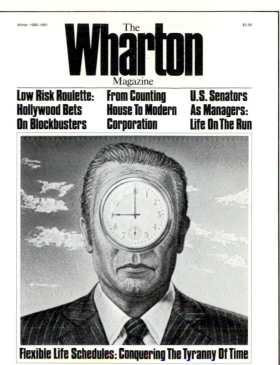

Winter 1980-1981 $5.00

The Wharton Magazine

Low Risk Roulette: Hollywood Bets On Blockbusters

From Counting House To Modern Corporation

U.S. Senators As Managers: Life On The Run

Flexible Life Schedules: Conquering The Tyranny Of Time

Economic Forecast: Page 49

The Wharton Magazine

Winter 1980-1981   Vol. 5 No. 2

Publisher
Donald C. Carroll

Editor in Chief
William K. West

Editorial Board
Jack M. Guttentag
Leonard M. Lodish
David N. Ness
Michael L. Wachter
Ross A. Webber

Advisory Board
Russell Ackoff
William Eagleson, Jr.
Alice F. Emerson
James Emery
Irwin Friend
Paul Green
Lawrence R. Klein
Irving Kravis
Michael R. Levy
Dan McGill
Dinah Nemeroff
Donald A. Pels
Almarin Phillips
David Solomons
Eric Trist
Charls E. Walker

Reviews Editor
Warren Bennis

Art Director
Mitch Shostak
Assistant Editor
Leslie Anne Whitaker
Scanning Editor
Michael F. Wolff

Associate Publisher
Eric van Merkensteijn
Advertising Director
Jack Aldrich
Circulation Director
Suzanne S. Becker
Operations Manager
Lois Ann Rose

Cover: Ed Soyka

U.S. Senators:
See How They Run,
page 36.

ARTICLES

The Wharton Magazine is published quarterly. Copyright © 1980 by the Trustees of the University of Pennsylvania. All rights reserved. No part of this publication may be reproduced or transmitted in any form or by any means, electronic or mechanical, including photocopy, recording, or any information storage and retrieval system, without permission in writing. Manuscripts and art should be accompanied by stamped, self-addressed envelope and mailed to: Editor, The Wharton Magazine, 3609 Locust Walk, University of Pennsylvania, Philadelphia, PA 19104. (215) 243-8999

Advertising: Jack Aldrich, Director of Advertising Sales, at same address. (215) 243-8999.

Publisher's Representatives: *New York.* Shippee Swift, Shippee Swift and Associates, Merkel Hill Road, Redding Ridge, CT 06876. (203) 938-3903. *New York and Stamford.* Russell Ward, National Representatives Company, 856 High Ridge Road, Stamford, CT 06905. (203) 322-5538. *Northern Connecticut and New England.* Joe DeLone, Joe DeLone and Associates, P.O. Box 271, 22 Welwyn Road, Riverside, CT 06878. (203) 637-2758. *Northern New Jersey.* Ed Walker, Coastal Trading Company, 222 Sandcastle Key, Secaucus, NJ 07094. (201) 865-6319. *Western States.* John MacKay, MacKay Advertising Sales, 681 Market Street, Room 1085, San Francisco, CA 94105. (415) 957-1575. *Southern*

California and Arizona. William Muhat, Collegiate Advertising Associates, 1888 Century Park East, Suite 910, Los Angeles, CA 90067. (213) 552-1167. *Midwest.* James O. Reilly, 709 Cooper Street, Des Plaines, IL 60018. (312) 824-2412. *Michigan and Ohio.* John O. Peters, 404 Fisher Building, Detroit, MI 48202. (313) 872-6331.

Staff: *Editorial Associates.* Janice MacKenzie. *Scanning Research.* Robert Halperin, Susan Hyman, Rob Kazanjian, Kenneth H. Thomas, Robert Thomas, Susan Tobin. *Computer Systems Consultant.* Howard Kirsner, Wharton Computer Center. *Office Assistants.* Rebecca Abel, Lisa Armstrong, Natalie Bowden, Eve Donovan, Marlies Fuchs, Aaron Groffman, Denise Lee, Edward Muhl, Roberta Todd.

Subscriptions: $14 a year in the United States. $16 in Canada and Mexico. $24 (by air) in Europe and Latin America. $26 (by air) in Asia, Pacific, and Africa. All subscription correspondence: The Wharton Magazine, Subscription Department, P.O. Box 581, Martinsville Center, Martinsville, N.J. 08836. Printed by The Winchell Company, Philadelphia, PA 19107. Prices for reprints and bulk orders on request. U.S.P.S. #432950. Second-class postage paid at Philadelphia, PA. Application for Audit Bureau of Circulations Membership has been made November 1980.

Vance Hall

PROPOSED DIETRICH HALL RENOVATION
THE WHARTON SCHOOL – UNIVERSITY OF PENNSYLVANIA
WARNER BURNS TOAN LUNDE – ARCHITECTS PLANNERS
724 FIFTH AVENUE   NEW YORK NEW YORK 10019

B4

Plans for the remodeled Dietrich Hall

Index